MW00909253

# COMPUTE!'s AMIGA MACHINE LANGUAGE PROGRAMMING GUIDE

by Daniel Wolf and Douglas Leavitt, Jr.

COMPUTE! Publications, Inc. abc
A Capital Cities/ABC, Inc. Company
Greensboro, North Carolina

Printed in the United States of America

10 9 8 7 6 5 4 3 2

ISBN 0-87455-128-5



COMPUTE! Publications, Inc., Post Office Box 5406, Greensboro, NC 27403, (919) 275-9809, is a Capital Cities/ABC Inc. company, and is not associated with any manufacturer of personal computers. Amiga and AmigaDOS are trademarks of Commodore-Amiga, Inc.

# Contents

## Section 6. Graphics



## Section 7. Amiga Floating-Point Math



## Section 8. The Applications Programs



## Appendices

# Foreword

For most people who learned machine language on the Apple II, the Commodore 64, and the Atari 8-bit machines, the prospect of progressing into the 16/32-bit territory of the Amiga—with its multitasking environment, windows and mouse input, and libraries of subroutines—can be daunting.

Until now, there was no simple way to get started.

But now, with *COMPUTE!'s Amiga Machine Language Programming Guide,* Daniel Wolf and Douglas Leavitt, Jr. provide an easy path to learning Amiga machine langage programming. In this book, you'll find sample programs that cover nearly all of Amiga's special features, along with helpful hints and suggestions on programming technique and organization.

*COMPUTE!'s Amiga Machine Language Programming Guide* provides a thorough explanation of the use of Intuition, including Intuition windows, menus, and requesters. You'll understand how to use button, string, and slider gadgets, and how to write programs that interact with the user through CLI and console windows.

Structures and fields (the individual bytes, words, or long words within a structure) are covered in detail, and their use in AmigaDOS function calls is explained. Floating-point math is explored, along with a look at "transcendental" math functions used in trigonometry. And, sample graphics programs that use these high-level math functions to provide fractals and three-dimensional graphics are included.

Appendices explaining 68000 instructions and addressing modes, macros, pseudo-ops, and assembler directives round out the book.

In short, this feature-packed book is perfect for anyone interested in programming the Amiga in machine language.

Please note: Because of the advanced nature of machine language programming, it would be difficult to work with an unexpanded Amiga and a single disk drive. For this reason, the material in this book was written with the assumption that the programmer has an Amiga computer with at least 512K and two disk drives.

The programs in COMPUTE!'s Amiga Machine Language Programming Guide are available on a disk, along with the *ASM68010* assembler. If you wish to purchase this disk, call toll free 1-800-346-6767 (in New York, 212-887-8525). Or, use the coupon found in the back of this book.


## Acknowledgments

Special thanks to Mark Riley who stimulated interest in using machine language for Amiga programming and helped explain enough to get me (DW) started on a simplified programming system. Also, thanks to Gary Koffler, of Everyware, for hints, tips, Amiga information, and personal contacts in the Amiga programming community.

Thanks to Carolyn Sheppner, and many other technical support people at Commodore, for helping with sticky programming problems. Thanks also to Mr. Fred Fish, the Amicus Network, VAUX, and other public domain software librarians.

Stephen Levy, of COMPUTE! Publications, gets special thanks for encouragement, constructive criticism, and belief in my ability to produce this book.


## Dedication

For my father.

# Introduction

The Amiga family of microcomputers includes three members: the original Amiga 1000 and the newer models 500 and 2000. They are software compatible and share a complement of hardware features that make them among the most powerful personal computers in today's market. Amigas have especially versatile color graphics capabilities and a multitasking operating system that permits operation of different programs simultaneously.

The architecture of these computers integrates a Motorola MC68000 microprocessor and special-purpose processor chips for graphics, sound, and input/output. The Amigas can be expanded with a variety of memory boards, disk drives, graphics devices, and other peripherals. Amigas feature a built-in user interface consisting of mouse-based interaction with windows, menus, and icons. The Amiga system is well suited to a wide variety of productivity, business, artistic, and entertainment applications. Amigas are used in professional television broadcasting, program art production, personal word processing and desktop publishing, as well as in business management.

## Programming the Amiga

With such a capable system of hardware and software, programmers find the Amiga inviting as well. Already, several programming language packages are available for the Amiga, including C, Fortran, LISP, and several dialects of BASIC. Because the Amiga's microprocessor is a Motorola MC68000, existing language packages that operate on other MC68000-based systems have been easy to transport to the Amiga. The MC68000 is the same 16/32-bit processor used in the Apple Macintosh family and the Atari ST series. Machine language is just another programming language for the Amiga, similar to these others, except that it executes much faster and takes up less space than most languages.

## Why Machine Language

With such a range of high-level languages (C and BASIC, for instance) available for the Amiga, some justification seems required for programming in machine language.

First, since all microprocessors (such as the 8080, Z80, 8088, and the 6502) have their own machine languages, there is a community of programmers already familiar with machine language techniques. Some programmers, who have already used MC68000 machine language on other computers, will naturally prefer similar working methods for Amiga software development.

Second, regardless of the type of microprocessor, machine language is the most direct means of programming the microprocessor. All high-level languages translate their programs into machine language, either through an interpreter or by means of a compiler. Compiled languages (C and Fortran, for instance) run their code through compilers, which translate their programs into machine language. BASIC usually has an interpreter that translates the BASIC program into machine language, instruction by instruction, as the program runs.

## Machine Language Source Code and Object Code

Machine language is written in a kind of shorthand. The machine language programmer arranges short-hand codes for instructions, in a sequence, to accomplish a specified task.

Translating these shorthand codes (collectively known as *source code*) into the numbers that instruct the computer (known as *executable code*) is accomplished by a program called an *assembler*. An assembler is like a compiler in that the code is translated only once and the result is a program that will run on its own, without an interpreter. The only way to program the microprocessor more directly is to place the numerical instructions in memory yourself. The assembler relieves programmers of the need to work with long binary numbers—strings of ones and zeros that are confusing and difficult to read.

The assembler examines the three- or four-letter opcode in the source code, looks up its numeric equivalent on a table, and places the object code in a memory location. When a machine language program is assembled, there's nearly an exact correspondence between the source code instructions and the object code instructions. When high-level languages are compiled, a more complicated translation usually takes place, and it's difficult for the programmer to anticipate what the object code will look like. It is likewise difficult for the high-level language programmer to predict the size and speed of the compiled program. Usually, the translation process for high-level languages is not a direct line-by-line replacement of code with numbers. A single statement in a high-level language might be translated into a long sequence of numerical instructions for the microprocessor.

One advantage of machine language is the fact that it is the most direct means of controlling the microprocessor. In addition, machine language usually provides the most compact finished programs because of the direct translation to instructions for the microprocessor.

A third advantage of machine language is that the programmer can and must make decisions about the use of internal registers of the MC68000 and almost all other aspects of a program's size and speed.

The proper use of registers powerfully affects a program's efficiency of operation. High-level languages leave these decisions to the compiler or interpreter. When using machine language, such decisions must be made expressly by the programmer. Because some instructions run faster when using registers, this means the machine language programmer may produce faster programs by using the registers intelligently. This aspect of programming is called *optimization.*

In summary, machine language for the Amiga offers these advantages:

- Similarity to other microprocessor machine languages
- Direct and concrete step-by-step microprocessor control
- Absolute programmer control over the program's speed and size (which affect the program's overall efficiency)

The disadvantages of machine language include:

- Explicit control of the microprocessor requires thorough knowledge of the instructions and how they work.
- Machine language provides a maximum of freedom which must be harnessed by a maximum of programmer responsibility.
- Source program size can be a problem. A single line of source code may accomplish a great deal in a BASIC program. A single line of machine language source code is often a single microprocessor instruction; therefore, a machine language source program may require a large number of lines of code to accomplish even the simplest task.

For the programmer who wishes to have complete control of the machine and who is willing to accept the responsibility for detailed programming, machine language is the language of choice.

## A Note on the C Language and Amiga

C is a language that was developed during the 1970s at Bell Laboratories. It became the native language of the UNIX operating system. Because C has a fairly simple structure, it is easily moved (or *ported*) to other microprocessors. The process involves writing a C compiler for the particular microprocessor (a process that takes place in either C itself or in the machine language for the microprocessor in question). There are C compilers available for most of the popular microprocessors and personal computers.

Since C compilers are available on so many machines, it's usually possible to move a C program to a new system simply by compiling the existing source code on the new machine, using its C compiler. Moving machine language programs is usually more complex and may not be possible when two computers use different microprocessors.

The C language has also become a very popular system programming language for professional programmers. Its features make it convenient as a high-level language, but it also has many low-level features surprisingly similar to machine language source code. These low-level features make C similar enough to machine language that professionals call it the system programmer's machine language. Such professional programmers heavily exploit the low-level features of C and the result is like a machine language that can be easily ported from computer to computer.

A small part of each C compiler must deal with the specific microprocessor. Fortunately, this machine-dependent part is transparent to the programmer. The C programmer usually is insulated from the specifics of the computing hardware. It isn't surprising that C was also the language chosen by the Amiga software development team.

The early Amiga programmers couldn't even use Amigas for writing programs. They used Sun Microsystems computers (also equipped with MC68000 microprocessors) or IBM PC systems (with 8088 microprocessors) and sent programs over a cable to the Amiga's memory.

C provided a common and (as high-level languages go) efficient programming language for the complex Amiga hardware while it was still under development. That means that the history of Amiga software development has been strongly influenced by C.

Much of the documentation provided for the Amiga programmer assumes programs are written in C. Since C is close to machine language in efficiency, speed, and program size, this is not a disadvantage. Some C compilers actually include an assembler. In these compilers, the C language source code program is first translated into an equivalent machine language source program, and then it is assembled.

Nearly anything that can be done using C on the Amiga can also be done using machine language, and vice versa. On the Amiga, machine language and C have a very close relationship: C is the Amiga's native language, and machine language is the MC68000 microprocessor's native language.

One important feature of machine language on the Amiga is that it provides access to all the C-based aspects designed by the Amiga's system programmers, without requiring a knowledge of C itself.

In summary, a choice between C and machine language on the Amiga is one of personal taste and style. They are nearly equivalent in power. Assembly language is still more efficient and direct and, of course, doesn't require that the programmer learn C (which does have some complicated and tricky features). Machine language is sometimes used to streamline the performance of a critical section of a C program.

Commodore has provided program developers with complete machine language development packages, but there has been less documentation publicly available about Amiga machine language programming. This book integrates some of the needed information into one volume to make machine language more accessible to Amiga programmers.

## About This Book

The purpose of this book is to introduce Amiga machine language programming to a wide audience, including both new and experienced programmers. Examples of programming methods as well as complete programs are provided to show

how readers can construct their own applications that take advantage of the Amiga's powerful features. The example programs demonstrate:

- AmigaDOS console use
- AmigaDOS function calling
- Intuition window open, close, user interactions
- Intuition menu layout and interactions
- Intuition button, string, and slider gadgets
- Intuition window graphics
- Intuition requesters
- Floating-point math

In addition to the short example programs that demonstrate the Amiga's features, there are four program listings that show how Intuition, Graphics, Math, and AmigaDOS features may be combined into larger programs:

- QUADRIX.ASM demonstrates 3-D graphics.
- LENS.ASM is a Workbench screen/window that provides a variable magnifying window.
- POLYFRAC.ASM demonstrates fractal line drawings.
- ASMINT.ASM provides an Intuition interface for machine language development.

The information topics covered include the following:

- Overview of important CLI commands
- Organizing your working environment
- Using an Amiga-compatible assembler
- A first program
- The MC68000 instructions
- The MC68000 addressing modes
- MC68000 techniques:
  Macros
  Subroutines
  Branches and loops
  Arithmetic
  Strings
- Amiga programming techniques:
  Symbol definitions for ROM Kernel software include files
  Library calls and register parameter passing
  Memory and multitasking
  Startup program requirements

- AmigaDOS and files (open, close, read, write)
- Intuition (windows, text, menus, gadgets, requesters, screens)
- Graphics (rastports, pixels, colors, lines, fills)
- Floating-point math (text conversion to floating point, hex dump)

The appendices have tables of important Amiga symbols and data for the assembler. Complete type-in listings are also provided for all the Amiga symbols used in the programs. By using these files (or the companion disk to this book), you can enter, assemble, and use these programs as well as write your own applications. The Intuition section presents topics in a building-block order, developing windows and text concepts, following with gadgets and menus (typically associated with text), and then requesters (which typically use gadgets and text).

For each appropriate section, there's an associated type-in file of useful macros and subroutines that are used as program building blocks throughout the succeeding parts of the book. These macros and subroutines were tested and designed to reduce repetitive coding. This is typical of Amiga programs, which have many modular data tables (or structures). In many cases, the use of complex Amiga features in a program can be accomplished with just a few lines of source code consisting of these macros and calls to the related subroutines. Source code is readable and easily modified, with text structure declarations limited to the text strings themselves.

At the end of the book is a complete listing of MC68000 and MC68010 microprocessor instructions, assembler directives, and pseudo-ops. Where the assembler documentation might be specific to the *ASM68010* assembler, included on the companion disk available from COMPUTE! publications, a note is made: Those using other assemblers (*Metacomco,* for instance) can refer to these notes and use the alternative syntax appropriate to their particular assembler. A great deal of effort has been expended to make this assembler documentation section compatible with both *ASM68010* and the *Metacomco* assembler.

## About the Companion Disk

A disk is available from COMPUTE! Books which provides readers with all the program listings and files presented in the book. It can make your use of the book's programs easier by eliminating almost all of the typing.

The disk also has a machine language development system for the Amiga. This includes *ASM68010,* a fast Amiga assembler. There is also the ASMINT program, which provides the *ASM68010* with a mouse interface. ASMINT has Intuition gadgets to handle most user interactions and is ideal for beginners with little CLI experience. The disk is designed to be used with any Amiga with two disk drives and 512K (or more) memory. See the inside back cover for information on how to order the companion disk.

## What You Should Know to Use This Book

This book assumes you're familiar with your Amiga. You should know about and feel comfortable using the mouse, disk drives, monitor, and keyboard. You should be used to the Preferences program.

General experience using the Amiga CLI (Command Line Interface) is also assumed. Use Preferences to assure that you can access a CLI by clicking the CLI ON gadget in the Preferences program, and then save the new Preferences. When you reboot the Amiga, the System Drawer on your Workbench disk will have a CLI program icon available. This icon can always be used to start a CLI.

You'll use the CLI to type commands directly into the Amiga. If you're not familiar with the CLI, you should review your Amiga system documentation. Some of the commonly used CLI commands needed by programmers are discussed with examples, but if you want a complete explanation of the CLI, you should consult the AmigaDOS Manual published by Bantam Books.

The AmigaDOS Manual also contains a very good presentation on the *Metacomco* assembler and linker. Readers are also assumed to be familiar with binary and hexadecimal numbers as well as how to use a text editor (such as MicroEmacs, provided with Amigas on the Extras disk) or word processor program to type in source code. Some acquaintance with either MC68000 machine language or machine language on some other microprocessor will be helpful, but not essential. Those with a good background in machine language should be able to skip over some of the beginner-oriented sections and directly approach the Amiga programming information.

## What You Should Have to Use This Book

You need an Amiga (any model) with two disk drives and at least 512K. Expanded memory to one megabyte or more is always a great convenience, since a large ramdisk speeds up file access. A printer is also convenient for reading complete program listings, but not essential.

You should have the Amiga V1.2 Enhancer software package that includes the Extras disk. The Extras disk has a high-quality text editor for program source code entry and editing, called MicroEmacs (referred to in this book as Emacs). It is a variation of a widely used text editor. All of the programs in this book assume the use of V1.2 Amiga operating system, which is also part of the Enhancer package.

If you do not have the Enhancer package, you can get it from your Amiga dealer. V1.2 is the latest version of the operating system at the time of this writing.

You also need an Amiga-compatible macroassembler and linker. At the time of writing this book there are several popular assemblers:

- The *Metacomco* assembler package
- ASM68010
- The *Manx* C compiler

**The *Metacomco* assembler package.** The Metacomco assembler package includes the AmigaDOS Developer's Manual, which contains assembler and linker documentation. This information is now reprinted in the AmigaDOS Manual, available separately.

Included in the package, along with the *Metacomco* assembler, is the Amiga linker (named *ALINK*). The *Metacomco* package also contains the official Amiga include files, which consist of numerous symbol definitions and small macros and subroutines. These files are large and heavily commented. They have been reprinted in the ROM Kernel manuals (see below).

This package also provides AMIGA.LIB on disk. AMIGA.LIB is a large file of program code and symbol definitions provided for use with ALINK. Because the programs in this book only use the simplest applications of linking, AMIGA.LIB is not used. Programmers who intend to work beyond the scope of this book with advanced linker features will be well advised to have the *Metacomco* package. Even when using the *Metacomco* system, the type-in files in this book will be required for use with the book's programs. The included files are not used here because of their size and enormously complex scope.

***ASM68010.*** *ASM68010* is an Amiga assembler with a built-in linker suitable for the simple linking tasks required by programs in this book. The *ASM68010* macroassembler (named ASM) is provided on the companion disk for this book. Also provided on the disk are all the files and program listings in this book. The book-disk is an alternative assembler development package because it also has the necessary include files in precisely the format required by the book's programs. *ASM68010* has the advantage of also being fully compatible with the MC68010 microprocessor (a slightly more advanced version of the MC68000), which many Amiga programmers have substituted for their systems' MC68000s (the two are interchangeable on the Amiga).

**The *Manx C* compiler package.** The *Manx C* compiler package includes an Amiga assembler and linker. Once again, the files in the book have to be typed in to be used with the *Manx C* assembler. Use of the *Manx C* compiler's assembler will not be covered in this book.

The only other thing you may desire to get the most out of this book is more Amiga technical documentation. This book cannot substitute for the official Amiga publications, but they're not necessary to get started. Here's a partial list of related books. They contain a wealth of Amiga programming information:

- *Programming the MC68000* (Sybex)
- Amiga ROM Kernel Manuals (Addison-Wesley) covering:
  Intuition
  Libraries and Devices
  Hardware
  Exec
- The *AmigaDOS Manual* (Bantam Books)—official DOS reference

The following programming guides concentrate mostly on C language but can help with Amiga programming concepts:

- *Programming Guide to the Amiga* (Sybex)
- *Amiga Programmer's Handbook, Volumes 1 and 2* (Sybex)
- *Inside the Amiga* (Sams)
- *Amiga Programmer's Guide* (COMPUTE! Books)

The last volume also has a section specifically on machine language Amiga programming, with some program listings that can be easily converted for use with this book's equate and include files. The popular Amiga publication, *Amazing Computing,* has also printed a series of beginner-oriented articles on MC68000 machine language.

Machine language is the most detailed way to program the Amiga, and the most efficient. This book provides the information and organization to help programmers bypass potential problems and complications of Amiga programming. It can stimulate beginners and advanced programmers to exploit the speed and efficiency of machine language to harness the power of the Amiga. With some concentration, study, and practice, you should find machine language Amiga programming a straightforward and effective way of expressing your Amiga applications. Since the Amiga is such a complex machine, no single book about it can be truly complete. Throughout the *Amiga Machine Language Programming Guide,* you'll find references to additional Amiga programming information to guide you in experimenting beyond the specifics of this book.

# SECTION 1

# MC68000 Microprocessor Architecture and Programming

# CHAPTER 1
# The MC68000 Architecture

## The Chip Family

The purpose of this chapter is to familiarize you with the MC68000 microprocessor so that you'll be able to read the program listings throughout the book. The following chapters provide practical instruction sequences using the most common MC68000 instructions, while this chapter presents a brief overview of the MC68000 and its instruction set. For further information, you should also consult the MC68000 manual in Appendix A.

If you're a machine language programmer who's already familiar with the MC68000, you might want to skip the rest of this chapter.

In the late 1970s, in response to the growing demand for greater microcomputer power and speed, Motorola developed the MC68000 microprocessor. The company showed foresight when they chose not to add functions to their current microprocessor, the 6809. Instead, they took a step backward and designed a new microprocessor line: the M68000 series. The MC68000, first in the new series, has many advanced features and has become the processor of choice in the computer workstation market. It has also become popular in the home computer market, having been adopted by such manufacturers as Commodore, Apple, and Atari.

The Motorola-designed MC68000 microprocessor is one of a family of five closely related microprocessors, including the MC68008, MC68000, MC68010, MC68020, and the newest MC68030. Their internal operations are very similar and most instructions are shared by all of them. The differences in these microporcessors are related to the amount of memory each can access during a single operation. The MC68008 reads a byte at a time, the MC68000 and MC68010 each read one word (16 bits, two bytes), and the MC68020 and MC68030 both read one long word (32 bits, four bytes) in a single operation.

Since most of the internal operations of the M68000 family take place in 32-bit registers, it's obvious that the MC68008 has to perform more read operations per instruction than a

MC68020; therefore, the MC68008, by its very nature, is slower than the other members of its family.

Because its internal operations use 32-bit registers, the MC68000 is sometimes called a 32-bit processor. Because it reads memory 16 bits at a time, it is sometimes called a 16-bit processor.

The MC68010 and MC68000 are similar. Both work equally well in the Amiga. In the MC68010, some common instructions are faster than MC68000 equivalents. The Amiga's performance is snappier with the MC68010 installed.

The MC68020 and MC68030 are not only faster than the MC68000, they also have some new 32-bit instructions that do not exist in the MC68000 and the MC68010. These two are true computing powerhouses, and they're about four to ten times faster than the MC68000. Since they read data 32 bits at a time and require more pins, they won't plug directly into the Amiga MC68000 socket. The MC68010, on the other hand, is electrically compatible with the MC68000. In many cases, replacing a MC68000 with a MC68010 can increase the performance of an Amiga as much as 15 percent.

There is one caveat: The early versions of the Amiga operating system (1.1 and earlier), will not work correctly with the MC68010. Version 1.2 of the Amiga operating system fixed those problems and will work properly with the MC68010. Commodore has always supplied version 1.2 for the Amiga 500 and 2000. Amiga 1000 owners without version 1.2 can purchase it through any Amiga dealer.

The M68000 series has many advantages over its 8-bit predecessors. These include a set of over 200 instructions for manipulating 1-, 8-, 16-, and 32-bit data values. The M68000-series microprocessors have 16 general purpose registers and 12 addressing modes. As a result, the Amiga has over 1000 machine language instruction combinations.

## The Registers

The M68000 family microprocessors have 17 32-bit registers, 16 of which are available at any given moment. There are two types: *data* (D) registers and *address* (A) registers, and there are eight of each. The MC68000 also has some specialized registers, including the program counter, status register, and condition code register. Different microprocessors within the family may have one or more special system registers.

The MC68000, unlike some other microprocessors, does not limit the use of these registers. If an instruction can use one of the two types of registers, any register of that type may be used. For example, you can add any two data registers together with an ADD instruction. This provides much greater flexibility because there are fewer hardware constraints.

**The data registers.** These are used in various ways: in arithmetic, as accumulators, as frequently referenced variables, and as index values for indexed addressing modes. Any data register can be the source or destination of an arithmetic or move operation. In the MC68000 processor, these registers cannot be used to fetch data from memory (this restriction was removed in the MC68020).

The register names for the data registers are D0, D1, D2, D3, D4, D5, D6, and D7. While these registers are 32 bits in size, an MC68000 instruction can limit itself to the lower 8- or 16-bit portion of a register when necessary. Therefore, the data registers can be used to add two bytes, two words, or two long words. (See Figure 1-1.)

**Figure 1-1. Layout of the MC68000 data register.**

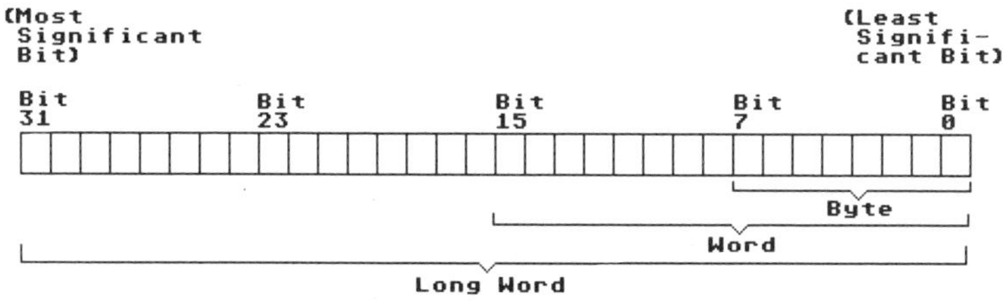


All operations performed on data registers set the *condition code bits.* Condition codes are used in branching; for instance, if the result of an operation is 0, you may want to branch to another part of your program. Condition codes, which allow the computer to make decisions like this, will be discussed in detail later.

**The address registers.** These usually contain addresses or address constants. They are used as stack pointers, or as pointers to data, lists, or other data structures. Their names are A0, A1, A2, A3, A4, A5, A6, and A7. Register A7 is also known as the stack pointer, or *SP*.

**Figure 1-2. Layout of an MC68000 address register.**

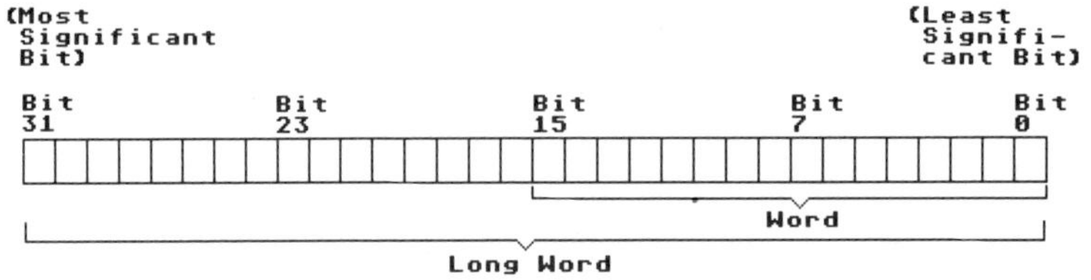


The MC68000 can perform arithmetic operations on address registers. The most common of these that are performed on addresses—such as addition and subtraction—are available, but other operations, such as Boolean, are not available. Address registers may only be accessed in word and longword quantities (never as bytes). Most operations performed on an address register will not set the condition codes. The major exception to this is the compare instruction, which will be discussed in more detail later.

One interesting feature of address registers is that when they're loaded with 16-bit values, they're automatically *sign extended* to 32 bits. When a 16-bit value is sign extended to a 32-bit value, the uppermost bit of the 16-bit value is duplicated in the 16 upper bits. This means that a 16-bit negative binary number will become the same negative number when stored in an address register, except that it will be 32 bits long. This is helpful for situations in which 32-bit calculations occur, and most or all of the data registers are in use. When an 8- or 16-bit value is stored in a data register, the upper bits of the data register are unmodified. On the MC68000, the EXT.L instruction (which will be discussed in detail later) performs this conversion on a data register.

While the address registers of the MC68000 are 32 bits long, only the lower 24 bits are used to address memory (the high-order 8 bits are ignored). You should still treat addresses as 32-bit quantities, however, to insure compatibility with future Amigas (which may contain an MC68020 and, therefore, be capable of dealing with 32-bit addresses).

## Special Registers

Register A7 is special, as mentioned above. This register was chosen by Motorola as the stack pointer, so it's also known as *SP*. Although it can be used just like any other address register, it would not be a good idea to do so. Register A7 normally points to the program stack. Many instructions implicitly use the SP as part of their operation, such as the instructions to call subroutines and to return from subroutines. This register must always point to an *even word* boundary in memory. That is, it must always point to the beginning of a 16-bit word, such as location 0, location 2, location 4, and so on. To assure that this happens, the MC68000 automatically aligns all MOVE instructions using the SP. There is additional discussion of stack operations later on.

Other special registers include the program counter (or *PC*), the status register (or *SR*), and the condition code register (or *CCR*) which is normally the lower eight bits of the status register.

The PC is a 32-bit register that points to the next executable instruction. Each time an instruction is fetched from memory, the MC68000 updates the PC to point to the address following the instruction. The address in the PC may be modified by some instructions, such as a branch or subroutine call, before the next instruction is fetched. Except when a machine language program executes branches, subroutine calls, traps, and certain other instructions, the program cannot modify the PC.

Neither the status register (SR) nor condition code register (CCR) are normally referenced directly by a program.

Condition codes are bits that are tested when a program wants to change program flow as the result of some condition. The following code compares a data register to the number 10, and branches if the data register contains a value larger than 10.

```
CMP.L   #10,D0          ;COMPARE D0 WITH 10, AND
                        ;SET THE CONDITION CODES
BGT     NEW_LOCATION    ;BRANCH IF D0 > 10
```

The SR is a 16-bit register, and the CCR is the lower 8 bits of the SR. For this book, only the bottom 8 bits, or the CCR will be discussed. The upper 8 bits are used in system software, and are beyond the scope of this discussion. The status register is depicted in Figure 1-3.

**Figure 1-3. The Status Register.**

| Most significant byte | | | | | | | | Least significant byte | | | | | | | |
|---|---|---|---|---|---|---|---|---|---|---|---|---|---|---|---|
| I | % | S | % | % | I2 | I1 | I0 | % | % | % | X | N | Z | V | C |
| F | E | D | C | B | A | 9 | 8 | 7 | 6 | 5 | 4 | 3 | 2 | 1 | 0 |

As you probably know, the letters *A–F* represent the values 10–15 in hexadecimal notation.

% Unused bit of the status register.

C Carry bit. This bit is *set* (made equal to 1) when a carry operation occurs, and *reset* (or *cleared*—made equal to 0) when a borrow operation occurs. These may occur as the result of addition or subtraction. For example, say the addition of two 16-bit numbers generates a 17-bit result. The bottom 16 bits of the result would be placed in the destination register, and the carry bit would be set to 1.

V Overflow bit. This bit is set when an arithmetic result is too large to be stored in a register. An example of overflow is adding two very large 32-bit numbers. If the sum of the two numbers is greater than the number that can be stored in 32 bits, overflow occurs. In this case, the overflow bit would be set to alert the program that the result is too big to be stored in a register.

Z Zero bit. This bit is set when the result of an operation is 0. Any nonzero result clears this bit.

N Negative bit. This bit is set to the value of the most significant bit of the result of an operation. A 1 indicates a negative result, while a 0 means the result is positive.

X Extend bit. This bit is used in many Extend instructions, such as ADDX. It provides a mechanism for multiprecision arithmetic. The extend bit is usually set or reset the same as the C bit.

The programmer should use caution programming the status register. The Amiga provides a special system function call (GETCC) to read the condition code bits of the status register (SR). Only the MC68000 allows user programs to modify this instruction. For compatibility with the MC68010 and the MC68020, Amiga programmers should use the GETCC function provided by Commodore. Although this function is not used in any of the programs in this book, it is similar in many respects to some of the system functions that will be discussed in greater detail. Please refer to the appendices or one of the Amiga ROM kernel manuals for more details. GETCC is a function in the Exec library.

The Amiga operating system can execute code in *supervisor* or *user mode*. Supervisor mode is used only when it is necessary to have unrestricted access to all parts of the machine. Because the Amiga programmer has been given a wealth of operating system calls, few Amiga programmers will feel the need to use this mode. Until you become an advanced machine language programmer, you'll probably utilize the User mode exclusively.

All of the M68000 family of processors provide additional registers only accessible in supervisor mode. On the MC68010, these include the vector base register (*vbr*), the source function code register (*sfc*), and the destination function code register (*dfc*). Supervisor mode also permits access to a second stack pointer on all M68000 family machines (this is the seventeenth register, mentioned above). The name of this register is the supervisor stack pointer (*ssp*). For further information about these registers, please consult the Appendix at the back of the book, or consult the appropriate Motorola reference manual.

## Memory Layout

The MC68000 is one of the first microprocessors to provide a large linear address space. The M68000 series processors were expressly designed to directly address four gigabytes (32 address bits, approximately 4 billion bytes) of data. On the MC68000, a byte is a sequence of 8 bits of binary data. A word is 2 bytes or 16 bits, and a long word is two words or 4 bytes, or 32 bits of data. An MC68000 based computer is only capable of accessing the first 16 megabytes (24 address bits, approximately 16 million bytes) of this address space. Machine language programmers should not try to store information in the upper 8 bits of an address. Two members of the M68000 family, the MC68020 and the MC68030, use the full 32 bits and can address the entire four gigabytes. Programs using those extra 8 bits may fail on a future Amiga computer using one of these microprocessors.

With the continued reduction in the cost of computer memory, future Amigas may have many megabytes (millions of bytes) of memory. In contrast, the 80X86 microprocessors designed by Intel (used in IBM PCs and compatibles) were not capable of linear addressing more than 64K at a time until 1986 and the arrival of the 32-bit 80386.

The M68000 family of microprocessors address memory differently than other microprocessors. Other microprocessors consider addresses to be in low-byte/high-byte form. If you're familiar with the 6502 microprocessor, used in many Apple computers and all eight-bit Commodore and Atari computers, you're probably accustomed to this format. The M68000 family of microprocessors stores addresses in the more natural high-byte/low-byte format.

Words and long words must have even addresses. Your word may start at location 0, location 2, and so on. Long words must start at locations divisible by four, such as locations 0, 4, 8, and so on. The new MC68020 does away with this requirement, but the programmers still advise adherence to this rule, as programs run faster this way.

**Figure 1-4. Long word 0.**

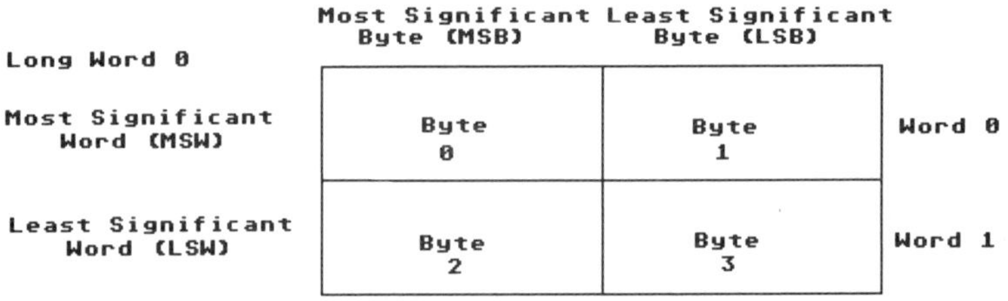


As you can see in Figure 1-4, byte 00000000 is the most significant byte of word 0. Similarly, word 0 is the most significant word of long word 0. The most significant byte of long word 1 would be byte 00000004.

The first kilobyte, or 1024 bytes, of the address space on the MC68000 is reserved for use by the MC68000 processor. Although it's beyond our scope to explain each location, it's enough to say these locations are reserved as trap and interrupt vectors. A trap or interrupt vector is an address of a subroutine to execute when the MC68000 recognizes an exception (for instance, a divide by zero error, a bus error, or possibly a disk interrupt).

You should become familiar with the MC68000 instructions, as well as the organization of memory, through the presentations here and/or a MC68000 manual. During the design of machine language programs, you need to decide on the proper use of byte, word, and long-word instructions and data. Here are some rules of thumb:

- Text characters (ASCII) are usually in byte form.
- Integers (−32768 to 32767) are usually in word form.
- Floating-point numbers (for example, 2.335987) are usually long words.
- Addresses are always long words.

In a program you may need to have data in various sizes to suit the needs of your application. If you plan to store pointers to arrays or pointers to other important memory locations (variables, for instance) you must store them as long words. Text strings are usually byte arrays.

**Caution:** The most common mistake made by MC68000 machine language programmers is forgetting to be sure that words and long words begin on even-numbered addresses.

*Be sure that words and long words always begin on even-numbered addresses.* The assembly programmer's term for this is that words and long words must be *word-aligned* in memory. Data stored in byte form can be in consecutive odd- and even-numbered addresses, and address registers can point to both odd- and even-numbered addresses, but if you try to MOVE a word or long word to or from an odd address, you'll crash the machine with a Guru meditation— #00000003.XXXXXXXX—an address bus error.

You can be sure you're at an even-numbered address at any time by using the EVENPC macro provided later in this book. EVENPC should be used every time a string of byte data is declared, just to make sure the next address is an even number. When in doubt, use the EVENPC macro.

It's possible to make a mistake by specifying the wrong data size in an instruction. At best, unpredictable data may be stored; at worst, you'll crash the machine. The system may crash immediately from the instruction, or possibly later on as a result of writing over an important nearby memory location. Imagine you've laid out four important byte-size variables next to each other in memory. If you write to the first variable with a long word, you'll unintentionally overwrite the other variables.

## CHAPTER 2

# MC68000 Instruction Formats

A machine language program consists of a sequence of lines. Each line is a machine language statement.

### Format of a Statement

For Amiga assemblers, most statements follow a general format. The exceptions to this rule are the *assembler directives* or *pseudo-ops*. The term pseudo-op means pseudo operation. A discussion of the general format for machine language source code follows. You'll find an in-depth discussion of pseudo-ops in an upcoming section.

A line of machine language source code can contain three fields; each of these fields is optional. They are:

- A label field
- An opcode field and the operands associated with that opcode
- A comment field

Consider the following example:

```
EXLAB:   MOVEQ   #10,D0   ;SET D0 TO BE THE VALUE 10
```

In the above example, EXLAB: is a label, MOVEQ is the opcode, #10 and D0 are operands, and the text following the semicolon is a comment.

### Labels

A label (also known as a *symbol*), is a string of alphanumeric characters that refers to an absolute or a PC-relative (Program Counter-relative) address. A label may consist of an upper- or lowercase ASCII character, a number, a period, or the underscore character. The first character of a label may not be a number because the assembler will attempt to parse it as a number. Do not use opcodes for labels.

The *Metacomco* Amiga assembler imposes an upper limit of 30 characters on the label. The *ASM68010* assembler is more flexible, but for backward compatibility with the *Metacomco* assembler, you should still limit labels to 30 characters.

Unlike opcodes, register names, and assembler directives, labels are case sensitive. This means the labels Assem, ASSEM, and AsSeM are all different. For consistency, only uppercase labels will be used in examples. If you don't want case sensitivity, use the assembler option -c C. See the section on assembler options in the Appendix at the back of this book for more information.

Here are examples of legal and illegal labels:

| **Legal Labels** | | |
|---|---|---|
| a | Aa | R2d2 |
| FooBar | .L1 | VERY_long_LaBeL.STILL_LEGAL |
| _MAIN | ____0...9 | .9 |

| **Illegal Labels** | **Reason** |
|---|---|
| 3.141PI | Leading digit |
| Bad?Label | Illegal character (?) |
| quote_notlegal' | Illegal character (') |
| ADD | Has the same name as an opcode |

Some labels are predefined by the *Metacomco* and *ASM68010* assemblers. The following is a list of these predefined labels:

| Label | Definition |
|---|---|
| * | This special label is the value of the location counter. The location counter is the assemble-time version of the program counter. This symbol can be used whenever it's necessary to find out the current offset from the beginning of the file. Usually, this symbol is used in calculating the length of some data. |

The following example shows how * is used to calculate the length of a string. The pseudo-ops EQU and DC.B, used in this example, are covered in more depth in the next chapter. The label LEN will contain the value 20 after the second line has been processed.

```
STRING: DC.B   '20 character string.'
LEN     EQU    STRING-* ;GET THE LENGTH OF STRING
```

**NARG** This special label contains the number of arguments sent to a macro invocation when the assembler is processing it. Macros and macro invocations are discussed in detail in the next section.

**Register names** All register names (d0, D0, d1, D1, a0, A0, sp, SP, pc, PC, and so on) are considered symbols by the assembler. All lower- and uppercase versions of the registers are set aside by the assembler as reserved labels.

Labels are used in two different locations. The first is the label definition, and the second is in a label reference. The definition of a label is the location in the program where the label is assigned a value. A label reference is any place where a label is used to refer to the label's value.

Label definitions take two forms: A label may be set to a value using an assembler directive such as EQU, EQUR, SET, or REG; or, it may be an address. The following is an example of a label assigned a value with an assembler directive:

```
TEN    EQU    10
```

In the example above, TEN is the label, EQU is the assembler directive, and 10 is the value. (Assembler directives are discussed in detail in Chapter 7.)

This example assigns the constant 10 to the label TEN. This is an example of an absolute label definition.

When the assembler sees an address label definition, it assigns the current relative address to the label. This address is the same as the location counter. This label may be used to change the flow of execution or as part of some other calculation at the time of program assembly. In other words, an address label definition is a way of accessing a piece of data without having to know exactly where its physical address is. Since the assembler will automatically manage this information, the programmer is only required to keep track of the label that points to the data. This is the most common use of a label. In this situation, a label refers to a data location in memory or to an address to which the program will jump.

An address label definition has two formats: If the first character of the label starts in column 1 of an input line, the label name will terminate either at the first blank character, a colon, or at the end of the input line; if the label does not start in column 1, the label must be terminated with a colon. Any other form will cause an assembly-time error.

The following are some examples of address label definitions:

Assume this delineates left margin
↓

```
STRING:                            ; A SAMPLE DATA LOCATION WHOSE
                                   ;ADDRESS IS
          DC.B     'HELLO',0       ; THE START OF THE STRING
                                   ; "HELLO"

          STRING2:                 ; ANOTHER SAMPLE DATA LOCATION
          DC.B     'GOODBYE',0     ;

JUMPHERE:                          ; A SAMPLE INSTRUCTION
                                   ;LOCATION
          LEA      STRING,A0       ; THIS INSTRUCTION LOADS THE
                                   ;ADDRESS OF THE
                                   ; DATA LOCATION STRING INTO
                                   ; THE ADDRESS
                                   ; REGISTER A0. THIS IS AN
                                   ; EXAMPLE OF A
                                   ; LABEL REFERENCE. THE CODE
                                   ; WILL BE DISCUSSED
                                   ; IN DETAIL LATER.

          BRA      JUMPHERE        ; ANOTHER EXAMPLE OF A LABEL
                                   ; REFERENCE. THIS
                                   ; REFERENCE MAKES THE PROGRAM
                                   ; CHANGE ITS
                                   ; EXECUTION DIRECTION, AND
                                   ; START EXECUTING
                                   ; AT THE LOCATION 'JUMPHERE'
```

Normal labels, as described in the previous paragraphs, may be externally defined or referenced. The assembler directives XDEF and XREF signal the assembler that a label is accessible outside the file (XDEF), or the label is defined in another file (XREF). If these directives are not used, then labels are only meaningful within the current assembly input file and must be defined there. The latter method is used in all programs. None of the examples seen here use the XREF or XDEF directives.

Another type of label, known as the *local label,* has a much shorter life span. A local label has the form *n*$, where *n* is a sequence of decimal digits. Some examples are 3$, 1$, and 10$.

Local labels exist only between the definition of two normal labels. This means that a local label must follow a normal label definition, and it ceases to exist at the next definition of a normal label.

The advantage of local labels is that they may be redefined and reused after each normal label definition. Local labels are never used outside the range of the two normal label definitions. Standard assemblers cannot detect which local label is being referenced in that case.

The following example shows local labels:

```
left margin
↓START:
        BRA     TEST    ; GOES TO LABEL TEST
 FOO
        BRA     1$      ; GOES TO THE NEXT STATEMENT
 1$:    NOP
        BRA     2$      ; LEGAL INSTRUCTION (GOES TO NEXT
                        ; STATEMENT)
 2$:
 TEST:  BRA     1$      ; GOES TO THE STATEMENT BELOW
 1$:
        BRA     2$      ; ILLEGAL (THERE IS NO LABEL TO GO TO
                        ; FROM HERE)
                        ; THE LABEL 2$ IS NOT DEFINED AFTER THE
                        ; LABEL
                        ; TEST.
 QUIT   BRA     START
```

## Opcode and Operand Formats

The second field of a line of source code is usually the MC68000 instruction mnemonic, or *opcode*, and the corresponding operands (opcode is a contraction of operation and code). MC68000 mnemonics always begin indented at least one space from the beginning of the line. This distinguishes an opcode from a label. The general format of instruction opcodes is a set of three or more ASCII characters, possibly followed by a period and a size specifier. These opcodes were defined by the MC68000 design engineers.

An opcode is a shorthand definition of a machine operation. For example, the opcode that was chosen by the MC68000 engineers to represent the instruction to "perform a binary ADDition of two operands'' was ADD. As a second example, the opcode LEA stands for ''Load Effective Address'' (note that the capitalized letters denote the characters used in forming the mnemonic). This part of an opcode is sometimes called the *base*, because the opcode refers to the base or *basic* part of the operation. It does not necessarily refer to the size of the instruction. The base usually has some form of size specifier appended. When a size specifier does not exist on a MC68000 instruction, the implied size is usually a 16-bit word opcode (an opcode that expects to perform an operation on a word-sized operand, symbolized by the letter *W*).

The following size specifiers are used in the MC68000 machine language:

**B** Signifies a byte-sized opcode.
**W** Signifies a word-sized opcode.
**L** Signifies the long-word sized opcode. If this size specifier is applied to a branch instruction, it tells the assembler to force a 16-bit relative offset, allowing your program to branch about 32K forward or back, relative to the current location specified by the program counter.
**S** This size specifier is only applied to branch instructions and tells the assembler to force an 8-bit relative offset.

A complete list of the opcodes and their various formats appears in Appendix A. Some of the most important opcodes will be discussed later in this chapter.

The second part of the second field in a line of source code consists of the *operand*(s). Opcodes on the MC68000 may be accompanied by zero, one, or two operands. Operands are the data on which the opcode operates (remember that opcode is a contraction of operation and code), or a reference to the data that the instruction uses.

**Two-operand opcodes.** Usually, when an opcode needs two operands, it's obvious when you look at the meaning of the opcode. MOVE and ADD, for instance, require two operands. The first would require two locations, and the second would require two quantities.

When an opcode requires two operands, the first is the *source operand* and the second is the *destination operand*. Source and destination make sense in this context because, as in a MOVE instruction, the source operand gets moved to a destination. The ADD instruction adds a source operand to a destination operand. MC68000 assemblers do not distinguish between upper- and lowercase opcodes. For the sake of consistency, all opcodes in this book are in uppercase. This, however, is not a sign that opcodes must be written in this manner.

**Zero- and one-operand opcodes.** When only one operand is involved, it is considered the destination operand. Generally, an opcode that requires a single operand performs only one function, such as pulling a value from the stack, storing a value, comparing a value, and so on. An opcode that requires no operand is one that performs a function within the microprocessor itself, or the NOP (No OPeration) opcode, which simply tells the computer to do nothing.

Operands and addressing modes will be discussed in greater detail later in this book.

## The Comment Field

In many respects, comments are the most important part of any program. This includes machine language as well as high level languages such as C, Pascal, or BASIC. Comments are just one more aspect of good programming practice. Most of the life of a program is actually maintenance, such as debugging and adaptation to new situations. Comments are essential to this process.

There are three ways to denote a comment:

- When the first character of a line is an asterisk, the entire line is treated as a comment.
- Any time a semicolon is encountered, the rest of the line is treated as a comment.
- Any characters at least one space after the last operand on a line are considered comments (*ASM68010* assembler only).

A comment signals the assembler to ignore the rest of the current line and to proceed to the next line.

Because the third method of denoting a comment is not standard, it should be avoided if you are planning to use an assembler other than the *ASM68010* assembler.

# CHAPTER 3

# Most Frequently Used MC68000 Instructions

Explaining machine language instructions before explaining the addressing modes they employ is almost as difficult as explaining the addressing modes first, and then the instructions afterward. If you're a beginner, you may need to read this and the next chapter more than once. The first time, try to read for the definitions of terms. The second time through, you'll begin to understand the concepts involved.

## The MOVE Instruction

The most fundamental instruction in the M68000 family is the MOVE instruction. It performs most of the memory and register handling in almost any M68000 program.

Since it is so heavily used, and is the first opcode discussed here, the discussion will be much more detailed than the discussion of opcodes to follow. Even if you're not interested in the MOVE opcode at the moment, it would be a good idea to read this section for the background material.

MOVE is actually a group of related instructions. It performs the function of LOAD and STORE instructions found in many other microprocessors (such as LDA or LDX on the 6502 microprocessor, as well as STA or STX). The MOVE instruction requires two operands—a source and a destination.

The MOVE instruction uses any of the three standard sizes, byte (B), word (W), or long word (L). On the MC68000, the standard MOVE instruction may use any of the legal addressing modes for both the source and destination. (Addressing modes will be discussed later in this book.) Many MC68000 assembly programmers take this capability for granted—until they have to write assembly code on a different microprocessor, such as the 8086, on which the MOVE instruction does not operate in all modes.

With some of the following examples, you can recognize the breadth of utility of the MOVE instruction. Here are some examples of its many forms:

| | |
|---|---|
| **MOVE.B D1,D2** | Move one byte from data register D1 to data register D2. |
| **MOVE INFO,D1** | Move one word from location INFO to data register D1. Note: This uses the implied W size specifier. As a result of using this form of the instruction rather than the MOVE.W (below), the upper 16 bits of the data register won't change. This may result in a sign change (from positive to negative, or negative to positive) of the value moved. The sign will be that of the value previously in the register. |
| **MOVE.W D0,A0** | Move a word from data register D0 to address register A0. Note: When the MOVE instruction loads an address register with a word value, the MOVE instruction automatically *sign extends* the 16-bit value to a 32-bit value, thus, retaining the sign of the value moved, and consequently destroying whatever data had been in the upper 16 bits of the address register. |
| **MOVE.L D1,D2** | Move a long word (32 bits) from data register D1 to data register D2. |
| **MOVE.W #1,FLAG** | Set the data location at the label FLAG to the value of 1. |
| **MOVE.L A0,−(SP)** | Move the long word in address register A0 to the top of stack. Note: This is the equivalent of the PUSH instruction commonly found in other computers. This will be discussed later in more detail. |
| **MOVE.W (SP)+,D6** | Move a word from the top of stack to data register D6. Note: This is the equivalent of the POP instruction commonly found in other computers. This will be discussed later in more detail. |
| **MOVE.L D2,(A0)** | Move the contents of data register D2 to the address in address register A0. |
| **MOVE.W VAR1,VAR2** | Move the data at label VAR1 to the location of label VAR2. |

| | | |
|---|---|---|
| **MOVE.B** | **5(A0,D0),0(SP,A1)** | A move instruction with complex addressing modes. |
| **MOVE.W** | **10(PC),8(A1,D1)** | A move instruction with complex addressing modes. |

In addition to the standard MOVE instruction, there is a faster subset of the most-used forms of MOVE.

**MOVEQ.** A variation of MOVE to put *immediate data* directly into a register. Immediate data is data specified on the same line as the MOVE instruction, as in MOVE.W #1,FLAG in which #1, is the immediate data moved to FLAG.

MOVEQ is specialized. It can only move an 8-bit numerical value into the data registers. The key thing to remember is that although only 8 bits are specified, they're sign extended to a full 32 bits before the data register is loaded. Here are some examples:

| | | |
|---|---|---|
| **MOVEQ** | **#3,D1** | Move the value 3 into data register D1. |
| **MOVEQ** | **#'?',D0** | Move the ASCII character ? (hexadecimal value #$3F) into data register D0. |
| **MOVEQ** | **#$FF,D7** | Move the value $FFFFFFFF (the sign-extended version of #$FF) into data register D7. |

The advantage of MOVEQ is that it is the fastest instruction for moving a small number into a register. It is used in many of the programs in this book to clear a data register, as in

```
MOVEQ   #0,D0
```

This is faster than the following instruction, which accomplishes the same thing:

```
CLR.L   D0
```

**MOVEM.** A single MOVEM (MOVE Multiple registers) instruction can move more than one register to or from the stack. This instruction is similar to MOVE, but it has a different set of operands. The operands required by MOVEM are a *register list* and memory address. A register list is a set of register names that specify which registers are to be copied to the data locations, or from the data locations to the registers. Here are some examples of register lists:

| | |
|---|---|
| D0 | Data register D0 only. |
| D0–D3 | Data registers D0, D1, D2, D3. |
| D2–D5/A0 | The registers D2, D3, D4, D5, A0. |
| D5–D7/A3–A6 | The registers D5, D6, D7, A3, A4, A5, A6. |
| D6/A6 | The registers D6 and A6. |

Two items separated by a dash (–) indicate an inclusive list of registers, and the slash (/) is used to separate register names or register lists.

When storing a list of registers to memory, the following addressing modes are allowed (more information on addressing can be found in Chapter 4):

| | | |
|---|---|---|
| (A*n*) | −(A*n*) | d16(A*n*) |
| d8(A*n*,R*n*) | ABS.W | ABS.L |

When loading a list of registers from memory, the following addressing modes are allowed:

| | | |
|---|---|---|
| (A*n*) | (A*n*)+ | d16(A*n*) |
| d8(A*n*,R*n*) | ABS.W | ABS.L |
| d16(PC) | d8(PC,R*n*) | |

Here are some examples:

| | | |
|---|---|---|
| **MOVEM.L** | **D0–D1/A0–A1,(A2)** | Moves D0, D1, A0, A1 to the address in address register A2. |
| **MOVEM.L** | **D0–D7/A0–A6,−(SP)** | This pushes all registers except A7 onto the stack. |
| **MOVEM.L** | **(SP)+,D0–D7/A0–A6** | This pulls all registers except A7 from the stack. This is the opposite of the operation immediately above. |
| **MOVEM.L** | **DATAREGS,D0–D7** | Moves data from the location marked by the label DATAREGS into the data registers. |

In MC68000 machine language, the opcode MOVE allows all of the legal addressing modes for either of its operands. MC68000 machine language provides extra error checking when restricted versions of the instruction are used. Most commonly, the restricted version of the opcode is the opcode followed by I, A, and sometimes M.

- The I appendage implies that the source operand must be an immediate operand.
- The A appendage implies that an address register is the destination.
- The M appendage implies that both the source and destination will be memory addresses.

For the MOVE instruction, only MOVEI and MOVEA are acceptable. The M appendage doesn't exist for the MOVE instruction. It would conflict with the MOVEM instruction described above.

Here are some legal examples of the MOVEA, and MOVEI instructions:

```
MOVEI      #10,D0          ; LOAD IMMEDIATE VALUE 10 INTO D0
```

This is the same as:

```
MOVE       #10,D0
```

or:

```
MOVE.W     #10,D0
```

The instruction:

```
MOVEA      JUNK,A0         ; MOVE CONTENTS OF MEMORY LOCATION
                           ; JUNK INTO A0
```

is the same as:

```
MOVE.W     JUNK,A0
```

Here are illegal examples of MOVEA and MOVEI:

```
MOVEI.L    JUNK,(A0)       ;THE SOURCE OPERAND ISN'T IMMEDIATE
MOVEA.L    (A0)+,(A1)+     ;THE DESTINATION ISN'T AN ADDRESS
                           ; REGISTER
```

The MOVEA instruction is often confused with the LEA (Load Effective Address) instruction. This is due to the misinterpretation of the MOVEA instruction as MOVe Effective Address, which is incorrect. The real meaning of MOVEA is MOVE to Address register.

## The LEA Instruction

The LEA (Load Effective Address) instruction loads the address of a labeled location in memory into an address register.

Normally, every time an instruction is executed, the microprocessor reads the instruction, calculates the addresses of the operands, uses these addresses to get the real operands, performs the specified operation on the source operand, and finally, stores the result in the specified destination operand address.

When the source or destination operand is a register, the microprocessor has a very easy time figuring out where the data operand is. Other times, the MC68000 microprocessor must precalculate the actual memory address of the data that will be used in the instruction. Once the address has been calculated, the MC68000 microprocessor can fetch the data from that address and perform the operation. This calculated address is called the *effective address* of an operand.

It is useful to have the effective address calculated and stored for later use in the program. This is the most common application of the LEA instruction. It calculates the address of the source operand and loads the calculated address into an address register. For example, you might have a labeled location in your program which is the beginning of an array of data. You might want to move the starting address of the array into an address register this way:

```
LEA         ARRAY,A1
```

To demonstrate the difference between MOVE and LEA, examine the following lines. For the sake of the example, say the label ARRAY is at memory location 1A007A:

```
MOVE.L      ARRAY,A1        ;MOVES THE CONTENTS OF MEMORY LOCA-
                            ; TION 1A007A TO A1
LEA.L       ARRAY,A2        ;MOVES THE NUMBER 1A007A TO A2
```

LEA always moves a long-word address. That address can then be used as part of another instruction as in the following source code:

```
LEA.L       ARRAY,A2
MOVE.L      (A2),A1
```

This source code would assemble into a program that loads the address of ARRAY into register A2, and then moves the value in the memory location labeled ARRAY into register A1.

The operation performed by LEA can be accomplished in

another way, using the MOVE or MOVEA instruction:

```
MOVE.L     #ARRAY,A2
```

or

```
MOVEA.L    #ARRAY,A2
```

are equivalent to the LEA instruction:

```
LEA        ARRAY,A2
```

These three instructions all load the 32-bit address of the label ARRAY into register A2. These forms are equivalent, but not identical (they result in different object codes, with LEA executing faster).

The LEA instruction can use many of the MC68000 addressing mode calculations, including:

| | | |
|---|---|---|
| (A*n*) | (A*n*) + | −(A*n*) |
| d16(A*n*) | d8(A*n*,R*n*) | ABS.W |
| ABS.L | d16(PC) | d8(PC,R*n*) |

Here are some examples of the use of the LEA instruction:

| | | |
|---|---|---|
| **LEA** | **(A1),A2** | Moves A1 to A2. |
| **LEA** | **1(A2),A2** | The address in register A2 is incremented by one and loaded into register A2. |
| **LEA.L** | **$AA(A2),A3** | Adds hexadecimal number $AA to A2, and loads the sum into A3. |
| **LEA** | **0(PC),A2** | This instruction loads the address of the next instruction (located in the program counter) into A2. |
| **LEA.L** | **−4(PC),A0** | This line of source code loads its own address into A0. |
| **LEA** | **0(A2,D2.L),A0** | Adds the contents of registers A2 and D2 and the number 0, and stores the sum in A0. |

When programming, you can easily tell when you need to use LEA and when you need MOVEA instead. Always use the LEA instruction rather than the MOVE immediate form. This practice makes programs easier to read and debug.

## The ADD and SUB Instructions

The MC68000 microprocessor provides a basic set of arithmetic functions. These are addition, subtraction, multiplication, and division. All four of these arithmetic functions are available for 16-bit values. Addition and subtraction can be used for 8- and 32-bit values as well.

There are three *ADD binary* and three *SUBtract binary* instructions. The MC68000 microprocessor can ADD:

- Any data value to any data register
- Any data register to any memory location
- Any word or long-word value to any address register
- Any immediate value to any data location

There's also the ADDQ instruction, which stands for ADD Quick. It allows very rapid addition of small integer values between one and eight.

Similarly, the MC68000 can subtract:

- Any data value from any data register
- Any data register from any data location
- Any word or long-word value from any address register
- Any immediate value from any data location

The SUB instruction also has the SUBQ (for SUBtract Quick) form for small integer values between one and eight.

One additional note: When adding or subtracting a 16-bit (word) value from an address register, the word value is automatically sign extended first and treated as a signed 32-bit value.

Here is a list of some of the possible ADD and SUBtract combinations:

| | | |
|---|---|---|
| **ADD** | **D4,D5** | Add the word in register D4 to the word in register D5. Remember that this operation sign extends the 16-bit word to 32 bits. This also happens in the next example. |
| **ADD.L** | **(A0),D4** | Find the long word in the address referenced by A0 and add it to D4. |
| **ADD.B** | **D4,BVAL** | Add the byte in D4 to the data at the address at label BVAL. |
| **ADD.W** | **#12345,A1** | Add the decimal constant 12345 ($3039 hexadecimal) to address register A1. |
| **ADD.W** | **#$3039,A1** | Same as last example, but in hexadecimal. You must use a dollar sign ($) to indicate hexadecimal. |
| **ADD.W** | **D4,A2** | Add the word in D4 to A2. This will result in sign extension. |
| **ADDQ.L** | **#1,D0** | Add one to D0. This is like an increment instruction on other microprocessors. |

| | |
|---|---|
| **ADDQ.W #4,D0** | Add four to D0. This allows incrementing by the value 4 (or any other integer) instead of 1. |
| **SUB.W #55,A0** | Subtract the value 55 from the value in register A0. |
| **SUB.B D0,D4** | Subtract the byte contained in D0 from the value in D4. Remember that the carry flag is also set if a borrow occurs. |
| **SUBQ.W #3,WVAL** | Subtract the value 3 from the word at the location labeled WVAL. This is a more general version of the *decrement* instruction found in other computers. |
| **ADD.L D0,D0** | A fast arithmetic shift left by one bit. This effectively multiplies the value in register D0 by two (the same action as if all bits in the long word in register D0 were shifted one location to the left). |

## The MUL and DIV Instructions

The MC68000 microprocessor doesn't have a complete set of 8-, 16- and 32-bit arithmetic multiply and divide instructions.

The microprocessor can perform 16-bit × 16-bit multiplication, yielding a 32-bit product. It can also divide a 32-bit dividend by a 16-bit divisor to yield a 16-bit quotient stored in the lower 16 bits of the destination register. If there is a remainder, it will be stored in the upper word of the destination register as a result.

**Multiplication.** The two multiplication instructions are MULS (MULtiply Signed) and MULU (MULtiply Unsigned). They can take the following as multiplier operands.

- As a source:
  A data register
  An immediate value
  A memory location
- As a destination:
  A data register

Some sample multiplications are:

| | |
|---|---|
| **MULS #5,D0** | Multiply D0 by five (signed) and store the product in D0. |
| **MULU DATA,D2** | Multiply the word at location DATA with the contents of D2 (unsigned) and leave the product in D2. |

After multiplication, the destination data register contains a full 32-bit result.

**Division.** The two divide instructions are the DIVS (DIVide Signed) and DIVU (DIVide Unsigned). They divide a 32-bit value in the destination register by a 16-bit value specified by the source operand.

The result of the division comes in two parts: the quotient and the remainder. After performing the division, the microprocessor places the quotient in the lower 16 bits of the destination register and the remainder in the upper 16 bits of the same register.

Because some division operations will result in a quotient too large to fit in the lower 16 bits of the destination register, an overflow condition may occur. When overflow takes place, the overflow status bit in the status register is set to 1.

If D1 contains the value 26 and D0 contains the value 5, the following code:

```
DIVS   D0,D1    ;SAME AS SAYING D1 = D1 / D0
```

stores a value of 5 in the low word of D1, and a value of 1 in the high word of D1.

Here are more examples:

**DIVS #5,D0** Divide D0 by five and store the results in D0.
**DIVU D2,D3** Divide the value in register D3 by the value in register D2 and store the results in D3.

Since the MC68000 does not provide a 32-bit × 32-bit multiply or divide instruction, this operation must be done in software. Below is an example of a 32-bit × 32-bit multiplication routine yielding a 32-bit result. Note that an extra multiply must be performed to yield a full 64-bit result.

```
* MULTIPLY A 32-BIT D0 BY A 32-BIT D1. PLACE THE RESULT
* OF THE MULTIPLY IN D2. USE D3 AND D4 AS TEMPORARY VALUES.
* THIS IS A SIGNED MULTIPLY , SO THE SIGN PRESERVATION CODE
* IS ALSO IN THIS EXAMPLE
    MOVEQ    #1,D4                ; THE TEMP USED TO HOLD THE SIGN
                                  ; OF THE RESULT
    TST.L    D0                   ; CHECK THE FIRST 32-BIT VALUE FOR
                                  ; NEGATIVITY
    BGE      POSITIVE_FIRST
    NEG.L    D0                   ; MAKE POSITIVE FOR MULTIPLY
    NEG      D4                   ; KEEP SIGN
POSITIVE_FIRST:
```

```
    TST.L    D1                 ; CHECK THE SECOND 32-BIT VALUE FOR
                                ; NEGATIVITY
    BGE      POSITIVE_SECOND
    NEG.L    D1                 ; MAKE POSITIVE FOR MULTIPLY
    NEG      D4                 ; KEEP SIGN
POSITIVE_SECOND:
; NOW MULTIPLY 2 POSITIVE 32-BIT NUMBERS
    MOVE.W   D0,D2
    MULU     D1,D2              ; MULTIPLY LOW16*LOW16
    MOVE.W   D0,D3
    SWAP     D0                 ; SWITCH TOP/BOTTOM REGISTER HALF
                                ; OF D0
    MULU     D1,D0              ; MULTIPLY HIGH16*LOW16
    SWAP     D1                 ; SWITCH TOP/BOTTOM REGISTER HALF
                                ; OF D1
    MULU     D1,D3              ; MULTIPLY LOW16*HIGH16
    ADD.L    D0,D3              ; COMBINE THE MIDDLE 32 BITS OF THE
                                ; 64-BIT MULTIPLY
    SWAP     D3
    CLR.W    D3                 ; PREPARE TO COMBINE LOWER 32 BITS
    ADD.L    D3,D2              ; COMBINE THE LOWER 32 BITS OF THE
                                ; 64-BIT NUMBER
    TST      D4                 ; NEED TO CHANGE THE SIGN??
    BGE      EXIT               ; NO
    NEG.L    D2                 ; YES, MULTIPLY BY -1
EXIT:
* REGISTER D2 NOW CONTAINS THE 32-BIT RESULT
* AND REGISTERS D0, D1, D3, D4 CONTAIN GARBAGE
* THIS SEQUENCE DOES NOT SET UP THE OVERFLOW BITS
```

## Logical Instructions (OR, EOR, AND, NOT, and NEG)

By now you should be getting the idea of how MC68000 instructions are organized. The logical instructions (AND, OR, EOR, NEG) operate directly on registers or memory, and on all three sizes of data (byte, word, and long word).

Logical operators affect data bit-by-bit. In order to understand their operation, it is necessary to think of values in terms of binary numbers. You're probably already familiar with logical operators and the binary number system. If not, you should consult a text such as *Machine Language for Beginners* from COMPUTE! Publications, or *Assembly Language Programming* from Howard W. Sams.

The logical operators operate by very special rules in the MC68000 microprocessor. For instance, the source operand of an EOR must be a data register. Also, the AND and OR instructions cannot use an address register, and either the source or destination must be a data register

The NOT and NEG instructions are not as widely known as the others. They each take only one operand—which may not be an address register. NOT reverses all the bits in the destination and NEG performs a two's compliment NEGation operation, changing the sign of a signed integer.

Below are truth tables for the AND, OR, EOR, NOT, and NEG instructions, as well as some examples of each.

**Logical AND (AND).**

| | | Binary | Hexadecimal |
|---|---|---|---|
| 0 AND 0 = 0 | | 11001010 | CA |
| 0 AND 1 = 0 | AND | 10111000 | B8 |
| 1 AND 0 = 0 | | ________ | — |
| 1 AND 1 = 1 | | 10001000 | 88 |

Program example:

```
AND.W   #1,D0         ; CHECK FOR ODD OR EVENNESS (IN A
                      WORD)
BEQ     WASEVEN       ; BRANCH TO LABEL WASEVEN, IF IT WAS
                      ; EVEN
AND.L   #$FFFFFFFE,D0 ; MAKE D0 EVEN
```

**Inclusive OR (OR).**

| | | Binary | Hexadecimal |
|---|---|---|---|
| 0 OR 0 = 0 | | 11001010 | CA |
| 0 OR 1 = 1 | OR | 10111000 | B8 |
| 1 OR 0 = 1 | | ________ | — |
| 1 OR 1 = 1 | | 11111010 | FA |

Program examples:

```
OR.L    D1,D0    ;UNION THE TWO LONG-WORD REGISTERS
OR.W    #1,D3    ;MAKE D3's LOW WORD ODD
```

**Exclusive OR (EOR).**

| | | Binary | Hexadecimal |
|---|---|---|---|
| 0 EOR 0 = 0 | | 11001010 | CA |
| 0 EOR 1 = 1 | EOR | 10111000 | B8 |
| 1 EOR 0 = 1 | | ________ | — |
| 1 EOR 1 = 0 | | 01110010 | 72 |

Program examples:

```
EOR.L   D0,D0    ;SET D0 TO 0
EOR.B   D0,VAL   ;EOR D0 WITH BYTE AT LOCATION VAL
```

**Logical NOT (NOT).**

| | | | |
|---|---|---|---|
| | | Binary | Hexadecimal |
| NOT 0 = 1 | NOT | 11001010 | CA |
| NOT 1 = 0 | | ________ | |
| | | 00110101 | 35 |

Program example:

```
NOT.B   FLAG   ;INVERT THE BITS AT BYTE LOCATION 'FLAG'
```

**Arithmetic NEGate (NEG).**

Program examples:

```
NEG.L   D2       ;MULTIPLY D2 BY -1
NEG.W   RESULT   ;MULTIPLY WORD AT LOCATION RESULT BY -1
```

## Shift and Rotate Instructions (LSL, LSR, ASL, ASR, ROL, and ROR)

These instructions perform Logical Shifts Left (LSL), Logical Shifts Right (LSR), Arithmetic Shifts Left (ASL), Arithmetic Shifts Right (ASR), ROtations Left (ROL), and ROtations Right (ROR).

Shifts and rotations have three different forms. The first two forms involve multiple shifts (shifting or rotating the bits) in a data register. The first of these two forms uses an immediate value between 0 and 7 to specify the number of shifts (this is called a *shift count*—a value of 0 causes a shift of 8 bits). The second form uses a data register to specify the number shift count. The six least significant bits of the source register specify a shift count of between 0 and 63 (a value of 0 causes a shift of 64 bits).

The destination operand must always be a data register.

The third form performs a shift or rotate of only one bit position on an operand in memory, rather than a data register. The first two forms may shift or rotate data registers containing byte, word, or long-word values, but single-bit shifts are restricted to word-sized (16-bit) values.

The following diagrams show the operation sequence for a single-bit shift or rotate. In these examples the letter *C* stands for the carry bit and *X* stands for the extend bit (both of these bits are in the status register).

The figures below represent an entire 32-bit register. The arrows in these diagrams indicate the direction in which data moves within the register. During shifts and rotates, the last bit on the left or right is pushed out of the register. The diagrams indicate whether that bit is lost or stored in the X and C bits of the status register.

When discussing bits on the MC68000 family, the high-order bit is bit #7 for a byte, #15 for a word, and #31 for a long-word value.

**Arithmetic Shift Left (ASL).** The first shift is ASL. A graphic depiction of this instruction can be found in Figure 3-1. Each bit is shifted to the left. The high-order bit (in this case, Bit 31) is shifted into the C and X bits in the status register, and a 0 is shifted into bit 0 at the far right. The overflow bit is set if a sign change occurs during the shift.

**Figure 3-1. Arithmetic Shift Left (ASL)**

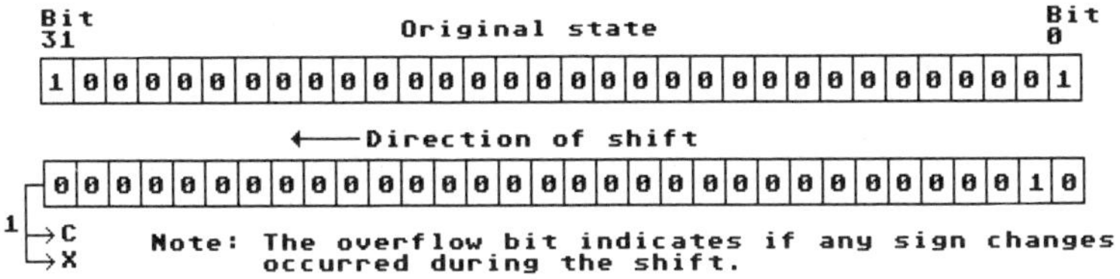


Examples of Arithmetic Shift Left:

```
ASL.L   #2,D0   ;SHIFT LONG WORD IN D0 LEFT BY TWO BITS
ASL     D0,D1   ;SHIFT WORD IN D1 LEFT BY SHIFT COUNT (IN D0)
                ; BIT POSITIONS
```

**Arithmetic Shift Right (ASR).** Figure 3-2 shows the action of an ASR instruction. Each bit is shifted to the right. Bit 0 is shifted into the C and X bits in the status register. The sign bit is duplicated from the high-order bit of the shift (in this case, Bit 31).

**Figure 3-2. Arithmetic Shift Right (ASR)**

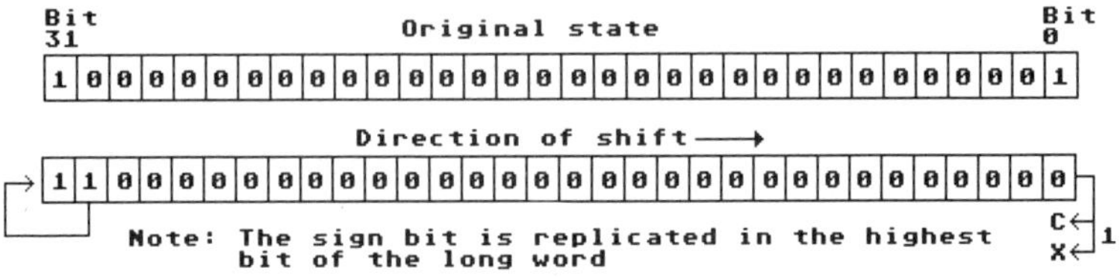


Examples of Arithmetic Shift Right:

```
ASR.L   #2,D0   ; SHIFT LONG WORD IN D0 RIGHT BY TWO BITS
ASR     D0,D1   ; SHIFT WORD IN D1 RIGHT BY SHIFT COUNT (IN D0)
                ; BIT POSITIONS
```

**Logical Shift Left (LSL).** Figure 3-3 shows the effect of an LSL instruction. Each bit is shifted to the left. The high-order bit (in this case, Bit 31) is shifted into the C and X bits of the status register and a 0 is shifted into Bit 0.

**Figure 3-3. Logical Shift Left (LSL)**

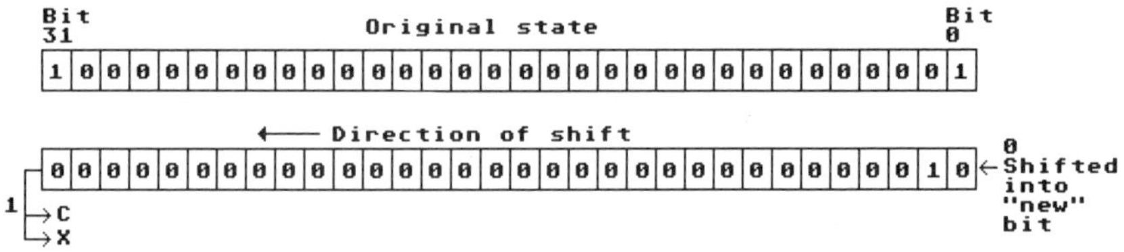


Examples of Logical Shift Left (LSL):

```
LSL.L   #3,D0   ;SHIFT LONG WORD IN D0 LEFT BY 3 BITS
LSL     D0,D1   ;SHIFT WORD IN D1 LEFT SHIFT COUNT (IN D0) BIT
                ;POSITIONS
```

**Logical Shift Right (LSR).** The LSR instruction (Figure 3-4) shifts each bit to the right. A 0 is shifted into the high-order bit (in this case, Bit 31), and Bit 0 is shifted into the C and X bits of the status register.

**Figure 3-4. Logical Shift Right (LSR)**

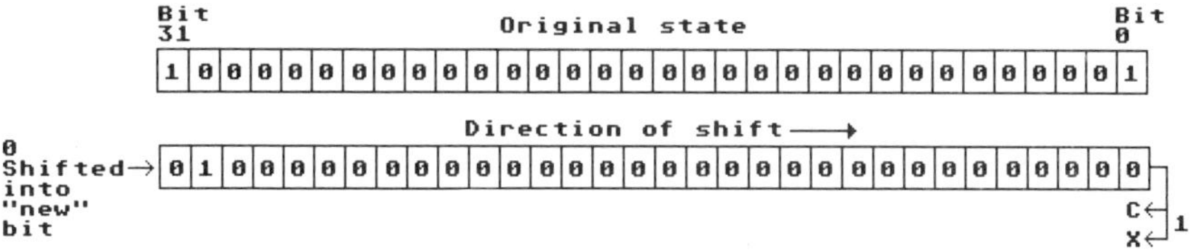


Examples of Logical Shift Right (LSR):

```
LSR.L   #4,D0   ;SHIFT LONG WORD IN D0 RIGHT BY 4 BITS
LSR     D0,D1   ;SHIFT WORD IN D1 RIGHT BY SHIFT COUNT (IN D0)
                ;BIT POSITIONS
```

**ROtate Left (ROL).** ROL rotates each bit to the left, placing the high-order bit of the rotation (in this case, Bit 31) into the C bit of the status register and into Bit 0 at the far right (see Figure 3-5).

**Figure 3-5. ROtate Left (ROL)**

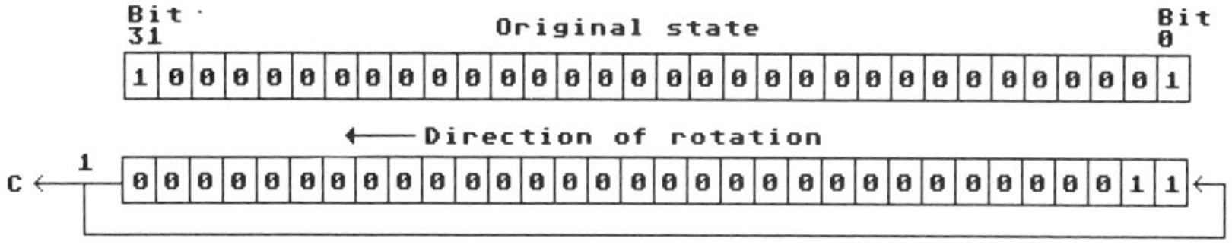


Examples of ROtate Left (ROL):

```
ROL.L   #3,D0   ;ROTATE LONG WORD IN D0 LEFT BY 3 BITS
ROL     D0,D1   ;ROTATE WORD IN D1 LEFT BY SHIFT COUNT (IN D0)
                ;BIT POSITIONS
```

**ROtate Right (ROR).** ROR performs a mirror image of ROL. Each bit is rotated to the right. Bit 0 is placed in the C bit of the status register and in the high-order bit of the rotation (in this case, Bit 31). See Figure 3-6.

**Figure 3-6. ROtate Right (ROR)**

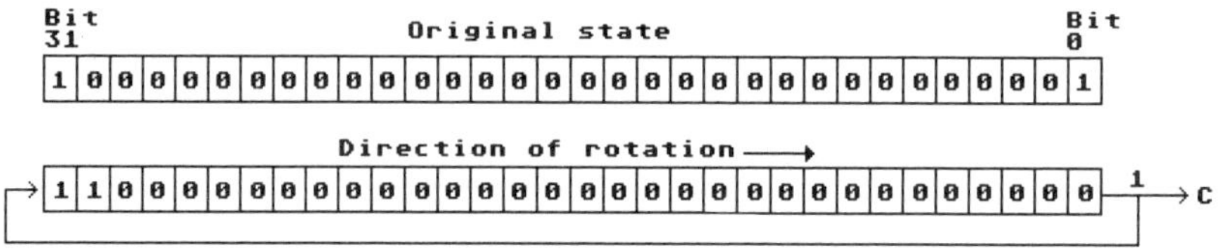


Examples of ROtate Right (ROR):

```
ROR.L   #4,D0   ;ROTATE LONG WORD IN D0 RIGHT BY 4 BITS
ROR     D0,D1   ;ROTATE WORD IN D1 RIGHT BY SHIFT COUNT (IN D0)
                ;BIT POSITIONS
```

## Bit Manipulation

Another group of MC68000 instructions are those that test and/or set individual bits. These instructions work on any of the 32 bits in a data register, or any of 8 bits of a byte location in memory. When using these instructions, you can specify the bit in question with either an immediate value or a data register.

The BTST, Bit TeST, instruction tells if any one of a data register's 32 bits is set (1) or cleared (0). Alternatively, it can test any one of 8 bits of a memory location for the same information. The result of the bit test is deposited in the Z (zero) bit in the status register. The BTST instruction can be followed by either a BNE, Branch on Not Equal, if the bit is set, or a BEQ, Branch on EQual, if the bit is cleared. The MC68000 also provides three other bit instructions. These are BSET (Bit SET), BCLR (Bit CLeaR), and BCHG (Bit CHanGe). BCHG is normally considered a bit *toggle* because the instruction inverts the state of the specified bit, turning it on if it was off, or off if it was on.

Here's a code example:

```
;                                ; FIND THE FIRST SET BIT IN D1
            MOVEQ     #0,D0      ;INITIALIZE THE BIT COUNT
LOOP:
            BTST      D0,D1      ;CHECK THE NEXT BIT
            BNE       FOUND      ;FOUND A SET BIT
            ADDQ.W    #1,D0      ; CHECK THE NEXT BIT
            CMP.W     #32,D0
            BLT       LOOP
```

```
NOTFOUND:                    ;NO BIT FOUND
          BSET    #0,D1      ;SET THE LOW ORDER BIT
;                            ;MORE CODE HERE
FOUND:                       ;A BIT WAS FOUND
          BCHG    D0,D1      ;TURN OFF THE BIT THAT WAS FOUND
```

## Branch and Loop Instructions

One important difference between a computer and a simple adding machine is the computer's ability to make yes-or-no decisions and to change the program flow based on these decisions. This process is called *branching*. All computers have this feature in some form or another.

A loop is a series of instructions that must either repeat a certain number of times, or repeat until a given condition changes. For instance, to print a line of dashes across the screen, you would set up a loop to print a hyphen 80 times. This loop repeats or *iterates* a given number of times.

Another example is when a program waits for input from the keyboard; it will probably use a subroutine to check the keyboard constantly until a key is pressed, and then continue with the program. This loop tests for a change in conditions.

**Branching instructions.** The MC68000 microprocessor has a group of branch instructions to branch on a variety of conditions. A branch must go to a memory location that is within ±32768 bytes from the branch instruction itself. This restriction is rarely a problem, but when longer branches are required, a JMP (JuMP) instruction provides the programmer with the ability to directly branch to any location in memory.

Branch instructions operate on values stored in the status register bits (known as condition code bits) discussed earlier. After almost any instruction has completed execution, the MC68000 tests the value of the result and sets up the condition code register. An MC68000 machine language program can then test for condition codes with the B*cc* instructions, and change the flow of execution elsewhere if the condition has been met.

There are three types of condition code tests. These are signed tests, unsigned tests, and miscellaneous tests. Signed condition code tests are performed as the result of a signed arithmetic operation. Unsigned condition code tests are performed as the result of unsigned arithmetic operations. Miscellaneous tests are performed when testing for side effects of an operation, such as overflow or carrying (marked by a set overflow or carry bit of the status register, respectively).

The following branching conditions are recognized by the MC68000:

- Signed conditions:
  BEQ Branch EQual
  BGE Branch Greater or Equal
  BGT Branch Greater Than
  BLE Branch Less or Equal
  BLT Branch Less Than
  BNE Branch Not Equal
- Unsigned conditions:
  BEQ Branch EQual
  BHI Branch HIgh
  BHS Branch High or Same
  BLO Branch LOw
  BLS Branch Low or Same
- Miscellaneous conditions:
  BCC Branch Carry Clear
  BCS Branch Carry Set
  BMI Branch MInus
  BPL Branch PLus
  BVC Branch oVerflow Clear
  BVS Branch oVerflow Set
- Unconditional branch:
  BRA BRanch Always

All of these terms are self-explanatory. BEQ, for instance, will cause the program flow to branch if the two given operands are equal.
Some simple branching examples:

```
;                        ; THIS EXAMPLE DOES A SIGNED COM-
                         ; PARISON AGAINST THE VALUE
;                        ; IN D0, AND BRANCHES IF D0 IS GREATER
                         ; THAN 20
;                        ;
;                        ; IN BASIC THIS WOULD BE:
;                        ;
;                        ; IF D0 > 20 THEN D2 = 1
;                        ;
;                        ; IN C THIS WOULD BE:
;                        ;
;                        ; if ( D0 > 20 ) D2 = 1;
```

```
        CMP.W   #20,D0      ; COMPARE D0 AND 20
        BGT     SETD2       ; IF THE OPERATION D0 - 20 IS > 0
                            ; GOTO SETD2
        BRA     EXIT        ; IF NOT GO TO EXIT
SETD2:
        MOVEQ   #1,D2       ; SET D2
EXIT:
;                           ;
;                           ; ANOTHER WAY TO DO THE SAME THING
                            ; (AND FASTER)
;                           ; IS TO REVERSE THE LOOP TEST:
;                           ;
        CMP.W   #20,D0      ; COMPARE D0 AND 20
        BLE     EXIT        ; IF THE OPERATION D0 - 20 IS <= 0
                            ; GOTO EXIT
        MOVEQ   #1,D2       ; SET D2
;                           ;
;                           ; THIS EXAMPLE DOES AN UNSIGNED
                            ; COMPARISON AGAINST TWO
;                           ; ADDRESSES, AND BRANCHES IF THE AD-
                            ; DRESS IN A0 IS <= THE ADDRESS
;                           ; IN A1
;                           ;
        CMP.L   A0,A1       ; COMPARE A1 WITH A0
        BLS     ISLE        ; BRANCH IF A0 <= A1
ISHI:
;                           ; A0 MUST BE STRICTLY GREATER THAN
                            ; A1
;                           ; CHECK TO SEE IF FLAG IS SET OR NOT
;                           ;
        TST.W   FLAG
        BEQ     NOTSET      ; BRANCH IF NOT SET (FLAG=0)
;                           ;
;                           ; ADD TWO VALUES AND BRANCH IF THE
                            ; RESULT IS ZERO
;                           ;
        ADD     D0,D1
        BEQ     ADDTOZERO
```

**CoMPare (CMP).** As shown in the example code above, the CMP (CoMPare) instruction is often an essential part of a branch. CMP always takes two operands. Source operands can be any data value and destination operands can be data or address registers. When the source operand is an immediate value, the destination operand can be a memory location.

The CMP instruction does not change the source or destination operands. It subtracts the source operand from the destination operand, sets the condition code bits, and throws away the result.

**The TeST instruction.** The TST (TeST) operation, similar to the compare operation, tests the one operand against zero, sets the condition codes, and throws away the results. The following two lines are equivalent:

```
TST.W   D0
```

is the same as

```
CMP.W   #0,D0
```

**The DB*cc* instruction.** Another looping construct is the DB*cc* instruction. This instruction provides a looping mechanism similar to the REPEAT UNTIL looping construct of Pascal. The DB*cc* instruction repeats a loop UNTIL either the condition becomes true, or the loop counter goes below 0 (assuming the loop counter was initially set to a positive value).

The format of the DB*cc* instruction is DB*cc* D*n*,LABEL. The *cc* may be any of the following condition codes.

- Signed conditions:
  DBEQ Decrement and Branch EQual
  DBGE Decrement and Branch Greater or Equal
  DBGT Decrement and Branch Greater Than
  DBLE Decrement and Branch Less or Equal
  DBLT Decrement and Branch Less Than
  DBNE Decrement and Branch Not Equal
- Unsigned conditions:
  DBHI Decrement and Branch HIgh
  DBHS Decrement and Branch High or Same
  DBLO Decrement and Branch LOw
  DBLS Decrement and Branch Low or Same
- Miscellaneous conditions:
  DBCC Decrement and Branch Carry Clear
  DBCS Decrement and Branch Carry Set
  DBMI Decrement and Branch MInus
  DBPL Decrement and Branch PLus
  DBVC Decrement and Branch oVerflow Clear
  DBVS Decrement and Branch oVerflow Set

- Special conditions:
  DBF Decrement and Branch False (conditional test is never true)
  DBT Decrement and Branch True (conditional test is always true)

The DB*cc* instruction works in the following manner: If the specified condition is true, the loop terminates and execution continues with the next instruction; if it is false, the lower 16 bits of the specified register are decremented by one. If the result is −1, the loop terminates and execution continues with the next instruction. If the result is not −1, the program branches back to the top of the loop.

The DB*cc* instruction only uses the bottom 16 bits of the destination data register for a loop counter. The effect is that loop counters cannot be larger than 32,767. Larger loop counts can be accomplished, however, simply by using nested loops.

The MC68010 processor has a special *loop mode* for DB*cc* instructions with a relative offset of −4 (see the example below). The MC68010 has a two word prefetch queue in addition to a one word instruction decode register. In a DB*cc* loop with a displacement of −4, the DB*cc* instruction and its branch displacement are held in the prefetch queue, and all opcode fetches are suppressed and only operand reads and writes are performed until an exit condition is met. This means that any single-word MC68010 instruction used inside the loop will run faster because the MC68010 doesn't refetch the loop and DB*cc* instructions with each loop. It holds them and reuses them without reading them in from memory over and over again.

Some of the more important cases include fast block moves such as:

```
        LEA.L    SOURCEADDRESS,A0          ; GET THE SOURCE
                                           ; ADDRESS
        LEA.L    DESTINATIONADDRESS,A1     ; GET THE DESTINATION
                                           ; ADDRESS
        MOVE.W   #LENGTHOFMOVE,D0          ; LOAD THE NUMBER OF
                                           ; LOOPS
LOOP:
        MOVE.B   (A0)+,(A1)+               ; MOVE 1 BYTE IN THE
                                           ; LOOP
        DBEQ     D0,LOOP                   ; NOTE DISPLACEMENT OF
                                           ; −4
```

The bits tested in condition codes for a B*cc* or DB*cc* have not been discussed in this section. For beginning assembly programmers, it's not critical. For a reference on the bits tested for each of the different condition codes, see the B*cc* instruction in the Appendix at the back of this book, or see a MC68000 reference manual.

### Subroutine Calls and Returns

There are two instructions for calling subroutines: BSR (Branch to SubRoutine) and JSR (Jump to SubRoutine). The BSR is used when you're absolutely certain that the beginning of the subroutine is within 32,768 bytes of the BSR instruction. This instruction has the same constraints as the B*cc* instructions.

The JSR instruction is more flexible. It can jump to a subroutine anywhere in memory.

These instructions allow the program to temporarily branch to another place in the program, and later return to the instruction following the BSR or JSR. This is accomplished by saving the return address on the stack. The return address is the program counter (PC) address at the time the BSR or JSR is executed. Later, when an RTS (ReTurn from Subroutine) instruction is executed, the old PC address is removed from the stack and reloaded into the PC. This forces the program to begin executing code where it left off when it encountered the JSR or BSR.

The following example pushes two long words on the stack and calls a subroutine. The subroutine adds the two values and returns the result in register D0.

```
;                                       ; SUBROUTINE CALL SETUP
;                                       ;
          MOVE.L    VALUE1,-(SP)        ; PUSH THE FIRST ARG ON THE
                                        ; STACK
          MOVE.L    VALUE2,-(SP)        ; PUSH THE SECOND ARG ON
                                        ; THE
                                        ; STACK
          JSR       ADDSUBR             ; CALL THE ADDSUBR
          ADDQ.L    #8,SP               ; REMOVE VALUE1 AND VALUE2
;                                       ; .
;                                       ; . MORE CODE HERE
;                                       ; .
;                                       ; THE ADDSUBR SUBROUTINE—
                                        ; ADD TWO STACK ELEMENTS
```

```
                                        ; AND
                                        ; RETURN
;                                       ; A VALUE IN REGISTER D0
ADDSUBR:
          MOVE.L    4(SP),D0
          ADD.L     8(SP),D0
          RTS                           ; ALL SUBROUTINES END WITH
                                        ; RTS
```

## Sign Extension

It is often necessary to increase or decrease the size of data. Decreasing the size is easy. If the data was a 16-bit word value, and has now become an 8-bit byte value, simply start accessing the data with byte addresses. Don't forget to update the address pointer when converting down to a smaller size, especially if the data is not in a register. To increase, or sign extend, the value of a piece of data, use the EXT (EXTend sign bit) instructions. Sign extension is the process of propagating the sign bit (MSB) of a data value to the upper part of a word or long word.

Consider the following problem. A program needs to add together two numbers. These numbers (for this example) are −5 and −1. The obvious answer to this is:

```
   In decimal      In 32-bit binary arithmetic
     -5               FFFFFFFB
   + -1             + FFFFFFFF
     --               --------
     -6               FFFFFFFA
```

As long as all the operators are long words, you will receive the correct result, but consider for a moment what happens when −5 is a word and −1 is a long word. If your arithmetic doesn't use sign extension, the upper bits of the −5 are filled with zeros and the result is not −6:

```
   In 32-bit arithmetic without sign extension:
   0000FFFB     (-5 as a word with no sign extension)
 + FFFFFFFF     (-1 as a long word)
   ---------
   10000FFFA    (not -6)
```

Without sign extension of small values, incorrect results may occur. The MC68000 microprocessor provides two instructions to sign extend values. The instruction EXT.W forms a 16-bit word from a byte by extending its sign bit (bit 7) through bits 8–15 of a data register word. If the EXT.L instruction is used to change a 16-bit value to a 32-bit value, bit 15 of the 16-bit word is extended through bits 16–31 of a data register.

The following example loads a byte variable and sign extends it's value to a full 32 bits.

```
MOVE.B VAR,D0
EXT.W       D0   ;CONVERT BYTE TO WORD
EXT.L       D0   ;CONVERT WORD TO LONG WORD
```

There are a variety of instructions not covered in detail here, but these are among the most common and most powerful instructions available on the MC68000 microprocessor. You will want to learn others. Please refer to a MC68000 microprocessor manual or the Appendix at the end of this book for more information about other instructions.

You should also note that this book does not cover the MC68000 supervisor mode. If you're interested in system-level programming on the MC68000 and the instructions available when a program executes in supervisor mode, study the Appendix or an MC68000 microprocessor manual.

# CHAPTER 4
# MC68000 Addressing Modes

An address is a number or symbol that stands for a memory location. When a microprocessor performs an instruction, the instruction must first be loaded from memory. The same is true of loading or storing data. To load instructions or data from memory, the microprocessor uses the address of its memory locations. Each memory location has a numerical address. In programs, the numerical addresses can be given symbolic names for convenience.

When the MC68000 reads from or writes to a memory location, it uses a 32-bit number as an address. The microprocessor can calculate the address to be used by combining a variety of numbers. In some cases it may add together two registers to form an address. In other cases it may add a constant value to a register to form an address. In yet other cases, the address of a piece of data is simply the number presently held in one of the address registers.

The method used to combine numbers and registers to form an address is called an *addressing mode*. Each instruction dictates an addressing mode used for that instruction. If the instruction manipulates data in a register, the addressing mode is called *register direct*. If the same instruction manipulates data at a memory location pointed to by an address register, the addressing mode is called *address register indirect*. The MC68000 microprocessor has 11 different addressing modes. Some are obvious and simple; others are complex and require study.

As mentioned before, all machine language can be generally divided into two parts: the *opcode* (the instruction given to the machine) and the *operand* (the memory location affected by the instruction). If the data immediately follows the opcode, the microprocessor doesn't have to look somewhere else in memory for it. This is called *immediate addressing*.

As you might suspect, other forms of addressing are more

complex. The microprocessor can look for operands at a specified address. If you were to think of the microprocessor's operation as if it were a post office, this would be analogous to delivering mail based on the address on the envelope. This is called *absolute addressing*.

Sometimes people move and leave forwarding addresses with the postmaster. When running across a letter written to such people, the mail carrier has to go to a central file and look up the new address. This situation is very similar to *register direct addressing*. You store the address of the operand in a data or address register, and tell the microprocessor to look there for the address.

When the mail carrier goes to the address on the envelope and discovers that it's a trailer court or an apartment complex, he or she has to have a little more information, such as lot or apartment number, to find the right address. This is analogous to *register indirect with displacement addressing*.

In all, the Amiga's MC68000 and MC68010 microprocessors have 11 basic addressing modes. MC68000 machine language programs can also directly access other registers not covered here. The 11 addressing modes discussed here are:

| **Name** | **Format** |
|---|---|
| Inherent | |
| Register Direct | R*n* |
| Address Register Indirect | (A*n*) |
| Address Register Indirect with Postincrement | (A*n*)+ |
| Address Register Indirect with Predecrement | −(A*n*) |
| Address Register Indirect with Displacement | d16(A*n*) |
| Address Register Indirect with Index and Displacement | d8(A*n*,R*n*) |
| Absolute | value |
| Program Counter Relative with Displacement | d16(PC) |
| Program Counter Relative with Index and Displacement | d8(PC,R*n*) |
| Immediate Value | #value |

The following is a summary of the 11 different addressing modes and some of their possible uses. The major heads contain the technical name of the addressing mode and the format for its use. D*n*, for instance, refers to any data register. The addressing modes with indexes start with d16 or d8, which indicates that an 8- or a 16-bit index is the first element of the format. R*n* refers to any data or address register. The + and − signs refer to increment and decrement. If the + or − sign leads the addressing mode format, it is an indication that the increment or decrement occurs before the address is accessed. A trailing + or − sign indicates that the increment or decrement occurs after the address is accessed.

## Inherent

Inherent addressing is the easiest of all—the microprocessor knows from the opcode alone which addresses to use. For example, an RTS instruction has no operand field, yet the microprocessor knows to fetch the return address from the stack. Two instructions that require no operands are NOP (No OPeration) and RESET.

## Register Direct R*n*

In the register direct addressing mode, the operand is in the specified address, or data register. Most instructions use either a data register or an address register as one of the operands. Registers are most commonly intermediate values or heavily-used variables in a section of code.

## Address Register Indirect (A*n*)

In the address register indirect addressing mode, the address of the operand is in the specified address register. This 32-bit value is used to fetch the operand for calculation. On the MC68000 and MC68010, only the lowest 24 (out of a possible 32) bits of the address are used. On the MC68008, only the bottom 20 bits are used. The programmer, however, should not use the upper 8 bits of address for flag bits or nonaddress data. This trick was used in some early MC68000 programs—much to their detriment when they were ported to the MC68020, a microprocessor that uses all 32 address bits.

The address register indirect mode is commonly used just after an address has been calculated, or when the same address is used repeatedly. For example, the following code uses the same address multiple times in a loop, but only calculates it once. After it's calculated, it's placed in address register A0:

```
        LEA       USEDALOT,A0
LAB:
        MOVE.W    (A0),D0          ; LOAD A COMMON VARIABLE THAT
                                   ; GETS TRASHED
;.
;.                                 DO SOME WORK
;.
        BRA       LAB
```

This addressing mode does not modify the specified address register.

## Address Register Indirect with Postincrement (A*n*)+

Address register indirect with postincrement is similar to address register indirect, but as the name implies, the value in the address register is automatically increased after each use. If you use this addressing mode with a long-word instruction (like MOVE.L), the address register will be incremented by four. If you use it with a word instruction (like MOVE.W), it will be incremented by two. And if you use it with a byte instruction (like MOVE.B), it will be incremented by one. This addressing mode provides an easy means of processing arrays, stacks, queues, and other data structures.

If the address register is the stack pointer (SP or A7) and the operand size is a byte, then the stack pointer is automatically incremented by two instead of one. This keeps the stack properly aligned at all times.

If the assembly program uses a downward-growing stack, automatically available with the SP register, a stack pop operation is readily available.

```
;                          STACK POP (STACK GROWING DOWNWARD)
    MOVE.L   (SP)+,D0    ; TAKE THE TOP ELEMENT OFF THE STACK AND
                         ; SAVE IT IN D0
```

If the assembly program has created an upward-growing stack, then a stack push operation may be performed in the following way. (Although stacks normally grow downward on the Amiga, it is not necessary that the programmer use stacks in this manner.)

```
;                           ; STACK PUSH (STACK GROWING UPWARD) (AS-
                            ; SUMING A3 IS STACK POINTER)
    MOVE.L   D0,(A3)+       ; PUSH D0 TO THE TOP OF STACK FOR FUTURE
                            ; USE
```

Some more examples:

```
;                           ; QUEUE SAVE/RETRIEVE (ASSUME A2 IS HEAD
                            ; OF
;                           ; QUEUE, A3 IS TAIL OF QUEUE)
;                           ; CHECK QUEUE LIMITS
    MOVE.W   D1,(A3)+       ; SAVE ITEM
;                           ; CHECK QUEUE LIMITS
    MOVE.W   (A2)+,D1       ; GET ITEM

    MOVE.L   (A0)+,(A1)+    ; MOVE LONG WORD POINTED TO BY A0 TO
;                           ; LONG WORD POINTED TO BY A1, THEN
                            ; INCREMENT
;                           ; BOTH A0 AND A1 BY 4 AFTER THE
                            ; INSTRUCTION.
;                           ; THIS IS VERY USEFUL FOR COPYING LARGE
;                           ; CHUNKS OF DATA IN A LOOP
```

## Address Register Indirect with Predecrement −(A*n*)

Using address register indirect with predecrement causes the address of the operand contained in the address register to be decremented by one, two, or four, depending upon the size of the operand specified, *before* the operation takes place. The address in the specified address register is used to fetch the operand or store data. If the address register is the stack pointer (SP or A7), and the operand size is a byte, the stack pointer is automatically decremented by two instead of one. This keeps the stack properly aligned at all times.

Register indirect with predecrement mode has many uses. These include, among other things, array, stack, and queue manipulation.

If the assembly program uses a downward-growing stack, automatically available with the SP register, a stack push operation is readily available.

```
;                           STACK PUSH (STACK GROWING DOWNWARD)
    MOVE.L   D0,-(SP)       ; PUSH D0 TO THE TOP OF STACK FOR FUTURE
                            ; USE
```

If the assembly program has created an upward-growing stack, then a stack pop operation may be performed in the following manner:

```
;                          ; STACK POP (STACK GROWING UPWARD) (AS-
                           ; SUMING A3 IS STACK POINTER)
    MOVE.L    -(SP),D0     ; TAKE THE TOP ELEMENT OFF THE STACK AND
                           ; SAVE IT IN D0 FOR LATER USE
```

Some more examples:

```
;                             ; QUEUE SAVE/RETRIEVE (ASSUME A2 IS
;                             ; HEAD OF QUEUE, A3 IS TAIL OF QUEUE)
;                             ; CHECK QUEUE LIMITS
    MOVE.W    D1,-(A3)        ; SAVE ITEM
;                             ; CHECK QUEUE LIMITS
    MOVE.W    -(A2),D1        ; GET ITEM
    MOVE.W    -(A0),-(A1)     ; DECREMENT BOTH A0 AND A1 BY 2,
;                             ; THEN MOVE THE WORD POINTED TO BY A0
                              ; TO
;                             ; THE WORD POINTED TO BY A1. THIS IS
                              ; VERY
;                             ; USEFUL FOR COPYING LARGE CHUNKS OF
                              ; DATA ;
               ; IN A LOOP
```

Remember that the amount of increment or decrement depends on the size specifier on the actual instruction.

## Address Register Indirect with Displacement d16(A*n*)

Address register indirect with offset uses the address contained in the specified address register added to a 16-bit displacement value as the address of the operand to be fetched or stored. The address register is not modified by this addressing mode.

This addressing mode has many uses. The most common use is accessing stack variables that exist as constant locations. Consider the following example:

```
                MOVE.L    VAR3,-(SP)   ; SAVE THIRD VARIABLE
                MOVE.B    VAR2,-(SP)   ; SAVE SECOND VARIABLE
                MOVE.W    VAR1,-(SP)   ; SAVE FIRST VARIABLE
JSR SUBROUTINE
```

The stack now looks like Figure 4-1.

**Figure 4-1. Stack after loading variables.**

| | Even Byte | Odd Byte | |
|---|---|---|---|
| SP+10 | Variable number three high word | | SP+11 |
| SP+8 | Variable number three low word | | SP+9 |
| SP+6 | 0 0 0 0 0 0 0 0 | Variable number two | SP+7 |
| SP+4 | Variable number one | | SP+5 |
| SP+2 | Return program Counter high word | | SP+3 |
| SP+0 | Return program Counter low word | | SP+1 |

```
;                                ; TO RETURN VARIABLES FROM STACK
    JSR       SUBROUTINE
    MOVE.W    4(SP),D0           ; TO ACCESS VARIABLE 1
    ADD.B     7(SP),D0           ; TO ACCESS VARIABLE 2
    MOVE.L    8(SP),A0           ; TO ACCESS VARIABLE 3
    MOVE.L    D0,(A0)            ; (VARIABLE 3) = VARIABLE 1 + VARIABLE
                                 ; 2
;                                ; ANOTHER WAY TO RETURN VARIABLES
    JSR       SUBROUTINE         ; SAME AS ABOVE
    TST.W     (SP)+              ; POP VARIABLE 1
    TST.B     (SP)+              ; POP VARIABLE 2
    TST.L     (SP)+              ; POP VARIABLE 3
;                                ; MORE EFFICIENT WAY TO RETURN
                                 ; VARIABLES
    JSR       SUBROUTINE         ; SAME AS ABOVE
    ADDQ.L    #8,SP              ; POP ALL 3 VARIABLES SIMULTANEOUSLY
```

## Address Register Indirect with Index and Displacement d8(A*n*,R*n*)

In this addressing mode, the eight-bit displacement, the specified address register, and the specified index register are added together to generate the address of the operand. This calculated value is used to fetch or store the data used by the instruction.

The second register, commonly known as the index register, is either a data register or an address register. This register is referenced as a 16-bit or a 32-bit value. By default, the register acts as a 16-bit value. To specify the size of this register, append to the opcode either .L for a 32-bit value, or .W for a 16-bit value.

This addressing mode is very useful for array indexing. Consider an array of data structures, in which each structure is 16 words long. The following code fragment totals the second words of the array (see Figure 4-2).

```
        LEA.L    ARRAY_OF_STRUCTS,A0
        MOVE.L   NUM_OF_STRUCTS,D1
        LSL.L    #4,D1                 ; GET MAXIMUM INDEX
                                       ; (NUM*16)
        MOVEQ    #0,D0                 ; INIT INDEX
        MOVEQ    #0,D2                 ; SUM
LOOP:
        ADD.W    2(A0,D0),D2           ; SUM = SUM +
                                       ; NEXT_ELEMENT
        ADD.W    #16,D0                ; INDEX = INDEX +
                                       ; STRUCT_SIZE
        CMP.W    D1,D0                 ; IS D0 - D1 < 0?
        BLT      LOOP                  ; YES, DO NEXT ITERATION
                 (the rest of the code)
```

**Figure 4-2. The effect of address register indirect with index and displacement.**

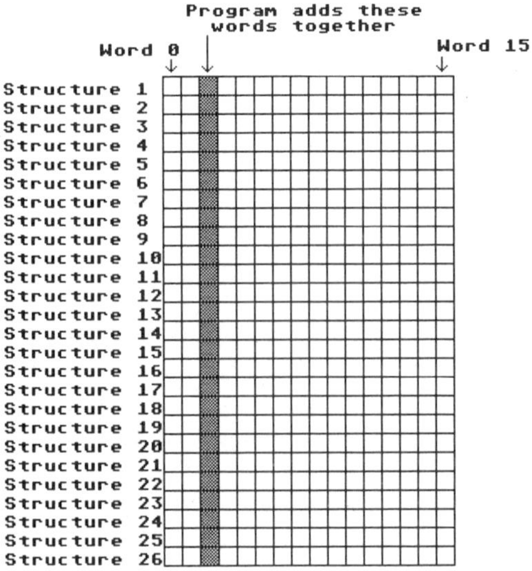

Another example is a quick multiply by two in an address register:

```
LEA.L    0(A0,A0.L),A0   ;MULTIPLY A0 BY 2
```

## Absolute Addressing value

The absolute addressing mode has two variations—absolute short and absolute long. With absolute short mode, the lower half of the effective address follows the opcode in memory as a word *value*. The specified word value is sign extended and then used as the address of the operand in question.

The absolute short addressing mode can only access the lowest or highest 32K memory locations. This mode provides a short, quick way to use programs or temporary storage. It is short and quick because it saves a word of memory and a read cycle.

The following example loads the TRAPV vector, and probably would only be executed in supervisor mode.

```
LEA.L    MY_TRAPV_ROUTINE,A0   ; GET A SUBROUTINE ADDRESS
MOVE.L   A0,$001C.W            ; SAVE IT IN TRAPV VECTOR
```

With absolute long addressing, the effective address occupies two words of memory immediately after the opcode. This addressing mode gives the user access to any memory location. The labels used are commonly called *global variables*. For example, if you assigned the label DATALOC to a memory location, you could store information in that location with the following line of code (which transfers a word of information from data register D7 to the memory location DATALOC):

```
MOVE.W   D7,DATALOC   ;SAVE SOME DATA
```

An Amiga machine language program should always use labels when referring to any type of absolute data. This allows the assembler to generate the correct relocation information. Without relocation information, the machine language program cannot execute correctly in the multiprocessing environment of the Amiga.

A multitasking environment must be able to move programs around in memory. If you assign absolute constants (such as telling the program to jump to a specific address) without relocation information, your program will crash whenever it is moved to a different location in memory. All the absolute addresses will be wrong.

### Program Counter Relative with Displacement d16(PC)

With this addressing mode, the 16-bit displacement value is added to the program counter and used as the address of the operand fetched or stored. The program counter is unmodified by this addressing mode.

This has three important uses:

- When the source code makes reference to a label, and the referenced label is within 32,768 bytes of the current location counter, as in the statement JMP LABEL
- For constant jumps through a jump table
- To find the address of the current instruction as in the following statement: LEA.L −4(PC),A0

### Program Counter Relative with Index and Displacement d8(PC,R*n*)

In program counter relative with index and displacement addressing, the eight-bit displacement, the program counter, and the specified secondary register are added together to generate the address of the operand. This calculated value is used to fetch or store the data used by the instruction.

Either a data or address register can play the role of the secondary register, commonly known as the *index* register. This register may act as a 16- or 32-bit value. By default, the register will be accessed as a 16-bit value. To specify the size of this register, append to the opcode either .L (as in LEA.L) for a 32-bit value, or .W (as in LEA.W) for a 16-bit value.

This addressing mode is most useful when doing a variable jump through a jump table as in this example:

```
        MOVE.W  INDEX,D0        ; GET JUMP TABLE INDEX
        LSL.L   #2,D0           ; MULTIPLY BY 2
        JMP     2(PC,D0)        ; CALL SUBROUTINE IN TABLE
        BRA     EXIT
        DC.L    SUBROUTINE0     ; INDEX 0
        DC.L    SUBROUTINE1     ; INDEX 1
        DC.L    SUBROUTINE2     ; INDEX 2
EXIT:
```

### Immediate #value

The specified value is used as the source operand for the instruction.

This addressing mode is used to load a constant value. Every time this addressing mode is used, there is one less constant to store in data space. The data follows immediately after the opcode. The data can be a byte, a word, or long word.

The MC68000 has a special immediate mode for small operands. In this mode, the data is actually contained within the opcode itself. This *quick* mode can move a number in the range −128 to +128 to a register or memory location, or add or subtract numbers from 1 to 8.

The following is an example of immediate addressing mode.

```
          AND.L   #$7F,D0      ; MASK OUT UPPER 25 BITS
          OR.W    #$8000,D0    ; TURN ON SIGN BIT (WORD SIZED
                               ; VALUE)
          BMI     CONTINUE     ; BRANCH IF MINUS
          NOP                  ; THIS IS NEVER EXECUTED
CONTINUE:
     (rest of program here)
```

## Differences between the MC68000 and the MC68010

There are four important differences between the MC68000 and the MC68010. One of the most important changes is the MC68010 microprocessor's ability to continue an instruction correctly after a bus error has occurred. Because of the organization of the *instruction prefetch queue,* this is not always possible on the MC68000 microprocessor. The difference between the two chips in this area is the manner in which the MC68010 writes out its bus error stack frame. Enough information is saved so the MC68010 can continue the instruction when the processor returns from bus error exception processing.

Another difference between the MC68000 and the MC68010 microprocessors is that the MOVE to Status Register instruction can only be executed in supervisor mode on the MC68010.

One of the most noticeable modifications in the MC68010 microprocessor is the speedup of the multiply and divide instructions. The MC68010 multiplies and divides 16-bit numbers approximately 50 percent faster than the MC68000.

The last difference between the MC68000 and the MC68010 is the DB*cc* LOOP MODE, described previously (under the heading "DB*cc* Instructions" in Chapter 3). This modification provides for fast execution of tight two-instruction loops. Two extra bus cycles are saved for each iteration of the loop, providing a substantial speed improvement. The key to this MC68010 feature is that the instruction within the inner loop of the DB*cc* must be exactly one word, or two bytes long. When the MC68010 detects this situation, it terminates instruction fetching and simply executes the prefetched instructions until the loop completes. When DB*cc* instructions appear frequently, a MC68010 microprocessor can increase the speed of programs by as much as 15 percent.

## 16-bit Programming Considerations

Users of the MC68000 and MC68010 consider this set of processors to be *16-/32-bit machines*. This term comes from the fact that although these microprocessors have many 32-bit operations, they were designed as 16-bit machines. The most notable evidence for this is the lack of 32-bit × 32-bit multiply and divide instructions, the fact that 32-bit instructions actually operate more slowly than their 16-bit counterparts, and the fact that the data path for these computers is physically 16 bits wide. On a true 32-bit machine, these three deficiencies would not exist.

With this information in mind, however, the MC68000 programmer can make better decisions about optimizing code. One of the best choices to make when coding for the MC68000 microprocessors is to use 16-bit data values wherever possible. In many instances, 16 bits are sufficient.

Thoughtful planning is the key when writing source code. In some instances, such as large data moves, 32-bit operations might seem superior. Since the physical data path is only 16 bits wide, all 32 operations take at least two extra cycles to execute. By using 32-bit counters throughout a program, the speed of execution may be degraded considerably.

Since the 32-bit × 32-bit multiplies and divides must be

simulated, a 16-bit multiply or divide is always superior in terms of speed. It takes at least three 16-bit multiplies to simulate a 32-bit × 32-bit multiply.

Another situation concerns large arrays. One addressing mode common on 32-bit machines is *register indirect with 32-bit displacement.* This is useful when accessing arrays, because the displacement can be the starting address of the array and the register can contain the index. Since this addressing mode does not exist on the MC68000 or MC68010 microprocessors, the register indirect with index and displacement addressing mode must be used. The machine language programmer performing array indexing must keep reloading the base offset of the array. The alternative is to cache the base offset in an address register. Keep this in mind for good array indexing performance.

The MC68000 and MC68010 microprocessors do not have *barrel shifters.* A barrel shifter is a piece of hardware that speeds up shifts and multiply instructions. Since the MC68000 doesn't have a barrel shifter, a shift of three bits takes longer than a shift of two bits. The longer the shift, the more time it takes. On more complex microprocessors, like the MC68020, all shift instructions take the same amount of time.

Beware of MOVEM instructions for small numbers of registers. The MOVEM instruction is very fast when loading or storing large numbers of registers. Like any complex instruction, it has a setup time. Whenever moving only one or two registers, it's faster to use one or two MOVE instructions. If three or more registers are moved at one time, it's faster to use a single MOVEM instruction.

Although the MC68000 microprocessor has the CLR instructions to clear data registers, the MOVEQ #0,D*n* is faster and always clears all 32-bits.

It is wise to use some registers as temporaries and others to hold register variables. On the Amiga, it is conventional to use the registers D0, D1, A0, and A1 as temporary registers, and the other registers as variables. Most Amiga ROM kernel subroutines don't preserve the contents of D0, D1, A0, and A1. They are treated as *scratch* registers. If you write subroutines that behave the same way, you'll have consistent performance, and other Amiga programmers will more easily understand them.

# SECTION 2

# Amiga Machine Language Concepts

# CHAPTER 5

# The Amiga CLI (Command Line Interface)

In order to use the programs and programming methods presented in the rest of this book, you'll need to use a small group of Amiga CLI commands. The following short presentation is intended as a refresher, not a substitute for the *AmigaDOS Manual* (Bantam Books), nor is it a complete discussion of even these few commands. If you're totally unfamiliar with the Amiga CLI, it's a good idea to put this book down and study and practice with the CLI until you're satisfied that you understand the CLI and its commands. The Amiga system documentation (which accompanies each Amiga) gives much more detail than is presented here, and the *AmigaDOS Manual* provides a complete reference on all CLI commands.

## Getting to the CLI

There is a special command file that gets executed every time you boot your Amiga from your Workbench disk. This command file, which is a series of AmigaDOS commands, can be found in the S directory of your Workbench disk, with the name STARTUP-SEQUENCE. Its job is to get the Amiga started and bring in the Workbench system, and then clear the screen and quit.

While the startup sequence is being executed, you can see the CLI window (also known simply as the CLI) in action, executing commands. The last command in the standard startup sequence file is an ENDCLI, which eliminates the CLI window. If this last command is deleted from the startup sequence command file, the CLI window will remain visible and usable after the startup process is finished.

You can make a copy of your Workbench disk using the Workbench duplicate menu option, and edit the startup sequence found in the S directory with a text editor. Remove the ENDCLI instruction to maintain your CLI window on the screen.

The other way to get access to a CLI window is to use the Preferences program on the Workbench disk:

- Start the Amiga using the Kickstart and Workbench disks.
- Double-click on the Workbench disk icon.
- Double-click on the Preferences icon within the Workbench disk window.
- When the Preferences screen appears, locate the CLI on/off gadget and use the mouse to click once on the ON side of the gadget.
- Use the Save gadget (click it once) to save the new preferences to disk.
- Reboot the Amiga (press CTRL and both the left and right Amiga keys simultaneously). The Amiga keys are the keys to the right and left of the space bar. (The left Amiga key has been changed to a Commodore key on the Amigas 500 and 2000).

This will cause the Amiga to perform the startup-sequence again and the new Preferences will take effect when the Workbench screen appears.

Now you can open a CLI window by following these steps:

- Double-click on the Workbench disk icon.
- Double-click on the System Drawer icon in the Workbench disk window.
- You'll see an icon for CLI in the System Drawer window.
- Double-click on the CLI icon.
- Click on the close window gadgets for the Workbench disk window and the System Drawer window.
- You should be left with a CLI window which can be resized to your convenience, but with no close gadget.

The CLI window is an Amiga programmer/user interface which operates like most traditional computers that have no mouse, windows, or drop-down menus. This window permits you to type in commands to the Amiga and have the Amiga perform them. The Workbench disk contains a directory named C, which contains many useful commands. Some of the C directory commands are:

| | |
|---|---|
| COPY | Copy files |
| DELETE | Delete files |
| RENAME | Rename files |
| MAKEDIR | Make a directory |
| LIST | List contents of directory |
| NEWCLI | Start a CLI |
| ENDCLI | Quit a CLI |
| ASSIGN | Give a directory or device a logical name |
| EXECUTE | Execute a file of CLI commands |
| RUN | Execute a CLI command or a program as a *background* process |
| CD | Current directory |

The short list of commands above is intended to get you started. If you are a beginner, it would be well worth your time to practice the commands.

It's necessary to have the Workbench disk inserted in a disk drive (*DF0:*, also known as drive 0) in order for the Amiga to be able to find the commands when you type them in. The Amiga knows to look in the C directory on the boot disk for the command's program code. The program code is then loaded in from disk and executed by the Amiga.

## The COPY Command

The COPY command is used to copy a file. You must specify a source name (*from*) and a destination name (*to*). Recall that a file name can be preceded by a directory specification. The following examples show a few of the many ways to use the COPY command to move files around.

**COPY DF0:S/STARTUP-SEQUENCE TO DF1:** Copies the file STARTUP-SEQUENCE from the S directory of the disk in DF0: to the main (root) directory of the disk in DF1: (the external disk drive, which is also known as drive 1).

**COPY DF0:S/STARTUP-SEQUENCE TO RAM:TEMPORARY_STARTUP** Copies the STARTUP-SEQUENCE file from the S directory of the disk in drive 0 to the ramdisk, and simultaneously gives it the name TEMPORARY_STARTUP.

**COPY RAM:SOURCE_FILE TO DF1:SOURCES/** Copies a file named SOURCE_FILE from the ramdisk to the sources directory on the external disk drive. Notice that in order to do this COPY you don't have to type the name of the file a second time. The

Amiga will simply assume the name of the file is unchanged. This is identical to the following command (which requires a little more typing): **COPY ram:source_file to DF1:sources/source_file.**

COPY is one of the Amiga's most useful commands and is very frequently used.

## The DELETE Command

The DELETE command is used to eliminate a file completely. The DELETE command uses only a single filename, which can be prefixed with a directory specification.

**DELETE DF1:SOURCES/UNNEEDED_FILE** Deletes the file named UNNEEDED_FILE from the SOURCES directory on the disk in drive 1.

**DELETE RAM:INCLUDES/SYSEQUATES.ASM** Deletes the file SYSEQUATES.ASM from the INCLUDES directory in the ramdisk.

**DELETE RAM:INCLUDES ALL** Will delete all the files in the INCLUDES directory in the ramdisk. The directory itself (named INCLUDES in this example) will also be deleted.

**DELETE DF1:SOURCES/#?.ASM** Will delete all the files in the SOURCES directory, on the disk in drive 1, that end with the extension *.ASM* (any characters separated from the main filename by a period are referred to as an *extension*). This is a quick way to delete multiple files that all have the same extension and that are in the same directory. This wildcard-matching technique for identifying multiple files is described more thoroughly in the *AmigaDOS Manual.* You can sometimes use it with other commands.

The DELETE command must be used cautiously. Once a program is deleted from an Amiga device (disk or ramdisk) it is irretrievable. Never use the DELETE command unless you're sure the file is really not needed, or you have a backup of the file.

## The RENAME Command

RENAME is used to change the name of a file. It's very useful for manipulating the names of files to conform with your personal taste and style. The following simple example is typical:

**RENAME DF1:TOOLS/MICROEMACS TO DF1:TOOLS/EMACS** Changes the name of the MICROEMACS program in the tools directory on DF1: to EMACS (using a shorter name for a file can minimize typing of repetitive commands).

**RENAME DF0:C/EXECUTE TO DF0:C/DO** Changes the name of the Amiga's EXECUTE command (which lives in the C directory of the Workbench disk) to DO. Whenever you need to use the EXECUTE command, you have to type in DO instead.

**RENAME RAM:SOURCE AS RAM:NEWSOURCE** Uses RENAME to change the name of a file in the ramdisk.

**RENAME DF0:STARTUP-SEQUENCE DF0:S/STARTUP-SEQUENCE** This RENAME is a bit sneaky. It changes the pathname of the file and, consequently, moves the file from the root directory of the disk in drive DF0: to the S directory on the same disk.

## The MAKEDIR Command

MAKEDIR allows you to create a new directory on a disk or in another existing directory. Sometimes it's convenient to COPY a group of related files to a single directory. For example, the companion disk has a directory called SOURCES, which contains all the source code program files for this book. If you're working on many source files at the same time, you might wish to follow the first example in this list:

**MAKEDIR RAM:MYSOURCES**
**COPY FROMWHEREVER:SOURCEFILE TO RAM:MYSOURCES/SOURCEFILE** This makes a directory within the ramdisk named MYSOURCES, and copies the SOURCEFILE from FROMWHEREVER to the new directory MYSOURCES in the ramdisk.

Remember that any disk or ramdisk can have directories, and directories can have *subdirectories*. There's always a *root* directory for DF0:, DF1:, and RAM:. It's always the first directory accessed. Any additional directories in that device will be *descendants* or *children* (subdirectories) of the root. Those subdirectories can also have subdirectories. (See Figure 5-1.)

**Figure 5-1. Directory Tree**

Partial tree diagram of V1.2 Workbench disk showing how directories may contain subdirectories as well as files.

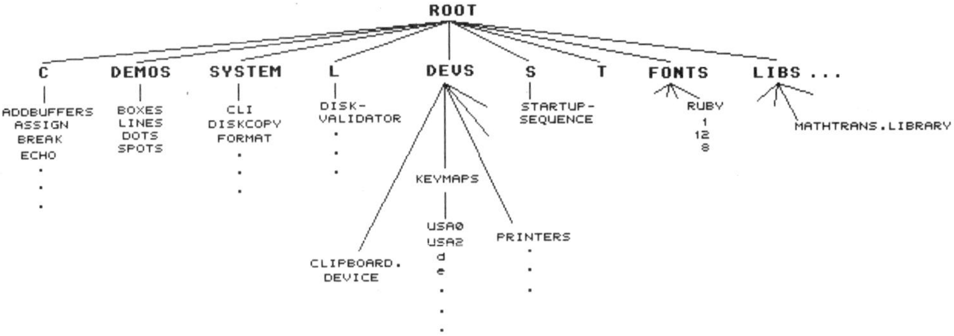


## The LIST Command

LIST prints the directory contents to the CLI window or printer (if you prefer). Here are some examples of how to examine the contents of a directory:

**LIST RAM:** Will make a list of the contents of the root directory of the ramdisk appear in the CLI window.
**LIST DF0: TO PRT:** Prints a list of the contents of the root directory of the disk in DF0: on your printer.
**LIST DF0:C** Will list the contents of the C directory on the disk in DF0: to your CLI window.
**LIST DF1:RAMIT/INCLUDES** Lists the contents of the INCLUDES directory within the RAMIT directory on the disk in DF1:, to the CLI window .
**LIST DF0: OPT A** This lists the names of every file on the disk in drive 0, including all directories and subdirectories.

## The NEWCLI and ENDCLI Commands

NEWCLI is used to start another CLI window. This window is entirely separate from the current CLI window. You can run programs or enter commands in this window while the first window is busy doing something else. To activate the new window, just point the mouse anywhere inside it and click the left button. It's almost like owning more than one computer. Of course, you can use the NEWCLI command in this window, which creates another CLI window. You can continue this process as long as you want—your only limit is the amount of memory in your machine. This is an excellent example of the multitasking ability of the Amiga. ENDCLI closes and removes the CLI window in which the command was entered.

**NEWCLI** Just type in the command and a new CLI window will immediately become available. You can type commands to it as if it were a second Amiga.

**ENDCLI** Just type in the command and the CLI window will close down and disappear.

This pair of commands is very useful. If you issue a command that will take a long time (copying a large file, for instance), you can type in NEWCLI before you issue the time-consuming command, in order to have a separate CLI to work with while the other one is occupied. When the time-consuming command is finished, you can type in the ENDCLI command to its window and carry on using the new CLI that was called up with the NEWCLI command.

## The ASSIGN Command

This command lets you assign one or more different logical names to a directory. This is useful if a program expects a group of files in a particular directory. If the files are in a directory with a different name, you don't have to make a directory with that name and copy the files to it. Simply assign the name of the directory the program is looking for to the directory that contains the files. The ASSIGN command tells the Amiga that whenever it sees a reference to an assigned name, it should look in the directory it is assigned to.

One example is very common. Many Amiga programs require that the C directory of CLI commands be available somewhere. It's a common practice to use the COPY command to move the C commands into a directory named C in the ramdisk, and then assign the logical name "C" to that directory with ASSIGN C: RAM:C. Now, whenever the Amiga wants something from the C directory, it will look in the directory RAM:C. Since files are loaded much faster from the ramdisk than a disk, commands will execute much faster.

**ASSIGN C: RAM:C** Tells the Amiga that whenever it needs something from the C directory, it can be found in the directory RAM:C.

**ASSIGN D: RAM:RAMIT** Tells the Amiga that whenever it needs something from the D: directory, it can be found in the directory named RAMIT in the ramdisk. This particular ASSIGN command is used with the ASMINT program on the companion disk. ASMINT assumes a logical directory named D: exists somewhere and contains the files ASM, HEADER, EMACS, and so on. You can copy these files to any directory you want and have ASMINT look there by assigning the logical name D: to that directory.

**ASSIGN** By itself prints a list of logical directory names and their physical equivalents.

## The EXECUTE Command

EXECUTE lets the Amiga execute a list of CLI commands written in a file. This type of file is called an *execute* file, a *batch* file, or a *command* file.

**EXECUTE DF1:RAMSTARTUP** Tells the CLI to treat the file RAMSTARTUP in the root directory of DF1: as a series of CLI commands, as if they were typed in at the CLI. The RAMSTARTUP file comes with the companion disk and contains all the commands required to copy the RAMIT directory and its files into the ramdisk. RAMSTARTUP also contains the ASSIGN commands needed by the ASMINT program.

**EXECUTE RAM:MAKE** Tells the CLI to treat the file MAKE as a sequence of CLI commands. A make file is a convenient command file that contains the entire sequence of CLI commands required to assemble and link a program. They're commonly used to reduce the amount of typing required to perform some task that requires multiple CLI commands. Use a text editor to write a make file or any other command file.

## The RUN Command

RUN allows you to perform a CLI command (or run a program from the CLI) without tying up the CLI you're using. RUN causes the command to execute in the background, which means the computer will execute the command and let you enter other commands at the same time.

**RUN DF0:C/COPY RAM:FILENAME TO DF1:FILENAME** Causes the COPY command to be executed in the background. The CLI window is left free for other commands.

**RUN RAM:MYPROGRAM** Causes the CLI to start executing the program named MYPROGRAM from the ramdisk, while preserving the current CLI window for use with other commands.

## The CD Command (Change Directory/Current Directory)

This command lets you move around within a group of directories. When you're in a directory, it's as if that directory is the root directory. Other commands need not be preceded by that directory's specification. Here's an example:

**CD DF1:**
**LIST** You'll see the same thing as LIST DF1:.
**CD DF1:RAMIT/INCLUDES**
**COPY A TO B** Does the same thing as COPY DF1:RAMIT/INCLUDES/A TO DF1:RAMIT/INCLUDES/B.
**CD** Prints out the current directory's name to the CLI window.

Once you've used CD to move to a different directory, you'll stay there until you use CD to move again.

# CHAPTER 6

# The Three-Step Development of an Amiga Machine Language Program

This chapter covers the preparation of the source code that forms the foundation of any Amiga machine language program. The source code, as mentioned before, is a text file of MC68000 machine language instructions and program data.

On the Amiga, as on many other computers, machine language programs are written using a text editor or word processor. The text file is then translated by the assembler and linked with a linker. A machine language executable program is the final result. From the Amiga user's point of view, running a finished machine language program is just like calling any command (such as COPY) on the Amiga. To run the file from the CLI, simply type the filename of the finished program.

There are three steps in the construction of an Amiga machine language program:

- Write a source program file with a text editor.
- Assemble the source program file, which creates an object file.
- Link the object file to form an executable program *load module.*

**Prepare the source (text) file of MC68000 instructions and Amiga system subroutine calls.** The source file is always text and should not contain the usual formatting codes provided by word processors. The simplest way to write source code files is to use the MicroEMACS program supplied with Amiga 1.2 Operating System upgrades by Commodore-Amiga. MicroEMACS is a high-performance editor that will make your composition easy because it uses the mouse and drop-down menus. It was used for the development of all program source file listings in this book and is usually referred to as simply *Emacs.*

**Assemble the source (text) file using the ASSEM or ASM command.** The ASSEM or ASM68010 creates a temporary file that needs a final touch (linking) to become a full-fledged executable program. Here is how the ASSEM (or ASM) command is invoked from the CLI:

```
ASSEM SOURCE -O OBJECT -C W150000   (Metacomco assembler)
ASM SOURCE -O OBJECT                (ASM68010 assembler)
```

Remember that ASM is the name of the *ASM68010* assembler that is found on the companion disk, and ASSEM is the name of *Metacomco*'s Amiga assembler, part of the Commodore-Amiga Assembly Language Development package.

These commands assemble file SOURCE to object code file OBJECT, using a work space of 150,000 bytes. It's very important to provide a sufficiently large workspace for the machine when using the *Metacomco* assembler. Usually 150,000 bytes is adequate, sometimes even more is necessary. Even if the source text file is short, it may be that many additional files are *included* in the assembly. That situation may require a very large workspace. (See Chapter 8 for more information about include files.)

The ASSEM command may be issued with additional parameters and modifiers to cause disk or printer listings of the assembly. ASM68010 automatically allocates its workspace and requires no special command to set up a workspace of a specific size. ASM68010 ignores *-C W150000* if it's present in the command.

The command example below instructs the assembler to create a program listing file in addition to a file for the object code. The program listing file can be treated like any other Amiga text file: It can be edited, printed, copied, and so on. It shows the numerical instruction codes for each line of the source code file.

```
ASSEM DF1:SOURCE -O DF1:OBJECT -C W150000 -L DF1:OBJ.LIST   (Metacomco)
ASM DF1:SOURCE -O DF1:OBJECT -L DF1:OBJ.LIST                (ASM68010)
```

This example assembles a source file on DF1: to object file OBJECT on DF1: while creating a listing file OBJ.LIST (also on DF1:). The -L parameter causes a listing file to be created. Even if the source file is short, a large listing file may result if there are other included files.

**Link the temporary file with the ALINK command.** This converts the temporary file created by the assembler into a finished executable program with a name of your choice. The linking is required to knit sections of your program with memory references that are sometimes located in separate link files.

To understand linking, you must first realize that in the Amiga, no fixed memory addresses (except one—memory location 4) are used in programming. This is because all programs must be able to operate anywhere they are placed in memory by the loading process. Unlike most eight-bit computers, which run only one program at a time in a fixed memory space, the Amiga runs many programs simultaneously. All the Amiga programs are in memory at once, and can be loaded in any order. There is no way to know in advance where a program may reside when it's loaded and run.

Therefore, an Amiga program is really a *load module* consisting of your code and the information required to adjust the addresses in the code according to the location in memory where it is loaded. The linker supplies some of this relocation information which makes up the load module.

Sometimes numerical values that cannot be found in the include files are required by the assembler. Commodore has supplied a file named AMIGA.LIB (part of the *Metacomco* package) that contains these additional definitions. For the programs in this book, it isn't necessary to use the AMIGA.LIB file for linking. You can, therefore, always use the simplest forms of the ALINK command:

ALINK *OBJECT* TO *PROGRAM*

This example completes the simple assembly operation shown in the first example under ASSEM. First assemble SOURCE to OBJECT, and then link OBJECT to produce a final PROGRAM.

When the source has been assembled and linked, run the final PROGRAM by entering PROGRAM from the CLI.

If it were necessary to include AMIGA.LIB during linking, you could follow this example:

ALINK *OBJECT* TO *PROGRAM* LIBRARY *AMIGA.LIB*

The *ASM68010* assembler has an alternate way of linking when all the program symbols are defined somewhere in the program. Since that's true for all the programs in this book (symbols are defined either in the programs themselves or in include files merged with the program during assembly), it will be unnecessary to use any separate linker program with *ASM*. Its AUTOLINK feature can be used every time a program is assembled by preceding the source file name with an -A flag:

ASM -A *SOURCE* -O *OBJECT*

This command will assemble the file named SOURCE to an object file called OBJECT, and then AUTOLINK it. The result will be an executable program (a load module) named OBJECT that requires no further linking. Note that because *ASM68010* is compatible with ASSEM from *Metacomco*, you can use it the same way as ASSEM, and use the usual method of linking with ALINK. Simply ignore the -A (AUTOLINK) feature if you wish to use *ASM68010* with ALINK.

A third alternative for linking is a public domain program called BLINK, which can substitute completely for ALINK. BLINK is available from many sources including user groups, bulletin boards, and vendors of public domain disks for the Amiga.

A complete description of *ASM68010* use, features, runtime flags (for instance, -A, -O, -L, and -I), and directives (conditional assembly, macros, listing control, and so on) is in Appendix B.

The ASSEM and ALINK commands are completely described in the *AmigaDOS Manual,* published by Bantam Books. Pages 186–217 are devoted to descriptions of the ASSEM and ALINK programs. The linking process can be quite complex with scanned libraries, overlay files, and other features not required for the programs presented in this book.

## A First Program: Assembling and Linking a Source Program

The following sample program is called HELLO.ASM. It prints a short text message to the same CLI from which it is called. HELLO.ASM can only be used from the CLI. It's not compatible with the Workbench and icon system. Here is the sequence of steps required to create and run HELLO.ASM:

- Use a text editor to type in the program code for Program 1. (When saving the file from the text editor, use the filename RAM:HELLO.ASM.)

- Insert the assembler disk (either *Metacomco* or the companion disk to this book) into DF1:.
- Type the following CLI commands if using the *Metacomco* assembler:
  DF1:ASSEM RAM:HELLO.ASM -O RAM:HELLO.OBJ -C W50000
  DF1:ALINK RAM:HELLO.OBJ TO RAM:HELLO
  DELETE RAM:HELLO.OBJ

  These three commands assemble, link, and delete the temporary object file created by the *Metacomco* assembler prior to linking. The finished program will be waiting for use in the ramdisk. To run the program, just type RAM:HELLO from the CLI.
- Type the following command using the CLI to perform both assembly and linkage using the *ASM68010* assembler:
  DEV:RAMIT/ASM -A RAM:HELLO.ASM -O HELLO

  To run the program, just type RAM:HELLO from the CLI.

Before attempting to assemble any of the programs on the companion disk available with this book, you need to execute one or more of the three batch files included on the companion disk.

- If you purchase the companion disk and have an Amiga with one megabyte or more of memory, you can speed up the assembly process by putting everything in the ramdisk. There are two batch files that will do this automatically for you. To put the system commands in the ramdisk, type EXECUTE DEV:RamDisk. This batch file will copy the system commands into the ramdisk (it will take a few minutes but it will be well worth your time). When it finishes, your commands will execute much faster, and you won't have to keep the Workbench disk in a disk drive. To move the assembler and include files into the ramdisk, type EXECUTE DEV:RamStartUp. This will copy the assembler and all include files into the ramdisk (again this will take a few minutes). The assembler will now operate much faster than when working with a disk-based system.
- If you purchase the companion disk but have an Amiga with only 512K of memory, type EXECUTE DEV:StartUp. This will perform the assignments necessary to use the *ASM68010* assembler.
- If you're using the *Metacomco* assembler, check the assembler's manual for any necessary preparations.

## Listing 6-1. HIWORLD.ASM

```
;HIWORLD.ASM BY DANIEL WOLF
;COPYRIGHT 1987 BY COMPUTE! PUBLICATIONS
;09/10/87

;*** A SIMPLE PROGRAM TO PRINT TO THE CLI WINDOW AND EXIT ***

 BRA _START               ;BRANCH DIRECTLY TO BEGINNING OF PROGRAM

SYSBASE EQU 4             ;THE ONLY FIXED AMIGA ADDRESS, THE SYSTEM BASE!
                          ;IT CONTAINS THE ADDRESS OF THE EXEC LIBRARY BASE

LVO.OPENLIBRARY EQU $FFFFFDD8            ;EXEC LIBRARY OFFSET
LVO.CLOSELIBRARY EQU $FFFFFE62           ;EXEC LIBRARY OFFSET
LVO.OUTPUT EQU $FFFFFFC4                 ;DOS LIBRARY OFFSET
LVO.WRITE EQU $FFFFFFD0                  ;DOS LIBRARY OFFSET

JUST MACRO; ROUTINE       ;A MACRO TO CALL SPECIFIC NAMED ROUTINE
 JSR LVO.\1(A6)
 ENDM

;*** BEGIN HERE ***

_START
 MOVEA.L SYSBASE,A6
 LEA _DOSNAME,A1          ;PUT POINTER TO NAME IN A1
 MOVEQ.L #0,D0            ;DON'T CARE WHICH KICKSTART VERSION
 JUST OPENLIBRARY         ;OPEN DOS LIBRARY
 MOVE.L D0,A6             ;KEEP LIBRARY POINTER IN A6 NOW
 BEQ _STARTERROR          ;0 MEANS ERROR

 JUST OUTPUT              ;SET UP CLI WINDOW AS OUTPUT FOR TEXT

 MOVE.L D0,D1             ;ADDRESS OF OUTPUT FILE HANDLE
 MOVE.L #MESSAGE,D2       ;ADDRESS OF MESSAGE TEXT
 MOVE.L #LENGTH,D3        ;NUMBER OF CHARACTERS IN MESSAGE
 JUST WRITE               ;PRINT MESSAGE TO CLI WINDOW

;*** NOW CLEAN UP AND EXIT TO SYSTEM ***

 MOVE.L A6,A1             ;CLOSE THE DOS LIBRARY
 MOVEA.L SYSBASE,A6
 JUST CLOSELIBRARY
 RTS                      ;EXIT BACK TO WHERE THIS PROGRAM CAME FROM!

_STARTERROR
 MOVE.L #20,D0            ;PUT ERROR CODE IN D0 IF DOS WON'T OPEN
 RTS                      ;AND EXIT NOW!

;*** DATA DECLARATIONS ***

_DOSNAME
  DC.B 'dos.library',0                ;NAME AS REQUIRED BY OPENLIBRARY

MESSAGE
 DC.B ' HELLO WORLD ',13,10           ;TEXT MESSAGE WITH RETURN, LINEFEED

LENGTH EQU *-MESSAGE                  ;PC-LABEL = LENGTH OF MESSAGE

 DC.W 0                               ;WORD-ALIGN THE PROGRAM COUNTER

 END                                  ;END DIRECTIVE TO ASSEMBLER
```

## Reference Section

### Text Entry, Assembly, and Link Commands for this Book

The steps used with this example are also used to enter, assemble, and link all the other programs in this book. The procedures are repeated below, step by step, for reference.

### Text Entry Procedure for all Files and Program Listings in this Book

- Use the EMACS text editor to type in text.
- Use the *save as* project menu selection to save the text file with the appropriate name.

### Assembly and Link Procedure for Program Listings in this Book—*Metacomco* Assembler

- Use the CLI to type in the following assembler command:
  ASSEM SOURCEFILENAME -O OBJECTFILENAME
- Use the CLI to type in the following linking command:
  ALINK OBJECTFILENAME TO PROGRAMFILENAME
- Use the CLI to delete the intermediate object code file:
  DELETE OBJECTFILENAME
- Use the CLI to run the program:
  PROGRAMFILENAME

### Assembly and Link Procedure for Program Listings in this Book—*ASM68010* Assembler

- Use the CLI to type in the following assembler autolink command:
  ASM -A SOURCEFILENAME -O PROGRAMFILENAME
- Use the CLI to run the program:
  PROGRAMFILENAME

SOURCEFILENAME, OBJECTFILENAME, and PROGRAMFILENAME are dummy names to indicate that some directory/file name combination is required here. Complete examples of these command sequences are shown above for real source, object, and program files.

# CHAPTER 7
# Macro Assembler Directives

Commands to the assembler, called *directives* or *assembler directives*, make programming more convenient. This chapter introduces directives and presents enough information to get you started using the more common ones. A comprehensive reference section on assembler directives is found in Appendix A.

Directives are sometimes called *pseudo-ops* because they look like op-codes, but are not recognized by the MC68000 microprocessor. They are only read and interpreted by the assembler.

Three of these directives are so important that separate chapters are devoted to them. Those three directives are INCLUDE, MACRO, and IF (conditional assembly).

The simpler directives DS.*x*, DC.*x*, EQU, and END are presented below.

## The DS.*x* Directive

The DS.*x* directive Declares Storage for program data. It is used frequently in machine language programs to set aside memory at the time of assembly. You may wish to limit the use of this directive and use dynamic memory allocation in your program to create storage areas and delete them as needed. The techniques for dynamic memory allocation in programs are shown later. Here are examples of using DS.*x* (where *x* stands for the MC68000 size specifier, B, W, or L):

```
MESSAGE
   DS.B   80     ; DECLARING AN 80-BYTE STORAGE AREA AT 'MESSAGE'
BUFFER
   DS.B   132    ; DECLARING A 132-BYTE STORAGE AREA AT 'BUFFER'
POINTERLIST
   DS.L   16     ; DECLARING 16-LONG WORD POINTER ARRAY NAMED
                 ; 'POINTERLIST'
```

When the assembler sees a DS.*x* directive, it makes room in the object code accordingly. The above examples show how a block of memory can be incorporated directly into a program.

## The DC.*x* Directive

The DC.*x* directive Declares a Constant value. In addition to declaring specific memory storage requirements using the DS.*x* directive, you can declare specific labeled variable values and constants in your code using the DC.*x* (where *x* stands for the size specifier). All the programs in this book make extensive use of the DC.*x* directive to provide initial values for certain program variables, and to create labeled storage locations for pointers that have an initial null (0) value. As you read through the program listings, you'll see dozens of examples of DC.*x* that lay out text strings as well. Text strings in the Amiga usually end with a 0 byte. Here are some examples of DC.*x* usage:

```
WINDOWPTR
   DC.L   0                  ; STORAGE FOR LONG-WORD POINTER, FILLED
                             ; LATER
MYMESSAGE
   DC.B   'Hello World',0    ; EXAMPLE OF NULL-TERMINATED AMIGA TEXT
WINDOWTITLE
   DC.B   'My Window',0      ; EXAMPLE OF TEXT FOR A WINDOW TITLE
POINTERARRAY
   DC.L   0,0,0,0,0,0,0,0    ; Layout for EIGHT LONG-WORD POINTERS
                             ; (ADDRESSES) INITIALIZED TO NULL (0)
```

When the assembler finds the DC.*x* directive, it places the data constant that follows it into the program.

## The EQU Directive

The EQU (EQUate) directive assigns a label to a specific numerical value. This is handy for parameters best defined at the beginning of the program.

For example, you may want to create size values for all the windows in a program, at the beginning. You could create equates called WINDOWH and WINDOWV. To assign window sizes to windows within the program, you would merely enter these two labels when the window size parameter is requested. Then, if you want to change all the window sizes, rather than search through the program for every window definition, you can simply change the values in the EQUate statements at the beginning of the program.

This is how the equates files are written (INTEQUATES.ASM, for instance). Here are some examples:

```
MAX_XSIZE  EQU  639   ; SETS MAX_XSIZE EQUAL TO 639 (DECIMAL)
MAX_YSIZE  EQU  $20   ; SETS MAX_YSIZE EQUAL TO HEX 20 (32
                      ; DECIMAL)
```

Later on you can use these values in the following way:

```
MOVE.W  #MAX_XSIZE,D1  ; THIS MOVES WORD VALUE 639 INTO D1
MOVE.L  #MAX_YSIZE,D2  ; MOVES LONG-WORD VALUE $20 (32
                       ; DECIMAL) INTO D2
```

The programs in this book use the EQU directive extensively. In most of the programs the EQU directive is used at the very beginning of the program to define certain symbols that control conditional assembly in other parts of the program. Conditional assembly (using the IF directive) is presented in a separate chapter. Here are some examples of using EQU simply to define a symbol:

```
DOS  EQU  1
INT  EQU  1
GFX  EQU  1
```

An equate does not reserve storage in your program. Instead, the EQU directive is used to define a value in the symbol table during assembly. Then, other portions of the program can use references to these symbols to control conditional assembly.

### END Directive

END may appear only once in a source file being assembled. It tells the assembler to stop. It's not necessary to have an END directive, but if you want the assembler to assemble only the first half of your program, the END pseudo-op will allow this.

## Arithmetic Operators

There are several directives that can be used to perform some simple arithmetic computations (operations) during assembly. Here are some examples:

**The logical OR operator (!).** The following code illustrates the use of the logical OR operator, symbolized by the exclamation point (!):

```
MOVE.L  #MEMF_CHIP!MEMF_CLEAR,D0  ; USED WHEN ALLOCATING
                                  ; MEMORY
```

This line of source code means the assembler should combine (using the Boolean OR function) two different symbols' numeric values into a single numeric value. In this case MEMF_CHIP has the decimal value of 2 (0000 0010 binary) and MEMF_CLEAR has a decimal value of 16 (0001 0000 binary). When the assembler encounters the ! directive, it combines these two values into a single decimal value of 18 (0001 0010 binary) in the object code.

**The integer division operator (/).** The following line of source code demonstrates the use of the integer division operator (/):

```
MOVE.L  #TICKSPERSECOND/2,D1
```

This line of code tells the assembler to divide the value of TICKSPERSECOND by two, prior to generating code for it. The TICKSPERSECOND symbol has the numerical value of 50 in the Amiga (see DOSEQUATES.ASM). In this example, the assembler would place the value 25 into D1. This type of code is used, in several of the programs in this book, along with the AmigaDOS DELAY function to cause a program to wait for a specified period of time without tying up the microprocessor. A typical usage of this construction is:

```
MOVE.L  #TICKSPERSECOND,D1
DOSLIB  DELAY                  ; USE AMIGADOS TO DELAY 1 FULL
                               ; SECOND
MOVE.L  #TICKSPERSECOND/4,D1
DOSLIB  DELAY                  ; USE AMIGADOS TO DELAY 1/4
                               ; SECOND
```

Integer division should only be used with integers.

**The shift left operator (<<).** The shift left operator, symbolized by two less-than signs (<<), shifts a binary number one bit to the left, essentially multiplying it by two, as in the following example:

```
MOVE.L  #TICKSPERSECOND<<,D1  ; SHIFTS TICKSPERSECOND 1 BIT
                              ; LEFT
DOSLIB  DELAY                 ; USE AMIGADOS TO DELAY 2 FULL
                              ; SECONDS
```

There are several other arithmetic operators used in the same ways shown in the preceding examples. They include:

| **Operator** | **Effect** |
|---|---|
| + and − | Add and subtract |
| * and / | Multiply and divide |
| ! | Logical OR |
| & | Logical AND |
| >> | Right shift (divide by two) |
| << | Left shift (multiply by two) |

Refer to Appendix A for comprehensive information on the use of assembler directives and arithmetic operators.

# CHAPTER 8
# Include Files

In preceding chapters, you've seen references to *include files*. Include files are pieces of source code that are merged with a program during assembly. They provide programmers with a sensible way to manage program development. Include files are generally short, easily read, easily altered files that perform a single function or provide a library of equates for the main program to use. They bring modular programming to machine language.

## The Include Files and the Kernel

The Amiga is equipped with 256 kilobytes of kernel software. The kernel is full of useful routines and system constants that do most of the Amiga's work. The ROM kernel code contains routines for opening and managing windows, operating the mouse, keyboard sensing, multitasking control, and more.

Many of the kernel routines have names and known entry points for use by C and machine language programmers. There are also hundreds of system constants, most of which are offsets relative to known memory locations. The art of programming the Amiga, whether in C or machine language, includes the proper use of these kernel routines, system constants, and offsets.

Probably the most common use of include files is providing a library of the kernel routines, along with labels. If these equates had to be defined in each piece of source code, the programmer could waste hours looking up addresses and typing. The include files allow you to take care of this time-consuming chore only once, after which a simple include directive will insure that the necessary equates will be provided at the time of assembly. This also keeps source code files smaller (because the equates are part of a separate file) and reduces the likelihood that a difficult-to-find typing error will interfere with the program's operation.

## Amiga Include Files

The include files provided with the *Metacomco* assembler are lists of the named kernel routines and constants, and their values or addresses. The include files are numerous, and each one contains name and value information for a related group of kernel routines and constants. The machine language include files all end with .I (such as TYPES.I, INTEQUATES.I).

The *Amiga ROM Kernel Reference Manual: Libraries and Devices*, published by Commodore, contains printouts of the include files. You can also read the include files by printing them out (from the *Metacomco* disk) using AmigaDOS CLI commands such as TYPE FILENAME TO PRT:.

Because the early machine language development system for Amiga was actually a SUN Microsystems workstation with a UNIX operating system and many megabytes of memory, the Amiga include files are fairly complex.

- The include files are extremely long. The disk versions are nearly identical to those printed in the *Libraries and Devices* manual. They include much descriptive system documentation commentary. This makes them valuable reference documents, but a little unwieldy when using a "plain vanilla" Amiga as the development system. They are so large that it's difficult to use them when programming an unexpanded Amiga.
- The include files from Amiga contain special macros that automatically convert the structure field names from the format in which they're presented (similar to the way they would be declared in a C program) into their numerical equivalents, during assembly. That means the actual numerical values of most structure field names are not given explicitly in the include files. Because library offset values are not explicitly stated either (they are found in AMIGA.LIB), it is necessary to link with AMIGA.LIB when using these include files.
- Experienced machine language programmers should take advantage of the clever and complete constructions available in the Amiga include files. It's probably wise to make a separate working copy of each of them with comment lines deleted to make them more manageable in length. You could write a program to strip any lines beginning with a semicolon or an asterisk.

## Include Files for Use with This Book

This book presents several include files that contain:

- Lists of symbolic equates for use with DOS, Graphics, Exec, and Intuition. These are all fairly short (total of about 10K) and can be expanded by studying the ROM kernel manuals. For additional library vector offsets, see Appendix D of the Exec manual. For additional named structure field offsets, compare the tables in this volume with the listings in the Intuition manual.

  SYSEQUATES.ASM—Numerical definitions of general Amiga system variables.
  DOSEQUATES.ASM—Same for those specific to AmigaDOS (DOS library).
  GFXEQUATES.ASM—Same for those specific to Graphics (Graphics library).
  INTEQUATES.ASM—Same for those specific to Intuition (Intuition library).

- Convenient macros for use with the listings in this book and your own programs. This is a fairly short list that you can expand with additional macros of your own design.

  MACROS.ASM—68000, system, DOS, graphics, intuition, and math macros. There are a few additional macros that are in the other specific support files. Since these additional macros are specific to the tasks carried out by the support code files, they've been placed there. The MACROS.ASM file only contains the most general and widely used macros.

- Special support code for parts of the Intuition system (windows, text, menus, gadgets, requesters). These have been written to simplify use of the Intuition resources and to demonstrate their use in the sample programs, and contain both subroutines and a few specific macros that can simplify your source programs.

  WINDOWS.ASM
  TEXTS.ASM
  MENUS.ASM
  GADGETS.ASM
  REQS.ASM

- Additional support code files to simplify program development when using floating-point and transcendental math.

  MATH.ASM

- A program fragment, which is needed for almost all programs on the Amiga, that performs the functions of a graceful start and ending of a program. This program fragment permits the Amiga operating system to recognize the program when it starts running, and then perform appropriate preliminary tasks, depending on whether the program is activated from the Workbench (clicking an icon) or started by a CLI command (by entering *programname* or RUN *programname* at the CLI). This universal program fragment is called: STARTUP.ASM

You should type in and copy these files to the INCLUDES directory of your machine language work disk. In a later chapter you'll find instructions for creating a work disk for machine language program development. The include files mentioned above are required by the other programs in this book. The typing job is long, but it can be avoided if you have the companion disk to this book, which contains all of these files. The include files on the *Metacomco* disk are not used by the programs in this book.

If you opt to type the include files, you can leave out the comments in order to reduce the amount of typing necessary. Using MICROEMACS or another text editor will simplify your work. In the end, you'll have a set of compact, versatile, and easily expanded include files.

## Using Include Files in a Program

Include files are called into your program at the time of assembly with the INCLUDE assembler directive. There should be one directive for each of the files to be included. You should write the include directives at the beginning of your source code. As the assembler scans the source file, each time it comes upon an include directive, it will locate the named file and merge it into the workspace used by the assembler. That means that the workspace contains one long file built from your source file and all the include files.

In the following examples, it is assumed there is some directory called INCLUDES that contains all the include files. For convenience, this is often a ramdisk directory.

```
INCLUDE    "INCLUDES:MENUS.ASM"          ; PUTS INCLUDES:MENUS.ASM IN
                                         ; WORK AREA
INCLUDE    "INCLUDES:MATH.ASM"           ; PUTS INCLUDES:MATH.ASM INTO
                                         ; WORK AREA
INCLUDE    "INCLUDES:SYSEQUATES.ASM"     ; PUTS INCLUDES:SYSEQUATES.ASM
                                         ; INTO WORK AREA
```

The assembler will look for the listed files in the INCLUDES directory. If they're found, they are loaded into the assembler's workspace at exactly the point in the source file where the include directive appears.

## The Header File

The header file provides a shortcut to including files based on the fact that any file can be included within another.

A header file is simply a list of include commands. (The header file used with all the programs in this book is printed in Chapter 9, under the heading Conditional Use of the Include Directive.) Because many of the same include files are needed by most programs, the include process was simplified by using the header to take care of all the other includes needed for a program. In order to understand the operation of the header file fully, you'll need to understand conditional assembly, which is discussed in Chapter 9.

The header file is called with a single include command:

```
INCLUDE   "HEADER"
```

The header file will then choose the include files needed for the program being assembled.

## Within the Equate Files

When you write your program, you'll call the needed kernel routines by name. The equate files remove the responsibility of entering the addresses of these routines and constants. They enter the addresses of the constants and routines for you.

The equate files also provide definitions of system tables called *structures,* which will be discussed in more detail at a later time. Here is a section of the INTEQUATES.ASM include file that contains values of constants used by Intuition:

```
BOOLGADGET       EQU  $1
BORD.BACKPEN     EQU  $5
BORD.COUNT       EQU  $7
BORD.DRAWMODE    EQU  $6
BORD.FRONTPEN    EQU  $4
```

This equate file contains constant values for dozens of symbolic labels used by Intuition. Those shown here are mostly offsets into the BORDER structure (a type of memory data table). For example, BORD.COUNT is equal to seven. This is because the COUNT for a border is found seven bytes into the structure. The COUNT is the number of pairs of *x,y* points that make up the border endpoints. If a BORDER has five endpoints, the number 5 should be located exactly seven bytes from the beginning of the BORDER structure. Putting a value of 5 in that location could be done in the following way:

```
    LEA       BORDER,A0             ; PUT ADDRESS OF THE BORDER
                                    ; STRUCTURE INTO A0
    MOVE.W    #5,BORD.COUNT(A0)     ; PUT FIVE INTO A WORD LOCATED
;                                   ; SEVEN BYTES FROM ADDRESS IN A0
                                    ; (THE
;                                   ; BASE ADDRESS OF THIS BORDER
                                    ; STRUCTURE)
```

Programmers don't have to memorize the fact that BORD.COUNT equals seven, or look it up on a table. They only need to include an equate file and keep handy a list of the shorthand names for constants and routines in the kernel.

As you read through this book, you will see many examples in which names are used where you might expect to see numbers. Remember that numerical values are assigned to these names in an equate file.

It's important to use the names instead of actual numeric values whenever possible. The reason is that the manufacturer might change the locations of these constants and routines within the kernel. If there are such changes in the future, the equate files will also be changed so that using the familiar names will result in the correct numerical values being generated by the assembler.

Whenever you see a strange variable name or odd combination of characters used without any apparent definition, try looking up the unfamiliar word or characters in the include files.

It's wise to be careful about the order of your include assembler directives within the source code. For instance, while it is permissible to include a file within an included file, be careful not to nest included files so deeply that they're difficult to follow. It would be better programming practice to do all including early in the main source code.

If you fail to include a file with necessary symbol definitions for your program, the assembler will report undefined symbol errors and the assembly will fail. When you see this sort of error, check your include files first to make sure you have included all necessary files.

CHAPTER 9

# Macros and Conditional Assembly

## Macros

A macro is typically a short, frequently used sequence of machine language instructions. Once you've assigned a name to the macro, the assembler treats it as if it were a new instruction. When assembled, the macro is expanded into its defined list of instructions at that point in your program. You can see that a macro is similar to an include file, but it contains instructions rather than data.

Macros usually have one or more parameters as well. The parameters are symbols from the source program. The macro utilizes them as input data. This is a feature that allows macros to do things subroutines cannot.

Macros can contain directives (commands) to the assembler, so that as they are encountered in the source program, the assembler may arrange them in different ways in the assembled code. Once you use a few macros, they become indispensable power tools and can make your programming much easier. Macros are widely used throughout this book, and a listing of them is provided in MACROS.ASM. You're free to make additional macros and add them to the MACROS.ASM file. Macros make machine language extensible; you can define efficient new instructions with the names and syntax of your choice.

Here is an example macro:

```
ZERA   MACRO             ; AN
       SUB.L    \1, \1
       ENDM
```

This short macro definition is called ZERA. Its purpose is to clear an address register (set it to 0). It turns out that there is no direct instruction to do this on the MC68000. There is a CLR.L D*n* instruction, which can clear a data register, but you can't use it with an address register. Use the macro as a shorthand instruction name to clear an address register. When you want to use it in your program to clear address register A2, write:

```
ZERA   A2
```

It will behave as if it were an instruction to clear address register A2. When the assembler encounters this macro, it substitutes the instruction SUB.L A2,A2 at that point in the code. The A2 in the usage example is called a *parameter*. It's matched with the symbol \1 found in the macro definition. When you see the symbol \1 in a macro definition, it should be read as *parameter number 1*. In this case, there is one parameter, A2. So when the assembler sees:

```
ZERA   A2
```

it assembles it as:

```
SUB.L   A2,A2
```

This instruction tells the MC68000 microprocessor to subtract A2 from itself. Therefore, it has the effect of clearing A2.

As you can see, Macro definitions make MC68000 machine language extendible with as many additional instructions as you wish to create. A clever and energetic programmer can create a higher-level language by using macros.

The following example creates a macro to simplify the process of calling a ROM kernel library subroutine:

```
LIBCALL  MACRO                       ; LIBRARY, ROUTINE (TWO
                                     ; PARAMETERS)
         MOVE.L     \1,A6
         JSR        LVO.\2(A6)
         ENDM
```

This macro uses two parameters, the first (\1) is the label at which you have previously stored a library base address. The second parameter (\2) is the short name of the routine you want to use in that library. The *ASM68010* assembler starts the names of all library routines with *LVO.*, and this macro puts those letters in place for you. Here's an example showing how this macro is used in a program:

```
LIBCALL    DOSBASE,WRITE
```

The program code generated by this macro invocation is:

```
MOVE.L   DOSBASE,A6       ; PUTS PARAMETER #1 INTO A6
JSR      LVO.WRITE(A6)    ; JSR TO LVO.PARAMETER #2
```

## Nesting Macros

A macro may contain another macro's name. Encountering such a circumstance, the assembler will expand one macro within the other. The following example nests the LIBCALL macro inside another macro:

```
DOSLIB  MACRO
        LIBCALL _DOSBASE, \1
        ENDM
```

For the sake of this example, you must imagine that elsewhere in the program you stored an address from the DOS library at an address labeled DOSBASE. This macro uses LIBCALL. LIBCALL's \1 (parameter number 1) becomes DOSBASE. The DOSLIB macro only has one parameter—the name of the DOS library routine you wish to call. Here's an example of using DOSLIB:

```
DOSLIB  READ
```

This is the code the assembler will generate when it encounters this macro:

```
MOVE.L  _DOSBASE,A6
JSR     LVO.READ(A6)
```

This code is identical to the code generated by

```
LIBCALL _DOSBASE,READ
```

The LIBCALL macro nested in the DOSLIB macro is shorter and quicker to type in.

## Macros vs. Subroutines

Using macros can make programming in machine language almost as easy as programming in C or some other high-level language. Convenient symbolic macro names with simple, sensible parameters can substitute for a great deal of repetitive typing. Macros make it convenient to create new instructions when no simple MC68000 instruction will do the job. From the programmer's perspective, macros turn lengthy sequences of code into short symbolic names, almost like keywords in BASIC.

Macros are especially useful when code sequences are used repeatedly with slight variations which can be accommodated by passing parameters. In fact, the ease of passing parameters to macros is one of their principal advantages over subroutines.

Using subroutines instead of macros is a programming design decision. If you use many long macros, you'll end up with a very long object file, while your source code remains compact. Using large numbers of subroutines may have the opposite effect, to some degree: The object code generated by the assembler will be more compact.

Subroutines only appear in your code once. They can be used repeatedly without generating additional code, but in order to use them, you'll probably have to create code that passes parameters to them.

## Some Macro Examples

A family of macros used throughout the programs in this book is printed in the next chapter. This family is used in almost all the programs and should be typed in according to the instructions given. Here are some additional examples of macros as a review, to insure that you understand the concept.

```
ZERO  MACRO
      MOVEQ.L #0, \1
      ENDM
```

This macro clears a data register. For example, if you wish to clear data register D0, you simply write:

```
      ZERO D0
```

The following macro pushes the contents of the desired register or registers onto the stack.

```
PUSHREG  MACRO
         MOVEM.L  \1,-(SP)
         ENDM
```

If you wish to save the contents of D0, D1, and D2 while those registers are temporarily used for something else, you can use the following line of code:

```
   PUSHREG   D0-D2
```

The following macro pulls data from the stack and places

it into the registers specified in \1:

```
PULLREG   MACRO
          MOVEM.L (SP)+,\1
          ENDM
```

If you wish to restore the contents of D0, D1, and D2 from the previous example, use the following line of code:

```
  PULLREG   D0-D2
```

## Conditional Assembly

Another group of assembler directives allow the programmer to write source code which may or may not become part of the executable program when it's assembled. These conditional assembly directives are instructions to the assembler either to assemble a section of code or skip over it, based on whether certain conditions are satisfied.

The conditionals do not affect the actual program except by controlling what code is assembled into the object program. Don't confuse these conditional assembly directives with the condition codes of the MC68000 microprocessor, which are used with other MC68000 instructions to control the program flow.

### IF*x* and ENDC

Four of the conditional directives are used frequently in the programs in this book. Comprehensive documentation on conditional assembly can be found in Appendix B. The four commonly used conditionals are:

IFD Assemble if a symbol is defined.
IFND Assemble if a symbol is not defined.
IFC Assemble if a symbol is the same as another symbol.
IFNC Assemble if a symbol is not the same as another symbol.

Whenever the IF*x* conditional directive is used, it precedes the section of program source code to be affected by the condition. After the section of code that is under control of the conditional, you must use:

ENDC Ends conditional assembly.

Here are some examples. The first example shows a combination of assembly directives.

```
IFD         DOS
INCLUDE     'DOSEQUATES.ASM'
ENDC
```

The DOSEQUATES.ASM file will only be included if the symbol *DOS* is defined somewhere in the program.

The next example sets JAM1 equal to 0 only if it has not been defined elsewhere.

```
        IFND  JAM1
JAM1    EQU   0        ; DEFINE THE LABEL IF NOT ALREADY DEFINED
        ENDC
```

The next example uses the DOSPRINT macro to print out a message if the symbol named STRING contains the value *HELLO* at assembly time.

```
IFC         STRING,'HELLO'       ; COMPARE STRING TO HELLO
DOSPRINT    STDOUT,#MESSAGE
ENDC
```

The last example is used frequently with macros. In effect, it says, "If the first parameter ( \1) is not equal to a blank (empty string), then move that parameter into D0."

```
IFNC      '\1',''      ; IF PARAMETER ONE IS NOT BLANK
MOVE.L    \1,D0
ENDC
```

To see more examples of conditional assembly, review the MACROS.ASM file and the HEADER file under the heading "Conditional Use of the Include Directive," below.

## Conditional Assembly Within Macros

Macros can use conditional assembly to make them even more flexible. In this example, the macro sets up a pen color for graphics (the graphics functions are presented later). The macro uses D0 to hold the pen number. If the program already has the color number in D0, the macro doesn't need to move it there. The macro can skip over that part and just call the SETAPEN graphics function.

```
SETAPEN  MACRO                     ; PARAMETER ONE IS RASTPORT
;                                  ; PARAMETER TWO IS COLOR #
         GFXPUSH                   ; MACRO NESTED WITHIN THIS
                                   ; MACRO TO SAVE REGISTERS
         IFNC      '\2',''         ; IF SECOND PARAMETER EXISTS
                                   ; (IS NOT A BLANK)
         MOVE.W    \2,D0           ; MOVE SECOND PARAMETER TO
                                   ; D0
         ENDC                      ; END OF CONDITIONAL ASSEMBLY
         GFXLIB    SETAPEN,\1      ; CALL THE GRAPHICS FUNCTION
                                   ; SETAPEN
         GFXPULL                   ; RESTORE THE REGISTERS
                                   ; PUSHED WITH GFXPUSH
         ENDM
```

In the next two examples that use the macro above, the macro takes advantage of the conditional assembly. In the first example, the assembler will recognize that there is no second parameter (color number) specified and won't assemble the part of the SETAPEN macro that contains the instruction MOVE.W \2,D0.

```
MOVE.W   #3,D0   ; PLACE COLOR NUMBER INTO D0
SETAPEN  RP      ; DON'T USE SECOND PARAMETER COLOR
                 ; NUMBER
;                ; BECAUSE ITS ALREADY IN D0
```

In the next example, the assembler recognizes that the second parameter has been provided and the line containing MOVE.W #3,D0 will be assembled as part of the macro.

```
SETAPEN  RP,#3  ; USE MACRO TO PLACE COLOR NUMBER THREE
                ; INTO D0
;               ; AND CALL THE SETAPEN FUNCTION
```

Conditional assembly within the SETAPEN macro allows you to enter a color number in D0 one time and subsequently use the SETAPEN macro several times with that color number. The assembler leaves out the unnecessary line of code (MOVE.W \2,D0) in each case. This shortens the object file generated by the assembler and makes it run faster.

The MACROS.ASM file printed in the next chapter shows other examples of conditional assembly within macros. Most of the program listings use this flexibility by making reference to macros with different numbers of parameters. Using conditional assembly within macros lets a macro do several slightly different things, depending on the needs of the programmer.

## Conditional Use of the Include Directive—The Header File

Another valuable use for conditional assembly was shown briefly above: the use of conditional assembly to control the include process.

Several include directives may appear near the beginning of a program. They are used early in the source code to bring relevant symbol definition files, macro files, and other files into the object code before they're called on by the code that follows.

As mentioned earlier, a header file can serve as a handy tool to simplify this section of a program. The best way to use a header file is to conditionally assemble all available include files. Then, the programmer can simply define the symbols that control, including the specific files needed by the program.

Program 9-1 is a header file used by all the programs in this book. There are a few includes that are always needed, and they're not controlled by conditional assembly. For instance, all the programs need the SYSEQUATES.ASM, MACROS.ASM, and the STARTUP.ASM files.

The symbols used to control most include directives are simple three-letter codes that are easy to remember.

If you write the following opening lines of a program source file:

```
DOS EQU       1
INT EQU       1
    INCLUDE  "HEADER"
```

the header will insure that the following files are included:

- DOSEQUATES.ASM
- INTEQUATES.ASM
- SYSEQUATES.ASM
- MACROS.ASM
- STARTUP.ASM

All the other files controlled by conditional assembly in the HEADER will be ignored since their control symbols are not defined. In other words, IFD is false for the other files, and conditional assembly will skip GFXEQUATES.ASM, WINDOWS.ASM, MENUS.ASM, GADGETS.ASM, and the rest (see Program 9-1.)

All the programs in this book, except HIWORLD.ASM, use the HEADER file and the corresponding symbols. Table 9-1 is a list of the three-letter symbols used to control conditional assembly in this book.

**Table 9-1. Conditional Assembly Symbols for HEADER and STARTUP.ASM**

| Symbol | HEADER will include | STARTUP.ASM will open/close | Comments |
|---|---|---|---|
| INT | INTEQUATES.ASM | Intuition Library | |
| DOS | DOSEQUATES.ASM | AmigaDOS Library | |
| GFX | GFXEQUATES.ASM | Graphics Library | |
| MAT | MATH.ASM | MathFFP Library | |
| TRA | | TransMath Library | |
| WIN | WINDOWS.ASM | | |
| MEN | MENUS.ASM | | |
| GAD | GADGETS.ASM | | |
| REQ | REQS.ASM | | |
| TXT | TEXTS.ASM | | |
| HEX | | | Controls assembly of HEX MATH part of MATH.ASM |
| FFP | | | Controls assembly of FFP MATH part of MATH.ASM |
| WBC | | | Controls assembly of WORKBENCH CONSOLE in STARTUP.ASM |

## Listing 9-1. The HEADER File Used in Programs in This Book

```
;******************************** HEADER.ASM BY DANIEL WOLF
;COPYRIGHT 1987 BY COMPUTE! BOOKS
;08/12/87

 NOLIST

 IFND DOS       ;MAKE SURE DOS IS THERE
DOS EQU 1
 ENDC

 IFND INT       ;MAKE SURE INTUITION IS THERE
INT EQU 1
 ENDC

 IFD DOS        ;MAKE SURE THE EQUATES GET INCLUDED IF MAIN SYMBOL DEFINED
DOSE EQU 1
 ENDC

 IFD INT
INTE EQU 1
 ENDC

 IFD GFX
GFXE EQU 1
 ENDC
```

```
 IFD DEV
DEVE EQU 1
 ENDC

 INCLUDE "INCLUDES:SYSEQUATES.ASM"
 IFD DOSE
 INCLUDE "INCLUDES:DOSEQUATES.ASM"
 ENDC
 IFD GFXE
 INCLUDE "INCLUDES:GFXEQUATES.ASM"
 ENDC
 IFD INTE
 INCLUDE "INCLUDES:INTEQUATES.ASM"
 ENDC
 IFD DEVE
 INCLUDE "INCLUDES:DEVEQUATES.ASM"
 ENDC

 IFND JAM1
JAM1 EQU Ø
 ENDC

 INCLUDE "INCLUDES:MACROS.ASM"
 IFD WIN
 INCLUDE "INCLUDES:WINDOWS.ASM"
 ENDC
 IFD TXT
 INCLUDE "INCLUDES:TEXTS.ASM"
 ENDC
 IFD GAD
 INCLUDE "INCLUDES:GADGETS.ASM"
 ENDC
 IFD MAT
 INCLUDE "INCLUDES:MATH.ASM"
 ENDC
 IFD MEN
 INCLUDE "INCLUDES:MENUS.ASM"
 ENDC
 IFD REQ
 INCLUDE "INCLUDES:REQS.ASM"
 ENDC

 INCLUDE "INCLUDES:STARTUP.ASM"

 LIST
```

Use EMACS to type in and save HEADER to the RAMIT/INCLUDES directory. Type the CLI command: DEV:RAMIT/EMACS DEV:RAMIT/INCLUDES/HEADER. Before typing in HEADER, you should read Chapter 10 for more complete instructions.

# CHAPTER 10
# Organizing Development Files

If you're working with the companion disk from COMPUTE! Publications, there's no need to create a working disk. The companion disk is already organized with a complete set of development files and an assembler program. You may wish to skip this chapter or quickly skim it for reference. Be sure to follow the instructions that accompany the companion disk.

## Organization

Before getting underway with machine language programming, it's wise to organize a working disk with a convenient set of directories and files. The purpose of this section is to help you set up a working disk.

You'll need three disks for this procedure: a new blank disk; the EXTRAS disk that comes with the 1.2 system *Enhancer* software, from Commodore; and the *Macroassembler Development System* disk, which can be purchased from your Amiga dealer.

- Open a CLI in the Workbench environment to allow you to execute DOS commands, such as COPY and ASSIGN.
- Use the Workbench Initialize Menu command to format a new blank disk in the external disk drive (DF1:) with the name *DEV*. This procedure prepares your blank disk to hold programs and files in the format required by the Amiga. New disks must be formatted before you use them.
- In the CLI, type the commands:

  **MAKEDIR DF1:RAMIT**
  **MAKEDIR DF1:RAMIT/INCLUDES**

- Now, remove the DEV disk from drive DF1: and insert the Metacomco disk.
- Type in these commands to move the assembler and linker into a ramdisk temporarily:

**DELETE RAM: ALL**
**COPY DF1:C/ASSEM TO RAM:ASSEM**
**COPY DF1:C/ALINK TO RAM:ALINK**

- Remove the Macroassembler Development System disk and insert the EXTRAS disk into DF1:
- In order to move the MICROEMACS text editor from the Tools directory of the EXTRAS disk into the ramdisk, with a new name *EMACS*, type the command:

**COPY DF1:TOOLS/MICROEMACS TO RAM:EMACS**

- Remove the EXTRAS disk and insert the DEV disk in drive DF1:.
- Type in the commands:

**COPY RAM: TO DF1:RAMIT ALL**
**DELETE RAM: ALL**

After this sequence of steps, the RAMIT directory on DEV contains the ASSEM, ALINK, and EMACS files, and the ramdisk is empty again.

In order to complete the construction of a working development disk (DEV), use the MICROEMACS program to type in the listings in this book and save them to the DEV disk.

- Use EMACS to type in and save the SYSEQUATES.ASM file to the RAMIT/INCLUDES directory. Type the CLI command:

**DEV:RAMIT/EMACS DEV:RAMIT/INCLUDES/SYSEQUATES.ASM**

This will run the EMACS program placed on the DEV disk earlier, and it will start by creating a new file named SYSEQUATES.ASM in the RAMIT/INCLUDES/ directory on the DEV disk.

- Type in the SYSEQUATES.ASM file found at the end of this chapter. While you're typing in the file, it's wise to use the SAVE option from the EMACS menu periodically. When you're finished typing in the file, use the SAVE-EXIT option in the EMACS menu.

You should now have a complete SYSEQUATES.ASM file on your DEV disk, located in the RAMIT/INCLUDES directory.

- Use EMACS to type in the following additional files, which are listed at the end of this chapter:

SYSEQUATES.ASM (Save as file DEV:RAMIT/INCLUDES/SYSEQUATES.ASM)
DOSEQUATES.ASM (Save as file DEV:RAMIT/INCLUDES/DOSEQUATES.ASM)
MACROS.ASM (Save as file DEV:RAMIT/INCLUDES/MACROS.ASM)

Now the DEV disk is ready for use. It has a set of include files in its RAMIT/INCLUDES directory, and it also has the ASSEMBLER, LINKER, EMACS, and HEADER files in its RAMIT directory. These files are all you need to get started with some fairly sophisticated Amiga machine language programming.

- Make a copy of the DEV disk using the DISKCOPY command (in the CLI) or the WorkBench DUPLICATE menu selection.

The equate files presented here are short versions that contain the necessary symbol definitions required for programs in this book only. They are short enough to type in. More complete versions of these files are on the companion disk, or you can add to these files by examining the includes files on the Metacomco Assembly Development disk, or by copying in the relevant information from the Amiga kernal reference manuals.

The longer versions of the equate files may be too large for a 150K workspace, which is a concern if you have a 512K Amiga. If you have expansion RAM, you may wish to use the longer versions available on the companion disk. If you do so, you should also pay attention to the 150K workspace used in most of the examples in this book. A larger workspace can be arranged for the *Metacomco* assembler, if you have enough memory in your Amiga. Just change the *-c w150000* option in the assembler command line to accomodate large files (for instance, *-c w300000* to accomodate 300K).

There are two additional equate files that you may find useful at another time, but which you can leave alone for now. These are GFXEQUATES.ASM and INTEQUATES.ASM. They contain the required symbol definitions for programs that use Intuition features (such as windows and menus) and the Graphics functions (RECTFILL, AREADRAW, and others). These are discussed in later chapters. There are also a number of additional include files used by some of the programs presented later in the book (WINDOWS.ASM, GADGETS.ASM, MATH.ASM, and so on).

As these additional include files are introduced in later chapters, you'll need to type them in and save them in the RAMIT/INCLUDES directory, with the procedure outlined above.

> Because naming conventions and methods differ slightly, the programs in this book can *only* be assembled using the files in this book. Likewise, existing source code programs written for the *Metacomco* include files can *only* be assembled using their files.

## Listing 10-1. SYSEQUATES.ASM

```
;******** SYSEQUATES.ASM
; COPYRIGHT 1988 COMPUTE! Publications
;03/24/87

;*** SYSTEM (EXEC) LIBRARY ROUTINE OFFSETS (PARTIAL LIST FROM AMIGA.LIB)

LVO.ALLOCMEM                    EQU $FFFFFF3A
LVO.CLOSELIBRARY        EQU $FFFFFE62
LVO.FINDTASK                    EQU $FFFFFEDA
LVO.FORBID              EQU $FFFFFF7C
LVO.FREEMEM                     EQU $FFFFFF2E
LVO.GETCC               EQU $FFFFFDF0
LVO.GETMSG              EQU $FFFFFE8C
LVO.OPENLIBRARY         EQU $FFFFFDD8
LVO.PERMIT              EQU $FFFFFF76
LVO.REPLYMSG                    EQU $FFFFFE86
LVO.WAIT                EQU $FFFFFEC2
LVO.WAITIO              EQU $FFFFFE26
LVO.WAITPORT                    EQU $FFFFFE80

;*** MEMORY ALLOCATION CONSTANTS

MEMF_CHIP     EQU $2
MEMF_CLEAR    EQU $10000
MEMF_FAST     EQU $4
MEMF_LARGEST          EQU $20000
MEMF_PUBLIC           EQU $1

SYSBASE       EQU $4
ABSEXECBASE       EQU $4
```

## Listing 10-2. DOSEQUATES.ASM

```
;******** DOSEQUATES.ASM
; COPYRIGHT 1988 COMPUTE! Publications
;03/24/87

;*** DOS LIBRARY ROUTINE OFFSETS (PARTIAL LIST FROM AMIGA.LIB)

FH.TYPE EQU $8

LVO.CLOSE               EQU $FFFFFFDC
LVO.CURRENTDIR                  EQU $FFFFFF82
LVO.PARENTDIR                   EQU $FFFFFF2E
LVO.DELAY               EQU $FFFFFF3A
LVO.INPUT               EQU $FFFFFFCA
LVO.OPEN                EQU $FFFFFFE2
LVO.OUTPUT              EQU $FFFFFFC4
```

```
LVO.READ            EQU $FFFFFFD6
LVO.WRITE           EQU $FFFFFFDØ
LVO.EXECUTE                 EQU $FFFFFF22
LVO.LOCK            EQU $FFFFFFAC

MODE_NEWFILE                EQU $3EE
MODE_OLDFILE                EQU $3ED
ACCESS_READ             EQU -2
SHARED_LOCK         EQU -2
EXCLUSIVE_LOCK              EQU -1
ACCESS_WRITE                EQU -1

;*** PROCESS STRUCTURE OFFSETS

PROC.CLI            EQU $AC
PROC.CONSOLETASK    EQU $A4
PROC.MSGPORT                EQU $5C
PROC.STACKBASE              EQU $9Ø
PROC.STACKSIZE              EQU $84
PROC.TASK           EQU $Ø
PROC.TASKNUM                EQU $8C
PROC.WINDOWPTR              EQU $B8

TICKSPERSECOND              EQU 5Ø
```

## Listing 10-3. MACROS.ASM

```
;******************************** MACROS.ASM BY D. WOLF
;COPYRIGHT 1987 BY COMPUTE! BOOKS
;08/04/87

;*** SYSTEM MACRO DEFINITIONS ***

EVENPC MACRO     ;USED TO WORD-ALIGN THE PROGRAM COUNTER !
 DS.W 0
 ENDM

ZERO MACRO
 MOVEQ #0,\1
 ENDM

ZERA MACRO
 SUBA.L \1,\1
 ENDM

PUSHREG MACRO    ;REGISTERS
 MOVEM.L \1,-(SP)
 ENDM

PUSHALL MACRO
 PUSHREG D0-D7/A0-A6
 ENDM

PULLREG MACRO    ;REGISTERS
 MOVEM.L (SP)+,\1
 ENDM

PULLALL MACRO
 PULLREG D0-D7/A0-A6
 ENDM

LIBCALL MACRO    ;LIBRARY,ROUTINE
 MOVE.L \1,A6
 JSR LVO.\2(A6)
 ENDM

SYSLIB MACRO     ;ROUTINE
 LIBCALL SYSBASE,\1
 ENDM

DOSLIB MACRO     ;ROUTINE
 LIBCALL _DOSBASE,\1
 ENDM

GFXLIB MACRO     ;ROUTINE[,*RASTPORT]
 IFNC '\2',''
 MOVE.L \2,A1
 ENDC
 LIBCALL _GFXBASE,\1
 ENDM

INTLIB MACRO     ;ROUTINE
 LIBCALL _INTBASE,\1
 ENDM

MATHLIB MACRO    ;ROUTINE
 LIBCALL _MATHBASE,\1
 ENDM

TRANSLIB MACRO   ;ROUTINE
 LIBCALL _MATHTRANSBASE,\1
 ENDM

ICONLIB MACRO    ;ROUTINE
 LIBCALL _ICONBASE,\1
 ENDM

JUST MACRO       ;ROUTINE
 JSR LVO.\1(A6)
 ENDM
```

```
EMERGENCY MACRO  ;ERROR CODE (DØ)      PUTS ERROR IN DØ AND MAKES FAST EXIT!
 MOVE.L #\1,DØ
 JMP _ERROR
 ENDM

ALLOCPUBMEM MACRO ;SIZE
 MOVE.L \1,DØ
 MOVE.L #MEMF_PUBLIC!MEMF_CLEAR,D1
 SYSLIB ALLOCMEM
 ENDM

FREEMEM MACRO      ;ADDRESS,SIZE
 MOVE.L \1,A1
 MOVE.L \2,DØ
 SYSLIB FREEMEM
 ENDM

;*** DOS MACRO DEFINITIONS ***

DOSREAD MACRO     ;*FILEHANDLE (D1),*BUFF (D2),LEN (D3)
 MOVE.L \1,D1
 MOVE.L \2,D2
 MOVE.L \3,D3
 DOSLIB READ
 ENDM

DOSPRINT MACRO    ;*FILEHANDLE (D1),*BUFF (D2), [LEN (D3)]
 PUSHREG D1-D3/AØ-A1
 MOVE.L \1,D1
 MOVE.L \2,D2
 IFC '\3',''
 BSR DOSTEXTLEN   ;IF NO LENGTH SPECIFIED, GO CALCULATE IT
 ENDC
 IFNC '\3',''
 MOVE.L \3,D3
 ENDC
 DOSLIB WRITE
 PULLREG D1-D3/AØ-A1
 ENDM

 IFD DOS

DOSTEXTLEN        ;CALCULATES LENGTH OF NULL-TERMINATED STRING INTO D3 FOR DOS
 MOVE.L D2,AØ
1$
 TST.B (AØ)+
 BNE.S 1$
 MOVE.L AØ,D3
 SUB.L D2,D3
 SUBQ.L #1,D3
 RTS

 ENDC

;**** INTUITION MACRO DEFINITIONS ***

REMEMBERCHIPMEM MACRO ;*REMEMBERKEY,SIZE  (AØ,DØ)
 LEA \1,AØ
 MOVEQ.L #Ø,DØ
 MOVE \2,DØ
 MOVE.L #MEMF_CLEAR!MEMF_CHIP,D1
 INTLIB ALLOCREMEMBER
 IFNC '\3',''
 TST.L DØ
 BEQ \3
 ENDC
 ENDM

REMEMBERPUBMEM MACRO ;*REMEMBERKEY,SIZE (AØ,DØ)
 LEA \1,AØ
 MOVEQ.L #Ø,DØ
 MOVE \2,DØ
 MOVE.L #MEMF_CLEAR!MEMF_PUBLIC,D1
 INTLIB ALLOCREMEMBER
 IFNC '\3',''
 TST.L DØ
 BEQ \3
 ENDC
 ENDM
```

```
;*** GRAPHICS MACRO DEFINITIONS ***

GFXPOINT MACRO ;[*X,*Y]
 IFNC '\1',''                          ;IF FIRST ARGUMENT *NOT* A 'BLANK'
 MOVE.W \1,DØ                          ;PUT X,Y INTO REGISTER WORDS
 MOVE.W \2,D1                          ;ONLY IF NECESSARY
 ENDC
 EXT.L DØ                              ;EXTEND REGISTERS TO LONG WORDS
 EXT.L D1                              ;THIS PUTS HIGHEST BIT OF 'LOW' WORD INTO
 ENDM                                  ;ALL BITS OF 'HIGH' WORD IN SAME REGISTER

GFXPUSH MACRO                          ;PUSH 4 MAIN REGISTERS
 PUSHREG DØ-D1/AØ-A1
 ENDM

GFXPULL MACRO                          ;PULL 4 MAIN REGISTERS
 PULLREG DØ-D1/AØ-A1
 ENDM

LOADRGB MACRO                          ;*VIEWPORT,COLORMAP,COUNT
 GFXPUSH
 MOVEA.L \1,AØ                         ;GET ADDRESS OF VIEWPORT INTO AØ
 LEA \2,A1                             ;POINTER TO LABELLED COLORVALUE LIST
 MOVEQ #\3,DØ                          ;HOW MANY COLOR REGISTERS TO FILL
 GFXLIB LOADRGB4                       ;PUT COLORVALUES INTO USE FOR THIS VIEWPORT
 GFXPULL
 ENDM

SETOPEN MACRO                          ;*RASTPORT[,*COLOR]
 IFNC '\2',''                          ;SET OUTLINE PEN COLOR #
 MOVE.W \2,DØ
 ENDC
 MOVE.L \1,A1                              ;PTR TO RASTPORT INTO A1
 MOVE.B DØ,RP.OPEN(A1)                     ;THERE IS NO LIBRARY FUNCTION FOR THIS!!!
 ENDM

SETAPEN MACRO                          ;*RASTPORT[,*COLOR]
 GFXPUSH                               ;SET FOREGROUND DRAWING PEN FOR JAM1
 IFNC '\2',''
 MOVE.W \2,DØ
 ENDC
 GFXLIB SETAPEN,\1
 GFXPULL
 ENDM

SETBPEN MACRO                          ;*RASTPORT[,*COLOR]
 GFXPUSH                               ;SET BACKGROUND DRAWING PEN FOR JAM2
 IFNC '\2',''
 MOVE.W \2,DØ
 ENDC
 GFXLIB SETBPEN,\1
 GFXPULL
 ENDM

SETDRMD MACRO      ;*RASTPORT, MODE (JAM1, JAM2, COMPLEMENT)
 GFXPUSH
 IFNC '\2',''
 MOVE.W \2,DØ
 ENDC
 GFXLIB SETDRMD,\1
 GFXPULL
 ENDM

FILLWIN MACRO     ;WINDOW, [COLOR REG #]     FILLS A WINDOW WITH A SOLID COLOR
 ZERO DØ
 MOVEA.L \1,AØ
 MOVE.L WW.RPORT(AØ),RP
 IFNC '\2',''
 MOVE.W #\2,DØ
 ENDC
 SETAPEN RP
 MOVE.W WW.WIDTH(AØ),D2
 SUBI.W #4,D2
 MOVE.W WW.HEIGHT(AØ),D3
 SUBI.W #2,D3
 MOVE.W #2,DØ
 MOVE.W #1Ø,D1
 RECTFILL RP
 ENDM
```

```
RECTFILL MACRO      ;*RASTPORT[,*X1,*Y1,*X2,*Y2]
 PUSHREG DØ-D3
 MOVEA.L \1,A1      ;POINTER TO RASTPORT TO DRAW INTO IN A1
 IFNC '\2',''       ;IF SECOND ARGUMENT IS *NOT* A 'BLANK'
 MOVE.W \2,DØ       ;THEN MACRO CALL SHOULD CONTAIN ALL ARGUMENTS!
 MOVE.W \3,D1       ;MOVE X,Y COORDINATES TO REGS.
 MOVE.W \4,D2       ;EITHER AS IMMEDIATE DATA (# IN MACRO CALL)
 MOVE.W \5,D3       ;OR FROM LABELLED LOCATIONS (LABELS ARE THE ARGUMENTS THEN)
 ENDC
 EXT.L DØ           ;IF DATA WERE IN MEMORY, NEED TO EXTEND TO LONG WORD
 EXT.L D1           ;IF THEY WERE ALWAYS #IMMEDIATE DATA, THESE EXT.L'S
 EXT.L D2           ;WOULDN'T BE NEEDED - WE COULD USE MOVE.L's (ABOVE) INSTEAD.
 EXT.L D3
 GFXLIB RECTFILL    ;CALL GRAPHICS ROUTINE FOR THIS RASTPORT 'DRAW'
 PULLREG DØ-D3
 ENDM

DRAWPOINT MACRO ;*RASTPORT[,*X,*Y]
 GFXPUSH
 GFXPOINT \2,\3             ;SET THE X,Y COORDINATES IN REGISTERS
 GFXLIB WRITEPIXEL,\1       ;NOW DO THE WRITEPIXEL IN THIS RASTPORT
 GFXPULL
 ENDM

READPOINT MACRO             ;*RASTPORT[,*X,*Y]
 PUSHREG D1
 GFXPOINT \2,\3             ;SET THE X,Y COORDINATES IN REGISTERS
 GFXLIB READPIXEL,\1        ;NOW DO THE READPIXEL FROM THIS RASTPORT
 PULLREG D1
 ENDM

DRAWLINE MACRO              ;*RASTPORT[,*X1,*Y1,*X2,*Y2]
 PUSHREG DØ-D3              ;SIMILAR TO THE RECTFILL FORMAT, SEE ABOVE
 MOVE.L \1,A1
 IFNC '\2',''
 MOVE.W \2,DØ
 MOVE.W \3,D1
 MOVE.W \4,D2
 MOVE.W \5,D3
 ENDC
 BSR _DRAWLINE
 PULLREG DØ-D3
 ENDM

 IFD GFX

_DRAWLINE                  ;ENTER WITH RASTPORT IN A1, POINTS IN DØ,D1,D2,D3
 PUSHREG DØ-D1
 PUSHREG A1
 EXT.L DØ
 EXT.L D1
 GFXLIB MOVE
 MOVE.W D2,DØ
 MOVE.W D3,D1
 EXT.L DØ
 EXT.L D1
 PULLREG A1
 JUST DRAW
 PULLREG DØ-D1
 RTS

 ENDC

;*** FLOATING POINT MACROS ***

RMATH MACRO ;
 MOVE.L _MATHBASE,A6
 ENDM

TMATH MACRO ;
 MOVE.L _MATHTRANSBASE,A6
 ENDM

FLOAT MACRO;
 MOVE.W \1,DØ
 EXT.L DØ
 JUST SPFlt
 MOVE.L DØ,\2
 ENDM
```

## Comparing Equate Files To Amiga Include Files

The programs in this book use naming and symbol definition conventions different from those in the *.i* files on the *Metacomco* disk.

- The files in this book use all capital letters while the *Metacomco* files use combinations of upper- and lowercase letters:

  Example: This book ALLOCMEM
  *Metacomco* AllocMem

- Library routines are also in uppercase letters in this book, as opposed to *Metacomco*'s use of mixed upper- and lowercase letters.

  Example: This book LVO.*xxxxxxx*
  *Metacomco* _LVO*xxxxxxx*
  Example: This book LVO.OPENLIBRARY
  *Metacomco* _LVOOpenLibrary

- You'll sometimes find shortened names for structures and structure offsets in this book, to save typing.

  Example: This book WW.RPORT
  *Metacomco* Window.RastPort

- Library routine offsets in this book are defined as constants in equate files. The equate files are included during assembly and no linkage with external files is required. *Metacomco* defines the library routine offsets in a separate link file called AMIGA.LIB. The programmer must declare most library routines as external references using the XREF and XDEF directives, and later link the program with AMIGA.LIB.

  Example: This book LVO.OPENLIBRARY EQU $FFFFFDD8
  *Metacomco* XREF _LVOOpenLibrary

- Programs in this book define structure offsets as constants in equate files, also.

  Example: WW.LEFTEDGE EQU 0

*Metacomco* uses a very different method of defining structures. A complete explanation of that method is beyond the scope of this book. Using *Metacomco*'s method, the name of each field offset (in this case, Window.LeftEdge is the *Metacomco* equivalent name) is assigned a numeric value during assembly. This method is very flexible and clever, but it requires that the programmer have a detailed understanding of the macros in *Metacomco*'s Types.i include file. Those macros allow machine language programmers to mimic the C language style of structure definition and field naming. This approach has advantages for advanced programmers.

This summary comparison of the programming system used in this book and the approach used in the *Metacomco* include files points up advantages and disadvantages of each:

- Because a complete exposition on each of the more than 70 *Metacomco* include files would have been impossible within the scope of this book, four equate files were substituted for them.
- Because typing in a complete set of include files for the Amiga would have been a formidable job, the files for this book were shortened by limiting them to the library functions used here.
- Because the files in this book have explicit, constant definitions, you'll probably find them easier to understand and use than the *Metacomco* include files.
- You can convert from one style to the other fairly easily by referring to this section of the book. It doesn't matter which assembler is used (*ASM68010* on the companion disk, or ASSEM on the *Metacomco* disk). What is important is that the include files match the program code names and symbols.
- Because the files in this book are shorter (50K versus 300K), a 512K Amiga should have plenty of room for them. Shorter files also reduce the time required for assembly.
- The HEADER file does all the work of deciding which equate files are needed during assembly. Its not always clear which of the 70-odd include files are required when using the *Metacomco* system.

## Extending the Equate Files

To minimize the work of typing in the equate files (SYSEQUATES.ASM, and so on) the library offset definitions for all functions were not included. If you wish to write programs using functions that aren't defined in these files, you'll have to provide their library offset definitions yourself.

For example, say you want to use the BLITCLEAR function in the Graphics Library. If you examine the GFXEQUATES.ASM file, you'll find there's no mention of the BLITCLEAR function. You must add a line to the equate file that looks like:

```
LVO.BLITCLEAR   EQU   $FFFFFxxx
```

To find the information to plug into the empty bytes represented by lowercase *x*s in *$FFFFFxxx*, look in the *Amiga ROM Kernel Manual:Exec*. In Appendix D of that volume, there is a long list of the numbers you need. On Page D-6, you'll find the number for the BlitClear function, namely FFFFFED4. (It's shown as *0xfed4*, the C programmer's way of writing $FFFFFED4.)

Now you can add the following BLITCLEAR definition to the equate file:

```
LVO.BLITCLEAR   EQU   $FFFFFED4
```

Using EMACS, it's easy to add the one line and resave the GFXEQUATES.ASM file with the modification.

Later, when you're programming and need the BLITCLEAR, you can simply enter:

```
GFXLIB   BLITCLEAR   ; (USING APPROPRIATE REGISTER PARAMETERS)
```

and the assembler will have no trouble making the connection to the new version of the equate file.

If you don't happen to have the "Exec" manual, but you do have the *Metacomco* disk, you can also type out the AMIGA.LIB file and read the numerical versions of the _LVO*xxxxxxx* offsets there.

The equate files in this book are short enough to type in, and long enough to cover many Amiga library functions that give your programs most of the fundamentals (windows, menus, and so on). They're simple enough to expand with additional Amiga library functions.

If you need to add definitions of more structures to these files, please compare how they're specified in the equate files as opposed to the *Metacomco* include files. The numerical definitions of each of the offsets was established by counting from the beginning of the structure. Where *Metacomco* says a field is a BYTE, add one to the previous field's offset value. Here is a list of the equivalents between *Metacomco*'s structure definitions and the definitions used in this book:

| *Metacomco* Listing | Value | Meaning |
|---|---|---|
| BYTE | One byte | Signed byte |
| UBYTE | One byte | Unsigned byte |
| SHORT | Two bytes | Signed word |
| USHORT | Two bytes | Unsigned word |
| LONG | Four bytes | Signed long word |
| ULONG | Four bytes | Unsigned long word |
| APTR | Four bytes | Address pointer |
| STRUCT | Four bytes | Pointer to another structure |

This example is based on *Metacomco*'s NewWindow Structure Definition listed in the *Amiga Intuition Reference Manual,* Appendix B, page 12:

NewWindow

```
USHORT   LeftEdge
USHORT   TopEdge
USHORT   Width
```

Means: (using our notation in the equate files)

```
NW.LEFTEDGE  EQU  $0
NW.TOPEDGE   EQU  $2   ; 1 WORD FROM THE TOP OF THE STRUCTURE
NW.WIDTH     EQU  $4   ; 2 WORDS FROM THE TOP OF THE
                       ; STRUCTURE
```

# SECTION 3

# Amiga Special Programming Techniques

# CHAPTER 11
# Amiga Libraries

The Amiga is a multitasking computer. All of the programs in this book are intended to participate in the Amiga's multitasking environment. They utilize the wide range of the Amiga's resources.

## Intuition

Intuition is an internal library of programs used to manipulate windows, mouse, menus, and so on in the familiar Amiga user interface. Working with Intuition requires that you write your programs to conform to certain minimum standards of memory use and error checking. Here are a couple of things to keep in mind when designing Amiga programs:

- Your programs should be written in relocatable code.
- A program should free system resources (memory, libraries, devices, and so on) when finished with them.
- Programs should be polite to other programs running simultaneously.
- A program must begin and end its operations gracefully.

**Relocatable code.** The first requirement means you usually should not refer to specific memory addresses in programs. Programmers cannot be sure where their programs will reside when loaded. A programmer can't assume that a memory array resides at a particular address, either. It is also dangerous to write self-modifying code. Well-designed source code is written using labels and symbols, allowing the assembler and linker to assign relocatable addresses.

The AmigaDOS loader that brings a program into memory modifies it according to the address where it is loaded. In other words, a program is a template until it's loaded into memory. The file containing an executable program also contains the information required by the loader to perform a fill-in-the-blank process at load time. The disk file is actually called a *load module*.

Sometimes, you need to refer to some of the fixed hardware device addresses, like the serial ports, and others that are documented in the *Amiga Hardware Reference Manual*. Since these areas are never used as program storage or data storage, using their specific addresses is legal. Only the user RAM is jumbled up with programs and list structures by the operating system.

**Other requirements.** The other demands Intuition places on the programmer are that programs should have a special startup section, a main section for instructions, and a special ending section. The startup code sets up your access to system resources and looks up some needed addresses; then, your MAIN section operates using them; and finally, the ending section frees the resources claimed by the startup section and returns to the Workbench or CLI.

A STARTUP.ASM program is provided with this book (see Chapter 14). It gives complete startup and ending sections where you can sandwich your own code. When this STARTUP.ASM program is used, it's always easy to create a new program. Simply write a file named *source*, making sure one of its first lines is:

```
INCLUDE   STARTUP.ASM
```

Most programs in this book utilize STARTUP.ASM to simplify and unify the coding/assembly/link sequence. It opens libraries and sets up the environment for the application, and then closes libraries and performs the necessary graceful exit. There will be a closer look at STARTUP.ASM after we examine the concepts of memory allocation and the Amiga's libraries.

## Amiga Libraries

The Amiga provides hundreds of kilobytes of functions for use in applications programs. If you want to draw a circle on the screen, call a subroutine in the Graphics library. If you want to print text in a window, call a subroutine in the Intuition library.

To maintain software compatibility from release to release, *libraries* are conveniently organized for programmers. The Amiga libraries are organized as *jump tables*. A jump table is a list of addresses of the actual functions. Table 11-1 is a list of the libraries in the Amiga's ROM. The programmer opens a library by calling OPENLIBRARY. OPENLIBRARY returns the address of the jump table for the specified library. An apparent Catch-22 is that library access is controlled by the Exec library (that's where OPENLIBRARY and CLOSELIBRARY are). Exec is the one library that doesn't need opening. The base address of the Exec library's jump table is always located at memory location 4 in the Amiga's RAM. This one location is the only permanently assigned memory location for Amiga software. By making this one number a permanent resident of location 4, the rest of the system's libraries become accessible through Exec's OPENLIBRARY call.

Once the base address of a library's jump table is found, the address of each of that library's functions is lined up for easy access, relative to that base address. (See Figure 11-1.) To use a function whose address is in the library, a Jump to SubRoutine (JSR) is made to an offset from the jump table base address in A6. Examples of opening a library are shown in Listing 11-1. They demonstrate how to call the Exec library's OPENLIBRARY function and check for errors after its use. They also demonstrate that, in general, the Exec library functions require that their parameters be made available in address register A1.

**Figure 11-1. Amiga Library General Structure**

A typical Amiga library is organized into a jump table so that the actual location of the functions becomes irrelevant.

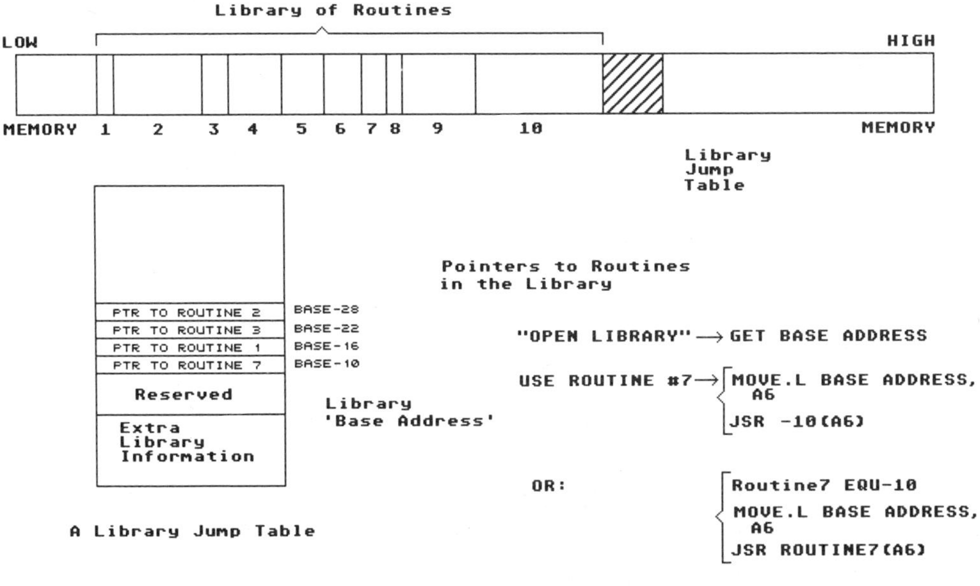

**Table 11-1. Amiga ROM Kernel Libraries**

| Library | Contents |
|---|---|
| Clist | Character string functions for the clipboard |
| DOS | AmigaDOS, I/O, file handling |
| Exec | Library access, memory allocation, message ports, and so on |
| Graphics | Sprites, color maps, rectangular fills, and so on |
| Icon | Workbench icon functions |
| Intuition | User Interface functions (menus, gadgets, windows, and so on) |
| Layers | Graphic layering functions (usually used only by system) |
| MathFFP | 32-bit fast floating-point math functions (Arithmetic) |
| MathIEEDoubBas | 64-bit IEEE floating-point math functions (Arithmetic) |
| MathTrans | 32-bit Transcendental math functions (sin, cosine, and so on) |
| Potgo | Pot bits functions, game port functions |
| Timer | Functions for reading, setting the Amiga timer |
| Translator | Translator functions for speech synthesizer output |

**Listing 11-1. Programming Examples: Opening a Library**

```
;                                          TO OPEN THE DOS LIBRARY -
        MOVEQ    #0,D0                     ; NO PARTICULAR VERSION
        MOVEA.L  4,A6                      ; EXEC LIBRARY JUMP TABLE
                                           ; ADDRESS INTO A6
        LEA      DOSNAME,A0                ; PUT POINTER TO NAME OF
                                           ; LIBRARY INTO A0
        JSR      LVO.OPENLIBRARY(A6)       ; USE THE EXEC OPENLIBRARY
                                           ; FUNCTION
        TST.L    D0                        ; DID THE OPEN SUCCEED?
        BEQ      ERROR_DOSLIB              ; NO, D0 CAME BACK EMPTY, SO
                                           ; HANDLE THE ERROR
        MOVE.L   D0,_DOSBASE               ; YES, D0 HAS THE ADDRESS OF
                                           ; THE DOS LIBRARY
;                                          SAVE THAT NUMBER FOR LATER
                                           USE
;                                          MORE PROGRAM CODE GOES
                                           HERE
;                                          AND THE FOLLOWING MUST BE
                                           PLACED IN YOUR DATA
                                           DECLARATIONS
DOSNAME DC.B     'DOS.LIBRARY',0           ; LABELLED TEXT OF OFFICIAL
                                           ; LIBRARY NAME
```

```
_DOSBASE  DC.L      0                        ; ROOM FOR STORING THE
                                             ; LIBRARY'S 'BASE'
;                                            TO OPEN THE INTUITION
                                             LIBRARY -
          MOVEQ     #0,D0                    ; DON'T SPECIFY ANY VERSION
                                             ; OF LIBRARY
          MOVEA.L   4,A6
          LEA       INTNAME,A0
          JSR       LVO.OPENLIBRARY(A6)
          TST.L     D0                       ; REMEMBER TO CHECK FOR AN
                                             ; ERROR
          BEQ       ERROR_INTLIB
          MOVE.L    D0,_INTBASE              ; NO ERROR OCCURRED, D0 HAS
                                             ; ADDRESS
;                                            MORE OF YOUR PROGRAM GOES
                                             HERE
;                                            IN YOUR CODE'S 'DATA DEC-
                                             LARATIONS SECTION' ARE:
INTNAME   DC.B      'INTUITION.LIBRARY',0
_INTBASE  DC.L      0
;                                            OPENING OTHER LIBRARIES FOL-
                                             LOWS THIS FORMAT PRECISELY
;                                            THERE MUST BE A LABELED LO-
                                             CATION FOR THE TEXT OF THE
                                             LIBRARY NAME
;                                            THERE USUALLY SHOULD BE A
                                             LABELLED LOCATION FOR THE
                                             LIBRARY BASE
;                                            WHICH COMES BACK IN D0
                                             AFTER A SUCCESSFUL CALL TO
                                             'OPENLIBRARY'
;                                            TO OPEN AND USE A LIBRARY
                                             FUNCTION - EXAMPLE OF USING
                                             THE 'MATHLIB'
;                                            TO ADD TOGETHER TWO 'FLOAT-
                                             ING POINT' NUMBERS
          MOVEQ.L   #0,D0
          MOVEA.L   4,A6
          LEA       MATHNAME,A0
          JSR       LVO.OPENLIBRARY(A6)
          TST.L     D0
          BEQ       ERROR_MATHLIB
          MOVE.L    D0,_MATHBASE             ; SAVE LIBRARY BASE ADDRESS
          MOVE.L    D0,A6                    ; MOVE IT INTO A6 TO USE THE
                                             ; LIBRARY FUNCTIONS
          MOVE.L    VARIABLE1,D0
          MOVE.L    VARIABLE2,D1
```

```
        JSR      LVO.SPADD(A6)          ; DOES FLOATING POINT ADDI-
                                        ; TION OF THE TWO
;                                       NUMBERS IN D0 AND D1
        MOVE.L   D0,SUMOF               ; SUM OF THE NUMBERS COMES
                                        ; BACK IN D0
;                                       WE CHOSE TO SAVE IT IN
;                                       'SUMOF'
;                                       MORE OF YOUR PROGRAM GOES
;                                       HERE
;                                       AND LATER, SOMEWHERE IN
;                                       YOUR DATA DECLARATIONS
MATHNAME  DC.B  'MATHFFP.LIBRARY',0
_MATHBASE DC.L  0
```

**Parameter passing.** If you review the code examples that demonstrate the OPENLIBRARY function, you'll notice that certain information must be placed in registers before the function can be called. Those parameters are required by OPENLIBRARY to do its job.

This is typical of Amiga library calls. The calling program sets up some required data in registers and then makes the call. Some calls also require a preexisting table of data (called a *structure*) prior to the call. Structures will be discussed in greater detail below.

**Libraries as system resources.** Libraries are *system resources*. As mentioned above, any system resources used by your program must later be returned to the system. That means that libraries opened at the beginning of the program should be closed at the end, or when the program is finished using them.

The Amiga's operating system must keep track of a library as long as it is open. If you have libraries open unnecessarily, you're wasting both memory space and processor time. Having your program open a library also places some restrictions on what the Amiga can do with that library internally. Usually, the Amiga operating system is free to move whole libraries anywhere in memory it finds convenient. But once a library is opened, the operating system knows it must not move the library.

Therefore, in Listing 11-1, each library is individually opened and closed by name. The CLOSELIBRARY function is part of the Exec library, whose base address is always in memory location 4. Since the Exec library is always open, you can always use the CLOSELIBRARY function to close any other library except the Exec library. Examples of using the CLOSELIBRARY function can be found in Listing 11-2.

**Listing 11-2. Using the Exec CLOSELIBRARY Function**

```
;                                          CLOSING THE DOS LIBRARY
;                                          (COMPANION TO EXAMPLE IN
;                                          LISTING 11-1)
          MOVE.L   4,A6                    ; PLACE BASE ADDRESS OF EXEC
                                           ; LIBRARY INTO A6
          MOVE.L   _DOSBASE,A1             ; MOVE STORED ADDRESS OF DOS
                                           ; JUMP TABLE TO A1
          JSR      LVO.CLOSELIBRARY(A6)    ; NOW USE EXEC'S CLOSELIBRARY
                                           ; FUNCTION
;                                          DATA DECLARATION
_DOSBASE  DC.L     0
                                           ; HERE'S WHERE TO PUT THE
;                                          ; DOS BASE ADDRESS
;                                          ; WHEN
;                                          THE LIBRARY WAS OPENED
;                                          THIS EXAMPLE ALSO SHOWS WHY
;                                          ITS A GOOD IDEA TO SAVE THE
;                                          BASE ADDRESS OF A
;                                          LIBRARY YOU OPEN - BECAUSE
;                                          LATER IT IS NEEDED TO CLOSE
;                                          THAT LIBRARY
;                                          CLOSING THE INTUITION LI-
;                                          BRARY (COMPANION TO EX-
;                                          AMPLE IN LISTING 1)
          MOVE.L   4,A6                    ; PLACE BASE ADDRESS OF EXEC
                                           ; LIBRARY INTO A6
          MOVE.L   _INTBASE,A1             ; MOVE STORED ADDRESS OF IN-
                                           ; TUITION LIBRARY INTO A1
          JSR      LVO.CLOSELIBRARY(A6)    ; NOW USE EXEC'S CLOSELIBRARY
                                           ; FUNCTION
;                                          DATA DECLARATION
_INTBASE  DC.L     0                       ; WHERE THE BASE ADDRESS OF
                                           ; LIBRARY WAS PLACED
```

Because the Exec library (called the Sys library by *ASM68010*) is always open, it has to have a stable base jump table address. As mentioned above, this base address is memory location 4. This location is called ABSEXECBASE or SYSBASE (by *ASM68010*). It's the only fixed memory location used by the Amiga operating system. Adventurous programmers can access the entire system using the functions in the

Exec library to access other libraries and their functions.

**Libraries as families of functions.** You must understand that libraries represent families of functions. All the functions in a given library perform either similar functions or related functions. To draw a line or a circle, you would call the Graphics library. To perform floating-point multiplication or division, you would have to call a function in the MathFFP (fast floating-point math) library.

This is a crucial concept in Amiga machine language programming. Libraries provide your program with access to built-in software functions for graphics, Intuition, AmigaDOS, floating-point math, and more. Both the OPENLIBRARY and CLOSELIBRARY functions are in the Exec library (which is always open).

OPENLIBRARY requires one parameter: a pointer to the name of the library declared as *null-terminated text.* As the name implies, null-terminated text is a string of characters that ends with a byte containing the value 0. An example would appear in memory as LIBRARYNAME0, where the 0 byte indicates the end of the string. The parameter passed when opening a library is the address of the first character in the string (in this case, the letter *L* ).

CLOSELIBRARY requires one parameter: the base address of the library being closed. Both the OPENLIBRARY and CLOSELIBRARY functions expect their parameters to be placed in address register A1, prior to their use.

Advanced programmers can build their own Amiga libraries by collecting the function addresses in a jump table. The techniques for this are described in the *Amiga ROM Kernel Manual: Exec*. They are beyond the scope of this book. The programs in this book will use the Amiga libraries for AmigaDOS, Intuition, graphics, fast floating-point math, and transcendental floating-point math.

An example of a non-Amiga library is the LIVE.LIB library of functions used by the A-Squared LIVE high-speed video digitizer. It contains functions just for use with that hardware accessory. The LIVE digitizer has such special timing requirements that its own library must be used. There are times, when LIVE is operating, that the Intuition library cannot be used at all. The A-Squared programmers had to supply an alternative to the Intuition library just for use with their hardware.

While none of the programs in this book require special libraries, advanced programmers may find it useful to learn how to make their own libraries for custom applications. Once you learn how to program with the Amiga's libraries, you'll easily adapt to using other specialized libraries.

The code for opening and closing libraries is similar among libraries. The main difference is the pointer to the name of the library used during the opening phase.

**Library macros.** Since opening libraries is a fairly standardized procedure, it's a perfect candidate for a macro. Listing 3 shows some relevant macros which are provided in the MACROS.ASM file. Library functions are called by placing the base address of the opened library into A6 and making a JSR relative to A6. Examples in this book almost always use the SYSLIB, INTLIB, MATHLIB, GFXLIB, or DOSLIB macros to simplify calling a library function. These macros assure that a library base address is placed into A6. They also code the JSR instruction and insert the *LVO.* prefix to all function names. These niceties reduce repetitive typing involved in calling library functions.

**Listing 11-3. Macros Useful for Accessing Libraries (See MACROS.ASM)**

```
;                                   A MACRO TO SET UP A CALL TO ANY LI-
;                                   BRARY FUNCTION (LIKE OPENLIBRARY)

LIBCALL  MACRO
         MOVE.L   \1,A6             ; PLACE LIBRARY'S BASE ADDRESS INTO A6
         JSR      LVO.\2(A6)        ; JUMP TO NAMED SUBROUTINE IN THE
                                    ; LIBRARY
         ENDM
;                                   A MACRO TO SET UP A CALL TO AN EXEC LI-
;                                   BRARY FUNCTION

SYSLIB   MACRO
         LIBCALL  SYSBASE,\1        ; USE LIBCALL MACRO, WITH SYSBASE (4) AS
                                    ; PARAMETER
         ENDM

;                                   A MACRO TO SET UP A CALL TO A DOS LI-
;                                   BRARY FUNCTION (ASSUMING LIBRARY
;                                   OPEN)

DOSLIB   MACRO
         LIBCALL  _DOSBASE,\1       ; USE LIBCALL MACRO, WITH DOSBASE AS
                                    ; PARAMETER
```

```
        ENDM
;                                   A MACRO TO SET UP A CALL TO A MATH LI-
;                                   BRARY FUNCTION
MATHLIB MACRO
        LIBCALL  _MATHBASE,\1
        ENDM
```

## Calling a Library Function

Table 11-2 provides a list of the Exec functions (functions found in the Exec Library) used in programs in this book, as well as the registers used to pass parameters

Most library functions require that you place pointers or data in registers before calling them. This is called *set-up*. Table 11-2 shows the set-up required by some of the Exec functions.

**Results.** All library function calls return a result. This result can usually be found in data register D0. Many functions simply place a 0 in data register D0 if the function failed, and a 1 if the function succeeded.

Later on, you'll encounter library functions that return a pointer to a structure created by the function. Floating-point math library functions leave the result of their operation in D0. Functions from different libraries pass parameters to registers in different ways. Exec functions usually use address register A1. DOS functions pass parameters in data registers D1, D2, and D3. INTUITION may use A0–A2, and D0–D3 for passing parameters to a function.

It should be noted that although all functions pass results, sometimes these results are irrelevant. Under some circumstances, you won't care what the result is, or you'll be able to tell without checking the result. For instance, when some functions fail, the computer will crash (cease operating), which would make it both impossible and redundant to check for a result.

**Four-step library-calling process.** When you read through Listing 11-5, try to see the four-step process used in calling a library function:

- Open the library.
- Place parameters for desired function in appropriate registers.
- Call the function.
- Test the number returned in D0 for errors or desired results.

Now that you've seen how to open and close libraries, and you've reviewed some macros that make programming with library functions easier, take a moment to reexamine some examples shown in Listing 11-1. Listing 11-4 shows two of the examples from Listing 11-1. The major difference between the examples in the two listings is the use of macros in place of long-hand source code.

**Listing 11-4. Opening Libraries Using Macros**

```
;                                   DATA DECLARATIONS NOT SHOWN
;                                   OPENING THE DOS LIBRARY

    LEA      DOSNAME,A1
    SYSLIB   OPENLIBRARY
    TST.L    D0
    BEQ      ERROR_DOSLIB
    MOVE.L   D0,_DOSBASE
;                                   OPENING THE INTUITION LIBRARY

    LEA      INTNAME,A1
    SYSLIB   OPENLIBRARY
    TST.L    D0
    BEQ      ERROR_INTLIB
    MOVE.L   D0,_INTBASE
```

Listing 11-5 illustrates the process of opening a library, placing the parameters in appropriate registers, and using macros to call library functions.

**Listing 11-5. Library Function Calls with Parameter Passing in Registers**

```
;                                           OPENING AND USING A MATH LI-
;                                           BRARY FUNCTION
;                                           PARAMETERS IN D0,D1

          LEA        MATHNAME,A1            ; PTR TO TEXT NAME OF LIBRARY
                                            ; INTO A1
          SYSLIB     OPENLIBRARY            ; EXEC LIBRARY 'OPEN OTHER
                                            ; LIBRARY'
          TST.L      D0
          BEQ        ERROR_MATHLIB
          MOVE.L     D0,_MATHBASE           ; SAVE POINTER TO MATH LIBRARY
                                            ; BASE
          MOVE.L     VARIABLE1,D1           ; PUT FLOATING POINT NUMBER 1
                                            ; INTO D1
          MOVE.L     VARIABLE2,D0           ; PUT FLOATING POINT NUMBER 2
                                            ; INTO D0
```

```
MATHLIB  SPADD                              ; ADD TWO NUMBERS WHICH
                                            ; WERE IN D0,D1
         MOVE.L      D0,SUMOF               ; RESULT OF ADDITION IS IN D0
;                                           OPENING AND USING AN INTU-
;                                           ITION LIBRARY FUNCTION
         LEA         INTNAME,A1             ; PARAMETER FOR OPENLIBRARY
                                            ; FUNCTION INTO A1
         SYSLIB      OPENLIBRARY
         TST.L       D0
         BEQ         ERROR
         MOVE.L      D0,_INTBASE            ; SAVE POINTER TO INTUITION
                                            ; LIBRARY BASE
         MOVE.L      NEWWINDOW,A0           ; PARAMETER FOR OPENWINDOW
                                            ; FUNCTION INTO A0
;                                           NEWWINDOW IS ADDRESS OF A
;                                           NEWWINDOW STRUCTURE
INTLIB   OPENWINDOW                         ; NOW CALL THE INTUITION
                                            ; LIBRARY FUNCTION
         TST.L       D0                     ; SEE IF RESULT IN D0 IS 0
         BEQ         ERROR                  ; IF IT WAS, THAT'S AN ERROR OF
                                            ; OPENWINDOW
         MOVE.L      D0,THISWINDOW          ; IF IT WASN'T, SET PTR TO
                                            ; WINDOW STRUCTURE
;                                           CAME BACK IN D0. LETS SAVE IT.
```

In closing this introduction to the concept of libraries, here's an example of using the SYSLIB macro to close a library in Listing 11-6.

**Listing 11-6. Closing Libraries Using the SYSLIB Macro (See MACROS.ASM)**

```
;                                CLOSING THE INTUITION LIBRARY
;                                DATA DECLARATIONS NOT SHOWN
   MOVE.L   _INTBASE,A1      ;PLACE LIBRARY BASE ADDRESS INTO A1
   SYSLIB   CLOSELIBRARY     ;CLOSE THE LIBRARY
;                                CLOSING THE DOS LIBRARY
   MOVE.L   _DOSBASE,A1
   SYSLIB   CLOSELIBRARY
```

Be sure you understand the fact that libraries are organized into families of software functions. For instance, all graphics functions may be found in the Graphics library; floating-point math functions are in the MathFFP library; functions relating to mouse input and windows are in the Intuition library; and so on.

This concept is central to the entire process of Amiga machine language programming.

## Beginners' Note

You will notice that whenever libraries are discussed, they are referred to by name. The functions within these libraries are also called by name. For instance, LVO.OPENLIBRARY is a function in the Exec library.

The MC68000 microprocessor has no idea what LVO.OPENLIBRARY is. The name must be defined as a number somewhere, because numbers are the only thing a microprocessor understands.

To see the numerical definitions of the Exec functions used by programs in this book, read the SYSEQUATES.ASM file in the previous chapter. There, you will find LVO.OPENLIBRARY has a numerical equivalent of $FFFFFDD8. The SYSEQUATES.ASM file must be included by the program's source code in order to allow the computer to understand what is meant by the text string LVO.OPENLIBRARY. If you read through the HEADER file in the previous chapter, you'll see that SYSEQUATES.ASM is always included.

The SYSEQUATES.ASM file provided in this book is very short. For the sake of space and typing time, it was limited to those numerical definitions required by the programs in this book. Exec contains many more LVO.*xxxxxx* functions. If you wish to see them all, open the *Amiga ROM Kernel Intuition Manual* to Appendix D for a brief discussion of Amiga library offsets, and then review the tables of numbers that follow.

**Table 11-2. Exec (SYS) Library Functions and Parameter Registers**

| Name | Description | Parameters | Registers | Result |
|---|---|---|---|---|
| ALLOCMEM | Allocate memory | Size,Type | D0,D1 | Ptr/0* |
| FREEMEM | Deallocate memory | Ptr,Size,Type | A1,D0,D1 | /crash |
| OPENLIBRARY | Open a library | Name,Version | A1,D0 | Ptr/0 |
| CLOSELIBRARY | Close a library | Ptr to library | A1 | /crash |
| FINDTASK | Get task structure | A1 = 0 | Ptr/0 | |
| FORBID | Stop task switching | | | |
| PERMIT | Allow task switching | | | |
| WAITPORT | Wait on port message | Ptr to port | A0 | |
| GETMSG | Get arrived message | Ptr to port | A0 | Ptr |
| REPLYMSG | Reply to message | Ptr to message | A1 | |

* The abbreviation *Ptr* indicates that the result returned by the function is a pointer. If 0 appears under the heading *Results,* a 1 indicates a success and a 0 indicates a failure. Crash indicates that the program will crash the computer if the function call fails. If no result is listed, the result is irrelevant.

# CHAPTER 12
# Memory Allocation

Because the Amiga is multitasking and loads programs and data into memory in different locations as needed, it must contain some internal functions to keep track of which parts of memory are filled and which are available for loading new data or programs.

## Allocating and Deallocating Memory

The Amiga operating system maintains a *heap* of memory and a *freelist* of addresses and amounts of memory not in use. Programs don't usually manipulate these lists because the operating system takes care of them automatically (although advanced programming techniques on the Amiga sometimes involve creation of *subtasks,* which manage their own memory heaps).

Allocating memory for use by a program (arrays and other data structures) is simple and straightforward. There are several methods for claiming memory when your program needs it.

**Using ALLOCREMEMBER and FREEREMEMBER.** The simplest method for claiming some free memory for your program's use involves two Intuition library functions called ALLOCREMEMBER and FREEREMEMBER.

When your program calls ALLOCREMEMBER, it must tell the operating system how much and which type of memory to allocate. (The types of memory will be explained in the next section.) When ALLOCREMEMBER returns, it provides the address of a free region of memory that has been allocated. The address is returned in D0. If the function fails, then D0 will contain a 0, instead. At the same time, ALLOCREMEMBER automatically adds the information about the allocated memory to a special REMEMBER list. That means a program may call ALLOCREMEMBER several times to secure several chunks of memory, which are automatically remembered without any further action on your part.

When your program is finished with the memory it has allocated, it must return it to the heap. This is accomplished with a single call to FREEREMEMBER. The only drawback to this procedure is that the separate chunks of memory obtained on a "chunk-by-chunk" basis must then be deallocated the same way, which is difficult to do. You should allocate memory using ALLOCREMEMBER when the memory is needed throughout the program. Then, at the end of the program, a call to FREEREMEMBER deallocates all of this memory at once.

The STARTUP.ASM program in Chapter 14 has a built-in call to FREEREMEMBER in its final section, so you won't have to be concerned with this function as long as you're using the conventions of this book. If you use STARTUP.ASM, all the memory allocated by ALLOCREMEMBER calls is automatically returned when your program shuts down. Remember that ALLOCREMEMBER and FREEREMEMBER are functions in the Intuition library. You must open that library before you call these functions.

ALLOCREMEMBER and FREEREMEMBER are very convenient functions to use because all the addresses of allocated memory chunks are remembered by the Amiga, enabling their simultaneous deallocation with FREEREMEMBER. In order for the Amiga to keep track of this list, both ALLOCREMEMBER and FREEREMEMBER use a long word declared in the program. Usually this long word is named REMEMBERKEY to indicate that it is the KEY to the REMEMBER list. The data declaration in a program is simply:

```
REMEMBERKEY   DC.L   0   ;PROVIDE A LONG WORD FOR AMIGA
;                        TO REMEMBER ALL THE ALLOCREMEMBER
;                        ALLOCATIONS
```

The STARTUP.ASM program has this data declaration built in. STARTUP.ASM, thus, assumes that you will use ALLOCREMEMBER in your programs. If you don't, the data declaration will keep its 0 value and STARTUP.ASM will skip over its FREEREMEMBER call. If you've used ALLOCREMEMBER somewhere in the program, the REMEMBERKEY value will change. STARTUP.ASM detects it and calls FREEREMEMBER when your program ends. If you use STARTUP.ASM as part of your program, you do not need to declare your own REMEMBERKEY. It's possible to declare several REMEMBERKEYs and handle more than one list of allocated chunks. Each list is associated with a different

REMEMBERKEY and can be deallocated by a separate call to FREEREMEMBER. If you wish to have multiple lists of allocated memory, consider using the following method instead.

**Using ALLOCMEM and FREEMEM.** Sometimes it's necessary to keep track of some memory allocations separately and directly through your program. In these cases, we may use two of the functions in the Exec library—ALLOCMEM and FREEMEM.

You don't have to open any libraries to use these, because Exec is always open. These are used when some memory will be returned to the heap, separately from a large list being managed by ALLOCREMEMBER. Use ALLOCMEM and FREEMEM (the address of the allocated memory comes back in D0 when you call ALLOCMEM) to get memory that is to be handled separately. These functions don't create a REMEMBER list, so they're more efficient than ALLOCREMEMBER and FREEREMEMBER.

Call ALLOCMEM with parameters designating the quantity and type of memory desired. (An explanation of the types of memory available can be found in the following section.) The address (or a 0 value, in the event of a failure) of the allocated chunk is returned in D0. Programs should store the addresses of memory chunks obtained in order to return them to the heap when the operation requiring extra memory is complete. You deallocate memory obtained using ALLOCMEM, by using the function FREEMEM.

You may recognize some similarity between this process and the opening/closing of libraries. Memory is another system resource that must be returned after use. The taking and returning of these resources is usually managed by pairs of functions like OPEN/CLOSE or ALLOCATE/FREE, or ALLOCREMEMBER/FREEREMEMBER.

It's possible to allocate one large memory chunk at the start of a program and subdivide it for use, but it's more convenient to call ALLOCREMEMBER whenever more memory is needed. This way, more memory remains on the heap, providing for smoother operation and more resources for other applications that may be running. The Amiga usually has a lot of small chunks of memory available for use, and only a few large ones. Be wise in your use of memory.

**Size of memory allocated.** The Amiga always allocates memory in multiples of 8 bytes. You may request a memory allocation of 3 bytes, but the Amiga will allocate 8. If you request 31 bytes, the Amiga will allocate 32 bytes.

Memory allocation has another important feature: All addresses of allocated chunks of memory start on *long-word boundaries.* That is, these addresses can be evenly divided by four. Because the MC68000 expects instructions and most data to be aligned on even addresses in memory, the allocation functions relieve you of the responsibility for aligning your arrays and other data.

Specific methods for using ALLOCREMEMBER/FREEREMEMBER and ALLOCMEM/FREEMEM are shown in Listing 12-1. You may also study the *Amiga ROM Kernel Reference Manual: Exec* and the *Amiga Intuition Reference Manual* for more information on memory allocation. Before showing the programming examples and macros for memory allocation, we need to learn about the different types of memory in an Amiga system.

## Types of Memory

The Amiga operating system uses three types of memory: chip, fast, and public memory.

**Chip memory.** The special graphics, sound, and I/O chips in an Amiga give it much of its power, but they also impose a limitation on programs. The special chips can only see *part* of the Amiga's potential memory range. In an Amiga with 512K or less memory, the special chips can see *all* of the memory. This lower 512K of the Amiga's total memory space is called *chip* memory (MEMF_CHIP is its symbolic name).

**Fast memory.** Any expansion memory beyond the first 512K is called *fast* memory. It's called fast because the special chips usually can't see it and, therefore, processing this memory is not momentarily blocked through *bus contention.* Bus contention is the result of several processors trying to use the same bus. It's analogous to two people trying to make telephone calls on a party line. Courtesy will result in one of the calls being made now and the other later, but for a few seconds, both people are trying to dial, to talk, and to figure out the problem at the same time. The Amiga has a party line to memory within the first 512K and a private line to fast (or expansion) memory. (The Amiga 500 may experience some bus contention even on expansion memory.)

The symbolic name for fast memory is MEMF_FAST.

**Public memory.** There is one other type of memory called *public memory*. Public memory may be fast memory (if it's available) as a first choice, and chip memory as a second choice. Its special symbol is MEMF_PUBLIC.

Public memory may have another meaning in the future if Commodore enhances the operating system to include *memory protection*, a feature of larger computers. Public memory is memory accessible to all active tasks. Other memory designated for use by a single task might be called *private memory*, and could be protected from interference by other tasks.

The current Amiga operating system doesn't provide protection, so it's easy for one task to interfere with another. That's one reason it's so important to allocate memory and resources for a task carefully, and to assure that they are carefully deallocated when the task is done.

When you ask for public memory, the operating system will decide which type you are given. Be sure to allocate chip memory to create a graphic image, or screen display, or sound. Fast memory is usually used for program code, data arrays, and variables. When you request public memory for data arrays, you'll be given fast memory if it's available. Since some users of your program may have expansion memory and some may not, asking for public memory allows for the greatest compatibility. The operating system's convention of using fast memory first allows you to keep chip memory clear for sound and graphics uses.

The symbols used to request memory are MEMF_FAST, MEMF_PUBLIC, and MEMF_CHIP. A fourth symbol you'll need to know is MEMF_CLEAR. When this symbol is used with the call for memory, the allocated memory will be cleared. Each bit within the allocated memory will be set to 0.

These symbols are defined in the SYSEQUATES.ASM file. Example program fragments that allocate, and free memory, are shown in Listings 12-1 and 12-2.

**Listing 12-1. Using the Intuition and Exec Library Memory Allocation Functions**

```
;                               USING ALLOCREMEMBER TO OBTAIN A
;                               CHUNK OF 40 BYTES FOR AN ARRAY

;                               THIS EXAMPLE ASSUMES THE INTUITION
;                               LIBRARY IS OPENED ELSEWHERE IN THE
;                               PROGRAM
```

```
;                                         AND ITS BASE ADDRESS HAS BEEN
;                                         STORED IN A LABELED LOCATION,
;                                         _INTBASE
    MOVE.L   _INTBASE,A6                  ; USING THE INTUITION LIBRARY
    MOVE.L   #40,D0                       ; YOU NEED 40 BYTES OF MEMORY IN
                                          ; ONE CHUNK
    MOVE.L   #MEMF_CHIP,D1                ; YOU WANT CHIP MEMORY THIS TIME
    MOVE.L   REMEMBERKEY,A0               ; A LABELED LOCATION USED AS REFER-
                                          ; ENCE TO THE
;                                         REMEMBER LIST BY THE OPERATING
;                                         SYSTEM
;                                         REMEMBERKEY IS FOUND IN THE
;                                         STARTUP.ASM
    JSR      LVO.ALLOCREMEMBER(A6)        ; GET SOME MEMORY
    TST.L    D0                           ; WAS AN ERROR MADE?
    BEQ      ERROR_ALLOCREMEM             ; IF YES, BRANCH TO AN ERROR
                                          ; SUBROUTINE
    MOVE.L   D0,ARRAYBASE                 ; If NO, SAVE THE ADDRESS OF THE 40-
                                          ; BYTE CHUNK AT
;                                         A LABELED LOCATION IN MEMORY
;                                         USING THE EXEC LIBRARY ALLOCMEM
;                                         FUNCTION TO GET SOME MEMORY
    MOVE.L   #40,D0                       ; AMOUNT IN D0
    MOVE.L   #MEMF_FAST,D1                ; TYPE OF MEMORY IN D1
    MOVE.L   4,A6                         ; EXEC LIBRARY BASE ADDRESS INTO A6
    JSR      LVO.ALLOCMEM                 ; GET SOME MEMORY
    TST.L    D0                           ; ERROR?
    BEQ      ERR_ALLOCMEM                 ; IF YES, BRANCH TO ERROR HANDLER
    MOVE.L   D0,ARRAYBASE                 ; IF NO, SAVE THE ADDRESS OF THE 40-
                                          ; BYTE CHUNK
```

**Listing 12-2. Returning Allocated Memory with FREEREMEMBER or FREEMEM**

```
;                                         THIS CODE FREES MEMORY ALLOCATED
;                                         BY FIRST EXAMPLE IN LISTING 12-1.
    MOVE.L   ARRAYBASE,A1                 ; ADDRESS OF MEMORY TO BE
                                          ; DEALLOCATED
    MOVE.L   #40,D0                       ; HOW MUCH MEMORY TO GIVE BACK
    MOVE.L   _INTBASE,A6                  ; USING THE INTUITION LIBRARY
    MOVE.L   REMEMBERKEY,A0               ; TELL SYSTEM WHERE THE LIST OF
                                          ; REMEMBERED
;                                         MEMORY ALLOCATIONS STARTS. THIS
;                                         REMEMBERKEY
;                                         IS IN YOUR DATA DECLARATIONS IF YOU
;                                         WANT TO
;                                         USE YOUR OWN NAME FOR IT
;                                         STARTUP.ASM HAS A REMEMBERKEY WITH
```

```
;                                          THAT
;                                          NAME
    JSR       LVO.FREEREMEMBER(A6)         ; GIVE THE MEMORY BACK
;                                          DEALLOCATING MEMORY USING THE EXEC
;                                          LIBRARY FREEMEM FUNCTION
    MOVE.L    4,A6                         ; USE THE EXEC LIBRARY BASE ADDRESS
                                           ; IN A6
    MOVE.L    ARRAYBASE,A1                 ; TELL SYSTEM WHERE THE CHUNK IS
    MOVE.L    #40,D0                       ; TELL SYSTEM HOW BIG CHUNK IS
    JSR       LVO.FREEMEM(A6)              ; FREE THE MEMORY
```

This is another situation in which macros are called for. The MACROS.ASM file has two macros that simplify the use of the ALLOCREMEMBER function. They're shown here, for reference, in Listing 12-3. (See the MACROS.ASM file for additional macro listings.) Note that both macros make use of the same REMEMBERKEY.

**Listing 12-3. Macros for Using Intuition Library ALLOCREMEMBER**

```
;                                                        MACRO FOR
;                                                        ALLOCREMEMBER WITH
;                                                        CHIP MEMORY
;                                                        ASSUMES INTUITION LI-
;                                                        BRARY IS OPEN
REMEMBERCHIPMEM   MACRO                                  ;POINTER TO
                                                         ; REMEMBERKEY,AMOUNT,
                                                         ; [ERRORBRANCH]
                  LEA      \1,A0                         ; ADDRESS OF
                                                         ; REMEMBERKEY POINTER
                                                         ; IN
                                                         ; A0
                  ZERO     D0                            ; MACRO TO CLEAR D0,
                                                         ; MAKE
                                                         ; D0 = 0
                  MOVE     \2,D0                         ;MOVE AMOUNT INTO D0
                  MOVE.L   #MEMF_CHIP!MEMF_CLEAR,D1      ; WE WANT CLEARED CHIP
                                                         ; MEMORY
                  INTLIB   ALLOCREMEMBER                 ; MACRO TO CALL
                                                         ; INTUITION
                                                         ; ALLOCREMEMBER
                  IFNC     '\3',''                       ; IF THERE IS AN 'ERROR'
                                                         ; PARAMETER
                  TST.L    D0                            ; THEN USE IT, OTHERWISE
                                                         ; ERROR CHECKING
                  BEQ      \3                            ; MUST BE IN YOUR OWN
                                                         ; CODE FOLLOWING THIS
                  ENDC                                   ;MACRO
                  ENDM
```

```
;                                                          MACRO FOR
;                                                          ALLOCREMEMBER WITH
;                                                          PUBLIC MEMORY
REMEMBERPUBMEM    MACRO                                    ; POINTER TO
                                                           ; REMEMBERKEY,AMOUNT,
                                                           ; [ERRORBRANCH]
                  LEA       \1,A0
                  ZERO      D0
                  MOVE      \2,D0
                  MOVE.L    #MEMF_PUBLIC!MEMF_CLEAR,D1
                  INTLIB    ALLOCREMEMBER
                  IFNC      '\3',''
                  TST.L     D0
                  BEQ       \3
                  ENDC
                  ENDM
```

Listing 12-4 shows the example from Listing 12-1, accessing the ALLOCREMEMBER function using macros instead of long-hand code.

**Listing 12-4. Macro Version of First Example in Listing 12-1.**

```
    REMEMBERCHIPMEM   REMEMBERKEY,#40,ERROR_ALLOCREMEM
    MOVE.L            D0,ARRAYBASE
;                     NOTE THIS EXAMPLE ASSUMES INTUITION LIBRARY IS
;                     ALREADY OPEN AND THAT THE
;                     PROGRAM'S DATA DECLARATIONS INCLUDE A
;                     REMEMBERKEY AND AN ARRAYBASE (BOTH
;                     SHOULD BE LONG WORDS BECAUSE THEY MUST EACH
;                     CONTAIN A MEMORY ADDRESS OF 32
;                     BITS.)
```

This example shows how most of the memory allocations are handled in this book's programs. Macros are used whenever possible to shorten and simplify the program source code. Proper memory allocation and deallocation are requirements common to most Amiga programs. Be sure this concept and the relevant library functions are familiar to you before trying to use these techniques. You'll find many additional examples in the program listings in subsequent chapters.

# CHAPTER 13
# Structures

The term *structure* is from the C language. Structures provide storage space for variables and data used by the operating system and application programs. The concept of structures goes hand-in-hand with the Amiga library software organization.

Structures are simply data tables. Dozens of structures were defined by the programmers of the Amiga, each with a name appropriate to its function. One of the essential documents of the Amiga is a list of the structure names and contents.

## Amiga's Data Tables

Much machine language work on the Amiga involves providing memory space for structures, filling them with data, and reading data from them during the operation of the program.

Before you can call most of the library functions, you must provide parameters or data. Some library functions require that data be placed in data or address registers. However, other library functions require far more data than you could fit into the 16 data and address registers. When that happens, you may be called upon to set up a structure and pass the address of the structure to a library function. A structure can be as large as necessary to contain the information the library function needs. It may contain subsections of byte, word, and long-word data.

An example is the OPENWINDOW function. Prior to calling it (it is in the Intuition library), a structure called NEWWINDOW must be created and filled with information about the window to be opened. Data about the size, title, gadgets, and other features you want the window to have, are placed into the NEWWINDOW structure. Then, when you call the OPENWINDOW function, the only data you put into the registers prior to the call is the address of the NEWWINDOW structure.

**Declaring structures in source code.** The machine language programmer can build structures in several ways. Use the DC.*x* assembler directives (DC.B, DC.W, DC.L, and

DCB.B) to declare storage space for a structure such as NEWWINDOW, in the program source code. If you use this method to make a separate structure allocation in code for each one that's required, you'll soon find that you have a huge source file with a lot of repetitive structures needed by the program.

Listing 13-1 is an example of using the DC.*x* directive to fill a NEWWINDOW structure. The use of NEWWINDOW structures will be discussed further in the INTUITION WINDOWS chapter. The point here is simply to show one way structures can be placed into your program source code.

**Listing 13-1. Declaring and Filling a Structure (NEWWINDOW) in Source Code**

```
NEWWINDOW                         ; LABELED BEGINNING ADDRESS OF THIS
                                  ; STRUCTURE
          DC.W   0,0              ; TWO WORDS, LEFTEDGE AND TOPEDGE
                                  ; VARIABLES
          DC.W   300,100          ; WINDOW WIDTH AND HEIGHT
          DC.B   0,1              ; TWO BYTES, THE COLOR REGISTERS FOR
                                  ; DRAWING WINDOW
          DC.L   CLOSEWINDOW      ; THIS IS AN IDCMP FLAG
          DC.L   WINDOWCLOSE!WINDOWDRAG!WINDOWSIZING!WINDOWDEPTH
;                                 THESE FLAGS DICTATE THE APPEARANCE OF
;                                 USUAL
;                                 WINDOW GADGETS LIKE CLOSE, DRAG, SIZE,
;                                 AND SO ON.
;                                 THE '!' MEANS 'OR' TO THE ASSEMBLER
          DC.L   0                ; NO GADGETS FOR THIS WINDOW
          DC.L   0                ; NO POINTER IMAGE FOR THIS WINDOW
          DC.L   TITLE            ; POINTER TO NULL-TERMINATED TEXT
                                  ; WINDOW TITLE
          DC.L   0                ; NO SPECIAL SCREEN FOR THIS WINDOW
          DC.L   0                ; NO SPECIAL BITMAP FOR THIS WINDOW
          DC.W   40,20            ; TWO WORDS, MINIMUM WINDOW WIDTH AND
                                  ; HEIGHT
          DC.W   630,200          ; TWO WORDS, MAXIMUM WINDOW WIDTH
                                  ; AND HEIGHT
          DC.W   WBENCHSCREEN     ; TYPE OF SCREEN WINDOW WILL BE IN
```

The program code to open the window specified by this structure is:

```
LEA      NEWWINDOW,A0     ; PUT ADDRESS OF THE NEWWINDOW STRUCTURE
                          ; IN A0
INTLIB   OPENWINDOW       ; USE INTLIB MACRO TO CALL OPENWINDOW
                          ; LIBRARY FUNCTION
```

**Using subroutines to allocate and fill structures.** Another method uses subroutines to allocate memory for each structure and fill the data fields with standard values. The programmer must then only make modifications to the standard values as needed.

This book includes a family of subroutines that allocate memory and fill structures used for menus, windows, gadgets, and other elements of the Intuition system. The drawback to using the subroutines is that they enlarge the source and object code. If you only need a structure of a certain type once, you may want to declare it in your code and leave out the related subroutine. For menus and other Intuition tools, it's easier to use the subroutines provided here (or your own) because many structures are created for most Intuition tools. The family of subroutines for handling structures, in this book, are in the support code files that are part of the type-in include files. The include files are named WINDOWS.ASM, GADGETS.ASM, and so on, and will appear in upcoming chapters.

The subroutines use standard sets of values for certain Intuition structures. These may not always be the ones you want in your own programs. Modify the subroutines any way you need, or write code that does the modifications your programs require. The latter method works well when only a slight modification on a structure is needed. Listing 13-2 is an example of the MAKEAWINDOW subroutine allocating memory, filling a NEWWINDOW structure, and then opening the window.

**Listing 13-2. Using a Subroutine (MAKEAWINDOW) to Allocate and Fill a NEWWINDOW Structure and Open a Window**

```
;                           USE CODE ONLY TO DICTATE THOSE field VALUES
;                           THAT ARE UNIQUE
    MOVE.W  #10,D0          ; PLACE LEFTEDGE VALUE OF 10 IN D0
    MOVE.W  #10,D1          ; PLACE TOPEDGE VALUE OF 10 IN D1
    MOVE.W  #300,D2         ; PLACE WIDTH VALUE OF 300 IN D2
    MOVE.W  #100,D3         ; PLACE HEIGHT VALUE OF 100 IN D3
    BSR     MAKEAWINDOW     ; LET THE SUBROUTINE DO THE WORK OF
                            ; ALLOCATING
;                           AND FILLING THE NEWWINDOW 'STANDARD' SLOT
;                           VALUES
;                           AND OPENING THE WINDOW
```

This example refers to the MAKEAWINDOW subroutine presented in a later chapter. It's used here to make the point that you're free to write your own subroutines for doing much of the drudgery of allocating and filling structures. The only alternative is to declare them within your program source code, as shown above. A program with more than a few simple structures can become very long. The subroutine method saves a lot of code and typing.

One more aspect of structures is important to program design: Each of the fields in a structure has a name defined in the include files. If you will think of databases for a moment, this may become clear. A database has records, which are similar to structures. Within each record are fields. Similarly, structures have fields. Generally, for the sake of order, database fields are named. They might bear names like Address or City. The first field of a NEWWINDOW structure is named *NW.LEFTEDGE*.

NW.LEFTEDGE is a word of data indicating how far the window should be from the left edge of the screen. When you wish to assign a value to it, use the name NW.LEFTEDGE as an offset to an address register, to fill that field with a value. The assembler finds the correct value and substitutes it at the time of assembly. Therefore, it isn't necessary to memorize all the numeric offset values of fields within a structure. Simply remember the field names. Like NW.LEFTEDGE, most field names are logical and easily understood.

The examples that fill structures with data values always use the field-naming scheme in the equate files. Since each data element of a structure is located at some fixed number of bytes (called an offset) from the beginning of the structure, the structure can be filled by using the base address and the offsets. Listing 13-3 is an example using address register indirect with displacement addressing to fill in part of a NEWWINDOW structure.

**Listing 13-3. Filling a NEWWINDOW Structure Using Indirect with Displacement Addressing**

```
LEA      NEWWINDOW,A0            ; PLACE ADDRESS OF STRUCTURE IN A0
MOVE.W   #10,NW.LEFTEDGE(A0)     ; MOVE 10 TO LEFTEDGE SLOT IN
                                 ; STRUCTURE
MOVE.W   #10,NW.TOPEDGE(A0)      ; MOVE 10 TO TOPEDGE SLOT IN STRUCTURE
MOVE.W   #300,NW.WIDTH(A0)       ; MOVE 300 TO WIDTH SLOT IN STRUCTURE
MOVE.W   #100,NW.HEIGHT(A0)      ; MOVE 100 TO HEIGHT SLOT IN STRUCTURE
MOVE.B   #2,NW.DETAILPEN(A0)     ; MOVE 2 TO DETAILPEN SLOT
MOVE.B   #3,NW.BLOCKPEN(A0)      ; MOVE 3 TO BLOCKPEN SLOT
```

In Listing 13-3., the offsets NW.LEFTEDGE, NW.TOPEDGE, and so on, are given numerical values by the assembler from the equate files. The four equate files GFXEQUATES.ASM, INTEQUATES.ASM, DOSEQUATES.ASM, and SYSEQUATES .ASM contain the definitions and offset field names of all the structures used in this book.

Figure 13-1 may help you develop a mental picture of a structure.

**Figure 13-1. A Structure's Image in Memory**

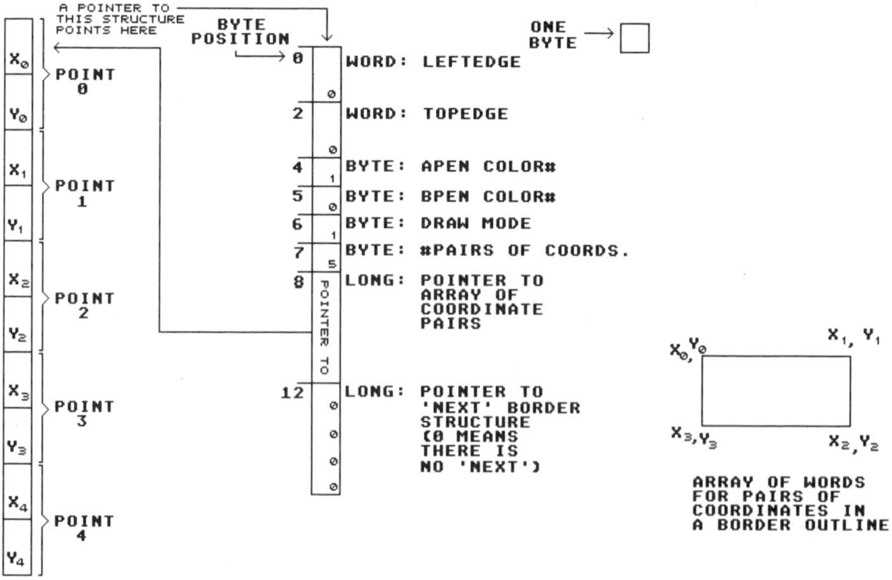

As a final note on offsets, you may be interested to know that neither the Amiga ROM kernel reference manuals nor the include files on the *Metacomco* assembler disk give individual numeric values for the named structure offsets.

The official method of defining offset values is much more complicated than using an equate file. The *Metacomco* assembler creates these numerical values as a program is assembled. Equate files were used in producing the programs for this book on the grounds that they are simpler, and they make machine language programming on the Amiga more familiar to those used to machine language on other personal computers.

# CHAPTER 14
# Amiga Program Startup Code

Now that you've been prepared with the necessary information about Amiga programming techniques, memory allocation, structures, and library usage, it's time to take a look at STARTUP.ASM. This program is intended to be used with most of the programs in this book. You already read a few references to it earlier in the text.

**Figure 14-1. Flow Chart of STARTUP.ASM Program Fragment**

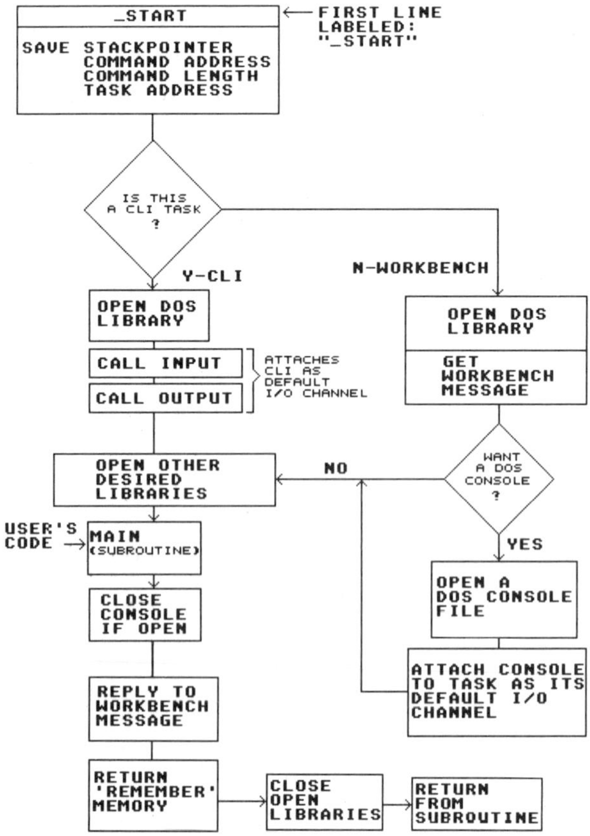

## Why is STARTUP.ASM needed?

Amiga machine language programs usually have startup and ending sections. The startup section opens system resources (like libraries) and the ending section returns the resources to the system. All of the programs in this book, except HIWORLD, use a universal STARTUP.ASM program to accomplish this.

At the end of the HEADER file is an INCLUDE directive for the STARTUP.ASM file. The middle of the STARTUP.ASM program has a BSR (Branch SubRoutine) instruction that directs the program flow to the entry point of your program file. Thus, the entry point of your SOURCE file should be labeled *MAIN*.

Once you understand the operation of STARTUP.ASM, you're free to add to it or modify it to conform to your own applications. The first few lines of STARTUP.ASM deal with multitasking. There are a few lines of code which determine if the program was started up from the Workbench or a CLI. Then, it opens appropriate libraries according to its needs. Programs may use DOS, Intuition, Graphics, MathFFP, and MathTrans libraries. STARTUP.ASM may open them all. Once STARTUP.ASM has determined the program's parent task (either Workbench or CLI) and opened the libraries, it branches with the instruction BSR MAIN to the start of your program.

Your program should end with an RTS instruction (ReTurn from Subroutine). This will return the program flow to the ending portion of STARTUP.ASM. The ending portion closes all the libraries opened earlier and exits to the operating system.

If you use the STARTUP.ASM file provided in this book, you'll only have to worry about programming. You won't have to open or close libraries; this will be done for you.

The STARTUP.ASM file also declares a few bytes of data for all programs, and checks for errors while opening libraries. If STARTUP.ASM detects an error at this early stage, it has an exit routine that closes things down quickly. Your program won't even begin unless the STARTUP.ASM program has successfully completed its job.

For more information about writing startup programs, see the *Amiga ROM Kernel Reference Manual: Libraries and Devices.*

## The STARTUP.ASM Program

Listing 14-1 contains the program code for the STARTUP.ASM program. Using EMACS or your favorite text editor, type in and save this file, since it will be required for all the other programs in this book. Save this file with the name:

**DEV:RAMIT/INCLUDES/STARTUP.ASM**

This will place the STARTUP.ASM include file in its proper place on the DEV disk you began building in Chapter 10.

STARTUP.ASM is the framework for a general-purpose Amiga machine language program. It plays the part of a template into which you can insert your own code, and which can be modified for your particular needs. Programs in this book are created by writing a source file and including STARTUP.ASM. The STARTUP.ASM file remains constant, entering and exiting from the multitasking operating system for all other programs.

Since STARTUP.ASM will play such an important role in all subsequent programming, it would be worthwhile to examine it to see how it works with your code.

The STARTUP.ASM performs several functions in a well-managed sequence:

- Saves critical registers
- Determines whether this code was started from the CLI or the Workbench
- Opens the DOS library
- Sets up I/O pointers using DOS functions (if it entered from the CLI)
- Opens default console I/O if entry was from the Workbench, and the Workbench console symbol is defined
- Opens libraries conditionally if there are GFX, INT, and MAT definitions, and so on
- Branches to user source code as a subroutine
- After returning from user program code, it replies to the Workbench message and closes the default console, if necessary
- Closes any open libraries
- Restores critical registers and returns from subroutine

> The first line of STARTUP.ASM is labeled _START. All programs that appear later in this book begin with a BRA _START instruction. That forces them directly to the beginning of this code.

Remember, the _START label is part of the STARTUP.ASM program. It marks the first instruction your programs should actually execute. It's the starting point for all programs except HIWORLD.ASM. Application program source code should start like this:

```
        BRA      _START      ; BRANCH AROUND THE EQU AND
                             ; INCLUDE
;                            DIRECTLY INTO THE STARTUP.ASM
WBC     EQU      1           ; THESE SYMBOLS CONTROL CONDITIONAL
GFX     EQU      1           ; ASSEMBLY ELSEWHERE
        INCLUDE  "HEADER"    ; INCLUDE THE EQUATES AND
;                            STARTUP.ASM WHICH HAS THE _START
;                            LABEL AS ITS FIRST INSTRUCTION
MAIN                         ; WHEN STARTUP.ASM IS READY, IT
;                            PERFORMS A BSR MAIN AND RUNS YOUR
;                            CODE
;                            YOUR PROGRAM CODE HERE
        RTS                  ; END PROGRAMS WITH RETURN FROM
                             ; SUBROUTINE
```

Now, examine the rest of the STARTUP.ASM source code. Note the source code's appearance. Semicolons set off comments; labels always appear in the first column of text; and unlabeled lines are always indented. Note the extensive use of macros to call Amiga kernel functions that make the code readable and short.

EVENPC (EVEN Program Counter) is a macro that insures the next address used will be word-aligned in memory. Remember that word and long-word data must be on an even address, and whenever a string of bytes is set up (with a DC.B pseudo op), it may end on an odd address. Whenever an address must be even, and you're not certain it is, use the EVENPC macro. It's used extensively throughout listings in this book. It is not necessary to use it if you always declare even numbers of bytes, but that can be difficult with long character strings.

> Remember that failure to insure word-alignment where it is necessary will cause the machine to crash.

STARTUP.ASM also contains some strange labels, like PROC.MSGPORT, and WA.LOCK, with no apparent meaning. These are all *named structure fields* (or *position offsets)*—they have numerical equivalents in the equate files and refer to fields in structures. Although they seem to make no sense, be assured that they all have numerical equivalents. The assembler will know what they mean.

Note, also, that after accomplishing entry to the operating system, the actual source code program is called as a subroutine named *MAIN*. That means that source code files should have a label called MAIN as the entry point.

For simplicity, this STARTUP.ASM startup/ending code skips doing any Workbench message analysis. None of the programs in this book use Workbench messages. The code provided does make it possible to start programs that were made using STARTUP.ASM from the Workbench by double-clicking the mouse pointer on an icon. Simply copy a tool-type icon and give it the name of your finished program file. The parameters (the Tooltypes window and Comments window of the icon) are ignored by STARTUP.ASM.

After program control returns from executing the MAIN subroutine, the STARTUP.ASM closes down the opened libraries and returns with whatever the MAIN code left in D0. If an error occurred during startup, a direct route is provided to exit with a system error code in D0.

You can easily expand and modify the STARTUP.ASM to suit your needs. Add more libraries (for instance, the Timer library or Icon library), remove unneeded libraries, or eliminate the Workbench portion if your program only runs from the CLI.

Familiarize yourself with the STARTUP.ASM program now. As long as everything is operating properly, no further thought need be given to STARTUP.ASM. Note that your code file is usually named *SOURCE* and its entry point should be *MAIN*. At assembly, the assembler will always look for a file named SOURCE, which includes the STARTUP.ASM via the HEADER file.

## Listing 14-1. STARTUP.ASM: The standard start/end routine for programs in this book.

```
;******************************** STARTUP.ASM BY DANIEL WOLF
;COPYRIGHT 1987 BY COMPUTE! BOOKS
;06/10/87

;ERROR CODES

CANTINITSYSTEM EQU 20
CANTOPENWINDOW EQU 21
CANTOPENSCREEN EQU 22
CANTALLOCMEM   EQU 23
CANTOPENDEVICE EQU 24

;*** SYSTEM STARTUP CODE ***

_START
 MOVE.L SP,_STACK           ;SAVE STACK POINTER
 MOVE.L A0,COMMAND          ;SAVE ADDRESS OF COMMAND STRING
 MOVE.L D0,CMDLEN           ;SAVE LENGTH  OF COMMAND STRING
 SUBA.L A1,A1               ;CLEAR ADDRESS REGISTER A1
 SYSLIB FINDTASK            ;FIND ADDRESS OF THIS TASK'S TASK STRUCTURE
 MOVE.L D0,_TASK            ;SAVE THE POINTER TO TASK STRUCTURE
NOWSTARTUP
 MOVE.L #1,ENDFROMWB        ;ASSUME ITS FROM WB
 MOVE.L D0,A2               ;A2 CONTAINS TASK STRUCTURE ADDRESS
 TST.L PROC.CLI(A2)         ;IS THIS TASK A CLI PROCESS?
 BEQ.S FROM_WB              ;NO, ITS FROM WORKBENCH

FROM_CLI                    ;DO THIS CODE IF FROM CLI
 MOVE.L #0,ENDFROMWB
 MOVE.L #1,ENDFROMCLI
 MOVE.L COMMAND,A0          ;CLEAR A BYTE AT END OF COMMAND TAIL
 MOVE.L CMDLEN,D0
 CLR.B -1(A0,D0.W)
 BSR OPENDOS                ;OPEN THE DOS LIBRARY, WE NEED IT
 DOSLIB INPUT
 MOVE.L D0,STDIN            ;SETUP CURRENT CLI WINDOW AS INPUT FILE
 DOSLIB OUTPUT
 MOVE.L D0,STDOUT           ;AND AS OUTPUT FILE
 MOVE.L D0,STDERR           ;AND AS ERROR  FILE
 BRA NOWDOMAIN              ;NOW OPEN LIBS AND RUN USER CODE

FROM_WB                     ;DO THIS CODE IF FROM WORKBENCH
 BSR OPENDOS
 LEA PROC.MSGPORT(A2),A0    ;WAIT FOR THE WORKBENCH MESSAGE
 SYSLIB WAITPORT
 LEA PROC.MSGPORT(A2),A0
 SYSLIB GETMSG
 MOVE.L D0,WBMSG            ;SAVE POINTER TO THIS MESSAGE

 IFD WBC    ;DOES USER WANT DEFAULT WB CONSOLE?
DEFAULTCONSOLE
 MOVE.L #NEWCONSOLE,D1
 MOVE.L #MODE_NEWFILE,D2
 DOSLIB OPEN   ;OPEN A 'DEFAULT' CONSOLE
 MOVE.L D0,STDIN
 MOVE.L D0,STDOUT
 MOVE.L D0,STDERR
 BEQ _STARTERROR    ;GIVE UP IF THE CONSOLE ISN'T THERE
SETCONTASK    ;THIS IS A BCPL POINTER
 LSL.L #2,D0    ;CONVERT IT TO 68000 ADDRESS
 MOVE.L D0,A0    ;ITS THE ADDRESS OF THE FILE HANDLE
 MOVE.L _TASK,A2    ;STRUCTURE FOR THE CONSOLE
 MOVE.L FH.TYPE(A0),PROC.CONSOLETASK(A2)    ;TELL THE TASK ABOUT THE CONSOLE
 ENDC

;*** NOW OPEN LIBRARIES AND RUN USER'S PROGRAM CODE 'MAIN' ***

NOWDOMAIN
 BSR OPENLIBS
 BSR MAIN    ;BRANCH TO SOURCE PROGRAM'S 'MAIN' LABEL
```

```
 TST.L ENDFROMWB            ;IF WORKBENCH PROGRAM, CLOSE DEFAULT CONSOLE WINDOW
 BEQ _ERROR
 MOVE.L STDOUT,D1            ;IF IT NEVER GOT OPENED, SKIP IT!
 BEQ _ERROR
 DOSLIB CLOSE

;*** NOW CLEAN UP AND EXIT TO SYSTEM ***
_ERROR                      ;RETURN HERE TO CLEAR THINGS UP AND EXIT
MOVE.L DØ,-(SP)             ;HIDE DØ FOR A MOMENT ON STACK
TST.L WBMSG                 ;WAS THERE A WORKBENCH MESSAGE
BEQ.S MORFINISH             ;NOPE
SYSLIB FORBID               ;THIS LINE IS CRITICAL FOR WORKBENCH PROGRAMS
MOVE.L WBMSG,A1
JUST REPLYMSG               ;REPLY THE MESSAGE
MORFINISH
 MOVE.L REMEMBERKEY,DØ ;GIVE BACK ANY 'REMEMBER' MEMORY ALLOCATED BY PROGRAM
 BEQ.S 2$
 LEA REMEMBERKEY,AØ
 MOVEQ.L #1,DØ
 INTLIB FREEREMEMBER
2$
 MOVE.L _GFXBASE,DØ     ;CLOSE ANY OPEN LIBRARIES
 BEQ.S 3$
 BSR _CLOSELIB
3$
 MOVE.L _INTBASE,DØ
 BEQ.S 4$
 BSR _CLOSELIB
4$
 MOVE.L _MATHBASE,DØ
 BEQ.S 5$
 BSR _CLOSELIB
5$
 MOVE.L _MATHTRANSBASE,DØ
 BEQ.S 6$
 BSR _CLOSELIB
6$
 MOVE.L _DOSBASE,DØ
 BEQ.S 7$
 BSR _CLOSELIB
7$
 MOVE.L (SP)+,DØ        ;GET BACK DØ FROM STACK
 MOVE.L _STACK,SP       ;RESTORE STACK POINTER
 RTS                    ;EXIT BACK TO WHERE THIS PROGRAM CAME FROM!

_STARTERROR
 MOVEQ #CANTINITSYSTEM,DØ
 BRA _ERROR

_OPENLIB
 MOVE.L #Ø,DØ
 SYSLIB OPENLIBRARY
 RTS

_CLOSELIB
 MOVE.L DØ,A1
 SYSLIB CLOSELIBRARY
 RTS

OPENDOS                              ;open the DOS library now
 LEA _DOSNAME,A1                     ;put pointer to name in A1
 BSR _OPENLIB                        ;open it
 MOVE.L DØ,_DOSBASE                  ;check for successful open
 BEQ _STARTERROR                     ;Ø means error
 RTS

OPENLIBS                             ;open all the libraries we need
 IFD GFX
 LEA _GFXNAME,A1
 BSR _OPENLIB
 MOVE.L DØ,_GFXBASE                  ;and save their jump table pointers
 BEQ _STARTERROR
 ENDC
 IFD INT
 LEA _INTNAME,A1
 BSR _OPENLIB
 MOVE.L DØ,_INTBASE
```

```
 BEQ _STARTERROR
 ENDC
 IFD FFP
 LEA _MATHNAME,A1
 BSR _OPENLIB
 MOVE.L DØ,_MATHBASE
 BEQ _STARTERROR
 ENDC
 IFD TRA
 LEA.L _MATHTRANSNAME,A1           ;optionally open MATHTRANS library
 BSR _OPENLIB
 MOVE.L DØ,_MATHTRANSBASE
 BEQ _STARTERROR
 ENDC
 RTS

;*** STARTUP DATA STORAGE ***

_STACK DC.L Ø                       ;temporary stack pointer storage
_TASK DC.L Ø                        ;pointer to this task structure
_DOSBASE DC.L Ø                     ;pointer to DOS      library jump table
_GFXBASE DC.L Ø                     ;           GRAPHICS
_INTBASE DC.L Ø                     ;           INTUITION
_MATHBASE DC.L Ø                    ;           MATHFFP
_MATHTRANSBASE DC.L Ø               ;           MATHTRANS
REMEMBERKEY DC.L Ø                  ;program-wide ALLOCREMEMBER 'hook'
COMMAND DC.L Ø                      ;address of CLI command string
CMDLEN DC.L Ø                       ;length of  CLI command string
WBMSG DC.L Ø                        ;address of WORKBENCH message, if any
STDIN DC.L Ø                        ;address of INPUT  file
STDOUT DC.L Ø                       ;address of OUTPUT file
STDERR DC.L Ø                       ;address of ERROR  file
ENDFROMWB DC.L Ø                    ; = 1 if from WORKBENCH
ENDFROMCLI DC.L Ø                   ; = 1 if from CLI
 EVENPC
_DOSNAME DC.B 'dos.library',Ø       ;these names are required by OPENLIBRARY
 EVENPC
_GFXNAME DC.B 'graphics.library',Ø
 EVENPC
_INTNAME DC.B 'intuition.library',Ø
 EVENPC
_MATHNAME DC.B 'mathffp.library',Ø
 EVENPC
_MATHTRANSNAME DC.B 'mathtrans.library',Ø
 EVENPC
NEWCONSOLE
 DC.B 'CON:2Ø/2Ø/4ØØ/1ØØ/PROGRAM I/O'
 EVENPC
```

# SECTION 4

# Programming with AmigaDOS

# CHAPTER 15
# AmigaDOS

The Amiga Disk Operating System (AmigaDOS) is the simplest level of Amiga programming. AmigaDOS provides the CLI system of keyboard interaction and command execution. Whenever you type a CLI command, AmigaDOS routines perform the function.

## AmigaDOS and Machine Language Programming

Machine language programs can call AmigaDOS routines, or use AmigaDOS to call other programs. One powerful AmigaDOS routine, EXECUTE, can execute any command in ASCII text. By using EXECUTE, your programs can operate other AmigaDOS functions like LIST, COPY, and CD.

AmigaDOS also provides a *console window,* which programs can use as an Input/Output (I/O) channel to the keyboard and screen. By combining various AmigaDOS features, your programs can do almost anything a user could do.

Some AmigaDOS routines are more specific to its role as a disk operating system (DOS). These include OPEN and CLOSE, for opening and closing files, respectively. AmigaDOS also has routines for *file locking*. The lock feature of AmigaDOS allows single files to be opened and read by several programs multitasking in the Amiga environment, or it can prevent more than one program from writing to a file (called *write-access*). Some sort of lock mechanism is required in multitasking systems with files. It would be unwise to have a file opened by two different tasks at once, which may alter the file in different ways.

The uses of the LOCK structure and related functions (LOCK, UNLOCK, PARENTDIR, CREATEDIR, CURRENTDIR, and DUPLOCK), and many other specialized and advanced features of AmigaDOS, are beyond the scope of this presentation. The reader is directed to a text that focuses more directly on the CLI or AmigaDOS, such as *AmigaDOS Developer's Manual* from Commodore or *AmigaDOS Manual* from Bantam. The programs in this book use AmigaDOS for text I/O and command execution only.

Table 15-1 is a list of some AmigaDOS functions showing their parameter requirements and register usage conventions.

**Table 15-1. AmigaDOS Library Functions Used in this Book**

| Name | Description | Parameters | Registers | Result |
|---|---|---|---|---|
| CLOSE | Close file | File Handle | D1 | |
| DELAY | Delay | How Long | D1 | |
| EXECUTE | Execute a CLI command | Command,Input,Output | D1,D2,D3 | 1/0 |
| INPUT | Get input file | None (CLI ONLY) | | File handle |
| OPEN | Open file | Name,AccessMode | D1,D2 | File handle |
| OUTPUT | Get output file | None (CLI ONLY) | | File Handle |
| READ | Read from file | File,Buffer,Length | D1,D2,D3 | # read/0 |
| WRITE | Write to file | File,Buffer,Length | D1,D2,D3 | # written/0 |

## AmigaDOS INPUT and OUTPUT Calls for CLI-Originated Programs

Information in this section applies only to programs started from the CLI.

When a program is started from the CLI by typing its name as a command, the program inherits the CLI window. STARTUP.ASM performs AmigaDOS INPUT and OUTPUT calls and saves the file pointers for just this purpose. They are saved in the variables called STDIN, STDOUT, and STDERR (which gets the same pointer as STDOUT). These variable names are holdovers from the C language. They stand for STandarD INput, STandarD OUTput, and STandarD ERRor, respectively. They're the names of files to be used for user input, output, and error messages.

INPUT and OUTPUT calls to identify the CLI's input and output streams. Since the program was started from the CLI, a console-type file is already OPEN. Therefore STARTUP.ASM makes INPUT and OUTPUT calls to find the OPEN console file—namely the current CLI. If the program opens another file, there's no need to call INPUT or OUTPUT for that file. These functions only identify the CLI I/O streams for programs started from a CLI.

STARTUP.ASM always opens the AmigaDOS Library and performs the INPUT and OUTPUT functions for CLI-based programs. Your SOURCE file doesn't need to include these opening calls. The STDIN, STDOUT, and STDERR file pointers are all directed to the CLI from which the program was called. The program can use these variables to help with text I/O.

**Text output to the CLI: AmigaDOS WRITE.** The simplest Amiga program can use the existing CLI window to display messages and respond to user keyboard input.

Listing 15-1 shows how to use the WRITE function in a program. The DOSPRINT macro takes two parameters: the address of a null-terminated ASCII text and the pointer to the OUTPUT file. STDOUT is used as a label for this file. DOSPRINT calls the WRITE function. The WRITE function takes three parameters: a pointer to the OUTPUT file (in D1), a pointer to the text (in D2), and the length of the text (in D3).

WRITE does not use null-terminated text. Rather, it operates under another widely used protocol. You must inform WRITE of the number of characters to print. But, since null-terminated text is so convenient in most situations, the DOSPRINT macro is programmed to count the characters in a string until a 0 byte is reached. Then it feeds the character count to WRITE. The alternative would be to count the characters yourself, "by hand," and adjust the value every time a string is altered. You can get a closer look at the DOSPRINT macro in the MACROS.ASM file.

Listing 15-1 is a program that outputs a few messages to the CLI using both the WRITE function and the DOSPRINT macro.

**Listing 15-1. CLIPRINT.ASM**

```
;CLIPRINT.ASM BY DANIEL WOLF
;COPYRIGHT 1987 BY COMPUTE! PUBLICATIONS
;09/10/87

;THIS PROGRAM WILL ONLY WORK FROM THE CLI!!
;THIS PROGRAM WILL CRASH IF STARTED FROM THE WORKBENCH!!


 BRA _START;BRANCH PAST INCLUDES TO FIRST LINE OF
;STARTUP.ASM WHICH HAS LABEL _START

;WBC EQU 1 ;IF THIS LINE IS INCLUDED, STARTUP.ASM
;WILL PROVIDE A CONSOLE WINDOW FOR WORKBENCH
;STARTUP AND THE PROGRAM WON'T CRASH!!

 INCLUDE "HEADER"

MAIN                            ;REQUIRED ENTRY LABEL OF THE PROGRAM
;USE WRITE FUNCTION TO DISPLAY MESSAGE
 MOVE.L STDOUT,D1               ;OUTPUT FILE HANDLE FOR CLI WINDOW INTO D1
 MOVE.L #MESSAGE,D2          ;ADDRESS OF TEXT MESSAGE INTO D2
 MOVE.L #LEN1,D3                ;LENGTH OF MESSAGE (# CHARACTERS) INTO D3
 DOSLIB WRITE                   ;NOW CALL THE DOS LIBRARY 'WRITE' FUNCTION

 DOSPRINT STDOUT,#MESSAGE2  ;USE MACRO TO PRINT SECOND MESSAGE - EASIER?

    ;***  NOW EXIT TO STARTUP.ASM  ***

DONE
 ZERO D0                ;NO ERRORS, SO PLACE 0 IN D0 AS RETURN CODE
 RTS                        ;RETURN TO 'CLEANUP' PORTION OF STARTUP.ASM
```

```
   ;*** DATA STORAGE ***

MESSAGE
 DC.B ' This is an example of printing text using AmigaDos WRITE ',10,10,0
 EVENPC

LEN1 EQU *-MESSAGE

MESSAGE2
 DC.B ' NOTE USE OF 10 AS A LINEFEED CHARACTER ',10
 DC.B ' AND 0 TO END THE TEXT STRING',10,0
 EVENPC

LEN2 EQU *-MESSAGE2

END
```

**Reading the command line.** Starting a program from the CLI sometimes involves typing more than just the program's name. It's common to follow the program name with a space and one or more parameters.

Most CLI commands also work this way. For example, you can type DIR to obtain a listing of the current directory, or you can type DIR OPT A to obtain a more complete directory listing. The latter command contains two parameters for the DIR program (OPT and A). Your programs can read the command line, too.

The first few lines of the STARTUP.ASM program insure that any program using it as a beginning/ending shell will be able to read the command line. When the Amiga operating system starts a program from the CLI, the address of the first parameter on the command line is stored in register A0, and register D0 contains the parameter's length. STARTUP.ASM preserves these registers in the variables COMMAND and CMDLEN, for use by the program.

The program can refer to these variables and use them to read the command line. Once again, COMMAND is the address of the parameter following the command (*OPT A* in the command DIR OPT A), sometimes called the *tail* of the command. CMDLEN contains the number of characters in the command tail (five in the example given).

Listing 15-2 shows a simple program that accepts command tails and prints them out. This program is only meaningful when started from the CLI. If the program is started from the Workbench, the variables COMMAND and CMDLEN will contain useless information.

## Listing 15-2. CMDTAIL.ASM

```
;CMDTAIL.ASM BY DANIEL WOLF
;COPYRIGHT 1987 BY COMPUTE! PUBLICATIONS
;09/10/87

 BRA _START

WBC EQU 1 ;MAKE SURE THERE'S A DOS FILE TO PRINT TO!
 ;BY MAKING STARTUP.ASM OPEN ONE IF THE
 ;PROGRAM IS CALLED FROM WORKBENCH
 ;STDIN, STDOUT WILL BE CLI OR CONSOLE DEPENDING
 ;ON WHERE THE PROGRAM IS STARTED FROM

 INCLUDE "HEADER"

MAIN                            ;THIS MUST BE THE LABEL OF THE PROGRAM

 DOSPRINT STDOUT,COMMAND        ;MACRO TO PRINT TEXT TO CLI OR CONSOLE WINDOW
 ;THE TWO LABELS ARE DEFINED IN STARTUP.ASM

 MOVE.L #TICKSPERSECOND,D1 ;WAIT 4 SECONDS TO SEE IT
 ASL.L #2,D1
 DOSLIB DELAY

    ;***  NOW EXIT TO STARTUP.ASM  ***

DONE
 ZERO D0                   ;NO ERRORS, SO PLACE 0 IN D0
 RTS                       ;RETURN TO 'CLEANUP' PORTION OF STARTUP.ASM

 END
```

**Reading the keyboard.** A program started from the CLI can use the CLI's open console file to read keyboard input from the user. Programming this operation is straightforward. The program must make a memory buffer available for the incoming characters.

To call the AmigaDOS READ function, three parameters are required:

- A pointer to the open file
- A pointer to the memory buffer
- The number of characters to READ

The READ function will accept incoming characters until:

- The buffer fills
- The specified number of characters is READ
- A carriage return is received

Listing 15-3 is a program that prints a message and then reads the user's reply, all within the CLI.

### Listing 15-3. CLIREAD.ASM

```
;CLIREAD.ASM BY DANIEL WOLF
;COPYRIGHT 1987 BY COMPUTE! PUBLICATIONS
;09/10/87

 BRA _START

WBC EQU 1 ;MAKE SURE THERE'S A DOS FILE TO PRINT TO!
 ;BY MAKING STARTUP.ASM OPEN ONE IF THE
 ;PROGRAM IS CALLED FROM WORKBENCH
 ;STDIN, STDOUT WILL BE CLI OR CONSOLE DEPENDING
 ;ON WHERE THE PROGRAM IS STARTED FROM

 INCLUDE "HEADER"

MAIN                            ;THIS MUST BE THE LABEL OF THE PROGRAM

 DOSPRINT STDOUT,#MESSAGE       ;MACRO TO PRINT TEXT TO CLI OR CONSOLE WINDOW

 MOVE.L STDIN,D1                ;READ FROM STDIN (EITHER CLI OR CON:)
 MOVE.L #KEYBUFFER,D2           ;TO KEYBUFFER DECLARED BELOW
 MOVE.L #80,D3                  ;MAX 80 CHARS OR TIL RETURN
 DOSLIB READ

 DOSPRINT STDOUT,#KEYBUFFER     ;PRINT IT BACK OUT

 MOVE.L #TICKSPERSECOND,D1
 ASL.L #2,D1
 DOSLIB DELAY

    ;***  NOW EXIT TO STARTUP.ASM  ***

DONE
 ZERO D0                   ;NO ERRORS, SO PLACE 0 IN D0 AS ERROR CODE
 RTS                       ;RETURN TO 'CLEANUP' PORTION OF STARTUP.ASM

   ;*** DATA STORAGE ***

MESSAGE
 DC.B ' Type in your message (up to 80 chars.) and press RETURN ',10,10,0
 EVENPC

KEYBUFFER DS.B 80     ;STORAGE FOR 80 CHARACTER KEYBOARD READ BUFFER

 END
```

## Opening a File

As you've seen, a program started from the CLI already has a file open for I/O—the CLI. There will be situations, however, when you'll want to open files directly. When a file is opened by the AmigaDOS OPEN function, the pointer returned in D0 is called a *file handle*. It has one unusual property: It is not a true MC68000 address. It is a *BCPL pointer*. BCPL is a popular language in Great Britain. BCPL also happens to be the language used to write most of AmigaDOS.

**Files not on floppy disks.** AmigaDOS permits you to open various kinds of files besides those on floppy disk. Here are some examples of file names you can open with AmigaDOS:

- A file on a disk in drive 1: DF1:MESSAGEFILE
- The printer: PRT:
- A console I/O window: CON:10/10/400/100/MYCONSOLE

When the printer is opened as a file, you should only use it for output. When using a CON: file, the input will come from the keyboard, and output will go to the window. It's possible to open other devices and file types. Read through the listings in this chapter as a guide to experimentation with other types of files. You'll find CON: and PRT: files used in the listings. The listing ASMINT.ASM involves some additional examples of AmigaDOS file usage.

The OPEN function requires two parameters:

- A pointer to the text name of the file in register D1
- An access mode in register D2

When OPEN is called, the parameters tell the Amiga whether to use an existing file or create a new one. The different modes for opening files are summarized in Table 15-2.

**Table 15-2. Access Modes**

| Mode | Value | Meaning |
|---|---|---|
| MODE_NEWFILE | 1006 | New file opened for writing only |
| MODE_OLDFILE | 1005 | Old file opened for reading and writing |
| MODE_READWRITE | 1004 | New file opened for reading and writing |
| MODE_READONLY | 1005 | Old file opened for reading and writing |

Register D0 will contain a value of 0 if the OPEN command fails. Be sure to test for this error condition.

Once a program is finished using a file, it should put the file's handle in register D0 and call the CLOSE function.

Listing 15-4 is DOSOPEN.ASM, a program that opens a file in the ramdisk and closes it.

**Listing 15-4. DOSOPEN.ASM**

```
;DOSOPEN.ASM BY DANIEL WOLF
;COPYRIGHT 1987 BY COMPUTE! PUBLICATIONS
;09/10/87

 BRA _START;BRANCH PAST INCLUDES TO FIRST LINE OF
;STARTUP.ASM WHICH HAS LABEL _START
WBC EQU 1

 INCLUDE "HEADER";BRING IN INCLUDES AND STARTUP.ASM

MAIN                          ;REQUIRED ENTRY LABEL OF THE PROGRAM

;THIS TIME THE PROGRAM OPENS A RAM FILE TO WRITE TO

 MOVE.L #FILE,D1              ;POINTER TO NAME OF RAM FILE
 MOVE.L #MODE_NEWFILE,D2      ;AS A NEW FILE
 DOSLIB OPEN
 TST.L D0
```

```
 BEQ QUIT                        ;SORRY, CAN'T OPEN THE CONSOLE
 MOVE.L DØ,RAMFILE               ;GIVE OURSELVES AN OUTPUT FILE TO WRITE INTO

;USE WRITE FUNCTION TO PUT A MESSAGE THERE
 MOVE.L RAMFILE,D1               ;OUTPUT FILE HANDLE FOR CONSOLE WINDOW INTO D1
 MOVE.L #MESSAGE,D2            ;ADDRESS OF TEXT MESSAGE INTO D2
 MOVE.L #LEN1,D3                 ;LENGTH OF MESSAGE (# CHARACTERS) INTO D3
 DOSLIB WRITE                    ;NOW CALL THE DOS LIBRARY 'WRITE' FUNCTION

 DOSPRINT STDOUT,#MESSAGE2  ;USE MACRO TO PRINT SECOND MESSAGE - EASIER?
;THIS ONE GOES TO THE USER (STDOUT)!

 MOVE.L #TICKSPERSECOND,D1
 ASL.L #1,D1
 DOSLIB DELAY;DELAY 2 SECONDS TO SEE THIS STUFF

    ;***  NOW FINISH UP, CLOSE FILE, AND EXIT TO STARTUP.ASM  ***

DONE
 MOVE.L RAMFILE,D1
 DOSLIB CLOSE;WE OPENED A CONSOLE, SO WE NEED TO CLOSE IT!

QUIT
 ZERO DØ                  ;NO ERRORS, SO PLACE Ø IN DØ AS RETURN CODE
 RTS                          ;RETURN TO 'CLEANUP' PORTION OF STARTUP.ASM

   ;*** DATA STORAGE ***

FILE
 DC.B 'RAM:RAMFILE'
 EVENPC

MESSAGE
 DC.B ' This is an example of printing TO A FILE using AmigaDos WRITE ',1Ø,1Ø,Ø
 EVENPC

LEN1 EQU *-MESSAGE

MESSAGE2
 DC.B 1Ø,' RAMFILE created IN RAM DISK.  It has a message waiting for you.',1Ø,Ø
 EVENPC

LEN2 EQU *-MESSAGE2

RAMFILE
 DC.L Ø;FILE HANDLE OF RAM:RAMFILE AFTER IT IS OPENED

END
```

## The Console Window

You've seen how programs started from the CLI inherit the CLI's console window for input and output. STARTUP.ASM automatically attaches the program's I/O streams to the CLI window, if the program starts from a CLI.

But what if the program starts from the Workbench, instead? Your programs should provide for this possibility. The CLI window may not be available for sending or receiving user messages.

The AmigaDOS *CON:* device (CONsole device) can substitute for the CLI window, when necessary. The CON: device has its own special features. It need not always function as a CLI substitute. The STARTUP.ASM program has a built-in call to open a CON: device file for programs that start from the Workbench. It is controlled by conditional assembly through the WBC (WorkBench Console) symbol (see the latter half of Chapter 9). If you define the WBC symbol, STARTUP.ASM will assemble the part that opens the CON: for Workbench programs. Listing 15-5 shows the part of STARTUP.ASM that opens the CON: window under control of the WBC conditional symbol.

**Listing 15-5. Part of STARTUP.ASM that opens CON: window for Workbench programs.**

```
;PORTION OF STARTUP.ASM WHICH SETS UP AMIGADOS INPUT AND OUTPUT FILE HANDLES
;THIS ISN'T A COMPLETE PROGRAM, SO DON'T EVEN TRY TO ASSEMBLE AND LINK IT!!

FROM_CLI                        ;DO THIS CODE IF FROM CLI
 MOVE.L #Ø,ENDFROMWB
 MOVE.L #1,ENDFROMCLI
 MOVE.L COMMAND,AØ              ;CLEAR A BYTE AT END OF COMMAND TAIL
 MOVE.L CMDLEN,DØ
 CLR.B -1(AØ,DØ.W)
 BSR OPENDOS                    ;OPEN THE DOS LIBRARY, WE NEED IT
 DOSLIB INPUT
 MOVE.L DØ,STDIN                ;SETUP CURRENT CLI WINDOW AS INPUT FILE
 DOSLIB OUTPUT
 MOVE.L DØ,STDOUT               ;AND AS OUTPUT FILE
 MOVE.L DØ,STDERR               ;AND AS ERROR  FILE
 BRA NOWDOMAIN                  ;NOW OPEN LIBS AND RUN USER CODE

FROM_WB                         ;DO THIS CODE IF FROM WORKBENCH
 BSR OPENDOS
 LEA PROC.MSGPORT(A2),AØ        ;WAIT FOR THE WORKBENCH MESSAGE
 SYSLIB WAITPORT
 LEA PROC.MSGPORT(A2),AØ
 SYSLIB GETMSG
 MOVE.L DØ,WBMSG                ;SAVE POINTER TO THIS MESSAGE

 IFD WBC   ;DOES USER WANT DEFAULT WB CONSOLE?
DEFAULTCONSOLE
 MOVE.L #NEWCONSOLE,D1
 MOVE.L #MODE_NEWFILE,D2
 DOSLIB OPEN    ;OPEN A 'DEFAULT' CONSOLE
 MOVE.L DØ,STDIN
 MOVE.L DØ,STDOUT
 MOVE.L DØ,STDERR
 BEQ.S _STARTERROR     ;GIVE UP IF THE CONSOLE ISN'T THERE
SETCONTASK    ;THIS IS A BCPL POINTER
 LSL.L #2,DØ     ;CONVERT IT TO 68ØØØ ADDRESS
 MOVE.L DØ,AØ     ;ITS THE ADDRESS OF THE FILE HANDLE
 MOVE.L _TASK,A2     ;STRUCTURE FOR THE CONSOLE
 MOVE.L FH.TYPE(AØ),PROC.CONSOLETASK(A2)     ;TELL THE TASK ABOUT THE CONSOLE
 ENDC

;*** NOW OPEN LIBRARIES AND RUN USER'S PROGRAM CODE 'MAIN' ***
```

When a program opens a CON: device, it can perform input and output through the CON: window, instead of the CLI. When the program calls WRITE or uses the DOSPRINT macro, the output will go to the CON: window as if it were going to a CLI. CLI windows and CON: windows look and work alike for this simple kind of I/O. Listing 15-6 is a program that does simple text I/O. If the program is started from a CLI, the messages will appear in the CLI window. If it starts from the Workbench, a CON: file window is opened (via the call built into STARTUP.ASM) and the messages will be printed there, instead.

## Listing 15-6. CONSOLE.ASM: Console from STARTUP.ASM

```
;CONSOLE.ASM BY DANIEL WOLF
;COPYRIGHT 1987 BY COMPUTE! PUBLICATIONS
;Ø9/1Ø/87

 BRA _START;BRANCH PAST INCLUDES TO FIRST LINE OF
;STARTUP.ASM WHICH HAS LABEL _START

 INCLUDE "HEADER";BRING IN INCLUDES AND STARTUP.ASM

MAIN                              ;REQUIRED ENTRY LABEL OF THE PROGRAM

;THIS TIME THE PROGRAM OPENS ITS OWN CONSOLE

 MOVE.L #CONSOLE,D1               ;POINTER TO NAME OF CONSOLE FILE
 MOVE.L #MODE_NEWFILE,D2          ;AS A NEW FILE
 DOSLIB OPEN
 TST.L DØ
 BEQ QUIT                         ;SORRY, CAN'T OPEN THE CONSOLE
 MOVE.L DØ,STDOUT                 ;GIVE OURSELVES AN OUTPUT FILE TO WRITE IN!
;STDOUT LABEL IS IN THE STARTUP.ASM FILE!

;USE WRITE FUNCTION TO DISPLAY MESSAGE
 MOVE.L STDOUT,D1                 ;OUTPUT FILE HANDLE FOR CONSOLE WINDOW INTO D1
 MOVE.L #MESSAGE,D2           ;ADDRESS OF TEXT MESSAGE INTO D2
 MOVE.L #LEN1,D3                  ;LENGTH OF MESSAGE (# CHARACTERS) INTO D3
 DOSLIB WRITE                     ;NOW CALL THE DOS LIBRARY 'WRITE' FUNCTION

 DOSPRINT STDOUT,#MESSAGE2  ;USE MACRO TO PRINT SECOND MESSAGE - EASIER?

 MOVE.L #TICKSPERSECOND,D1
 ASL.L #2,D1
 DOSLIB DELAY;DELAY 4 SECONDS TO SEE THIS STUFF

    ;***  NOW FINISH UP, CLOSE WINDOW, AND EXIT TO STARTUP.ASM  ***

DONE
 MOVE.L STDOUT,D1
 DOSLIB CLOSE;WE OPENED A CONSOLE, SO WE NEED TO CLOSE IT!

QUIT
 ZERO DØ                    ;NO ERRORS, SO PLACE Ø IN DØ AS RETURN CODE
 RTS                            ;RETURN TO 'CLEANUP' PORTION OF STARTUP.ASM

   ;*** DATA STORAGE ***

CONSOLE
 DC.B 'CON:1Ø/1Ø/5ØØ/9Ø/EASY CONSOLE'
 EVENPC

MESSAGE
 DC.B ' This is an example of printing text using AmigaDos WRITE ',1Ø,1Ø,Ø
 EVENPC

LEN1 EQU *-MESSAGE

MESSAGE2
 DC.B ' NOTE USE OF 1Ø AS A LINEFEED CHARACTER ',1Ø
 DC.B ' AND Ø TO END THE TEXT STRING',1Ø,Ø
 EVENPC

LEN2 EQU *-MESSAGE2

END
```

The CON: file window's keyboard interaction can be quite simple. The CON: file normally returns ASCII characters. A variation on the CON: file window is called RAW:. RAW: windows can read the keyboard as well, but the input is in raw form instead of ASCII characters. You'll use the RAW: window for input when you need to interpret individual keystrokes that aren't ASCII (function keys, for instance). See the *Amiga ROM Kernel Reference Manual: Libraries and Devices* for detailed information on the kinds of keyboard interpretations available with CON: and RAW:.

## Calling Other Programs with EXECUTE

The EXECUTE function puts all the power of AmigaDOS within your program's reach. EXECUTE accepts a CLI command or program name (with parameters) and executes it as if it were typed into a CLI window.

It's easy to confuse this DOS EXECUTE function with the CLI command of the same name. They aren't the same. DOS EXECUTE is really the same as the CLI RUN command. If you wish the EXECUTE function to operate a command file (like CLI's EXECUTE) it's equivalent to typing:

```
RUN EXECUTE 'COMMANDFILENAME'
```

This confusion is the result of a poorly named function. It would have been less confusing if the AmigaDOS EXECUTE function were named RUN to match its CLI equivalent. The AmigaDOS EXECUTE function actually calls the CLI RUN command to do its job. The RUN command must be in either the current or command (C:) directory, or the EXECUTE function will fail.

You can EXECUTE DELETE, CD, LIST, and other CLI commands. You can even run the ASM command (which is how the ASMINT program works).

The EXECUTE function, requires three parameters:

- A pointer to the null-terminated text of the CLI command string in register D0
- An input file handle in register D1
- An output file handle in register D2

The file handles in the last two parameters are usually the file handles of the CLI or CON: window currently in use.

> If the command to be EXECUTED has any chance of causing read or write operations, the last two parameters are absolutely necessary. If a command tries to write without an output file handle, the Amiga will crash.

Listing 15-7 shows an example of the use of the EXECUTE function. It uses the existing CLI or CON: window (depending on how the program was started) as I/O for the EXECUTE.

### Listing 15-7. DOSEXEC.ASM

```
;DOSEXEC.ASM BY DANIEL WOLF
;COPYRIGHT 1987 BY COMPUTE! PUBLICATIONS
;09/10/87

 BRA _START

WBC EQU 1 ;MAKE SURE THERE'S A DOS FILE TO PRINT TO!
 ;BY MAKING STARTUP.ASM OPEN ONE IF THE
 ;PROGRAM IS CALLED FROM WORKBENCH
 ;STDIN, STDOUT WILL BE CLI OR CONSOLE DEPENDING
 ;ON WHERE THE PROGRAM IS STARTED FROM

 INCLUDE "HEADER"

MAIN                              ;THIS MUST BE THE LABEL OF THE PROGRAM

 MOVE.L #EXECOMMAND,D1
 ZERO D2 ;MAKE INPUT = 0 OR THE CONSOLE WON'T CLOSE!
 MOVE.L STDOUT,D3 ;EITHER CLI OR CONSOLE (IF FROM WB)
 DOSLIB EXECUTE

    ;***  NOW EXIT TO STARTUP.ASM  ***

DONE
 ZERO D0                     ;NO ERRORS, SO PLACE 0 IN D0
 RTS                         ;RETURN TO 'CLEANUP' PORTION OF STARTUP.ASM

 EVENPC

EXECOMMAND
 DC.B 'LIST',0
 EVENPC

 END
```

# SECTION 5

# Intuition

# CHAPTER 16
# Intuition and Windows

Intuition is the name of the Amiga's user interface. It consists of

- Graphic windows (as opposed to the all-text console windows available through AmigaDOS)
- Mouse-activated drop-down menus
- Mouse-activated *gadgets* that act as buttons and sliders
- Keyboard interaction *string gadgets*
- Requester yes/no/continue *choice windows.*

Before beginning to experiment with machine language and Intuition, it will be necessary to prepare an equate file to define symbols used in Intuition. The programs in this chapter require the INTEQUATES.ASM file (Listing 16-1), which contains the numeric definitions of library function offset addresses, and field offsets, and so on. Enter this file with the EMACS text editor, according to the procedures in Organizing Development Files (steps 9 and 10). Using EMACS, save this file as:

DEVS:RAMIT/INCLUDES/INTEQUATES.ASM

### Listing 16-1. INTEQUATES.ASM

```
;******** INTEQUATES.ASM
; COPYRIGHT 1988 COMPUTE! Publications
;03/24/87

;*** INTUITION CONSTANTS, ROUTINE OFFSETS, AND STRUCTURE OFFSETS


ACTIVATE      EQU $1000
ACTIVEWINDOW      EQU $40000
ALTKEYMAP     EQU $1000
AUTOKNOB      EQU $1

BACKDROP      EQU $100
BEEPING       EQU $20
BOOLGADGET    EQU $1

;*** BORDER STRUCTURE OFFSETS

BORD.BACKPEN          EQU $5
BORD.COUNT  EQU $7
BORD.DRAWMODE         EQU $6
BORD.FRONTPEN         EQU $4
BORD.LEFTEDGE         EQU $0
BORD.NEXT   EQU $C
BORD.TOPEDGE          EQU $2
BORD.XY     EQU $8
```

```
BORDERLESS  EQU $800
BOTTOMBORDER        EQU $80

CHECKED     EQU $100
CHECKIT     EQU $1
CLOSE               EQU $80
CLOSEWINDOW         EQU $200
COMMSEQ     EQU $4
CUSTOM              EQU $40
CUSTOMBITMAP        EQU $40
CUSTOMSCREEN        EQU $F

DELTAMOVE   EQU $100000
DISKINSERTED        EQU $8000
DISKREMOVED         EQU $10000

ENDGADGET   EQU $4

FOLLOWMOUSE         EQU $8
FREEHORIZ   EQU $2
FREEVERT    EQU $4

;*** GADGET STRUCTURE OFFSETS

GADG.ACTIVATION EQU $E
GADG.FLAGS  EQU $C
GADG.HEIGHT         EQU $A
GADG.ID     EQU $26
GADG.LEFTEDGE       EQU $4
GADG.MUTUALEXCLUDE EQU $1E
GADG.NEXT   EQU $0
GADG.RENDER         EQU $12
GADG.SELECTRENDER EQU $16
GADG.SPECIALINFO  EQU $22
GADG.TEXT   EQU $1A
GADG.TOPEDGE        EQU $6
GADG.TYPE   EQU $10
GADG.USERDATA       EQU $28
GADG.WIDTH  EQU $8

GADGBACKFILL        EQU $1
GADGDISABLED        EQU $100
GADGET0002  EQU $2
GADGETDOWN  EQU $20
GADGETTYPE  EQU $FC00
GADGETUP    EQU $40
GADGHBOX    EQU $1
GADGHCOMP   EQU $0
GADGHIGHBITS        EQU $3
GADGHIMAGE  EQU $2
GADGHNONE   EQU $3
GADGIMAGE   EQU $4
GADGIMMEDIATE       EQU $2
GIMMEZEROZERO       EQU $400
GRELBOTTOM  EQU $8
GRELHEIGHT  EQU $40
GRELRIGHT   EQU $10
GRELWIDTH   EQU $20
GZZGADGET   EQU $2000

HIGHBOX     EQU $80
HIGHCOMP    EQU $40
HIGHFLAGS   EQU $C0
HIGHIMAGE   EQU $0
HIGHITEM    EQU $2000
HIGHNONE    EQU $C0

;*** INTUIMESSAGE STRUCTURE OFFSETS

IM.CLASS    EQU $14
IM.CODE     EQU $18
IM.IADDRESS         EQU $1C
IM.IDCMPWINDOW      EQU $2C
IM.MESSAGE  EQU $0
IM.MICROS   EQU $28
IM.MOUSEX   EQU $20
IM.MOUSEY   EQU $22
IM.QUALIFIER        EQU $1A
```

```
IM.SECONDS  EQU $24
IM.SPECIALLINK      EQU $30

INACTIVEWINDOW      EQU $80000
INREQUEST   EQU $4000
INTUITICKS  EQU $400000
ISDRAWN     EQU $1000

;*** INTUITEXT STRUCTURE OFFSETS

IT.BACKPEN  EQU $1
IT.DRAWMODE         EQU $2
IT.FONT     EQU $8
IT.FRONTPEN         EQU $0
IT.LEFTEDGE         EQU $4
IT.NEXT     EQU $10
IT.PAD              EQU $3
IT.TEXT     EQU $C
IT.TOPEDGE  EQU $6

ITEMENABLED         EQU $10
ITEMTEXT    EQU $2

KNOBHIT     EQU $100
KNOBHMIN    EQU $6
KNOBVMIN    EQU $4

LEFTBORDER  EQU $20
;*** INTUITION SUBROUTINE LIBRARY OFFSETS (PARTIAL LIST FROM AMIGA.LIB)

LVO.ADDGADGET               EQU $FFFFFFD6
LVO.ALLOCREMEMBER   EQU $FFFFFE74
LVO.AUTOREQUEST     EQU $FFFFFEA4
LVO.CLEARDMREQUEST  EQU $FFFFFFD0
LVO.CLEARMENUSTRIP  EQU $FFFFFFCA
LVO.CLOSESCREEN     EQU $FFFFFFBE
LVO.CLOSEWINDOW     EQU $FFFFFFB8
LVO.CLOSEWORKBENCH  EQU $FFFFFFB2
LVO.DISPLAYBEEP     EQU $FFFFFFA0
LVO.DRAWBORDER              EQU $FFFFFF94
LVO.DRAWIMAGE               EQU $FFFFFF8E
LVO.ENDREQUEST              EQU $FFFFFF88
LVO.FREEREMEMBER    EQU $FFFFFE68
LVO.INTUITEXTLENGTH         EQU $FFFFFEB6
LVO.MODIFYIDCMP     EQU $FFFFFF6A
LVO.MODIFYPROP              EQU $FFFFFF64
LVO.MOVESCREEN              EQU $FFFFFF5E
LVO.MOVEWINDOW              EQU $FFFFFF58
LVO.OFFGADGET               EQU $FFFFFF52
LVO.OFFMENU                 EQU $FFFFFF4C
LVO.ONGADGET                EQU $FFFFFF46
LVO.ONMENU          EQU $FFFFFF40
LVO.OPENSCREEN              EQU $FFFFFF3A
LVO.OPENWINDOW              EQU $FFFFFF34
LVO.OPENWORKBENCH   EQU $FFFFFF2E
LVO.PRINTITEXT              EQU $FFFFFF28
LVO.REFRESHGADGETS  EQU $FFFFFF22
LVO.REMOVEGADGET    EQU $FFFFFF1C
LVO.REPORTMOUSE     EQU $FFFFFF16
LVO.REQUEST                 EQU $FFFFFF10
LVO.SCREENTOBACK    EQU $FFFFFF0A
LVO.SCREENTOFRONT   EQU $FFFFFF04
LVO.SETDMREQUEST    EQU $FFFFFEFE
LVO.SETMENUSTRIP    EQU $FFFFFEF8
LVO.SETWINDOWTITLES         EQU $FFFFFEEC
LVO.SHOWTITLE               EQU $FFFFFEE6
LVO.SIZEWINDOW              EQU $FFFFFEE0
LVO.VIEWPORTADDRESS         EQU $FFFFFED4
LVO.WINDOWTOBACK    EQU $FFFFFECE
LVO.WINDOWTOFRONT   EQU $FFFFFEC8

MAXBODY     EQU $FFFF
MAXPOT              EQU $FFFF

;*** MENU STRUCTURE OFFSETS
```

```
MENU.BEATX   EQU $1A
MENU.BEATY   EQU $1C
MENU.FIRSTITEM        EQU $12
MENU.FLAGS   EQU $C
MENU.HEIGHT           EQU $A
MENU.JAZZX   EQU $16
MENU.JAZZY   EQU $18
MENU.LEFTEDGE         EQU $4
MENU.NAME    EQU $E
MENU.NEXT    EQU $Ø
MENU.TOPEDGE          EQU $6
MENU.WIDTH   EQU $8

MENUCANCEL   EQU $2
MENUDOWN     EQU $69
MENUENABLED           EQU $1
MENUHOT      EQU $1
MENUNULL     EQU $FFFF
MENUPICK     EQU $1ØØ
MENUSTATE    EQU $8ØØØ
MENUTOGGLE   EQU $8
MENUTOGGLED           EQU $4ØØØ
MENUUP                EQU $E9
MENUVERIFY   EQU $2ØØØ
MENUWAITING           EQU $3

;*** MENUITEM STRUCTURE OFFSETS

MI.COMMAND   EQU $1A
MI.FLAGS     EQU $C
MI.HEIGHT    EQU $A
MI.ITEMFILL           EQU $12
MI.LEFTEDGE           EQU $4
MI.MUTUALEXCLUDE EQU $E
MI.NEXT      EQU $Ø
MI.NEXTSELECT         EQU $2Ø
MI.PAD                EQU $1B
MI.SELECTFILL         EQU $16
MI.SUBITEM   EQU $1C
MI.TOPEDGE   EQU $6
MI.WIDTH     EQU $8

MIDRAWN      EQU $1ØØ
MOUSEBUTTONS          EQU $8
MOUSEMOVE    EQU $1Ø

NEWPREFS     EQU $4ØØØ
NEWSIZE      EQU $2
NOCAREREFRESH         EQU $2ØØØØ

;*** NEWWINDOW STRUCTURE OFFSETS

NW.BITMAP    EQU $22
NW.BLOCKPEN           EQU $9
NW.CHECKMARK          EQU $16
NW.DETAILPEN          EQU $8
NW.FIRSTGADGET        EQU $12
NW.FLAGS     EQU $E
NW.HEIGHT    EQU $6
NW.IDCMPFLAGS         EQU $A
NW.LEFTEDGE           EQU $Ø
NW.MAXHEIGHT          EQU $2C
NW.MAXWIDTH           EQU $2A
NW.MINHEIGHT          EQU $28
NW.MINWIDTH           EQU $26
NW.SCREEN    EQU $1E
NW.TITLE     EQU $1A
NW.TOPEDGE   EQU $2
NW.TYPE      EQU $2E
NW.WIDTH     EQU $4

OTHER_REFRESH         EQU $CØ

;*** PROPINFO STRUCTURE OFFSETS

PI.CHEIGHT   EQU $C
PI.CWIDTH    EQU $A
PI.FLAGS     EQU $Ø
```

```
PI.HORIZBODY            EQU $6
PI.HORIZPOT             EQU $2
PI.HPOTRES  EQU $E
PI.LEFTBORDER           EQU $12
PI.TOPBORDER            EQU $14
PI.VERTBODY             EQU $8
PI.VERTPOT  EQU $4
PI.VPOTRES  EQU $10

POINTREL    EQU $1
PREDRAWN    EQU $2
PROPBORDERLESS          EQU $8
PROPGADGET  EQU $3

RAWKEY                  EQU $400
REFRESHBITS             EQU $C0
REFRESHWINDOW           EQU $4
RELVERIFY   EQU $1
REQACTIVE   EQU $2000
REQCLEAR    EQU $1000
REQGADGET   EQU $1000
REQOFFWINDOW            EQU $1000
REQSET                  EQU $80
REQVERIFY   EQU $800
RIGHTBORDER             EQU $10
RMBTRAP     EQU $10000

SCREENTYPE  EQU $F
SCRGADGET   EQU $4000

;*** SCREEN STRUCTURE OFFSETS (PARTIAL LIST)

SCRN.MOUSEX             EQU $12
SCRN.MOUSEY             EQU $10
SCRN.RASTPORT           EQU $54
SCRN.VIEWPORT           EQU $2C
SCRN.TITLE  EQU $16
SCRN.WIDTH  EQU $C
SCRN.HEIGHT             EQU $E

SELECTDOWN  EQU $68
SELECTED    EQU $80
SELECTUP    EQU $E8
SHOWTITLE   EQU $10

;*** STRINGINFO STRUCTURE OFFSETS

SI.ALTKEYMAP            EQU $20
SI.BUFFER   EQU $0
SI.BUFFERPOS            EQU $8
SI.CLEFT    EQU $14
SI.CTOP     EQU $16
SI.DISPCOUNT            EQU $12
SI.DISPPOS  EQU $C
SI.LAYERPTR             EQU $18
SI.LONGINT  EQU $1C
SI.MAXCHARS             EQU $A
SI.NUMCHARS             EQU $10
SI.UNDOBUFFER           EQU $4
SI.UNDOPOS  EQU $E

SIMPLE_REFRESH          EQU $40

;*** VARIOUS STRUCTURE SIZES

SIZE.BORD   EQU $10
SIZE.GADG   EQU $2C
SIZE.IM     EQU $34
SIZE.IMAG   EQU $14
SIZE.IT     EQU $14
SIZE.MENU   EQU $1E
SIZE.MI     EQU $22
SIZE.NS     EQU $20
SIZE.NW     EQU $30
SIZE.PI     EQU $16
SIZE.REQ    EQU $70
SIZE.SCRN   EQU $15C
SIZE.SI     EQU $24
```

```
SIZEBBOTTOM           EQU $20
SIZEBRIGHT  EQU $10
SIZEVERIFY  EQU $1
SIZING                EQU $10

;*** STARTUP MESSAGE OFFSETS

SM.ARGLIST  EQU $24
SM.MESSAGE  EQU $0
SM.NUMARGS  EQU $1C
SM.PROCESS  EQU $14
SM.SEGMENT  EQU $18
SM.TOOLWINDOW         EQU $20

SMART_REFRESH         EQU $0
STRGADGET   EQU $4
STRINGCENTER          EQU $200
STRINGRIGHT           EQU $400
SUPER_BITMAP          EQU $80
SYSGAGET    EQU $8000
SYSREQUEST  EQU $4000

TOGGLESELECT          EQU $100
TOPBORDER   EQU $40

VANILLAKEY  EQU $200000

WA.LOCK     EQU $0
WA.NAME     EQU $4
WBENCHMESSAGE         EQU $20000
WBENCHSCREEN          EQU $1
WBENCHWINDOW          EQU $2000000

;*** WINDOW AND IDCMP FLAGS DEFINITIONS

WINDOWACTIVE          EQU $2000
WINDOWCLOSE           EQU $8
WINDOWDEPTH           EQU $4
WINDOWDRAG  EQU $2
WINDOWREFRESH         EQU $1000000
WINDOWSIZING          EQU $1
WINDOWTICKED          EQU $4000000

;***  WINDOW STRUCTURE OFFSETS (PARTIAL LIST)

WW.FLAGS    EQU $18
WW.HEIGHT   EQU $A
WW.IDCMPFLAGS         EQU $52
WW.MOUSEX   EQU $E
WW.MOUSEY   EQU $C
WW.RPORT    EQU $32
WW.SCREENTITLE        EQU $68
WW.TITLE    EQU $20
WW.USERPORT           EQU $56
WW.WINDOWPORT         EQU $5A
WW.WSCREEN  EQU $2E
WW.WIDTH    EQU $8
WW.TOPEDGE  EQU $6
WW.LEFTEDGE           EQU $4
```

Intuition is a powerful resource. If you've used commercial software packages for the Amiga, you're already familiar with the use of menus, gadgets, and so on. This interaction is supported by a family of routines in the Intuition library. A selected list of the Intuition library functions is presented in Table 16-1 below. By mastering their use, your own programs can have a professional appearance. Because Intuition windows are the key to Intuition's other features, they'll be examined first.

The following Intuition library functions are those used in the programs in this book. For complete list and descriptions, see the *Amiga Intuition Reference Manual,* Appendix A, pages 1–79.

## Table 16-1. Intuition Library Functions

**Gadget Functions**
(See list of abbreviations below.)

| *Function Name* | *Parameters* | *Registers* | *Result Succeed/Fail* |
|---|---|---|---|
| ADDGADGET | (Win, Gad, List Position) | A0,A1,D0 | Position added |
| REMOVEGADGET | (Win,Gad) | A0,A1 | Position removed |
| MODIFYPROP | (Gad,Win,(Req),Flags,HP, VP,HB,VB) A0–A2,D0–D4 | | |
| ONGADGET | (Win,Gad,(Req) ) | A0–A2 | |
| OFFGADGET | (Win,Gad,(Req) ) | A0–A2 | |
| REFRESHGADGETS | (Gad,Ptr,(Req)) If Gadget is not in a *requester,* (Req) = 0 | A0–A2 | |

**Memory Allocation**

| *Function Name* | *Parameters* | *Registers* | *Result Succeed/Fail* |
|---|---|---|---|
| ALLOCREMEMBER | (RememberKey,Size,Flags) | A0,D0,D1 | Pointer/0 |
| FREEREMEMBER | (RememberKey,ReallyForget) If ReallyForget = 1, then free entire Remember list and memory buffers If ReallyForget = 0, then free only the Remember list | A0,D0 | |

**Requester Functions**

| *Function Name* | *Parameters* | *Registers* | *Result Succeed/Fail* |
|---|---|---|---|
| AUTOREQUEST | (Win,BText,PText,NText,PFlg, NFlg,Width,Height) | A0–A3,D0–D3 | Win/ALERT |
| BUILDSYSREQUEST | (Win,BText,PText,NText,Flg, Width,Height) | A0–A3,D0–D2 | Win/ALERT |
| ENDREQUEST | (Req,Win) | A0,A1 | |
| REQUEST | (Req,Win) | A0,A1 | 1/0 |

**Menu Functions**

| *Function Name* | *Parameters* | *Registers* | *Result Succeed/Fail* |
|---|---|---|---|
| CLEARMENUSTRIP | (Win) | A0 | |
| SETMENUSTRIP | (Win,Menu) | A0,A1 | |

**INTUITEXT Functions**

| *Function Name* | *Parameters* | *Registers* | *Result Succeed/Fail* |
|---|---|---|---|
| INTUITEXTLENGTH | (IText) | A0 | pixel length |
| PRINTITEXT | (RastPort,IText,Left,Top) | A0,A1,D0,D1 | |

**Screen Functions**

| *Function Name* | *Parameters* | *Registers* | *Result Succeed/Fail* |
|---|---|---|---|
| CLOSESCREEN | (Scr) | A0 | |
| DISPLAYBEEP | (Scr) | A0 | |
| OPENSCREEN | (NewScreen Structure) | A0 | Scr/0 |
| SHOWTITLE | (Scr,Showit) | A0,D0 | |
| | If Showit = 1, then title will be shown | | |
| | If Showit = 0, then title will not be shown | | |

**Window Functions**

| *Function Name* | *Parameters* | *Registers* | *Result Succeed/Fail* |
|---|---|---|---|
| CLOSEWINDOW | (Win) | A0 | |
| MODIFYIDCMP | (Win,Flags) | A0,D0 | |
| MOVEWINDOW | (Win,dx,dy) | A0,D0,D1 | |
| OPENWINDOW | (NewWindow Structure) | A0 | Win/0 |
| SIZEWINDOW | (Win,dx,dy) | A0,D0,D1 | |
| VIEWPORTADDRESS | (Win) | A0 | |
| WINDOWTOBACK | (Win) | A0 | |
| WINDOWTOFRONT | (Win) | A0 | |

**Abbreviations used in this Table**

| | |
|---|---|
| Win | Pointer to Window Structure |
| Gad | Pointer to Gadget Structure |
| Req | Pointer to Requester Structure |
| Scr | Pointer to Screen Structure |
| *x*Text | Pointer to INTUITEXT Structure |
| P*xxxx* | 'Positive' Text or Flags for Requester |
| N*xxxx* | 'Negative' Text or Flags for Requester |
| HP | Value to be stored in a PropInfo HorizPot variable |
| VP | Value to be stored in a PropInfo VertPot variable |
| HB | Value to be stored in a PropInfo HorizBody variable |
| VB | Value to be stored in a PropInfo VertBody variable |

## Using Intuition Windows

For the purpose of this discussion, the screen for all windows is the Workbench screen. Custom screens will be discussed later.

Here is the sequence of events that must take place in order to use an Intuition window:

- Provide memory for a NEWWINDOW structure (48 bytes):
  By declaring explicit storage (DS.*n*)
  By declaring a sequence of constants (DC.*n*)
  By ALLOCATING 48 bytes
- Fill fields in the structure with data such as window width, height, type, and so on:
  - Using MOVE instructions
  - By using a special MACRO to define everything
- Call the Intuition library function OPENWINDOW. If this function succeeds, it creates a window structure somewhere in memory and returns its address in register D0. If this function fails, it returns a 0 in D0. If successful, a new window is opened.
- Now, you may eliminate the NEWWINDOW structure. Its function was only temporary. However, if you intend to open a series of windows, you may want to keep the NEWWINDOW table to use again.
- Now, perform any Intuition functions using the window, including printing text, sizing, or moving the window in front of or behind other windows in the same screen, and so on. Most of these functions require the address of the WINDOW structure (which was supplied by OPENWINDOW) in A0, and a call to an Intuition library function. For example:

```
MOVEA.L  WINDOW,A0        ; PUT ADDRESS OF WINDOW STRUCTURE
                          ; IN A0
INTLIB   WINDOWTOFRONT    ; MACRO CALL WINDOWTOFRONT
                          ; ROUTINE
```

- Close the window when you finish using it.

```
MOVEA.L  WINDOW,A0
INTLIB   CLOSEWINDOW
```

The CLOSEWINDOW gadget doesn't actually close a window. All it does is send your program a message saying that the CLOSEWINDOW gadget was clicked. The program must still close the window. More about communications through messages later.

## The NEWWINDOW Structure

Assuming the program has either provided a memory area (using DS.B 48) or successfully allocated memory (using SYSLIB ALLOCMEM), you begin to create a window by placing the pointer to the structure's memory area in address register A0 (or any other convenient address register). Table 16-2 takes a closer look at this structure to help determine which fields to fill.

**Table 16-2. The Intuition NEWWINDOW Structure**

**Symbol: NW**
**Size: 48 bytes (\$30 bytes)**

| *Field Size* | *Name* | *Offset* | *Description* |
|---|---|---|---|
| Word | NW.LEFTEDGE | 0 | How many pixels from left edge of screen |
| Word | NW.TOPEDGE | 2 | How many pixels from top edge of screen |
| Word | NW.WIDTH | 4 | How many pixels wide |
| Word | NW.HEIGHT | 6 | How many pixels high |
| Byte | NW.DETAILPEN | 8 | Color register number for gadgets and title |
| Byte | NW.BLOCKPEN | 9 | Color register number for block fills |
| Long | NW.IDCMPFLAGS | 10 | Bits control event communications |
| Long | NW.FLAGS | 14 | Bits control window standard gadgets |
| Long | NW.FIRSTGADGET | 18 | Pointer to your first gadget structure |
| Long | NW.CHECKMARK | 22 | Pointer to custom menu checkmark image |
| Long | NW.TITLE | 26 | Pointer to null-terminated text title |
| Long | NW.SCREEN | 30 | Pointer to custom screen (if any) |
| Long | NW.BITMAP | 34 | Pointer to custom bitmap (if any) |
| Word | NW.MINWIDTH | 38 | Minimum window width in pixels |
| Word | NW.MINHEIGHT | 40 | Minimum window height in pixels |
| Word | NW.MAXWIDTH | 42 | Maximum window width in pixels |

| *Field Size* | *Name* | *Offset* | *Description* |
|---|---|---|---|
| Word | NW.MAXHEIGHT | 44 | Maximum window height in pixels |
| Word | NW.TYPE | 46 | Type of screen |

A number of the fields in a NEWWINDOW structure (NW.SCREEN, NW.BITMAP, NW.FIRSTGADGET, and NW.CHECKMARK) are only used for exotic types of windows. They can be set to 0 values. If the NEWWINDOW structure is allocated with MEMF_CLEAR, they will already be 0 and can be ignored.

You must insure that the fields are filled in with valid data, or else suffer the consequences. Numbers for NW.WIDTH, NW.HEIGHT, NW.LEFTEDGE, NW.TOPEDGE, NW.MAXHEIGHT, NW.MINHEIGHT, NW.MAXWIDTH, and NW.MINWIDTH should be inserted into these fields (they are all word-size). Typical values might be:

| | |
|---|---|
| NW.LEFTEDGE | 20 |
| NW.TOPEDGE | 20 |
| NW.WIDTH | 300 |
| NW.HEIGHT | 80 |
| NW.MAXWIDTH | 640 |
| NW.MAXHEIGHT | 200 |
| NW.MINWIDTH | 50 |
| NW.MINHEIGHT | 20 |

And corresponding code for these values can use the MOVE instruction, as in the first example below:

```
;                                       ; EXAMPLE METHOD OF FILLING
;                                       ; A NEWWINDOW STRUCTURE
;                                       ; EXAMPLE 1
;                                       ; USING THE MOVE
;                                       ; INSTRUCTION
;                                       ; (ASSUMING THE BASE AD-
;                                       ; DRESS OF THE NEWWINDOW
;                                       ; STRUCTURE IS IN A0)
          MOVE.W   #20,NW.LEFTEDGE(A0)
          MOVE.W   #20,NW.TOPEDGE(A0)
          MOVE.W   #300,NW.WIDTH(A0)
          MOVE.W   #80,NW.HEIGHT(A0)
;                                       ; (AND SO ON)
;                                       ; EXAMPLE 2
;                                       ; USING DC.X DIRECTIVES TO
;                                       ; DECLARE PART OF A
```

```
;                                           ; NEWWINDOW STRUCTURE
NEWWINDOW                                   ; LABELED ADDRESS OF THE
                                            ; BASE OF A NEWWINDOW
                                            ; STRUCTURE
            DC.W    20
            DC.W    20
            DC.W    300
            DC.W    80
;                                           ; (AND SO ON)
```

Other fields that can be filled without much deliberation are NW.DETAILPEN and NW.BLOCKPEN. Since the Workbench screen is being used, you can place any number from 0–3 in these fields. The number in the DETAILPEN field selects which of the four Workbench colors set in Preferences will be used for window details, like gadgets and title text. The number in the BLOCKPEN field selects which Workbench color will be used for block fills.

The NW.TYPE field is filled with the word value WBENCHSCREEN, for the time being (all windows will use the Workbench screen).

The NW.TITLE field is filled with a pointer to some null-terminated text for the window title. If you don't want a title, leave the value of 0 in NW.TITLE.

Listing 16-2 shows the methods used to fill the NEWWINDOW structure fields that will appear in a program named WINDOW1.ASM later on. A NEWWINDOW structure is in the source code data declarations of WINDOW1.ASM (see Listing 16-3).

**Listing 16-2. Declaring a Full NEWWINDOW Structure with DC.*x***

```
NEWWINDOW
          DC.W  40                        ; LEFT
          DC.W  15                        ; TOP
          DC.W  300                       ; WIDTH
          DC.W  160                       ; HEIGHT
          DC.B  2                         ; DETAILPEN
          DC.B  1                         ; BLOCKPEN
          DC.L  CLOSEWINDOW               ; IDCMP - CAN RECEIVE THE
                                          ; 'CLOSEWINDOW' MESSAGE
          DC.L  WINDOWCLOSE               ; FLAGS - WINDOW HAS THE
                                          ; 'CLOSEWINDOW' GADGET
          DC.L  0                         ; POINTER TO FIRST GADGET
          DC.L  0                         ; POINTER TO USER-DEFINED
                                          ; CHECKMARK
          DC.L  TITLETEXT                 ; POINTER TO SOME TITLE TEXT,
                                          ; NULL-TERMINATED
```

```
        DC.L   0                        ; POINTER TO SOME CUSTOM SCREEN
        DC.L   0                        ; POINTER TO SOME CUSTOM BITMAP
        DC.L   50                       ; MINIMUM WIDTH IF 'RESIZING'
                                        ; GADGET IS WORKING
        DC.L   20                       ; MINIMUM HEIGHT
        DC.L   640                      ; MAXIMUM WIDTH
        DC.L   200                      ; MAXIMUM HEIGHT
        DC.L   WBENCHSCREEN             ; SYMBOLIC NAME OF TYPE OF SCREEN
TITLETEXT
        DC.B   'HERE IS THE WINDOW TITLE',0
```

Now you can concentrate on the two most complex fields.

**The NW.FLAGS field.** One of the most flexible and complex things to master in working with Intuition windows is the use of the NW.FLAGS field of the NEWWINDOW structure. The NW.FLAGS field is a long word (32 bits) in which each bit controls a standard gadget (window size, window close, window drag, and others) or a window feature (such as refresh mode, borders on, borders off, and so on).

In a program, individual bits of the NW.FLAGS field are ORed together to build up the NW.FLAGS data word. Here's a typical example:

```
LEA      NEWWINDOW,A0  ; PUT BASE ADDRESS OF STRUCTURE IN A0
MOVE.L   #WINDOWSIZING!WINDOWCLOSE!WINDOWDRAG,NW.FLAGS(A0)
```

The second statement tells the assembler to use the ! assembler directive (which represents a logical OR) to combine flag bits for a window size gadget, window drag bar, and the window close gadget. There are many other possible combinations of flags.

Table 16-3 lists the available gadgets and features, their bit designations and brief descriptions. You can combine them in your NEWWINDOW structure by using their symbolic names and the logical OR assembler directive (!), or write hexadecimal digits into your code representing desired combinations of the bits. The latter method is not only more complicated, but will make your software harder to maintain; future software releases might change the bit positions of the flags.

**Table 16-3. NW.FLAGS (NEWWINDOW FLAGS field)**

| Name | Hexadecimal Value | Function |
|---|---|---|
| WINDOWSIZING | $0001 | Adds window sizing gadget |
| WINDOWDRAG | 0002 | Adds window drag gadget |
| WINDOWDEPTH | 0004 | Adds window depth gadget |
| WINDOWCLOSE | 0008 | Adds window close gadget |
| SIZEBRIGHT | 0010 | Makes size gadget fill right edge |
| SIZEBBOTTOM | 0020 | Makes size gadget fill bottom edge |
| SMART_REFRESH | 0000 | System automatically redisplays uncovered parts |
| SIMPLE_REFRESH | 0040 | Program must refresh uncovered parts |
| SUPER_BITMAP | 0080 | Window refreshed from custom bitmap |
| BACKDROP | 0100 | This windows stays behind all others |
| REPORTMOUSE | 0200 | Set if you need continuous reports of mouse movement |
| GIMMEZEROZERO | 0400 | Puts system gadgets in separate bitmap |
| BORDERLESS | 0800 | No window outline |
| ACTIVATE | 1000 | Turns window on when first opened |
| WINDOWACTIVE | 2000 | Set by Intuition when window is active |
| RMBTRAP | 10000 | Setting this flag disables menu operations. Program receives normal MOUSEBUTTON events when the right mouse button is pressed. |
| NOCAREREFRESH | 20000 | Set this flag if you don't want to receive refresh messages. |

It would be a good idea to experiment with the WINDOW1.ASM program (Listing 16-7) using different combinations of NW.FLAG bits to see what effects they have in practice. The subroutine labeled MAKEAWINDOW uses one combination that is effective for many standard uses, but don't limit yourself to the structure in this subroutine. Some experimenting may turn up a subroutine more suited to your specific needs.

**The IDCMPFLAGS flag.** The communications channel between Intuition and your window is the window's Intuition Direct Communications Message Port (IDCMP). IDCMPFLAGS is a long word. Each bit controls one aspect of event communication with your program.

Using IDCMPFLAGS, you can alert your program to such events as mouse-button presses (and/or releases). You may wish to receive a WINDOWCLOSE message when the user clicks a CLOSEWINDOW gadget. Each of these is considered an event and is communicated by an Intuition message (INTUIMESSAGES) to your program, if your window is active and the program requests a look at the messages.

Intuition captures all keystrokes, mouse movements, mouse button events, disk insertions and removals, and many other events. Then, it sends messages to all Intuition programs that request them.

If you set the appropriate flags, your program will be notified when the specified event occurs. If you fail to set the correct flags, your program will never know about certain external events like mouse movement. Here's a typical IDCMP flags setting:

```
LEA      NEWWINDOW,A0
MOVE.L   #CLOSEWINDOW!MENUPICK,NW.IDCMPFLAGS(A0)
```

This arranges for your program to be notified of window close and menu events. Using this code will cause your program to be ignorant of all keystrokes and mouse movements. There will be more discussion of IDCMP FLAGS in Chapter 17.

Listing 16-3 contains the WINDOWS.ASM include file for use with the subsequent programs in this chapter, and later chapters as well. It has a complete subroutine for opening a window (MAKEAWINDOW) and a macro (MAKEWIN), which can be used to perform much of the work of opening Intuition windows. Using EMACS or your favorite text editor, enter WINDOWS.ASM and save it with the name:

**DEVS:RAMIT/INCLUDES/WINDOWS.ASM**

## Listing 16-3. WINDOWS.ASM

```
;******************************** WINDOWS.ASM BY DANIEL WOLF
;COPYRIGHT 1987 BY COMPUTE! BOOKS
;03/21/87

MAKEWIN MACRO ;PARAMETERS
 LEA _THISTITLE,A0
 MOVE.L \1,(A0)
 MOVE.W #\2,D4
 MOVE.W #\3,D5
 MOVE.W #\4,D6
 MOVE.W #\5,D7
 BSR MAKEAWINDOW
 TST.L D0
 BEQ \6
 IFNC '\7',''
 MOVE.L D0,\7
 ENDC
 ENDM

;NEW WINDOW STRUCTURE SUPPORT FOR USE WITH  OPENWINDOW  FUNCTION


MAKEAWINDOW ;SUBROUTINE ENTER WITH D4=LEFT,D5=TOP,D6=WIDTH,D7=HEIGHT
 ;                          _THISTITLE=POINTER TO NULL-TERMINATED WINDOW TITLE

 MOVE.L #SIZE.NW,D0               ;ALLOCATE ONE NEWWINDOW'S WORTH OF MEMORY
 MOVE.L #MEMF_CLEAR!MEMF_CHIP,D1;MAKING SURE ITS SET TO ZERO AND IN CHIPMEM
 SYSLIB ALLOCMEM                  ;ALLOCATE THIS MEMORY INDEPENDENT OF ALL ELSE
 TST.L D0                         ;IF NOT SUCCESSFUL WE GET A ZERO BACK IN D0
 BEQ ERR_MAKEAWINDOWMEM
 MOVE.L D0,NEWWINDOW              ;HANG ON TO THIS POINTER
 MOVE.L D0,A0                     ;WE CAN DELETE THIS MEMORY LATER
 MOVE.W D4,NW.LEFTEDGE(A0)        ;A NEWWINDOW STRUCTURE CAN BE DE-ALLOCATED
 MOVE.W D5,NW.TOPEDGE(A0)         ;AFTER IT HAS SERVED ITS PURPOSE
 MOVE.W D6,NW.WIDTH(A0)
 MOVE.W D7,NW.HEIGHT(A0)          ;NOW JUST FILL UP THE NEWWINDOW STRUCTURE
 MOVE.B #-1,NW.DETAILPEN(A0)      ;-1 IS ALWAYS BE HIGHEST COLOR REG #
 MOVE.B #-1,NW.BLOCKPEN(A0)       ;REGARDLESS OF # COLORS AVAILABLE IN SCREEN
 MOVE.L _THISIDCMP,NW.IDCMPFLAGS(A0)  ;PRE-SET IDCMP FLAGS
 MOVE.L _THISFLAGS,NW.FLAGS(A0)       ;PRE-SET WINDOWFLAGS
 MOVE.L _THISTITLE,NW.TITLE(A0)       ;POINTER TO TITLE TEXT
 MOVE.W #100,NW.MINWIDTH(A0)        ;REASONABLE MINIMUM WIDTH AND HEIGHT
 MOVE.W #25,NW.MINHEIGHT(A0)
 MOVE.W #700,NW.MAXWIDTH(A0)        ;MAXIMUM MAXIMUM WIDTH AND HEIGHT!
 MOVE.W #440,NW.MAXHEIGHT(A0)
 MOVE.W _THISTYPE,NW.TYPE(A0)       ;USE THE SCREEN TYPE STORED IN _THISTYPE
 MOVE.L _THISCREEN,NW.SCREEN(A0)    ;ATTACH TO CUSTOM SCREEN OR 0 (DEFAULT)
 INTLIB OPENWINDOW                  ;NOW OPEN IT!
 TST.L D0
 BEQ.S ERR_MAKEAWINDOW              ;POINTER TO WINDOW IN D0
 MOVE.L D0,_THISWINDOW              ;STASH POINTER FOR A SEC
 MOVE.L #SIZE.NW,D0
 MOVEA.L NEWWINDOW,A1
 SYSLIB FREEMEM                     ;FREE UP THE MEM USED FOR THE NEWWINDOW
 MOVE.L _THISWINDOW,D0              ;NOW RETURN WITH POINTER TO WINDOW IN D0
 ZERO D1                            ;CLEAR D1, NO ERROR!
 RTS
ERR_MAKEAWINDOWMEM
 MOVE.L #CANTALLOCMEM,D1            ;PUT ERROR CODE IN D1
ENDE_MAKEAWINDOW
 ZERO D0                            ;CLEAR D0, INDICATE ERROR!
 RTS
ERR_MAKEAWINDOW
 MOVEQ.L #CANTOPENWINDOW,D1         ;PUT ERROR CODE IN D1
 BRA ENDE_MAKEAWINDOW

 IFD GFX       ;ONLY ASSEMBLE IF GFX ROUTINES AND EQUATES ALSO INCLUDED!
_CLEARWINDOW; SUBROUTINE ENTER WITH POINTER TO WINDOW STRUCTURE IN A0
 ;                                  COLOR REG #                 IN D0

 ZERO D0                  ;USE BACKGROUND COLOR REG # IN D0
_FILLWINDOW               ;ENTER HERE IF YOU HAVE YOUR COLOR REG # IN D0
 MOVE.L WW.RPORT(A0),RP   ;FIND THIS WINDOW'S RASTPORT ADDRESS
 SETAPEN RP               ;SET THE -A- PEN FOR THIS RASTPORT (MACRO)
 MOVE.W WW.WIDTH(A0),D2
```

```
 SUBI.W #4,D2                   ;AVOID CREAMING BORDERS, DRAGBAR, ETC.
 MOVE.W WW.HEIGHT(A0),D3
 SUBI.W #2,D3
 MOVE.W #2,D0
 MOVE.W #10,D1
 RECTFILL RP                    ;USE GRAPHICS LIBRARY RECTFILL ROUTINE (MACRO)
 RTS
 ENDC

NEWWINDOW
 DC.L 0                   ;STORAGE FOR POINTER TO ALLOCATED NEWWINDOW STRUCTURE
_THISWINDOW
 DC.L 0                   ;STORAGE FOR POINTER TO WINDOW ONCE OPENED
_THISTYPE
 DC.W WBENCHSCREEN        ;CAN BE CHANGED TO CUSTOMSCREEN IF NECESSARY
_THISTITLE
 DC.L 0                   ;STORAGE FOR POINTER TO TITLE NULL-TERMINATED TEXT
_THISIDCMP
 DC.L CLOSEWINDOW!MENUPICK!MOUSEBUTTONS!NEWSIZE!GADGETUP!GADGETDOWN
_THISFLAGS
 DC.L ACTIVATE!WINDOWSIZING!WINDOWDRAG!WINDOWDEPTH!WINDOWCLOSE!SMART_REFRESH
_THISCREEN
 DC.L 0                   ;STORAGE FOR POINTER TO CUSTOM SCREEN
```

## Using the MAKEAWINDOW Subroutine

MAKEAWINDOW has its own standard variables to simplify the creation and filling of a NEWWINDOW structure. The MAKEAWINDOW subroutine will do most of the work.

MAKEAWINDOW allocates a NEWWINDOW structure, fills it with typical default window parameters, calls the library function OPENWINDOW, and deallocates the NEWWINDOW structure. Most programs in this book use MAKEAWINDOW to simplify programming windows. The code listing for MAKEAWINDOW is heavily commented.

Using MAKEAWINDOW requires very little preparation.

- Place a pointer to the window's title in _THISTITLE (a variable declared in the MAKEAWINDOW code).
- Specify the left, top, width, and height values in registers D4, D5, D6, and D7, respectively.
- Issue the instruction BSR MAKEAWINDOW.

If there is no error, your window will open and a pointer to the resulting WINDOW structure will be placed in register D0. If there is an error, D0 will contain a 0.

Listing 16-4 calls MAKEAWINDOW:

**Listing 16-4. Using the MAKEAWINDOW Support Routine**

```
LEA      _THISTITLE,A0
MOVE.L   #MYWINDOWTITLE,(A0)   ; PUT POINTER TO MY
                               ; TEXT INTO _THISTITLE
MOVE.W   #40,D4                ; LEFTEDGE
MOVE.W   #15,D5                ; TOPEDGE
MOVE.W   #300,D6               ; WIDTH
```

```
              MOVE.W  #100,D7                    ; HEIGHT
              BSR     MAKEAWINDOW                ; CALL THE SUBROUTINE
                                                 ; TO CREATE A WINDOW
              TST.L   D0
              BEQ     ERROR                      ; ERROR BRANCH IF
                                                 ; SUBROUTINE RETURNS
                                                 ; A 0
              MOVE.L  D0,WINDOW                  ; OTHERWISE, SAVE
                                                 ; POINTER TO WINDOW
                                                 ; STRUCTURE
MYWINDOWTITLE                                    ; LABEL FOR WINDOW
                                                 ; TITLE TEXT
              DC.B    ' THIS IS A WINDOW TITLE ',0 WINDOW
              DC.L    0                          ; STORAGE FOR THE
                                                 ; POINTER RETURNED
                      ; BY MAKEAWINDOW
```

Note that MAKEAWINDOW has standard FLAGS and IDCMPFLAGS which are used almost universally in Intuition window programming. If you wish to have a different combination of flags, either edit the WINDOWS.ASM file or use code to place your own flags into the _THISFLAGS and _THISIDCMP variables, prior to calling MAKEAWINDOW. You'll find examples of this in several of the program listings.

## The MAKEWIN Macro

In addition to the MAKEAWINDOW subroutine, the WINDOWS.ASM file contains a macro which itself calls MAKEAWINDOW. Depending on which style of programming is most convenient, you can substitute the macro MAKEWIN for a call to the MAKEAWINDOW subroutine. Listing 16-5 illustrates the use of the MAKEWIN macro.

**Listing 16-5. Examples of the MAKEWIN Macro**

```
;                                         ; USING MAKEWIN WITH 5 PARAM-
;                                         ; ETERS FOR AUTOMATIC ERROR
;                                         ; BRANCHING
   MAKEWIN   20,20,300,80,ERROR_WINDOW    ; MAKES 300 × 80 WINDOW AT
                                          ; 20,20
;                                         ; AUTOMATICALLY BRANCHES TO
;                                         ; ERROR_WINDOW
;                                         ; LABEL IF UNSUCCESSFUL

;                                         ; USING MAKEWIN WITH 4 PARAM-
;                                         ; ETERS AND DOING EXPLICIT
;                                         ; ERROR CHECKING
```

```
MAKEWIN   0,0,640,200          ; MAKES 640 × 200 WINDOW AT
                               ; 0,0
TST.L     D0
BEQ       ERROR                ; BUT WE DO OUR OWN ERROR
                               ; CHECKING THIS WAY
```

## The CLEARWINDOW (FILLWINDOW) Subroutine

You can use the CLEARWINDOW function to clear a window (set it to the background color), or the FILLWINDOW function to fill a window with a solid color.

To clear a window, place the address of the window structure in address register A0 and BSR CLEARWINDOW. If you wish to fill with another color, place the color register number (1–3) into D0, put the window address in A0, and BSR FILLWINDOW. An example is Listing 16-6.

**Listing 16-6. A Call to FILLWINDOW Colors a Whole Window**

```
MOVEA.L   WINDOW,A0     ; PUT ADDRESS OF WINDOW STRUCTURE
                        ; INTO A0
MOVE.L    #2,D0         ; USE COLOR #2
BSR       FILLWINDOW    ; FILL WINDOW WITH COLOR REGISTER #2
```

WINDOW1.ASM uses a direct declaration of the NEWWINDOW structure. WINDOW2.ASM uses the MAKEAWINDOW and CLEARWINDOW/FILLWINDOW routines. Note the loop in which both programs scan for a window close message from the user. This is an example of using the IDCMP messages, which will be explored at greater depth later on.

Before going further into the details of window varieties, you should take the time to experiment with the programs below (Listings 16-7 and 16-8).

**Listing 16-7. WINDOW1.ASM**

```
;WINDOW1.ASM BY DANIEL WOLF
;COPYRIGHT 1987 BY COMPUTE! PUBLICATIONS
;Ø9/1Ø/87

 BRA _START

 INCLUDE "HEADER"

MAIN                            ;THIS MUST BE THE LABEL OF THE PROGRAM

 LEA NEWWINDOW,AØ               ;PUT POINTER TO NEWWINDOW STRUCTURE INTO AØ
 INTLIB OPENWINDOW              ;AND OPEN THE WINDOW
 MOVE.L DØ,WINDOW               ;SAVE POINTER TO THIS WINDOW STRUCTURE
 BEQ ERROR                      ;WHOOPS, POINTER = Ø!
```

```
    ;***  NOW WAIT FOR IDCMP TO REPORT A CLOSEWINDOW MESSAGE  ***

LOOP
 MOVE.L WINDOW,A0              ;USE POINTER TO WINDOW TO FIND WINDOW'S I/O PORT
 MOVE.L WW.USERPORT(A0),A0     ;PLACE POINTER TO WINDOW'S PORT IN A0
 SYSLIB WAITPORT               ;WAIT FOR A SPECIFIED MESSAGE TO ARRIVE
 MOVE.L WINDOW,A0
 MOVE.L WW.USERPORT(A0),A0
 SYSLIB GETMSG                 ;MESSAGE SHOULD BE AVAILABLE AFTER 'WAITPORT'
 TST.L D0                      ;POINTER TO INTUIMESSAGE COMES BACK IN D0
 BEQ.S LOOP                    ;NO MESSAGE FOUND THERE, SO LOOP (SHORT BRANCH)
 MOVE.L D0,A1                  ;POINTER TO INTUIMESSAGE CAME BACK, USE IN A1
 MOVE.L IM.CLASS(A1),D2        ;CLOSEWINDOW AND MENUPICK MESSAGES APPEAR HERE
 MOVE.W IM.CODE(A1),D3         ;MENU AND MENUITEM APPEAR HERE
 MOVE.W IM.QUALIFIER(A1),D4    ;KEYS APPEAR HERE
 SYSLIB REPLYMSG               ;QUICK, SEND MESSAGE BACK NOW!

 CMP.L #CLOSEWINDOW,D2         ;COMPARE CONTENTS OF D2 WITH VALUE OF 'CLOSEWINDOW'
 BEQ.S DONE                    ;IF THEY'RE EQUAL, THIS IS A CLOSEWINDOW MESSAGE!
 BRA LOOP                      ;OTHERWISE, BRANCH ALWAYS (BRA) BACK TO LOOP

    ;***  NOW FINISH UP, CLOSE WINDOW, AND EXIT TO SKELETON  ***

DONE
 ZERO D0                       ;NO ERRORS, SO PLACE 0 IN D0 AS ERROR CODE
 PUSHREG D0                    ;HIDE D0 FOR A MOMENT ON THE STACK
 MOVE.L WINDOW,D0              ;CHECK FOR AN OPEN WINDOW
 BEQ.S QUIT                    ;IF 'WINDOW' = 0 , THEN NO WINDOW WAS OPENED
 MOVE.L D0,A0                  ;THERE IS A WINDOW
 INTLIB CLOSEWINDOW            ;SO CLOSE IT
QUIT
 PULLREG D0                    ;RESTORE D0 NOW
 RTS                           ;RETURN TO 'CLEANUP' PORTION OF SKELETON

ERROR
 MOVEQ #CANTOPENWINDOW,D0      ;PUT ERROR CODE #21, "CAN'T OPEN WINDOW"
 RTS                           ;EXIT TO SKELETON NOW!

   ;*** DATA STORAGE ***

MYWINDOWTITLE                  ;NULL-TERMINATED WINDOW TITLE TEXT

 DC.B ' WINDOW1  BY D.WOLF ',0

 EVENPC                        ;WORD-ALIGN MEMORY AFTER DC.B!

WINDOW DC.L 0                  ;STORAGE FOR POINTER TO THE WINDOW STRUCTURE
RP DC.L 0                      ;STORAGE FOR WINDOW'S 'RASTPORT' POINTER

NEWWINDOW
 DC.W 40              ;LEFTEDGE
 DC.W 15              ;TOPEDGE
 DC.W 300             ;WIDTH
 DC.W 160             ;HEIGHT
 DC.B -1              ;DETAILPEN (= FF, MAXIMUM REGARDLESS OF SCREEN DEPTH!)
 DC.B -1              ;BLOCKPEN
 DC.L CLOSEWINDOW
 DC.L ACTIVATE!WINDOWSIZING!WINDOWDRAG!WINDOWDEPTH!WINDOWCLOSE!SMART_REFRESH
 DC.L 0               ;POINTER TO FIRST USER-DEFINED GADGET
 DC.L 0               ;POINTER TO USER-DEFINED CHECKMARK
 DC.L MYWINDOWTITLE   ;POINTER TO TITLE TEXT
 DC.L 0               ;POINTER TO CUSTOM SCREEN
 DC.L 0               ;POINTER TO CUSTOM BITMAP
 DC.W 50              ;MINWIDTH
 DC.W 20              ;MINHEIGHT
 DC.W 640             ;MAXWIDTH
 DC.W 400             ;MAXHEIGHT
 DC.W WBENCHSCREEN    ;TYPE OF SCREEN THIS WINDOW IS IN

 END
```

## Listing 16-8. WINDOW2.ASM

```
;WINDOW2.ASM BY DANIEL WOLF
;COPYRIGHT 1987 BY COMPUTE! PUBLICATIONS
;09/10/87

 BRA _START

WIN EQU 1          ;SET DEFINITION OF SYMBOL TO BE USED BY THE HEADER

 INCLUDE "HEADER"  ;BRING IN THE 'WINDOWS' ROUTINES

MAIN                              ;THIS MUST BE THE LABEL OF THE PROGRAM

                                  ;NOW USE 'MAKEAWIN' MACRO FOR SEVERAL

 MAKEWIN #MYWINDOWTITLE,40,15,300,160,ERROR
 MOVE.L D0,WINDOW                 ;SAVE POINTER TO THIS WINDOW STRUCTURE

 LEA _THISFLAGS,A0
 MOVE.L #WINDOWDRAG,(A0)         ;NO CLOSEWINDOW GADGET IN THESE WINDOWS
               ;NO AMBIGUITY WHICH TO CLOSE TO END PROGRAM

 MAKEWIN #MYWINDOWTITLE,50,30,200,100,ERROR
 MOVE.L D0,WIN2
 MAKEWIN #MYWINDOWTITLE,60,40,150,80,ERROR
 MOVE.L D0,WIN3
 MAKEWIN #MYWINDOWTITLE,70,50,100,70,ERROR
 MOVE.L D0,WIN4

    ;***  NOW WAIT FOR IDCMP TO REPORT A CLOSEWINDOW MESSAGE  ***
    ;     ON LARGEST WINDOW ONLY!!!

LOOP
 MOVE.L WINDOW,A0            ;USE POINTER TO WINDOW TO FIND WINDOW'S I/O PORT
 MOVE.L WW.USERPORT(A0),A0   ;PLACE POINTER TO WINDOW'S PORT IN A0
 SYSLIB WAITPORT             ;WAIT FOR A SPECIFIED MESSAGE TO ARRIVE
 MOVE.L WINDOW,A0
 MOVE.L WW.USERPORT(A0),A0
 SYSLIB GETMSG               ;MESSAGE SHOULD BE AVAILABLE AFTER 'WAITPORT'
 TST.L D0                    ;POINTER TO INTUIMESSAGE COMES BACK IN D0
 BEQ.S LOOP                  ;NO MESSAGE FOUND THERE, SO LOOP (SHORT BRANCH)
 MOVE.L D0,A1                ;POINTER TO INTUIMESSAGE CAME BACK, USE IN A1
 MOVE.L IM.CLASS(A1),D2      ;CLOSEWINDOW AND MENUPIC MESSAGES APPEAR HERE
 MOVE.W IM.CODE(A1),D3       ;MENU AND MENUITEM APPEAR HERE
 MOVE.W IM.QUALIFIER(A1),D4  ;KEYS APPEAR HERE
 SYSLIB REPLYMSG             ;QUICK, SEND MESSAGE BACK NOW!

 CMP.L #CLOSEWINDOW,D2       ;COMPARE CONTENTS OF D2 WITH VALUE OF 'CLOSEWINDOW'
 BEQ.S DONE                  ;IF THEY'RE EQUAL, THIS IS A CLOSEWINDOW MESSAGE!
 BRA LOOP                    ;OTHERWISE, BRANCH ALWAYS (BRA) BACK TO LOOP

    ;***  NOW FINISH UP, CLOSE WINDOWS, AND EXIT TO STARTUP  ***

DONE
 ZERO D0                     ;NO ERRORS, SO PLACE 0 IN D0 AS ERROR CODE
 PUSHREG D0                  ;HIDE D0 FOR A MOMENT ON THE STACK
 MOVE.L WINDOW,D0            ;CHECK FOR AN OPEN WINDOW
 BEQ.S QUIT                  ;IF 'WINDOW' = 0 , THEN NO WINDOW WAS OPENED
 MOVE.L D0,A0                ;THERE IS A WINDOW
 INTLIB CLOSEWINDOW          ;SO CLOSE IT
 MOVE.L WIN2,D0
 BEQ.S QUIT
 MOVE.L D0,A0
 INTLIB CLOSEWINDOW
 MOVE.L WIN3,D0
 BEQ.S QUIT
 MOVE.L D0,A0
 INTLIB CLOSEWINDOW
 MOVE.L WIN4,D0
 BEQ.S QUIT
 MOVE.L D0,A0
 INTLIB CLOSEWINDOW

QUIT
 PULLREG D0                  ;RESTORE D0 NOW
 RTS                         ;RETURN TO 'CLEANUP' PORTION OF STARTUP
```

```
ERROR
 MOVEQ #CANTOPENWINDOW,DØ    ;PUT ERROR CODE #21, "CAN'T OPEN WINDOW"
 RTS                         ;EXIT TO STARTUP NOW!

   ;*** DATA STORAGE ***

MYWINDOWTITLE                ;NULL-TERMINATED WINDOW TITLE TEXT

 DC.B ' Window2  BY D.WOLF ',Ø

 EVENPC                      ;WORD-ALIGN MEMORY AFTER DC.B!

WINDOW DC.L Ø                ;STORAGE FOR POINTER TO THE WINDOW STRUCTURE
WIN2 DC.L Ø
WIN3 DC.L Ø
WIN4 DC.L Ø

 END
```

## The WINDOW Structure

Until now, our discussion has centered around the NEWWINDOW structure and its use with OPENWINDOW. Now, you're ready to look at the WINDOW structure table and its fields.

Here is an overview of the information in the WINDOW structure created by OPENWINDOW. A program can look up the values in the WINDOW fields as needed. By placing the address of the window structure in an address register, its fields can be accessed by means of offsets.

**Table 16-4. The Intuition WINDOW Structure**

**Symbol: WW**
**Size: 128 bytes ($80 bytes)**

| *Field Size* | *Name* | *Offset* | *Description* |
|---|---|---|---|
| Long | WW.NEXT | $0 | Pointer to next window |
| Word | WW.LEFTEDGE | 4 | Number of pixels from the left edge of screen |
| Word | WW.TOPEDGE | 6 | Number of pixels from top edge of screen |
| Word | WW.WIDTH | 8 | Number of pixels wide |
| Word | WW.HEIGHT | 10 | Number of pixels high |
| Word | WW.MOUSEX | 12 | Mouse X coordinate |
| Word | WW.MOUSEY | 14 | Mouse Y coordinate |
| Word | WW.MINWIDTH | 16 | Number of pixels minimum width |
| Word | WW.MINHEIGHT | 18 | Number of pixels minimum height |
| Word | WW.MAXWIDTH | 20 | Number of pixels maximum width |
| Word | WW.MAXHEIGHT | 22 | Number of pixels maximum height |

| *Field Size* | *Name* | *Offset* | *Description* |
|---|---|---|---|
| Long | WW.FLAGS | 24 | Window flag bits |
| Long | WW.MENU | 28 | Pointer to menu structure |
| Long | WW.TITLE | 32 | Pointer to window title |
| Long | WW.FIRSTREQUEST | 36 | Pointer to first requester |
| Long | WW.DMREQUEST | 40 | Pointer to double-click requester |
| Word | WW.REQCOUNT | 44 | Number of requesters blocking action |
| Long | WW.WSCREEN | 46 | Pointer to this window's screen |
| Long | WW.RPORT | 50 | Pointer to this window's rastport |
| Byte | WW.BORDERLEFT | 54 | Number of pixels left border thickness |
| Byte | WW.BORDERTOP | 55 | Number of pixels top border thickness |
| Byte | WW.BORDERRIGHT | 56 | Number of pixels right border thickness |
| Byte | WW.BORDERBOTTOM | 57 | Number of pixels bottom border thickness |
| Long | WW.BORDERRPORT | 58 | Pointer to rastport for border |
| Long | WW.FIRSTGADGET | 62 | Pointer to first gadget in window |
| Long | WW.PARENT | 66 | Used by system for open/close |
| Long | WW.DESCENDANT | 70 | Used by system for open/close |
| Long | WW.POINTER | 74 | Pointer to the mouse pointer sprite data |
| Byte | WW.PTRHEIGHT | 78 | Mouse pointer sprite height |
| Byte | WW.PTRWIDTH | 79 | Mouse pointer sprite width (<=16) |
| Byte | WW.XOFFSET | 80 | Mouse pointer sprite *x* offset |
| Byte | WW.YOFFSET | 81 | Mouse pointer sprite *y* offset |
| Long | WW.IDCMPFLAGS | 82 | The IDCMPFLAGS for this window |
| Long | WW.USERPORT | 86 | Pointer to message port |
| Long | WW.WINDOWPORT | 90 | Pointer to message port |
| Long | WW.MESSAGEKEY | 94 | Pointer to INTUIMESSAGE |
| Byte | WW.DETAILPEN | 98 | Drawing pen for borders and so on |
| Byte | WW.BLOCKPEN | 99 | Drawing pen for menu, dragbar, and so on |

| *Field Size* | *Name* | *Offset* | *Description* |
|---|---|---|---|
| Long | WW.CHECKMARK | 100 | Pointer to checkmark image |
| Long | WW.SCREENTITLE | 104 | Pointer screen title (if not 0, screen title when window is active) |
| Word | WW.GZZMOUSEX | 108 | Mouse *x* position if GIMMEZEROZERO-type window |
| Word | WW.GZZMOUSEY | 110 | Mouse *y* position if GIMMEZEROZERO-type window |
| Word | WW.GZZWIDTH | 112 | Width if GIMMEZEROZERO-type window |
| Word | WW.GZZHEIGHT | 114 | Height if GIMMEZEROZERO-type window |
| Long | WW.EXTDATA | 116 | Pointer to external data |
| Long | WW.USERDATA | 120 | Pointer to user data |
| Long | WW.WLAYER | 124 | Duplicates rastport layer pointer |

## Refreshing Windows

Refresh is a procedure that redraws a window and its contents on the screen after it has been covered or *damaged*. Although the Amiga's operating system makes the screen look as if it were multidimensional, with menus, windows, and other displays covering and uncovering each other, the fact is, there is only one dimension. If a menu is pulled down over a window, or another window appears "in front of" an existing window, damage is done. In order to maintain the illusion of a three dimensional screen, the damage must be repaired as quickly as it is sustained.

SIMPLE_REFRESH provides a strategy to conserve chip memory. SIMPLE_REFRESH means your program is responsible for refreshing when damage has been done. Use it when it's unlikely that a window will be covered and later uncovered. If the window will never be damaged, it doesn't need to be refreshed.

SMART_REFRESH makes the system set aside chip memory for any rectangular region of a window that is covered up. When the intruding window or menu is gone, a SMART_REFRESH window automatically redisplays the damaged section. Your program doesn't have to do anything at all. The rectangles saved are called *clipping rectangles.* Each clipping rectangle must be stored in chip memory.

SUPER_BITMAP refreshing sets aside bitmap memory (once again, in chip memory) for remembering the window's entire contents. The bitmap memory may be larger in area than the window itself. Although SUPER_BITMAP is very memory-hungry, it permits your window to be scrolled over a larger area, like looking at a page through a small rectangle cut out of a piece of cardboard.

In all, there are dozens of ways to present and use windows in Intuition programs. This book is intended to get you started using them, but it would take another book as large as this one to fully cover windows. When you've achieved a level of mastery over the use of windows described in this text, you should review the *Amiga Intuition Reference Manual* section on windows to move on to the more exotic window forms.

# CHAPTER 17
# The IDCMP and IntuiText

## The IDCMP Flags

This section of Chapter 17 is both a review and a closer look at the powerful control exercised by this particular NEW-WINDOW slot.

### NEWWINDOW Structure ICDMPFLAGS Field

Once again, the IDCMPFLAGS field in the NEWWINDOW structure provides the potential for dozens of combinations of features. The bits in this field control the flow of events to your program, via Intuitions's communications channel to your window. You can choose to receive messages about a wide variety of user actions, such as mouse button events, menu use, gadget clicks, and so on. You can also use these flags to make sure certain circumstances prevail before a user is allowed to complete some action. For example, you can set the SIZEVERIFY flag to assure that window sizing by the user takes place only when your window is not being drawn by code that requires the window size to remain constant.

Table 17-1 provides a review of the IDCMPFLAGS, hex values, and brief descriptions. For additional information, see how they're used in the program examples, and review the OPENWINDOW function description in the *Amiga Intuition Reference Manual.*

**Table 17-1. Intuition Window IDCMPFLAGS**

| Name | Hexadecimal Value | Description |
|---|---|---|
| SIZEVERIFY | 0001 | Report sizing request |
| NEWSIZE | 0002 | Report user changed window size |
| REFRESHWINDOW | 0004 | Report window needs refreshing |
| MOUSEBUTTONS | 0008 | Report non-Intuition mouse button use |
| MOUSEMOVE | 0010 | Report all mouse movements |
| GADGETDOWN | 0020 | Report left mouse button down on gadget |
| GADGETUP | 0040 | Report left mouse button up on gadget |

| Name | Hexadecimal Value | Description |
|---|---|---|
| REQSET | 0080 | Report first requester in window |
| MENUPICK | 0100 | Report menu selection made |
| CLOSEWINDOW | 0200 | Report user clicked windowclose gadget |
| RAWKEY | 0400 | Report all raw key codes |
| REQVERIFY | 0800 | Report attempt to open requester |
| REQCLEAR | 1000 | Report final requester removed |
| MENUVERIFY | 2000 | Report attempt to use menu |
| DISKINSERTED | 8000 | Report user inserted a disk |
| DISKREMOVED | 10000 | Report user removed a disk |
| ACTIVEWINDOW | 40000 | Report when window is activated |
| INACTIVEWINDOW | 80000 | Report when window is deactivated |
| DELTAMOVE | 100000 | Report relative mouse movements |
| VANILLAKEY | 200000 | Report ASCII keycodes |
| INTUITICKS | 400000 | Report timer events every tenth of a second |

Here are some things to bear in mind when using these flag bits to control the receipt of event messages by your program. The more bits you set, the more messages will arrive. Be sure that you need the incoming information, because communication requires memory and system time overhead. It also requires your programs SYSLIB GETMSG and SYSLIB REPLYMSG, frequently, to process the messages.

If you set the VERIFY bit, your program should get and reply to those messages quickly and, thereby, permit the requester, menu, or sizing operations to take place. These flags are for your convenience to prevent graphics disruption in your window, but don't let them tie up your program's progress or the user's apparent ability to interact with the window.

Review the WINDOW1 and WINDOW2 programs in the previous chapter to see how they receive and reply to messages. Listing 17-1 is a typical program fragment that monitors the IDCMP messages. It begins with the label LOOP for a reason. This segment of program code is repeatedly executed to determine if an IDCMP message has occurred. If an appropriate message has arrived (namely one specified by the IDCMP flags used with that window), this code will see it and the program can respond accordingly.

## Waiting for a Message

In the Amiga's multitasking environment, it's important to suspend the program's usual operations while awaiting the user's next message. This is accomplished using the EXEC WAITPORT library routine.

WAITPORT tells the program to wait until a message arrives at the IDCMP Port. WAITPORT needs to know on which port to wait. Put the address of the WINDOW STRUCTURE's IDCMP PORT in register A0, prior to calling WAITPORT. That makes the WAITPORT function look at the IDCMP for that window.

Waiting for messages could be accomplished by a loop of MC68000 instructions that repeatedly scan until a message is detected, but that would be wasteful of the Amiga's resources; using WAITPORT is much better. WAITPORT lets other tasks and processes run while the current program is suspended and awaiting a response. WAITPORT relieves the MC68000 microprocessor of continuously monitoring for a message.

In the round-robin operation of all Amiga tasks, the waiting program only uses a small portion of the time allotted to it when its turn comes around. If no messages have yet arrived, it quickly relinquishes its turn and allows other tasks to continue.

**Listing 17-1. WAITPORT Loop for IDCMP CLOSEWINDOW Messages**

```
LOOP
        MOVE.L   WINDOW,A0              ; PUT ADDRESS OF WINDOW
                                        ; INTO A0
        MOVE.L   WW.USERPORT(A0),A0     ; LOOK UP IDCMP'S ADDRESS
                                        ; FOR THIS WINDOW
        SYSLIB   WAITPORT               ; JUST WAIT TILL SOME MES-
                                        ; SAGE ARRIVES
        MOVE.L   WINDOW,A0              ; PUT ADDRESS OF WINDOW
                                        ; INTO A0
        MOVE.L   WW.USERPORT(A0),A0     ; GET IDCMP ADDRESS OF THIS
                                        ; WINDOW AGAIN
        SYSLIB   GETMSG                 ; MACRO GETMSG CALL FOR
                                        ; ADDRESS OF MESSAGE
        TST.L    D0                     ; WAS THERE REALLY NO
                                        ; MESSAGE?
        BEQ.S    LOOP                   ; NO MESSAGE, JUST GO BACK
                                        ; AND WAITPORT AGAIN
```

```
        MOVE.L   D0,A1                 ; MESSAGE ARRIVED, ADDRESS
                                       ; INTO A1
        MOVE.L   IM.CLASS(A1),D2       ; CLOSEWINDOW, GADGET, and
                                       ; MENU SELECT etc.
        MOVE.W   IM.CODE(A1),D3        ; MENU SELECTION NUMBERS
                                       ; APPEAR HERE
        MOVE.W   IM.QUALIFIER(A1),D4   ; KEYBOARD INFORMATION
                                       ; APPEARS HERE
        SYSLIB   REPLYMSG              ; MACRO CALL TO RETURN THE
                                       ; MESSAGE
        CMP.L    #CLOSEWINDOW,D2       ; DID THE CLOSEWINDOW MES-
                                       ; SAGE ARRIVE?
        BEQ.S    DONE                  ; IF SO, BRANCH TO (PERHAPS)
                                       ; PROGRAM END
        BRA      LOOP                  ; WE WERE ONLY LOOKING FOR
                                       ; CLOSEWINDOW,
;                                      ; WHICH WASN'T THE MESSAGE,
;                                      ; SO WAITPORT AGAIN
```

Exec library functions fetch a message and return it after it's processed in this loop. WAITPORT lets the program know that a message has arrived. Other Exec functions are used to handle the message. They are GETMSG and REPLYMSG. Messages are sent by the operating system to the IDCMP and consist of information regarding various input events specified in the IDCMP flags.

When a GETMSG call returns a message, an address is the result. The address is placed in register D0. It points to a location in an INTUIMESSAGE structure. Within the INTUIMESSAGE structure are the IDCMPCLASS and IDCMPCODE fields (long-word and word values, respectively). Once these fields have been examined by the program (and copied to registers or memory as necessary), you can SYSLIB REPLYMSG to unload the message back to its source. The IDCMPCLASS and IDCMPCODE fields contain a value that reflects which of the many possible messages was received. If the CLOSEWINDOW message was sent because the user clicked a closewindow gadget, the ICDMPCLASS field will be equal to CLOSEWINDOW.

If you wish, you can arrange for your window to receive a blizzard of event messages from the user and the system. Use the WINDOW1 and WINDOW2 programs to experiment with combinations of settings of the IDCMP flags in the NEWWINDOW structure.

Once the window is opened (by using the MAKE-AWINDOW routine or other code), you may change the IDCMPFLAGS during the operation of your program by selecting the combination of flags you desire, and by using the MODIFYIDCMP function (using register D0 to pass the value for flags and register A0 to pass the address of the WINDOW structure):

**Listing 17-2. Specifying a New IDCMP FLAGS Combination in an Existing WINDOW**

```
MOVE.L   #(DESIRED COMBINATION OF IDCMP FLAGS),D0   ; CHOOSE SOME
                                                     ; FLAGS
MOVEA.L  WINDOW,A0                                   ; SPECIFY THE
                                                     ; WINDOW
INTLIB   MODIFYIDCMP                                 ; MACRO CALL TO
                                                     ; FUNCTION
```

The best ways to learn about the variety of effects that can be achieved with FLAGS and IDCMPFLAGS, is to try your own combinations, study the example listings, and refer to the *Amiga Intuition Reference Manual.*

## INTUITEXT: Intuition Text Handling

There are two ways to get text onto the screen within a window on the Amiga:

- If a program is running from the CLI, it already has an INPUT file and OUTPUT file assigned by STARTUP.ASM, and you use AmigaDOS WRITE and READ calls to handle text directly in the CLI window.
- When the program has its own Intuition window open (perhaps the program started up from the Workbench), use the Intuition PRINTITEXT routine to output text.

Intuition window also requires IDCMP messages to read characters (IDCMP INTUIMESSAGE CODE field) from the keyboard. You can get the keystroke codes in RAW form or VANILLAKEY (ASCII code) form this way.

It is also possible to use AmigaDOS to open a separate CLI-like window for input and output. You'll recall that this was called a CONsole device. It represents a powerful way to use AmigaDOS library routines in a program that is also using Intuition windows. AmigaDOS text I/O was covered in the earlier chapter on AmigaDOS, so we'll concentrate here on the Intuition text concepts including INTUITEXT and the variety of ways INTUITEXT structures are used with other Intuition structures (Menus, MenuItems, Gadgets, and so on).

## Intuition Window Text Output: INTUITEXT STRUCTURE, PRINTITEXT

Intuition can place any null-terminated text anywhere in any open Intuition window, using any system font, style, or color. It uses graphics routines, internally, to draw the text into your window. A program must first transform simple ASCII text (declared using DC.B directives—see examples) into an INTUITEXT structure before Intuition can use it.

The INTUITEXT structure is a 20-byte structure that provides the data Intuition needs to render text graphically in a window.

See the INTUITEXT STRUCTURE table in Table 17-2. One of the fields of an INTUITEXT structure is a pointer to your text. Other fields specify the foreground and background colors for the text, drawing mode (JAM1, JAM2, or COMPLEMENT), pixel positions for the start of the text, font, and a pointer to the next INTUITEXT structure. You can leave a value of 0 in the FONT field. You can also leave a 0 value in the NEXT pointer. If the NEXT pointer is set to another INTUITEXT structure's address, a call to PRINTITEXT will print it as well. If the FONT pointer is set to 0, the default system font is used (TOPAZ8 or TOPAZ9—depending on whether you selected 60 or 80 characters on your preferences menu). If your code opens the Diskfont library, you can (by studying the *Amiga Intuition Reference Manual*) use the other fonts. For simplicity, these programs use subroutines that are preset to use the default system font.

**Table 17-2. Intuition INTUITEXT Structure**

**Symbol: IT**
**Size: 22 bytes ($16 bytes)**

| *Field Size* | *Name* | *Offset* | *Description* |
|---|---|---|---|
| Byte | IT.FRONTPEN | 0 | Color register number for foreground |
| Byte | IT.BACKPEN | 2 | Color register number for background |

| *Field Size* | *Name* | *Offset* | *Description* |
|---|---|---|---|
| Byte | IT.DRAWMODE | 4 | JAM1, JAM2, OR XOR |
| Word | IT.LEFTEDGE | 6 | Number of pixels from the left edge |
| Word | IT.TOPEDGE | 8 | Number of pixels from the top edge |
| Long | IT.ITEXTFONT | 10 | Pointer to a font or 0 for default font |
| Long | IT.ITEXT | 14 | Pointer to a null-terminated text string |
| Long | IT.NEXTTEXT | 18 | Pointer to next INTUITEXT structure |

For easier access to the Intuition text-handling routines and structures, this chapter has a listing to be added to the include files you've typed in during previous sections. This file is called TEXTS.ASM and consists of subroutines and macros for easily using Intuition text. Listing 17-3 has the code for TEXTS.ASM, which can be typed in using the EMACS editor. Following the conventions developed in Chapter 3, we refer to the disk to which you've been depositing the type-in files as the DEV disk. Using EMACS or the editor of your choice, type in TEXTS.ASM from Listing 17-3 and save it to the DEV disk with the name:

DEV:RAMIT/INCLUDES/TEXTS.ASM

**Listing 17-3. TEXTS.ASM**

Intuition Text Handling Support Routines and Macros

```
;******************************** TEXTS.ASM BY DANIEL WOLF
;COPYRIGHT 1987 BY COMPUTE! BOOKS
;03/21/87

;TEXT SUPPORT ROUTINES

;MAKE AND PRINT NEW ITEXT AND GET ADDRESS OF NEW ITEXT STRUCTURE BACK IN D0

PRINTNEWAT MACRO     ;WINDOW,TEXT,LEFT,TOP,ERROR
 MOVE.L \1,A0        ;POINTER TO EXISTING WINDOW
 LEA \2,A1           ;POINTER TO FRESH NULL-TERMINATED TEXT
 MOVE.W #\3,D0       ;LEFT
 MOVE.W #\4,D1       ;TOP
 BSR _PRINTTEXT      ;MAKE NEW ITEXT (IN D0 IF SUCCESSFUL) AND PRINT!
 TST.L D0
 BEQ \5
 ENDM

;PRINT EXISTING INTUITEXT STRUCTURE

PRINTOLDAT MACRO     ;WINDOW,ITEXT,LEFT,TOP,ERROR
 MOVE.L \1,A0        ;POINTER TO EXISTING WINDOW
 MOVE.L \2,A1        ;PUT ADDRESS OF EXISTING INTUITEXT INTO A1
 MOVE.W #\3,D0       ;LEFT
 MOVE.W #\4,D1       ;TOP
```

```
 BSR _PRINTTXT       ;JUST PRINT EXISTING INTUITEXT
 TST.L D0
 BEQ \5
 ENDM

;JUST MAKE AN INTUITEXT, RETURN ADDRESS IN D0

MAKEITEX MACRO      ;TEXT,ERROR,RESULTPTR
 LEA \1,A0      ;LOAD ADDRESS OF N.T. TEXT (\1 PARAMETER)
 BSR MAKEATEXT
 TST.L D0
 BEQ \2              ;IF ERROR, BRANCH TO \2 PARAMETER
 MOVE.L D0,\3        ;STORE ADDRESS AT \3 PARAMETER
 ENDM                    ;RETURNS ADDRESS IF SUCCESSFUL IN D0

MAKEATEXT          ;SUBROUTINE - ENTER WITH PTR TO N.T. TEXT IN A0
 PUSHREG A0        ;PUSH ADDRESS OF N.T. TEXT
 REMEMBERPUBMEM REMEMBERKEY,#SIZE.IT,ERR_MITEXT
 MOVE.L D0,A0
 PULLREG A1        ;GET PTR TO N.T. TEXT FROM STACK
 PUSHREG A0        ;SAVE PTR TO ITEXT MEM BLOCK ON STACK
 BSR CREATETEXT    ;FILL IN THE INTUITEXT STRUCTURE
 PULLREG D0
 RTS               ;RETURN WITH ADDRESS OF ITEXT IN D0
ERR_MITEXT
 PULLREG A0        ;RETURN WITH 0 IN D0 IF ERROR ALLOCATING
 RTS

CREATETEXT; SUBROUTINE  ENTER WITH POINTER TO INTUITEXT SIZED MEM BLOCK IN A0
          ;                    POINTER TO NULL-TERMINATED TEXT      IN A1
          ; THIS ROUTINE FILLS THE INTUITEXT STRUCTURE WITH REASONABLE STUFF
          ; IT PUTS THE TEXT 2 DOWN AND 2 OVER (PIXELS) FROM UPPER LEFT
          ; AND USES  PEN #2  FOR FOREGROUND

 MOVE.B #2,IT.FRONTPEN(A0)          ;SET FOREGROUND PEN #=2
 MOVE.B #JAM1,IT.DRAWMODE(A0)       ;DRAW TEXT IN JAM1 MODE
 MOVE.W #2,IT.LEFTEDGE(A0)          ;START TEXT 2 PIXELS IN FROM LEFT
 MOVE.W #2,IT.TOPEDGE(A0)           ;START TEXT 2 PIXEL  DOWN FROM TOP
 MOVE.L A1,IT.TEXT(A0)              ;POINTER TO NULL TERMINATED TEXT
 RTS


_PRINTTEXT      ;SUBROUTINE    ENTER WITH POINTER TO WINDOW IN A0
                ;                                   N.T. TEXT IN A1
                ;                        LEFTEDGE IN D0
                ;                        TOPEDGE  IN D1

 PUSHREG D0-D1/A0             ;SAVE THE REGISTERS FIRST
 PUSHREG A1
 REMEMBERPUBMEM REMEMBERKEY,#SIZE.IT  ;ALLOCATE MEMORY FOR AN INTUITEXT
 TST.L D0
 BEQ.S ERR_TEXT
 MOVE.L D0,A0                 ;USE ADDRESS OF INTUITEXT STRUCTURE
 PULLREG A1                   ;NOW FILL THE INTUITEXT
 BSR CREATETEXT               ;CREATES 2-DOWN AND 2-RIGHT POSITION OFFSET
 MOVE.L A0,A1                 ;PUT POINTER TO INTUITEXT INTO A1
 MOVE.L A1,_THISITEXT         ;AND SAVE IT SO IT CAN BE RETRIEVED
 PULLREG D0-D1/A0             ;WINDOW, LEFT, TOP OFFSETS (ADDED TO ITEXT)

_PRINTTXT                     ;ENTER HERE IF A1 IS PTR TO ITEXT, A0 TO WINDOW
 MOVE.L WW.RPORT(A0),A0
 INTLIB PRINTITEXT            ;AND PRINT IT
 MOVE.L _THISITEXT,D0         ;NO ERROR, D0 = ADDRESS OF NEW INTUITEXT
 RTS

ERR_TEXT
 PULLREG A1
 PULLREG D0-D1/A0
 ZERO D0                      ;PUT ERROR = 0 CODE INTO D0
 RTS

_THISITEXT
 DC.L 0            ;STORAGE FOR POINTER TO AN ALLOCATED INTUITEXT
```

**The CREATETEXT subroutine.** This routine, in the TEXTS.ASM file, is called with the address of a 20-byte block of memory for an INTUITEXT structure in register A0 and the address of the null-terminated text in A1. CREATETEXT fills out the INTUITEXT structure with some standard default values. The INTUITEXT structure's memory is declared (by a line similar to MYINTUITEXT DS.B 20) in the program code, or allocated by a call to ALLOCREMEMBER or ALLOCMEM. The examples of INTUITEXT usage in upcoming chapters make extensive use of allocation followed by a call to CREATETEXT.

**The _PRINTTEXT and _PRINTTXT subroutines.** This routine in the TEXTS.ASM file allocates and fills an INTUITEXT structure. All the calling program must supply is the *x,y* position of the text to be printed and a pointer to the null-terminated text. Register D0 is used for *x*, D1 for *y*, register A0 for the window structure pointer, and A1 for the text pointer.

Note that if you print the same text more than once, you shouldn't use the _PRINTTEXT subroutine repeatedly, because it allocates memory. _PRINTTEXT returns the address of an allocated INTUITEXT in a variable labeled _THISITEXT. This address can be saved and used later to call _PRINTTXT. The first time some text is printed to a window, use _PRINTTEXT and save the address returned. The second and subsequent times, call _PRINTTXT (which skips the allocation) using the known address of the INTUITEXT in question. This method is demonstrated in WINDOWPRINT.ASM.

**The PRINTNEWAT and PRINTOLDAT macros.** These two macros represent the simplest way to accomplish simple printing of text in an Intuition window. The PRINTNEWAT macro accepts the label of a null-terminated text declaration as its parameter. It calls the CREATETEXT subroutine to create a new INTUITEXT structure and calls _PRINTITEXT. The *x* and *y* positions in the window to which the text is printed are the other parameters for this macro. PRINTNEWAT should only be used to print a particular text the first time it is needed.

PRINTOLDAT accepts the address of an existing INTUITEXT structure (and *x* and *y* position values) as a parameter, and calls _PRINTTXT to print it to the window. This macro is used whenever an INTUITEXT structure already exists for the text you wish to display. It doesn't create a new structure, but rather recycles an existing one.

## Listing 17-4. WINDOWPRINT Program

Demonstration of INTUITEXT structure and TEXTS.ASM use.

```
;WINDOWPRINT.ASM BY DANIEL WOLF
;COPYRIGHT 1987 BY COMPUTE! PUBLICATIONS
;09/10/87

 BRA _START

TXT EQU 1

 INCLUDE "HEADER"

MAIN                            ;THIS MUST BE THE LABEL OF THE PROGRAM

 LEA NEWWINDOW,A0               ;PUT POINTER TO NEWWINDOW STRUCTURE INTO A0
 INTLIB OPENWINDOW              ;AND OPEN THE WINDOW
 MOVE.L D0,WINDOW               ;SAVE POINTER TO THIS WINDOW STRUCTURE
 BEQ ERROR                      ;WHOOPS, POINTER = 0!

   ;***  NOW PRINT SOME TEXT TO THE WINDOW WITH _PRINTTEXT SUBROUTINE  ***

 MOVE.L D0,A0                   ;PUT POINTER TO WINDOW INTO A0
 LEA MESSAGE,A1                 ;POINTER TO TEXT INTO A1
 MOVE.W #10,D0
 MOVE.W #15,D1
 BSR _PRINTTEXT                 ;USE SUBROUTINE TO PRINT TEXT TO WINDOW
 TST.L D0
 BEQ ERR_DONE
 MOVE.L D0,MSG                  ;SAVE POINTER TO INTUITEXT WHICH CAME BACK!

   ;*** NOW PRINT MORE TEXT TO WINDOW WITH PRINTNEWAT MACRO ***

 PRINTNEWAT WINDOW,MESSAGE1,10,30,ERROR ;MACRO EQUIVALENT TO PREVIOUS 5 LINES!
 MOVE.L D0,MSG1                 ;ALSO RETURNS INTUITEXT PTR, CALLS _PRINTTEXT

    ;***  NOW PRINT BOTH 'OLD' MESSAGES USING EXISTING INTUITEXTS ***

 PRINTOLDAT WINDOW,MSG,10,45,ERR_DONE
 PRINTOLDAT WINDOW,MSG1,10,60,ERR_DONE

    ;***  NOW WAIT FOR IDCMP TO REPORT A CLOSEWINDOW MESSAGE  ***

LOOP
 MOVE.L WINDOW,A0             ;USE POINTER TO WINDOW TO FIND WINDOW'S I/O PORT
 MOVE.L WW.USERPORT(A0),A0    ;PLACE POINTER TO WINDOW'S PORT IN A0
 SYSLIB WAITPORT              ;WAIT FOR A SPECIFIED MESSAGE TO ARRIVE
 MOVE.L WINDOW,A0
 MOVE.L WW.USERPORT(A0),A0
 SYSLIB GETMSG                ;MESSAGE SHOULD BE AVAILABLE AFTER 'WAITPORT'
 TST.L D0                     ;POINTER TO INTUIMESSAGE COMES BACK IN D0
 BEQ.S LOOP                   ;NO MESSAGE FOUND THERE, SO LOOP (SHORT BRANCH)
 MOVE.L D0,A1                 ;POINTER TO INTUIMESSAGE CAME BACK, USE IN A1
 MOVE.L IM.CLASS(A1),D2       ;CLOSEWINDOW AND MENUPICk MESSAGES APPEAR HERE
 MOVE.W IM.CODE(A1),D3        ;MENU AND MENUITEM APPEAR HERE
 MOVE.W IM.QUALIFIER(A1),D4 ;KEYS APPEAR HERE
 SYSLIB REPLYMSG              ;QUICK, SEND MESSAGE BACK NOW!

 CMP.L #CLOSEWINDOW,D2        ;COMPARE CONTENTS OF D2 WITH VALUE OF 'CLOSEWINDOW'
 BEQ.S PRINTMORE              ;IF THEY'RE EQUAL, THIS IS A CLOSEWINDOW MESSAGE!
 BRA LOOP                     ;OTHERWISE, BRANCH ALWAYS (BRA) BACK TO LOOP

   ;***  NOW PRINT MORE TEXT TO THE WINDOW  ***

PRINTMORE
 MOVEA.L WINDOW,A0
 LEA MESSAGE2,A1
 MOVE.L #10,D0
 MOVE.L #75,D1
 BSR _PRINTTEXT                     ;USE SUBROUTINE TO PRINT TEXT TO WINDOW
 TST.L D0
 BEQ SKIPIT
 MOVE.L D0,MSG2                     ;SAVE ADDRESS OF INTUITEXT WHICH CAME BACK
```

```
SKIPIT
 MAKEITEX MESSAGE3,ERR_DONE,MSG3        ;USE MACRO TO MAKE AN INTUITEXT
 PRINTOLDAT WINDOW,MSG3,10,90,ERR_DONE ;PRINT FRESH INTUITEXT (ITS OLD NOW!)

 MOVE.L #TICKSPERSECOND,D1        ;LEAVE IT THERE 1 SECOND
 DOSLIB DELAY

    ;***  NOW FINISH UP, CLOSE WINDOW, AND EXIT TO SKELETON  ***

DONE
 MOVEQ #0,D0                 ;NO ERRORS, SO PLACE 0 IN D0 AS ERROR CODE
ERR_DONE
 PUSHREG D0                  ;HIDE D0 FOR A MOMENT ON THE STACK
 MOVE.L WINDOW,D0            ;CHECK FOR AN OPEN WINDOW
 BEQ.S QUIT                  ;IF 'WINDOW' = 0 , THEN NO WINDOW WAS OPENED
 MOVE.L D0,A0                ;THERE IS A WINDOW
 INTLIB CLOSEWINDOW          ;SO CLOSE IT
QUIT
 PULLREG D0                  ;RESTORE D0 NOW
 RTS                         ;RETURN TO 'CLEANUP' PORTION OF SKELETON

ERROR
 MOVEQ #21,D0                ;PUT ERROR CODE #21, "CAN'T OPEN WINDOW"
 RTS                         ;EXIT TO SKELETON NOW!

   ;*** DATA STORAGE ***

MYWINDOWTITLE                ;NULL-TERMINATED WINDOW TITLE TEXT

 DC.B ' WindowPrint  by D. Wolf',0

 EVENPC                      ;WORD-ALIGN MEMORY AFTER DC.B!

MESSAGE
 DC.B ' This is an example of printing text using INTUITION ',0
 EVENPC
MESSAGE1
 DC.B ' And another example of Intuitext Printing ',0
 EVENPC
MESSAGE2
 DC.B ' Here is some more ',0
 EVENPC
MESSAGE3
 DC.B ' And even MORE ',0
 EVENPC

WINDOW DC.L 0                ;STORAGE FOR POINTER TO THE WINDOW STRUCTURE
RP DC.L 0                    ;STORAGE FOR WINDOW'S 'RASTPORT' POINTER
MSG DC.L 0    ;POINTERS FOR INTUITEXTS (TO USE WITH PRINTOLDAT)
MSG1 DC.L 0
MSG2 DC.L 0
MSG3 DC.L 0

NEWWINDOW             ;NEWWINDOW STRUCTURE DECLARED DIRECTLY IN CODE
 DC.W 40              ;LEFTEDGE
 DC.W 15              ;TOPEDGE
 DC.W 500             ;WIDTH
 DC.W 120             ;HEIGHT
 DC.B -1              ;DETAILPEN (= FF, MAXIMUM REGARDLESS OF SCREEN DEPTH!)
 DC.B -1              ;BLOCKPEN
 DC.L CLOSEWINDOW
 DC.L ACTIVATE!WINDOWSIZING!WINDOWDRAG!WINDOWDEPTH!WINDOWCLOSE!SMART_REFRESH
 DC.L 0               ;POINTER TO FIRST USER-DEFINED GADGET
 DC.L 0               ;POINTER TO USER-DEFINED CHECKMARK
 DC.L MYWINDOWTITLE   ;POINTER TO TITLE TEXT
 DC.L 0               ;POINTER TO CUSTOM SCREEN
 DC.L 0               ;POINTER TO CUSTOM BITMAP
 DC.W 50              ;MINWIDTH
 DC.W 20              ;MINHEIGHT
 DC.W 640             ;MAXWIDTH
 DC.W 400             ;MAXHEIGHT
 DC.W WBENCHSCREEN    ;TYPE OF SCREEN THIS WINDOW IS IN
 END
```

Be sure you understand the concepts related to text handling by Intuition. The INTUITEXT structures are always used to embellish simple null-terminated text in Intuition applications. Other Intuition features, such as menus and gadgets, also use INTUITEXT structures when they need text. When you use the familiar Amiga menus, be aware that each line of a menu also has its corresponding INTUITEXT structure. The concept is simple, but important, and comes up many times as we present more about the Intuition system features. The INTUITEXT structure contains the information required to color and style the text.

# CHAPTER 18
# Intuition Menus

The Amiga system that provides pull-down menus is extraordinarily flexible. Users interact with menu selections using the mouse and its right button. Making a selection is as simple as releasing the button over the desired selection. Each menu item can hold either text or special imagery; or, it can be checkmarked or highlighted by changing color or having a box surround it when selected; or, it can show an alternate command key.

Controlling all this can become complex. As with windows, there's a family of flags for most menu features. Don't forget that each menu is attached to a window. The menu sends its event messages to your program by way of that window's IDCMP Port.

Each menu may have many menu items. The menu itself usually has a title shown at the top of the menu. Each menu item is usually represented by text specifying the action that will take place when that item is selected. You can create several menus next to each other, each with its own features.

One drawback to using menus in a machine language program is that each item must have its own MENUITEM structure to specify how it is drawn, and each of these structures must have substructures for INTUITEXT, or images used when that menu item is drawn. Declaring (and making sure their pointers all point correctly to other structures) all the MENU, MENUITEM, and INTUITEXT structures needed for just a small menu is a chore and can cause source code to balloon to an unmanageable size.

**Table 18-1. Intuition MENUITEM Structure**

**Symbol: MI**
**Size: 34 bytes ($22 bytes)**

| *Field Size* | *Name* | *Offset* | *Description* |
|---|---|---|---|
| Long | MI.NEXT | 0 | Pointer to next MENU-ITEM structure |
| Word | MI.LEFTEDGE | 4 | Number of pixels from left edge |
| Word | MI.TOPEDGE | 6 | Number of pixels from top edge |
| Word | MI.WIDTH | 8 | Number of pixels wide |
| Word | MI.HEIGHT | 10 | Number of pixels high |
| Word | MI.FLAGS | 12 | Enable, render, and event flags |
| Long | MI.MUTUALEXCLUDE | 14 | Bits excluding other menu items |
| Long | MI.ITEMFILL | 18 | Pointer to INTUITEXT or IMAGE structure |
| Long | MI.SELECTFILL | 22 | Pointer to select text or image |
| Byte | MI.COMMAND | 26 | A command key |
| Long | MI.SUBITEM | 28 | Pointer to subitem MENUITEM structure |
| Word | MI.NEXTSELECT | 32 | Menu number of simultaneous selection |

One solution to this problem is to use routines needing only the text of each item and the menu title declared in the source code. That is, the philosophy behind the MENUS.ASM routines for this chapter.

Listing 18-1 contains the code for the MENUS.ASM include file which has subroutines and macros that dramatically simplify and shorten the code needed to work with Intuition menus. As with the type-in include files presented in earlier parts of this book, you should use EMACS or your favorite text editor to type in the file and save it on the DEV disk you're creating with the name:

DEV:RAMIT/INCLUDES/MENUS.ASM

This will add the MENUS.ASM program code and macros to your growing family of include files on your DEV disk.

## Listing 18-1. MENUS.ASM Intuition Menus-Support Code and Macros

```
;******************************** MENUS.ASM BY DANIEL WOLF
;COPYRIGHT 1987 BY COMPUTE! BOOKS
;03/21/87

;MENU SUPPORT ROUTINES

MITEMLIST MACRO ;MENU ITEM LIST FILLER
 LEA _POINTERLIST,A0
 MOVE.L #\1,(A0)+             ;ADDRESS OF FIRST ITEM (NOT 0!!)
 MOVE.L #\2,(A0)+             ;ADDRESS OF SECOND ITEM (OR 0! IF NO ITEM)
 MOVE.L #\3,(A0)+
 MOVE.L #\4,(A0)+
 MOVE.L #\5,(A0)+
 MOVE.L #\6,(A0)+
 MOVE.L #\7,(A0)+
 MOVE.L #\8,(A0)              ;ADDRESS OF SEVENTH ITEM (OR 0!)
 MOVE.L #\1,D2
 BSR DOSTEXTLEN                       ;GET WIDTH OF FIRST ITEM
 ASL.L #3,D3                          ;NUM CHARACTERS * 8
 ADD.L #30,D3                         ;ADD ROOM FOR ALT KEY AND CHEKMARK
 MOVE.L D3,D1
 MOVE.L #\9,D0                        ;NUMBER OF ITEMS -1
 ENDM

MAKEMEN MACRO ;ADDRESSES OF PARAMETERS
 LEA \1,A0
 LEA \2,A1
 LEA \3,A2
 BSR MAKEAMENU
 TST.L D0
 BNE \4
 ENDM

MENUEVENT         ;SEPARATES MENU #, MENUITEM #, AND (UPROGRAMMIT) SUBITEM #
 MOVE.L D0,D1
 ANDI.W #31,D0
 LSR.W #5,D1
 ANDI.W #63,D1
 RTS

CREATEMENU; SUBROUTINE ENTER WITH POINTER TO MENU SIZED MEM BLOCK IN A0
          ;                       POINTER TO MENU NAME INTUITEXT  IN A1
          ;                       POINTER TO FIRST MENUITEM       IN A2
          ; THIS ROUTINE FILLS THE MENU STRUCTURE WITH REASONABLE STUFF

 MOVE.W D0,MENU.LEFTEDGE(A0)
 MOVE.W D1,MENU.WIDTH(A0)
 MOVE.W _THISFONTHITE,MENU.HEIGHT(A0)    ;USE DEFAULT TEXT HEIGHT FOR MENU
 MOVE.W #MENUENABLED,MENU.FLAGS(A0)      ;ENABLE THIS MENU AT ONCE
 MOVE.L A1,MENU.NAME(A0)                 ;POINTER TO NULL-TERMINATED NAME TEXT
 MOVE.L A2,MENU.FIRSTITEM(A0)            ;POINTER TO FIRST MENUITEM STRUCTURE
 PUSHREG D0,A0
 LEA _MITEMPTR,A0
 MOVE.L #8,D0
CLRMITEMPTRS
 MOVE.L #0,(A0)+
 SUBQ.L #1,D0
 BNE.S CLRMITEMPTRS
 PULLREG D0,A0
 RTS

CREATEITEM
 MOVE.L A1,MI.NEXT(A0)            ;PTR TO NEXT MENU ITEM IN THIS MENU ITEM LIST
 MOVE.W #2,MI.LEFTEDGE(A0)        ;ITEM STARTS 2 PIXELS FROM LEFT EDGE
 MOVE.W D1,MI.TOPEDGE(A0)
 MOVE.W D2,MI.WIDTH(A0)                    ;MENU ITEM IS  D2 PIXELS WIDE
 MOVE.W _THISFONTHITE,MI.HEIGHT(A0)        ;MENU ITEM IS   9 PIXELS HIGH
 ADDI.W #2,MI.HEIGHT(A0)                   ;**TRY ADJUSTING HERE
 BCLR #0,MI.HEIGHT(A0)
 MOVE.W _THISMITEMFLAGS,MI.FLAGS(A0)
 MOVE.L D4,MI.MUTUALEXCLUDE(A0)   ;MUTUAL EXCLUDES      FOR ITEM
 MOVE.L A2,MI.ITEMFILL(A0)        ;INTUITEXT STRUCTURE FOR ITEM
 MOVE.B D0,MI.COMMAND(A0)         ;COMMAND KEY          FOR ITEM
```

```
 MOVE.L #Ø,MI.SUBITEM(AØ)          ;NO SUBITEMS
 MOVE #Ø,MI.NEXTSELECT(AØ)         ;NO CONNECTIONS
 RTS

MAKEAMENU
 ;TAKES AN ARRAY OF 8 LONGWORD ADDRESSES OF TEXTS  IN   _POINTERLIST
 ;ALLOCATES AND INITS UP TO 8 INTUITEXT STRUCTURES INTO _ITEXTPTR ARRAY
 ;ALLOCATES AND INITS UP TO 8 MENUITEM STRUCTURES  INTO _MITEMPTR ARRAY
 ;ALSO USES ARRAY OF 8 COMMAND KEY *BYTES*         IN   _CMDKEYPTR
 ;
 ;DØ=NUMMENUITEMS
 ;D1=WIDTH OF MENUITEMS
 ;AØ=ADDR OF COMMAND KEY LIST
 ;A1=ADDR OF MUTUAL EXCLUDES
 ;A2=ADDR OF NULL TERMINATED TEXT MENU STRIP TITLE

 MOVE.L DØ,NUMMENITEMS
 MOVE.W D1,_MENITEMWIDTH
 MOVE.L AØ,_CMDKEYPTR
 MOVE.L A1,_MUEXPTR
 MOVE.L A2,_THISMENUTITLE

 MOVE.L DØ,D7
 CMP.L #8,D7
 BGT ERR_MAKEAMENU              ;MORE THAN 8 TEXT STRUCTURES! ERROR!
 MOVEQ.L #Ø,D6                  ;OFFSET OF FOUR BYTES PER BIT OF D7
_NEXTMENTEXT
 LEA _POINTERLIST,AØ
 TST.L Ø(AØ,D6.L)               ;IS THERE A TEXT POINTER HERE??
 BEQ _ENDMAKEAMENU
 MOVEQ.L #Ø,DØ
MENUTEXTSIZE
 REMEMBERPUBMEM REMEMBERKEY,#SIZE.IT
 TST.L DØ
 BEQ ERR_MAKEAMENUMEM
 LEA _ITEXTPTR,AØ
 MOVE.L DØ,Ø(AØ,D6.L)           ;STASH PTR TO INTUITEXT STRUCT IN ITEXTPTR ARRAY
 MOVEQ.L #Ø,DØ
MENUITEMSIZE
 REMEMBERPUBMEM REMEMBERKEY,#SIZE.MI
 TST.L DØ
 BEQ ERR_MAKEAMENUMEM
 LEA _MITEMPTR,AØ
 MOVE.L DØ,Ø(AØ,D6.L)           ;STASH PTR TO MENUITEM  STRUCT IN MITEMPTR ARRAY
MAKEAMENUITEM
 LEA _POINTERLIST,A1
 MOVEA.L Ø(A1,D6.L),A1          ;A1 IS POINTER TO NULL-TERMINATED TEXT
 LEA _ITEXTPTR,AØ
 MOVEA.L Ø(AØ,D6.L),AØ          ;AØ IS POINTER TO AN INTUITEXT STRUCT IN MEM
 BSR CREATETEXT                 ;INIT THE INTUITEXT STRUCT FOR THIS MENUITEM
 ADDQ.L #4,D6                   ;ADD 1 LONGWORD'S WORTH TO D6 INDEX POINTER
 DBRA D7,_NEXTMENTEXT           ;DEC/NOTBRANCH ALWAYS ON D7 AS COUNTER
 MOVE.L NUMMENITEMS,D7
 MOVEQ.L #Ø,D6
 MOVEQ.L #Ø,D5
_NEXTMENITM
 LEA _MITEMPTR,AØ
 MOVEA.L 4(AØ,D6.L),A1              ;A1=ADDR OF MEM ALLOCATED FOR NEXT MENUITEM
 MOVEA.L Ø(AØ,D6.L),AØ              ;AØ=ADDR OF MEM ALLOCATED FOR MENUITEM
 LEA _ITEXTPTR,A2
 MOVEA.L Ø(A2,D6.L),A2              ;A2=ADDR OF MEM ALLOCATED FOR INTUITEXT
 MOVEA.L _CMDKEYPTR,A3
 MOVE.B Ø(A3,D5.L),DØ               ;DØ=COMMAND KEY BYTE FROM _CMDKEYPTR ARRAY
 MOVE.W MENUHITPARAM,D1             ;D1=CURRENT DISTANCE FROM TOP
 MOVE.W _MENITEMWIDTH,D2            ;D2=WIDTH OF THESE MENUITEMS
 MOVEA.L _MUEXPTR,A3
 MOVE.L Ø(A3,D6.L),D4               ;D4=MUTUAL EXCLUDE FOR THIS ITEM
 BSR CREATEITEM
 ADD.W _THISFONTHITE,D1             ;ADD FONT HEIGHT TO DISTANCE FROM TOP
 ADDI.W #2,D1                       ;ADD ADDITIONAL PIXELS CAUSE WE'RE PLACING
 BCLR.L #Ø,D1                       ;GUARANTEE ITS AN EVEN NUMBER!!!
 MOVE.W D1,MENUHITPARAM             ;TEXT 2 PIXELS IN FROM THE TOP IN THE
 ADDQ.L #4,D6                       ;INTUITEXT STRUCTURE (CREATETEXT, ABOVE)
 ADDQ.L #1,D5
 DBRA D7,_NEXTMENITM
_ENDMAKEAMENU
 REMEMBERPUBMEM REMEMBERKEY,#SIZE.MENU
 TST.L DØ
```

```
 BEQ.S ERR_MAKEAMENUMEM
 MOVE.L DØ,D1
 MOVE.L DØ,AØ                    ;POINTER TO ALLOCATED MEM FOR A MENU STRUCTURE
 MOVEA.L _THISMENUTITLE,A1
 MOVEA.L _MITEMPTR,A2            ;POINTER TO FIRST MENUITEM ALLOCATED
 MOVEQ.L #Ø,DØ                   ;RETURN WITH DØ = Ø     *SUCCEED*
                                 ;              D1 = PTR TO MENU STRUCTURE
 MOVE.W DØ,MENUHITPARAM          ;AND ZERO OUT THE HEIGHT MEASURE FOR NEXT ONE
 RTS                             ;CALLER CAN NOW PLACE LEFTEDGE IN DØ AND
                                 ;              PLACE WIDTH     IN D1 AND
                                 ;CALL CREATEMENU

ERR_MAKEAMENUMEM
 MOVE.L #CANTALLOCMEM,DØ         ;RETURN WITH DØ =       *CANTALLOCMEM*
 RTS
ERR_MAKEAMENU
 MOVE.L #1,DØ                    ;RETURN WITH DØ = 1     *FAIL*
 RTS

_ITEXTPTR               ;ARRAY OF 8 PTRS TO INTUITEXT STRUCTURES
 DC.L Ø,Ø,Ø,Ø,Ø,Ø,Ø,Ø
_MITEMPTR               ;ARRAY OF 8 PTRS TO MENUITEM  STRUCTURES
 DC.L Ø,Ø,Ø,Ø,Ø,Ø,Ø,Ø
_POINTERLIST            ;PUT PTRS TO UP TO EIGHT LABELLED DC.B TEXTS HERE
 DC.L Ø,Ø,Ø,Ø,Ø,Ø,Ø,Ø
_CMDKEYPTR              ;PUT PTR TO COMMAND KEY LIST FOR THESE MENUITEMS HERE
 DC.L Ø
MENUHITPARAM            ;KEEPS TRACK OF HEIGHT VALUE FOR SUCCESSIVE MENUITEMS
 DC.W Ø
_MENITEMWIDTH           ;STORAGE FOR WIDTH MEASURE (WORD)
 DC.W Ø
NUMMENITEMS             ;HOW MANY MENU ITEMS FOR THIS MENU
 DC.L 1
_THISMENUTITLE          ;POINTER TO TITLE NULL-TERMINATED TEXT
 DC.L Ø
_MUEXPTR                ;POINTER TO LIST OF MUTUAL EXCLUDE VALUES FOR MENITEMS
 DC.L Ø
_THISMITEMFLAGS         ;DEFAULT MENU ITEM FLAGS
 DC.W CHECKIT!HIGHCOMP!COMMSEQ!ITEMENABLED!ITEMTEXT
```

**The MAKEAMENU, CREATEMENU, and CREATITEM subroutines.** These subroutines can take the drudgery out of menu programming. They permit you to declare the text required for your menus, and then allocate and fill MENU, MENUITEM, and INTUITEXT structures. The structures are filled with standard default values shown in the listings. You can change them in the declarations or with your own code. Note the FLAGS settings, specifically, because those are the ones to alter for experimentation.

The most complex structure in the menu is the MENUITEM structure (Table 18-2). One MENUITEM structure is created and filled for each selection on the menu. This is difficult to do with an algorithm that will satisfy all programmers, so don't consider CREATITEM to be "the last word" in subroutines. You will undoubtedly want to do some experimentation and tailor it to fit your individual needs.

MAKEAMENU does some arithmetic to assure that the INTUITEXT structures (which are linked to each MENUITEM structure) are positioned properly. The settings used in these routines also specify CHECKMARK, assume you are supplying command keys to allow keyboard selection as well as mouse selection, HIGHCOMP (video reverse highlighting of selected Menu items), default font, JAM1 drawing mode, and so on. These default selections will be acceptable on most applications, but you're encouraged to alter the FgPen and BgPen settings, swap JAM2 for JAM1, use HIGHBOX instead of HIGHCOMP as the highlight mode, and so on.

The only limitation inherent in the routines as they are written is that MAKEAMENU only accepts up to eight items per menu. Changing that limit is easy, and it's a good programming exercise. If you want multiple menus, the program must link the NEXTMENU fields of the MENU structures, and must also arrange them so that the menus are positioned appropriately across the screen. The examples show both single and multiple menu usage (Listings 18-2 and 18-3, MENU1.ASM and MENU2.ASM).

**The MITEMLIST and MAKEMEN macros.** Like the other Intuition include files presented in this book, the MENUS.ASM file also has macros that call the subroutines in the file and make program coding even more efficient than using the subroutines themselves. In this file, there are two macros to shorten the programming chores. Their use is illustrated in the example programs of Listings 18-2 and 18-3.

## Programming Menus with the Support Routines

The application program must do several things to take advantage of the MAKEAMENU subroutine:

- Declare text strings using labels
- Setup _POINTERLIST with pointers to the labels (use the macro)
- Setup address registers with pointers to command key definitions, mutual excludes, and the title text
- Setup data registers with count and MENUITEM position information
- BSR MAKEAMENU (this produces the list of MENUITEM structures)
- Check for errors (this and the previous two tasks are performed by the MAKEMEN macro)
- Save the pointer to the MENU structure returned by MAKEAMENU

- Setup data registers for actual MENU position
- BSR CREATEMENU (this finalizes filling in the MENU structure)
- Repeat each of the above steps for each additional MENU required
- Link NEXTMENU fields of the MENU structures obtained
- Place address of the WINDOW structure into address register A0
- Place address of the first MENU structure into A1
- Call the Intuition routine SETMENUSTRIP to attach the menus to the window

The preparation for MAKEAMENU and CREATEMENU takes several lines of code in most cases, but this is much shorter than declaring the structures directly. The macros eliminate this chore. MAKEAMENU and CREATEMENU allocate memory, using the ALLOCREMEMBER function, so that all memory used by all the menu-related structures can be returned to the system at once with FREEREMEMBER, at the end of the program.

Public memory is used for these structures because they aren't absolutely required to reside in chip memory. Public memory allocation will first try to use any fast (or expansion) memory attached to the Amiga. This is a friendly way to coexist with the multitasking Executive, since all memory required for use with the structures is allocated in small chunks "on the fly" and scarce chip memory is conserved wherever possible.

When first implemented, these routines were used to replace a declaration of a four-item menu. There was a savings of nearly 2K in the source listing and hundreds of bytes in the assembled program (even though the routines themselves add to program size).

**The MAKEAMENU subroutine (CREATEITEM, CREATETEXT).** MAKEAMENU utilizes two additional routines to prepare a set of MENUITEM structures and their associated INTUITEXT structures, for a complete menu of up to eight items.

The CREATEITEM routine is called to fill in the MENUITEM structure allocated by MAKEAMENU. The CREATETEXT routine is called to fill the INTUITEXT structure allocated for each of the MENUITEM structures. MAKEAMENU allocates memory for the structures, including the final MENU structure, which points to the first MENUITEM structure. In addition, MAKEAMENU assures that text is positioned correctly within the menu selection strips.

MAKEAMENU links pointers among the structures, as well. When MAKEAMENU returns, it either supplies an address to a MENU structure (if it was successful), or returns an error code. It does not actually fill in the MENU structure because when several menus are made, they must be positioned correctly with data supplied from the application program. The final job of filling in the MENU structure is left to a later call to CREATEMENU.

Before exploring the other intricacies of Intuition menu programming, you should try the MENU1.ASM program in Listing 18-2. It pulls together the concepts presented so far and shows the use of the MENUS.ASM support code routines and macros.

### Listing 18-2. MENU1.ASM

This program creates a single menu with three items.

```
;MENU1.ASM BY DANIEL WOLF
;COPYRIGHT 1987 BY COMPUTE! PUBLICATIONS
;09/10/87

 BRA _START

DOS EQU 1
INT EQU 1
GFX EQU 1

WIN EQU 1
MEN EQU 1
TXT EQU 1

 INCLUDE "HEADER"

MAIN
 TST.L ENDFROMWB             ;IF INITIATED FROM WB,  THEN NO ANNOUNCEMENTS YET!
 BNE.S _BUILDAWINDOW
FROMUSER
 DOSPRINT STDOUT,#MYMESSAGE ;IF INITIATED FROM CLI, THEN OUTPUT TITLE MESSAGE
 MOVEQ #0,D0
 MOVEA.L COMMAND,A0          ;PUT ADDRESS OF COMMAND LINE IN A0
 CMPI.B #'?',(A0)            ;IF FIRST CHARACTER IS ? THEN
 BNE.S _BUILDAWINDOW
 BRA USAGE                   ;PRINT OUT INSTRUCTIONS AND QUIT

_BUILDAWINDOW

 MAKEWIN #MYWINDOWTITLE,40,15,500,160,ERROR
 MOVE.L D0,WINDOW            ;WINDOW OPENED HAS ITS POINTER IN D0
```

```
_BUILDMENU
 LEA _POINTERLIST,AØ          ;THE FIRST OF A BLOCK OF 8 POINTERS
 MOVE.L #MYITEMØ,(AØ)+        ;FILL BLOCK WITH POINTERS TO MENU ITEM TEXTS
 MOVE.L #MYITEM1,(AØ)+        ;THESE ARE MOVES OF THE ADDRESSES OF MYITEMØ ...
 MOVE.L #MYITEM2,(AØ)+        ;INTO THE FIXED ARRAY FOR 'MAKEAMENU'
 MOVE.L #2,DØ                 ;NUMBER OF MENUITEMS       FOR THIS MENU

;MITEMLIST MYITEMØ,MYITEM1,MYITEM2,Ø,Ø,Ø,Ø,Ø,2     ;MACRO FOR LAST 6 LINES

 MOVE.W #12Ø,D1               ;WIDTH  OF MENUITEMS       FOR THIS MENU
 LEA MYCMDKEYS,AØ             ;ADDR OF COMMAND KEY LIST FOR THIS MENU
 LEA MYMUEXES,A1              ;ADDR OF MUTUAL EXCLUDES  FOR THIS MENU
 LEA MYMENUTITLE,A2           ;ADDR OF TITLE            FOR THIS MENU
 BSR MAKEAMENU                ;ALLOCATE AND BUILD MENUITEM STRUCTURES
 TST.L DØ                     ;ALL'S WELL?
 BNE DONE

;MAKEMEN MYCMDKEYS,MYMUEXES,MYMENUTITLE,DONE          ;MACRO FOR LAST 6 LINES

 MOVE.L D1,_THISMENU          ;MAKEAMENU RETURNS WITH POINTER TO MENU IN D1
 MOVE.W #5,DØ                 ;LEFEDGE  FOR THIS MENU
 MOVE.W #12Ø,D1               ;WIDTH    FOR THIS MENU
 BSR CREATEMENU               ;THIS CREATES THE ACTUAL MENU ATTACHED TO THE ITEMS

_MENUATTACH
 MOVE.L WINDOW,AØ             ;SUPPLY POINTER TO WINDOW  IN AØ
 MOVE.L _THISMENU,A1          ;SUPPLY POINTER TO MENU #Ø IN A1
 INTLIB SETMENUSTRIP          ;AND ATTACH THE MENU TO THE WINDOW

 MOVE.L #TICKSPERSECOND,D1    ;SET UP 1 SECOND'S WORTH OF TICKS
 DOSLIB DELAY                 ;LET THE TIMER TICK DOWN TO ZERO

LOOP
 MOVE.L WINDOW,AØ
 MOVE.L #$FFFF,DØ             ;WAKE UP THE WHOLE MENU NOW
 INTLIB ONMENU
 MOVE.L WINDOW,AØ
 MOVE.L WW.USERPORT(AØ),AØ    ;LISTEN TO PORT ATTACHED TO THIS WINDOW
 SYSLIB WAITPORT              ;WAIT FOR A SPECIFIED MESSAGE TO ARRIVE
 MOVE.L WINDOW,AØ
 MOVE.L WW.USERPORT(AØ),AØ
 SYSLIB GETMSG                ;MESSAGE HAS ARRIVE WITHIN SPECIFICATIONS
 TST.L DØ                     ;POINTER TO INTUIMESSAGE COMES BACK IN DØ
 BEQ.S RELOOP                 ;NO MESSAGE THERE, SO LOOP
 MOVE.L DØ,A1                 ;POINTER TO INTUIMESSAGE CAME BACK, USE IN A1
 MOVE.L IM.CLASS(A1),D2       ;CLOSEWINDOW AND MENUPIC MESSAGES APPEAR HERE
 MOVE.W IM.CODE(A1),D3        ;MENU AND MENUITEM APPEAR HERE
 MOVE.W IM.QUALIFIER(A1),D4   ;KEYS APPEAR HERE
 SYSLIB REPLYMSG              ;QUICK, SEND MESSAGE BACK NOW!

 CMP.L #CLOSEWINDOW,D2
 BEQ DONE                     ;IF ITS A CLOSEWINDOW MESSAGE, THEN DO SO...
 CMP.L #MENUPICK,D2
 BNE RELOOP                   ;THIS ISN'T A CLOSE OR A MENUPICK, SO LOOP
 MOVEQ.L #Ø,DØ
 MOVE.W D3,DØ                 ;SETUP MENUCODE IN DØ FOR THIS SUBROUTINE
 BSR MENUEVENT
 TST.W DØ                     ;DØ IS THE MENU      NUMBER
 BNE HANDLEMENU1              ;IF THIS ISN'T MENU #Ø, THEN CHECK IF MENU #1
 CMPI.W #2,D1                 ;D1 IS THE MENUITEM NUMBER, SEE IF D1 = 2
 BEQ DONE                     ;IF MENUITEM = 2 THEN     *QUIT*
 CMPI.W #1,D1                 ;COMPARE IMMEDIATE, SEE IF D1 = 1
 BEQ.S DOITEM1_MENUØ          ;IF MENUITEM = 1 THEN DO *ITEM1* MENUØ
 CMPI.W #Ø,D1                 ;COMPARE IMMEDIATE, SEE IF D1 = Ø
 BEQ.S DOITEMØ_MENUØ          ;IF MENUITEM = Ø THEN DO *ITEMØ* MENUØ
 BRA.S RELOOP                 ;IF NONE OF ABOVE, THEN LOOP
DOITEM1_MENUØ
 BSR MENUØITEM1
 BRA.S RELOOP
DOITEMØ_MENUØ
 BSR MENUØITEMØ

HANDLEMENU1
 ;INTERCEPT MENU1 AND ITS MENUITEMS HERE, IF THEY EXIST

RELOOP
 BRA LOOP                     ;RETURN TO TOP OF LOOP AND SCAN FOR MESSAGES
```

```
DONE                          ;NOW CLEAN UP WINDOW AND EXIT
 MOVE.L WINDOW,DØ
 BEQ.S QUIT
 MOVE.L DØ,AØ
 INTLIB CLEARMENUSTRIP        ;MUST CLEAR THE MENU PRIOR TO CLOSING WINDOW
QUIT
 MOVEQ.L #Ø,DØ
 PUSHREG DØ
 MOVE.L WINDOW,DØ
 BEQ.S 1$                ; 1$ IS A LOCAL LABEL   A NUMBER$ LABEL IS LOCAL
 MOVE.L DØ,AØ            ; MEANING IT CAN BE USED BETWEEN TWO REGULAR LABELS
 INTLIB CLOSEWINDOW      ; MEANING THE SAME LABEL CAN BE USED MANY TIMES
1$                       ; BUT EACH TIME WITH A DIFFERENT 'LOCAL' MEANING
 PULLREG DØ
QUITNOW
 RTS

ERROR
 DOSPRINT STDOUT,#ERRORTEXT    ;USING DOS TO PRINT MESSAGE TO CLI WINDOW
 MOVE.L #21,DØ
 BRA QUITNOW

USAGE
 DOSPRINT STDOUT,#USAGETEXT    ;USING DOS TO PRINT MESSAGE TO CLI WINDOW
 BRA DONE

MENUØITEM1
 MOVE.L WINDOW,AØ
 BSR _CLEARWINDOW              ;CLEAR THE WINDOW, NO COLOR JUST BACKGROUND
 RTS

MENUØITEMØ                     ;FILL WITH COLOR

 MOVE.L WINDOW,AØ              ;PUT WINDOW POINTER IN AØ
 MOVE.L #3,DØ                  ;COLOR REGISTER SELECTION (Ø-3 ON WORKBENCH)
 BSR _FILLWINDOW               ;FILL THE WINDOW
 RTS

MYWINDOWTITLE
 DC.B ' Menu1  by D.WOLF ',Ø
 EVENPC
USAGETEXT
 DC.B 'Usage: Menu1',1Ø,Ø
 EVENPC
ERRORTEXT
 DC.B 1Ø,'Sorry, cannot open window ',1Ø,Ø
 EVENPC
MYMESSAGE
 DC.B 1Ø,'Menu1 by Daniel Wolf Copyright 1987 by Compute! Publications',1Ø,Ø
 EVENPC

WINDOW DC.L Ø                  ;POINTER TO WINDOW STRUCTURE
RP DC.L Ø                      ;POINTER TO WINDOW'S RASTPORT STRUCTURE
_THISMENU
 DC.L Ø                        ;POINTER TO 'FIRST' MENU STRUCTURE

MYMENUTITLE
 DC.B 'MENU EXAMPLE',Ø         ;TEXT FOR MENU TITLE
 EVENPC
MYITEMØ
 DC.B '   ITEM A  ',Ø          ;TEXT FOR FIRST MENUITEM, WITH ROOM FOR CHKMARK
 EVENPC
MYITEM1
 DC.B '   ITEM B  ',Ø          ;TEXT FOR SECOND MENUITEM
 EVENPC
MYITEM2
 DC.B '   QUIT    ',Ø          ;TEXT FOR THIRD MENUITEM
 EVENPC
MYCMDKEYS
 DC.B 'ABQ'                    ;LIST OF 'COMMSEQ' MENU ALTERNATE COMMAND KEYS
 EVENPC
MYMUEXES                       ;LIST OF MUTUAL-EXCLUDE VALUES TO RESTRICT
 DC.L 6,5,Ø                    ;CHECKMARK TO ONE ITEM AT A TIME
 EVENPC
_THISFONTHITE
 DC.W 9

 END
```

The MENU1.ASM program demonstrates some previously unexplained menu features.

The CREATEMENU and MAKEAMENU routines use standard values for some important flags that control how the menus appear and operate. You can think of these flags like WINDOW flags or IDCMP flags, but they control menu features.

Since these flags are specified by the routines in the MENUS.ASM file, they're hidden from the MENU1.ASM program. If you wish to manipulate them to vary the appearance and control features of your menus, you'll have to change the MENUS.ASM file or modify them after the menu has been created by your program. This can be done with code that looks up the flags within a MENU structure. Such changes should be made prior to actually calling the Intuition library SETMENUSTRIP function.

**The MENUITEM flags.** There are 12 flag bits that can be set prior to a call to MAKEAMENU. They control the actual MENUITEM structures and the appearance and use of menu items. These are set to default values in the MENUS.ASM include file for this chapter, but can easily be altered for experimentation (strongly encouraged due to the variety of combinations). A list of them is in Table 18-2.

**Table 18-2. The MENUITEM Flags**

| Name | Hexadecimal Value | Description |
|---|---|---|
| CHECKIT | $0001 | Setting this flag informs Intuition that this is an attribute item, rather than an action item |
| ITEMTEXT | 0002 | This flag is set if item is text, clear if its an image |
| COMMSEQ | 0004 | Set if a command key is supplied for the item |
| MENUTOGGLE | 0008 | Toggles the checkmark when selected |
| ITEMENABLED | 0010 | Set to enable this menu item's messages |
| HIGHIMAGE | 0000 | Displays user's select image when selected |
| HIGHCOMP | 0040 | Highlights selected item by complementing it |
| HIGHBOX | 0080 | Highlights selected item with a box border |
| HIGHNONE | 00C0 | No highlighting at all |

| Name | Hexadecimal Value | Description |
|---|---|---|
| CHECKED | 0100 | If CHECKIT is specified, Intuition sets this when item is selected |
| ISDRAWN | 1000 | Set by Intuition if subitems shown |
| HIGHITEM | 2000 | Set by Intuition if item is highlighted |
| MENUTOGGLED | 4000 | Set by Intuition if item already toggled |

Once again, a program can combine these using the ! (logical OR) assembler directive. Use the examples and experiment with other combinations of the flags, and try resetting the flags for a second menu.

**The MUTUALEXCLUDE bits.** You may make a menu even more intelligent by proper use of the MUTUALEXCLUDE feature for each MENUITEM. MUTUALEXCLUDE is used to indicate that selecting a menu item automatically deselects another menu item. This is like the buttons on a car radio. If you push a button to select a station, the old button gets "popped" back out.

A long word (32 bits) is used to specify a MUTUALEXCLUDE pattern. Two attribute menu items that have different MUTUALEXCLUDE fields will automatically deselect each other. For example, lets say your writing a printing program. In one menu, you want two menu items, "Letter Quality" and "Draft". Since printing in draft and letter quality mode are exclusive of each other, you can indicate this with their MUTUALEXCLUDE flags. Set a MUTUALEXCLUDE flag of $00 for the "Letter Quality" menu item and a flag of $01 for the "Draft" menu item. Selecting "Draft" will now automatically deselect "Letter Quality", and vice versa.

When MAKEAMENU is called, one parameter supplied is a pointer to a list of MUTUALEXCLUDE values for the associated list of menu items. MAKEAMENU expects you to declare the MUTUALEXCLUDE values with a labeled DC.B string of bytes. Examine the code examples for more instances of how the MUTUALEXCLUDE feature is utilized.

## The Command Key Feature

A command key selects a menu item, when pressed while holding down one of the AMIGA keys. Each menu item may be selected by a keypress, or with the mouse, if the programmer allows for this option by including certain information in the MENUITEM structure. The MENUITEM must have its COMMSEQ flag set to a value of 1, and a command key byte must be supplied. The user can then activate that menu item by pressing an AMIGA key and the specified command key together.

The code examples below utilize a string of byte values for the command keys associated with a list of menu items. When MAKEAMENU is called, one of the parameters supplied is the pointer to your list of command key definitions for that menu item list. Declare them with a labeled DC.B string of characters (see the examples).

Figure 18-1 may help you to understand the mutual exclude and command key features.

**Figure 18-1. Screen, Window, Menu with Menu Items, Mutual Excludes, and Command Keys**

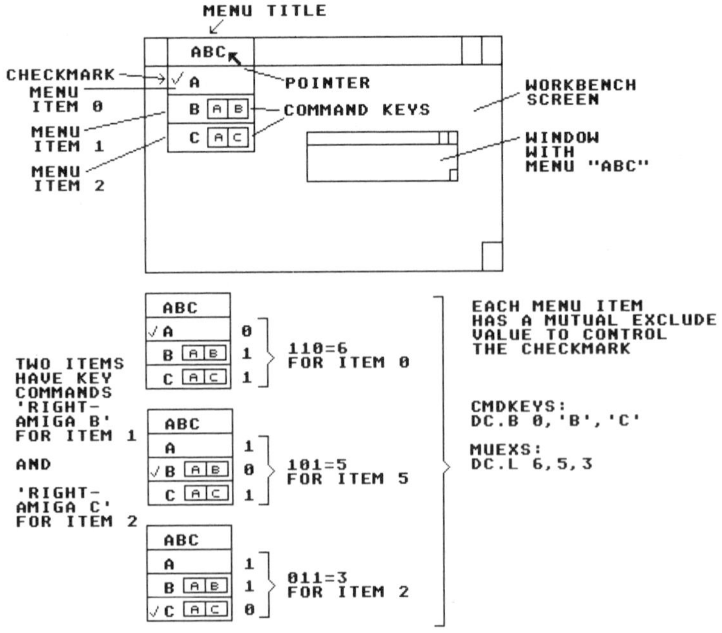

**The CREATEMENU subroutine.** This routine's purpose is to fill in the MENU structure allocated by MAKEAMENU. It's possible to adjust the flags field and variables relating to position, prior to this call, which finishes the process that creates the menu.

**MENU structure flags.** You can program a flag bit to enable a menu, or you can examine the flag bit to see if the menu is enabled. This flag bit can be manipulated in program code and also by Intuition. The other flag bit is set by Intuition if the menu is being shown on the screen. Here is a list of the flag bits and their values and descriptions:

| **Flag Bit** | **Bit Value** | **Description** |
|---|---|---|
| MENUENABLED | $0001 | Read/write flag, indicates or sets whether MENU is on or off |
| MIDRAWN | 0004 | Set by Intuition if menu is showing |

The full Menu Structure is defined in Table 18-3.

**Table 18-3. Intuition MENU Structure**

**Symbol: MENU**
**Size: 30 bytes ($1D bytes)**

| *Field Size* | *Name* | *Offset* | *Description* |
|---|---|---|---|
| Long | MENU.NEXT | 0 | Pointer to next MENU structure |
| Word | MENU.LEFTEDGE | 4 | Number of pixels from left edge |
| Word | MENU.TOPEDGE | 6 | Number of pixels from top edge |
| Word | MENU.WIDTH | 8 | Number of pixels wide |
| Word | MENU.HEIGHT | 10 | Height of one menu item |
| Word | MENU.FLAGS | 12 | Menu enabled, menu item drawn |
| Long | MENU.MENUNAME | 14 | Pointer to null-terminated title text |
| Long | MENU.FIRSTITEM | 18 | Pointer to first MENUITEM structure |
| Word | MENU.JAZZX | 22 | System use only |
| Word | MENU.JAZZY | 24 | System use only |
| Word | MENU.BEATX | 26 | System use only |
| Word | MENU.BEATY | 28 | System use only |

The MENU1.ASM program (Listing 18-2) shows a three-item menu added to a window. The first two items are dummies with no effect, and the last one is a QUIT option, which has the same effect in the program as clicking on the CLOSEWINDOW gadget. Notice once again how the IDCMP communications loop uses its analysis of the MENUPICK message to get the *class* (menu and menu item numbers). The MENUEVENT subroutine is a short one that extracts the combined numbers and provides them back to the program, separately, in registers D0 and D1. MENU2.ASM is a program example showing two complete multiitem menus. The code demonstrates how they become linked into a unified menu for the program.

**The MENUEVENT subroutine.** This routine is provided to extract the menu number, menu item number, and (if you use them) subitem number in separate registers.

The INTUIMESSAGE that occurs (when the MENUPICK IDCMP flag on an open window is set) combines all the numbers into one. They reside in three groups of five bits each. There can be up to 32 of them. The MENUEVENT subroutine separates these values for use by the program code. The program example shows how it is used.

NOTE: In order to receive messages about menu selections, you must include the MENUPICK flag bit in your windows IDCMP Port.

## Removing a Menu

When a program needs to switch menus or remove a menu from the title bar, a call is made to CLEARMENUSTRIP, an Intuition library function. You must call this function before closing any window that has a menu attached.

The listings below, MENU1.ASM and MENU2.ASM, show how to clear a menu before closing a window. To replace one menu entirely with another, use CLEARMENUSTRIP to eliminate the first menu before creating and attaching the new menu.

To round out this introduction to Intuition menus, Listing 18-3 contains an example of a menu strip with two menus. Each MENU structure has a set of menu items and its own title. Prior to calling SETMENUSTRIP in the Intuition library, insure that the first MENU structure points to the next MENU structure: Place the address of the second MENU structure in the NEXT field of the first. Then, SETMENUSTRIP makes both menus available at once.

### Listing 18-3. MENU2.ASM

Example program with two menus of three items each.

```
;MENU2.ASM BY DANIEL WOLF
;COPYRIGHT 1987 BY COMPUTE! PUBLICATIONS
;09/10/87

 BRA _START

DOS EQU 1
INT EQU 1
GFX EQU 1

MEN EQU 1
TXT EQU 1
WIN EQU 1

 INCLUDE "HEADER"

MAIN
 TST.L ENDFROMWB             ;IF INITIATED FROM WB,  THEN NO ANNOUNCEMENTS YET!
 BNE.S _BUILDAWINDOW
FROMUSER
 DOSPRINT STDOUT,#MYMESSAGE ;IF INITIATED FROM CLI, THEN OUTPUT TITLE MESSAGE
 ZERO D0
 MOVEA.L COMMAND,A0          ;PUT ADDRESS OF COMMAND LINE IN A0
 CMPI.B #'?',(A0)            ;IF FIRST CHARACTER IS ? THEN
 BNE.S _BUILDAWINDOW
 BRA USAGE                   ;PRINT OUT INSTRUCTIONS AND QUIT

_BUILDAWINDOW
 MAKEWIN #MYWINDOWTITLE,40,15,500,160,ERROR
 MOVE.L D0,WINDOW            ;WINDOW OPENED HAS ITS POINTER IN D0

 MOVE.L D0,A0                ;PUT WINDOW POINTER IN A0
 BSR _CLEARWINDOW            ;CLEAR THE WINDOW, NO COLOR JUST BACKGROUND

    ;*** NOW MAKE TWO MENUS USING MACROS FROM MENUS.ASM SUPPORT FILE ***

_BUILDMENU
 MITEMLIST MYITEM0,MYITEM1,MYITEM2,0,0,0,0,0,2
 MAKEMEN MYCMDKEYS,MYMUEXES,MYMENUTITLE,DONE
 MOVE.L D1,_THISMENU
 MOVE.L #5,D0
 MOVE.W #120,D1
 BSR CREATEMENU
```

```
_BUILDMENU2
 MITEMLIST MYITEMØ2,MYITEM12,Ø,Ø,Ø,Ø,Ø,Ø,1
 MAKEMEN MYCMDKEYS,MYMUEXES,MYMENUTITLE2,DONE
 MOVE.L D1,_THISMENU2
 MOVE.W #125,DØ           ;LEFEDGE  FOR THIS MENU (MOVED OVER FOR FIRST MENU)
 MOVE.W #12Ø,D1           ;WIDTH    FOR THIS MENU
 BSR CREATEMENU

_LINKMENUS
 MOVEA.L _THISMENU,AØ
 MOVE.L _THISMENU2,DØ
 MOVE.L DØ,(AØ)           ;PUT _THISMENU2 AS POINTER TO 'NEXT' MENU

_MENUATTACH
 MOVE.L WINDOW,AØ          ;SUPPLY POINTER TO WINDOW  IN AØ
 MOVE.L _THISMENU,A1       ;SUPPLY POINTER TO MENU #Ø IN A1
 INTLIB SETMENUSTRIP       ;AND ATTACH THE MENU TO THE WINDOW

LOOP
 MOVE.L WINDOW,AØ
 MOVE.L #$FFFF,DØ          ;WAKE UP THE WHOLE MENU NOW
 INTLIB ONMENU
 MOVE.L WINDOW,AØ
 MOVE.L WW.USERPORT(AØ),AØ  ;LISTEN TO PORT ATTACHED TO THIS WINDOW
 SYSLIB WAITPORT           ;WAIT FOR A SPECIFIED MESSAGE TO ARRIVE
 MOVE.L WINDOW,AØ
 MOVE.L WW.USERPORT(AØ),AØ
 SYSLIB GETMSG             ;MESSAGE HAS ARRIVED WITHIN SPECIFICATIONS
 TST.L DØ                  ;POINTER TO INTUIMESSAGE COMES BACK IN DØ
 BEQ RELOOP                ;NO MESSAGE THERE, SO LOOP
 MOVE.L DØ,A1              ;POINTER TO INTUIMESSAGE CAME BACK, USE IN A1
 MOVE.L IM.CLASS(A1),D2    ;CLOSEWINDOW AND MENUPIC MESSAGES APPEAR HERE
 MOVE.W IM.CODE(A1),D3     ;MENU AND MENUITEM APPEAR HERE
 MOVE.W IM.QUALIFIER(A1),D4 ;KEYS APPEAR HERE
 SYSLIB REPLYMSG           ;QUICK, SEND MESSAGE BACK NOW!

 CMP.L #CLOSEWINDOW,D2
 BEQ DONE                  ;IF ITS A CLOSEWINDOW MESSAGE, THEN DO SO...
 CMP.L #MENUPICK,D2
 BNE RELOOP                ;THIS ISN'T A CLOSE OR A MENUPICK, SO LOOP
 MOVEQ.L #Ø,DØ
 MOVE.W D3,DØ              ;SETUP MENUCODE IN DØ FOR THIS SUBROUTINE
 BSR MENUEVENT
 TST.W DØ                  ;DØ IS THE MENU     NUMBER
 BNE HANDLEMENU1           ;IF THIS ISN'T MENU #Ø, THEN CHECK IF MENU #1
 CMPI.W #2,D1              ;D1 IS THE MENUITEM NUMBER, SEE IF D1 = 2
 BEQ DONE                  ;IF MENUITEM = 2 THEN    *QUIT*
 CMPI.W #1,D1              ;COMPARE IMMEDIATE, SEE IF D1 = 1
 BEQ.S DOITEM1_MENUØ       ;IF MENUITEM = 1 THEN DO *ITEM1* MENUØ
 CMPI.W #Ø,D1              ;COMPARE IMMEDIATE, SEE IF D1 = Ø
 BEQ.S DOITEMØ_MENUØ       ;IF MENUITEM = Ø THEN DO *ITEMØ* MENUØ
 BRA.S RELOOP              ;IF NONE OF ABOVE, THEN LOOP
DOITEM1_MENUØ
 BSR MENUØITEM1
 BRA.S RELOOP
DOITEMØ_MENUØ
 BSR MENUØITEMØ
 BRA.S RELOOP

HANDLEMENU1                ;INTERCEPT IF MENU = 1
 CMPI.W #Ø,D1
 BEQ DOITEMØ_MENU1         ;SEE IF MENUITEM = Ø
 CMPI.W #1,D1
 BEQ DOITEM1_MENU1         ;SEE IF MENUITEM = 1
 BRA.S RELOOP
DOITEMØ_MENU1
 BSR MENU1ITEMØ
 BRA.S RELOOP
DOITEM1_MENU1
 BSR MENU1ITEM1


RELOOP
 BRA LOOP                  ;RETURN TO TOP OF LOOP AND SCAN FOR MESSAGES
```

```
DONE                         ;NOW CLEAN UP WINDOW AND EXIT
 MOVE.L WINDOW,DØ
 BEQ.S QUIT
 MOVE.L DØ,AØ
 INTLIB CLEARMENUSTRIP       ;MUST CLEAR THE MENU PRIOR TO CLOSING WINDOW
QUIT
 ZERO DØ
 PUSHREG DØ
 MOVE.L WINDOW,DØ
 BEQ.S 1$                  ; 1$ IS A LOCAL LABEL   A NUMBER$ LABEL IS LOCAL
 MOVE.L DØ,AØ              ; MEANING IT CAN BE USED BETWEEN TWO REGULAR LABELS
 INTLIB CLOSEWINDOW        ; MEANING THE SAME LABEL CAN BE USED MANY TIMES
1$                         ; BUT EACH TIME WITH A DIFFERENT 'LOCAL' MEANING
 PULLREG DØ
QUITNOW
 RTS

ERROR
 DOSPRINT STDOUT,#ERRORTEXT   ;USING DOS TO PRINT MESSAGE TO CLI WINDOW
 MOVE.L #21,DØ
 BRA QUITNOW

USAGE
 DOSPRINT STDOUT,#USAGETEXT   ;USING DOS TO PRINT MESSAGE TO CLI WINDOW
 BRA DONE

MENUØITEM1
 MOVE.L WINDOW,AØ
 BSR _CLEARWINDOW            ;CLEAR THE WINDOW, NO COLOR JUST BACKGROUND
 RTS

MENUØITEMØ                   ;FILL WITH COLOR
 MOVE.L WINDOW,AØ            ;PUT WINDOW POINTER IN AØ
 MOVE.L #3,DØ                ;COLOR REGISTER SELECTION (Ø-3 ON WORKBENCH)
 BSR _FILLWINDOW             ;FILL THE WINDOW
 RTS

MENU1ITEMØ
 RTS
MENU1ITEM1
 RTS

MYWINDOWTITLE
 DC.B ' Menu2  by D. Wolf ',Ø
 EVENPC
USAGETEXT
 DC.B 'Usage: Menu2',1Ø,Ø
 EVENPC
ERRORTEXT
 DC.B 1Ø,'Sorry, cannot open window ',1Ø,Ø
 EVENPC
MYMESSAGE
 DC.B 1Ø,'Menu2 by Daniel Wolf Copyright 1987 by Compute! Publications ',1Ø,Ø
 EVENPC

WINDOW DC.L Ø                   ;POINTER TO WINDOW STRUCTURE
RP DC.L Ø                       ;POINTER TO WINDOW'S RASTPORT STRUCTURE
_THISMENU
 DC.L Ø                         ;POINTER TO 'FIRST'  MENU STRUCTURE
_THISMENU2
 DC.L Ø                         ;POINTER TO 'SECOND' MENU STRUCTURE
MYMENUTITLE
 DC.B 'MENU EXAMPLE',Ø          ;TEXT FOR MENU TITLE
 EVENPC
MYITEMØ
 DC.B '    ITEM A   ',Ø         ;TEXT FOR FIRST MENUITEM, WITH ROOM FOR CHKMARK
 EVENPC
MYITEM1
 DC.B '    ITEM B   ',Ø         ;TEXT FOR SECOND MENUITEM
 EVENPC
MYITEM2
 DC.B '    QUIT     ',Ø         ;TEXT FOR THIRD MENUITEM
 EVENPC
MYCMDKEYS
 DC.B 'ABQ'                     ;LIST OF 'COMMSEQ' MENU ALTERNATE COMMAND KEYS
 EVENPC
```

```
MYMUEXES                              ;LIST OF MUTUAL-EXCLUDE VALUES TO RESTRICT
 DC.L 6,5,Ø                           ;CHECKMARK TO ONE ITEM AT A TIME
 EVENPC

MYMENUTITLE2
 DC.B ' EXAMPLE2 ',Ø                  ;TEXT FOR MENU TITLE
 EVENPC
MYITEMØ2
 DC.B '   HELLO    ',Ø                 ;TEXT FOR FIRST MENUITEM, WITH ROOM FOR CHKMARK
 EVENPC
MYITEM12
 DC.B '   GOODBYE  ',Ø                 ;TEXT FOR SECOND MENUITEM
 EVENPC
MYCMDKEYS2
 DC.B 'HG'                             ;LIST OF 'COMMSEQ' MENU ALTERNATE COMMAND KEYS
 EVENPC
MYMUEXES2                              ;LIST OF MUTUAL-EXCLUDE VALUES TO RESTRICT
 DC.L 2,1                              ;CHECKMARK TO ONE ITEM AT A TIME

_THISFONTHITE
 DC.W 9
 END
```

# CHAPTER 19
# Intuition Gadgets

The Intuition gadget system provides many ways to communicate with an application. Gadgets are dedicated regions of windows that act like buttons, knobs, slide controls, and switches when the mouse is clicked in them.

You're probably familiar with some of the built-in window gadgets like the drag bar, sizing gadget, close gadget, and front/back gadgets. Programmable gadgets can have special imagery, coloring, or text to attract the user's attention and explain their function.

Gadgets can substitute for menus. Sometimes they make options more prominent to the user than a menu would.

Producing effective gadgets takes planning and knowledge of the Intuition GADGET structure. The GADGET structure is linked to text, border outlines, icon-like imagery, and other substructures by way of pointers.

## Types of Gadgets

There are four types of gadgets:

- Boolean gadgets
- String gadgets
- Proportional gadgets
- Integer gadgets

The integer gadget is actually a special type of string gadget.

**Boolean gadget.** The Boolean gadget acts like an on/off switch. The user can activate it and deactivate it by clicking the left mouse button while the pointer is touching the gadget. The GADGET structure should have flags set to communicate the event to the application. If these flags are set, the application should test for receipt of GADGETUP and GADGETDOWN messages.

**String gadget.** The string gadget allows the user to edit and enter a text string. The text string can provide user input for file names, numerical values, and so on. When the amount of text input needed from the user, by a program, is limited, string gadgets provide a handy text entry for the user.

**Integer gadget.** The integer gadget allows the user to edit and enter a numerical whole-number value 0–65535 in a way similar to the string gadget. It's not covered specifically in the programs in this book.

**Proportional gadget.** The proportional gadget plays the role of a knob or variable slide control, and lets a user set a variable's value by manipulating the gadget's control knob with the mouse.

Proportional gadgets can have either vertical or horizontal slider bars, or a combination of both. The value represented by the position of the proportional gadget can be read by the application program. This, in turn, allows the program to set the position of the slider bar. Proportional gadgets are often used with windows in which only a portion of some available information is displayed. The slider bar is used to scroll, or otherwise move around, the larger information base and select a portion to appear in the window.

Proportional gadgets also have a mode in which they're appropriately resized and repositioned when the window size is changed by the user.

## The GADGET Structure

Table 19-1 shows the Intuition GADGET structure, its field names, and their numerical equivalents. It's similar, in some respects, to the MENU structure. A NEXT field points to the next GADGET structure for the window. It also contains LEFTEDGE, TOPEDGE, WIDTH, and HEIGHT fields for positioning the gadget within the window. There are fields for pointers to an INTUITEXT structure (if there is text in the gadget), the unselected (off) imagery (a BORDER structure or an IMAGE structure), and the gadget's selected (on) imagery. If the gadget is a string or proportional gadget, the SPECIALINFO field contains the address of a STRINGINFO structure or PROPINFO structure, as well (see below).

**Table 19-1. Intuition GADGET structure**

**Symbol: GADG**
**Size: 44 Bytes ($2C)**

| *Field Size* | *Name* | *Offset* | *Description* |
|---|---|---|---|
| Long | GADG.NEXTGADGET | 0 | Pointer to next GADGET structure |
| Word | GADG.LEFTEDGE | 4 | Number of pixels from left edge |
| Word | GADG.TOPEDGE | 6 | Number of pixels from top edge |
| Word | GADG.WIDTH | 8 | Number of pixels wide |
| Word | GADG.HEIGHT | 10 | Number of pixels high |
| Word | GADG.FLAGS | 12 | Highlighting and rendering flags |
| Word | GADG.ACTIVATION | 14 | Event communication flags |
| Word | GADG.TYPE | 16 | Boolean, string, prop, or integer |
| Long | GADG.RENDER | 18 | Pointer to custom image or border |
| Long | GADG.SELECTRENDER | 22 | Pointer to custom select image/border |
| Long | GADG.GADGETTEXT | 26 | Pointer to INTUITEXT for gadget |
| Long | GADG.MUTUALEXCLUDE | 30 | Mutual excludes for gadget activation |
| Long | GADG.SPECIALINFO | 34 | Pointer to special information |
| Word | GADG.GADGETID | 38 | User-definable data word |
| Long | GADG.USERDATA | 40 | Pointer to user-definable data area |

One gadget may need GADGET, INTUITEXT, IMAGE, BORDER, STRINGINFO and/or PROPINFO structures, all properly filled and linked by pointers. Like menus, this complexity can make programming with gadgets very tedious if the structure declarations are all in the source code.

It would be handy to have a routine that automatically builds a Boolean gadget with a line border, given only a labeled, null-terminated text string. For string and proportional gadgets, it would be handy to have routines that create and link all the necessary structures.

Later in this chapter, these utility routines will be introduced.

**Gadget FLAGS.** The individual bits of the FLAGS field in the GADGET structure, control its highlighting and position. Table 19-2 lists the names of these flags, their hexadecimal values, and functional descriptions.

**Table 19-2. Gadget FLAGS**

| Name | Hexadecimal Value | Description |
|---|---|---|
| GADGHCOMP | 0000 | Complements gadget when activated |
| GADGHBOX | 0001 | Draws box around gadget when activated |
| GADGHIMAGE | 0002 | Draws select render gadget image when activated |
| GADGHNONE | 0003 | No highlighting of activated gadget |
| GADGIMAGE | 0004 | Set if gadget is image, clear if border |
| GRELBOTTOM | 0008 | Makes gadget top edge relative to window bottom |
| GRELRIGHT | 0010 | Makes gadget left edge relative to window right |
| GRELWIDTH | 0020 | Makes gadget width relative to window width |
| GRELHEIGHT | 0040 | Makes gadget height relative to window height |
| SELECTED | 0080 | Turns gadget on when it first appears |
| GADGDISABLED | 0100 | Disables gadget selection |

**Gadget ACTIVATION flags.** The bits of the field in the GADGET structure provide for fine control of the user's interaction with a gadget. Table 19-3 lists the names, values, and descriptions of the gadget ACTIVATION flags.

**Table 19-3. Gadget ACTIVATION Flags**

| Name | Hexadecimal Value | Description |
|---|---|---|
| RELVERIFY | 0001 | Verifies that pointer was over gadget when button was released |
| GADGIMMEDIATE | 0002 | Sends gadget activated message to IDCMP |
| ENDGADGET | 0004 | Used in requester-based gadgets to end requester |
| FOLLOWMOUSE | 0008 | Gets continuous mouse position messages |
| RIGHTBORDER | 0010 | Adjusts size of windows right border to accommodate your gadget |

| Name | Hexadecimal Value | Description |
|---|---|---|
| LEFTBORDER | 0020 | Adjusts size of windows left border to accommodate your gadget |
| TOPBORDER | 0040 | Adjusts size of windows top border to accommodate your gadget |
| BOTTOMBORDER | 0080 | Adjusts size of windows bottom border to accommodate your gadget |
| TOGGLESELECT | 0100 | Sets gadget to on/off with successive clicks |
| STRINGCENTER | 0200 | Centers a string gadget in its region |
| STRINGRIGHT | 0400 | Right justifies a string gadget |
| LONGINT | 0800 | Permits entry of a long integer into a string |
| ALTKEYMAP | 1000 | String uses an alternate Amiga keymap |

This chapter provides a set of support-code subroutines and macros to simplify gadget programming. This utility is named GADGETS.ASM. It can be found in Listing 19-1. Like the include files introduced in the previous chapters, use EMACS or your favorite text editor to type in the file and save it with the following name on your DEV disk:

DEV:RAMIT/INCLUDES/GADGETS.ASM

### Listing 19-1. GADGETS.ASM

Support subroutines and macros for gadget programming.

```
;******************************* GADGETS.ASM BY DANIEL WOLF
;COPYRIGHT 1987 BY COMPUTE! BOOKS
;03/21/87

;GADGET SUPPORT ROUTINES FOR BOOLEAN, STRING, AND PROPORTIONAL TYPES

SIZE.BBORDER EQU 40              ;SPECIFIC SIZE OF A 4-POINT BORDER W/COORDS
BB.BUTTONLINES EQU 16            ;#BYTES FOR 4 POINT PAIRS

;NEWPGADG MACRO

NEWSGADG MACRO
 LEA \1,A0
 LEA \2,A1
 MOVE.W #\3,D4
 MOVE.W #\4,D5
 BSR MAKEASTRINGADGET
 MOVE.L \5,A0
 MOVE.L D0,A1
 BSR ADDNEWGADG
 ENDM

NEWBGADG MACRO
 LEA \1,A1
 MOVE.W #\2,D4
 MOVE.W #\3,D5
 BSR MAKEAGADGET
 MOVE.L \4,A0
 MOVE.L D0,A1
```

```
 BSR ADDNEWGADG
 ENDM

ADDNEWGADG
 ZERO DØ
 MOVE.W #-1,DØ
 INTLIB ADDGADGET
 MOVE.L _THISGADGET,DØ
 RTS

MAKEAGADGET ;SUBROUTINE ENTER WITH D4=LEFT,D5=TOP,D6=WID,D7=HEIGHT
 ;                                  A1=POINTER TO GADGET TEXT

 MOVE.L A1,_THISGTEXT
 REMEMBERPUBMEM REMEMBERKEY,#SIZE.BBORDER ;ALLOCATE ENOUGH FOR A BORDER STRUCT
 TST.L DØ                                 ;WHICH INCLUDES 4 COORDINATES
 BEQ ERR_MAKEAGADGETMEM
 MOVE.L DØ,_THISBBORDER                  ;JUST SAVE THE POINTER FOR NOW
 REMEMBERPUBMEM REMEMBERKEY,#SIZE.IT     ;REMEMBER MEM FOR INTUITEXT STRUCT
 TST.L DØ
 BEQ ERR_MAKEAGADGETMEM
 MOVE.L DØ,_THISGITEXT
 MOVE.L DØ,AØ                            ;AØ=POINTER TO ALLOCATED ITEXT MEM
 MOVE.L _THISGTEXT,A1                    ;A1=POINTER TO NULL-TERMINATED TEXT
 BSR CREATETEXT                          ;NOW SETUP THE INTUITEXT STRUCT
 INTLIB INTUITEXTLENGTH
 MOVEA.L _THISBBORDER,AØ                 ;USE LENGTH AND HEIGHT TO SET
 ADDA.L #SIZE.BORD,AØ                    ;ADD 16 TO GET TO THE BORDER COORDS
 ADDI.W #4,DØ
 BCLR.L #Ø,DØ
 MOVE.W DØ,4(AØ)                         ;THE BORDER COORDINATES
 MOVE.W DØ,8(AØ)
 MOVE.W DØ,D6
 MOVE.W _THISFONTHITE,D7                 ;ADD SOME ROOM TO THE BORDER,
 ADDI.W #4,D7                            ;ENOUGH FOR 2 PIXELS ABOVE AND BELOW
 BCLR.L #Ø,D7                            ;MAKE IT AN EVEN NUMBER
 MOVE.W D7,1Ø(AØ)                        ;THE TEXT IN THE GADGET
 MOVE.W D7,14(AØ)                        ;AND ADD OTHER COORDS IN THE BORDER
 MOVE.W #-1,DØ
 CMP.W #STRGADGET,_THISGTYPE
 BNE.S BORDERMINONE
 MOVE.W #-5,DØ
BORDERMINONE
 MOVE.W DØ,2(AØ)
 MOVE.W DØ,6(AØ)
 MOVE.W DØ,18(AØ)
 MOVE.W DØ,(AØ)
 MOVE.W DØ,12(AØ)
 MOVE.W DØ,16(AØ)
 MOVEA.L _THISBBORDER,A1                 ;NOW FILL OUT THE BORDER STRUCT
 MOVE.L AØ,BORD.XY(A1)
 MOVE.B #JAM1,BORD.DRAWMODE(A1)
 MOVE.B #1,BORD.FRONTPEN(A1)
 MOVE.B #5,BORD.COUNT(A1)
_JUSTTHEGADGET
 REMEMBERCHIPMEM REMEMBERKEY,#SIZE.GADG  ;REMEMBER MEM FOR GADGET STRUCT
 TST.L DØ
 BEQ ERR_MAKEAGADGETMEM
 MOVE.L DØ,_THISGADGET                   ;HANG ON TO THIS POINTER
 MOVE.L DØ,AØ                            ;POINTER TO THIS GADGET IN AØ
 MOVE.W D4,GADG.LEFTEDGE(AØ)
 MOVE.W D5,GADG.TOPEDGE(AØ)
 MOVE.W D6,GADG.WIDTH(AØ)
 MOVE.W D7,GADG.HEIGHT(AØ)               ;NOW FILL UP THE GADGET STRUCTURE
 MOVE.W _THISGTYPE,GADG.TYPE(AØ)         ;SET THE GADGET TYPE PRIOR TO ENTRY
 MOVE.W _THISGACTIV,GADG.ACTIVATION(AØ)  ;SET THE ACTIVATION FLAGS
 MOVE.L _THISGITEXT,GADG.TEXT(AØ)        ;POINTER TO INTUITEXT FOR GADGET
 MOVE.W _THISGFLAGS,GADG.FLAGS(AØ)       ;SET FLAGS PRIOR TO ENTRY
 MOVE.L _THISBBORDER,GADG.RENDER(AØ)     ;CORRECT LATER IF PROP GADGET
 ZERO D1                                 ;NO ERROR, GADGET PTR IN DØ
 MOVE.L _THISGADGET,DØ
 RTS

ERR_MAKEAGADGETMEM
 MOVE.L #CANTALLOCMEM,D1                 ;MOVE ERROR CODE TO D1
 ZERO DØ
 RTS
```

```
ERR_MAKEAGADGET
 MOVE.L #CANTALLOCMEM,D1                    ;MOVE ERROR CODE TO D1 (UPICKIT)
 ZERO DØ
 RTS

MAKEASTRINGADGET                             ;STRING GADGET ROUTINE
 MOVE.W #STRGADGET,_THISGTYPE
 MOVE.L AØ,_THISGBUFFER                      ;PTR TO NULL-TERMINATED STRING
 MOVE.L A1,_THISGUNDOBUF                     ;PTR TO A UNIVERSAL UNDO BUFFER
 REMEMBERPUBMEM REMEMBERKEY,#SIZE.SI
 TST.L DØ
 BEQ ERR_MAKEAGADGETMEM
 MOVE.L DØ,AØ                                ;NOW FILL IN THE STRINGINFO
 MOVE.L DØ,_THISGSTRINGINFO
 MOVE.L _THISGBUFFER,SI.BUFFER(AØ)
 MOVE.L _THISGUNDOBUF,SI.UNDOBUFFER(AØ)
 MOVE.W #1,SI.BUFFERPOS(AØ)
 MOVE.W #80,SI.MAXCHARS(AØ)
 LEA SIZESTRING,A1                           ;USE THE SIZING STRING BELOW
 BSR MAKEAGADGET
 MOVE.L _THISGSTRINGINFO,GADG.SPECIALINFO(AØ)
 MOVE.W #BOOLGADGET,_THISGTYPE               ;RESET DEFAULT BOOLEAN TYPE
 RTS

MAKEAPROPGADGET                                ;PROPORTIONAL GADGET ROUTINE
 MOVE.W #PROPGADGET,_THISGTYPE
 REMEMBERCHIPMEM REMEMBERKEY,#SIZE.IMAG        ;ALLOCATE A IMAGE STRUCTURE
 TST.L DØ                                      ;THIS IS A NECESSARY FORMALITY
 BEQ ERR_MAKEAGADGETMEM                        ;EVEN WITH THE AUTOKNOB!!!!!!!!
 MOVE.L DØ,_THISGIMAGE
 REMEMBERCHIPMEM REMEMBERKEY,#SIZE.PI          ;ALLOCATE A PROPINFO STRUCTURE
 TST.L DØ
 BEQ ERR_MAKEAGADGETMEM
 MOVE.L DØ,AØ                                  ;NOW FILL IN THE PROPINFO
 MOVE.L DØ,_THISGPROPINFO
 MOVE.W #AUTOKNOB!FREEHORIZ,PI.FLAGS(AØ)       ;DEFAULT IS HORIZONTAL
 CMP.B #'V',D3                                 ;SET BY CALLING PROGRAM FOR VERT
 BNE.S ITSHORIZONTAL
 MOVE.W #$8000,PI.VERTPOT(AØ)                  ;HALF MAX (MIDDLE OF RANGE)
 MOVE.W #$1000,PI.VERTBODY(AØ)                 ;THIN BODY (1000/FFFF = 1/16)
 MOVE.W #AUTOKNOB!FREEVERT,PI.FLAGS(AØ)        ;IF V PARAMETER, SET FREEVERT FLAG
ITSHORIZONTAL
 MOVE.W #$8000,PI.HORIZPOT(AØ)                 ;HALF MAX (MIDDLE OF RANGE)
 MOVE.W #$1000,PI.HORIZBODY(AØ)                ;THIN BODY (ABOUT 1/16)

 BSR _JUSTTHEGADGET                            ;NOW THE GADGET STRUCTURE
 MOVE.L _THISGADGET,DØ
 ZERO D1
 MOVE.L _THISGIMAGE,GADG.RENDER(AØ)
 MOVE.L #Ø,GADG.TEXT(AØ)                       ;AND LINK TO THE PROPINFO
 MOVE.L _THISGPROPINFO,GADG.SPECIALINFO(AØ) ;YOU CAN CONTROL SIZE, ETC.
ENDMAKEPROPGADG
 MOVE.W #BOOLGADGET,_THISGTYPE                 ;RESET BOOLEAN DEFAULT TYPE
 RTS

_THISGADGET
 DC.L Ø                                        ;STORAGE FOR POINTER TO GADGET
_THISGACTIV
 DC.W STRINGCENTER!RELVERIFY!GADGIMMEDIATE
                                            ;LET US KNOW IF GADGET HIT!
_THISGFLAGS
 DC.W GADGHCOMP                                ;HIGHLIGHT BY COMPLEMENTING
_THISGTYPE
 DC.W BOOLGADGET                               ;ITS BOOLEAN TYPE (SWITCH)
_THISGTEXT
 DC.L Ø                                        ;TEXT POINTER FOR GADGET
_THISGITEXT
 DC.L Ø                                        ;POINTER TO INTUITEXT FOR GADGET
_THISBBORDER
 DC.L Ø                                        ;POINTER TO BORDER FOR GADGET
SIZESTRING
 DC.B '                                          ',Ø;BLANK SIZING STRING
 EVENPC

_THISGSTRINGINFO    ;POINTER TO STRINGINFO STRUCTURE FOR STRING GADGET
 DC.L Ø
_THISGBUFFER        ;TEXT BUFFER FOR STRING GADGET
 DC.L Ø
```

```
_THISGUNDOBUF       ;UNIVERSAL UNDO-BUFFER FOR ALL STRING GADGETS IN WINDOW
 DC.L Ø
_THISGIMAGE         ;POINTER TO IMAGE FOR GADGET (MUST BE HERE, NOT USED!)
 DC.L Ø
_THISGPROPINFO      ;POINTER TO PROPINFO STRUCTURE FOR PROP GADGET
 DC.L Ø

;_BUTTONBORDER                          ;SAMPLE OF THE BORDER STRUCTURE
; DC.W Ø                                ;LEFTEDGE JUST OUTSIDE GADGET
; DC.W Ø                                ;TOPEDGE JUST OUTSIDE GADGET
; DC.B 1                                ;FRONTPEN
; DC.B Ø                                ;BACKPEN
; DC.B JAM1                             ;DRAWMODE
; DC.B 5                                ;# OF POINTS IN COORDINATE LIST
; DC.L _BUTTONLINES                     ;POINTER TO COORDINATE LIST
; DC.L Ø                                ;NEXT BORDER
;_BUTTONLINES
; DC.W Ø,-1,2Ø,-1,2Ø,1Ø,Ø,1Ø,Ø,-1      ;XØ,YØ  X1,Y1  X2,Y2  X3,Y3  .....
```

## Boolean Gadgets

The MAKEAGADGET routine in GADGETS.ASM helps create Boolean gadgets for your windows. The calling program only provides text for the gadgets. MAKEAGADGET first allocates a BORDER structure and an INTUITEXT structure for the text imagery used in the gadget. An arithmetic section uses the current font height and a call to INTUITEXTLENGTH to get size data for the gadget, and then creates a list of border coordinates for the BORDER structure. Finally, a GADGET structure is allocated and filled with appropriate default values. Those defaults for the Boolean gadgets are:

| | |
|---|---|
| GADGHCOMP | Mode for gadget highlighting |
| BOOLGADGET | Type for the gadget |
| TOGGLESELECT | Mode for gadget activation |

Pointer fields are filled with addresses of the INTUITEXT and BORDER structures.

Once the Boolean gadget has been created (using the supplied text) two additional calls are required to make it visible and usable.

- First, a call to ADDGADGET (INTLIB ADDGADGET) is made to place the GADGET structure on a list of GADGET structures for this window. The call to ADDGADGET specifies −1 as the list position to insure that the gadget is added to the top of the list.
- Then, once all gadgets have been made and added to the list, a call is made to REFRESHGADGETS. All the gadgets will appear and become usable at once.

The programs accompanying this section are called BOOLGADGET1 and BOOLGADGET2 (Listings 19-2 and 19-3). They show how to use MAKEAGADGET to create a Boolean gadget with the text *PRESS HERE*. In the program, when the user selects the gadget, the program ends. When you examine these listings, note how IDCMPFLAGS and IDCMP messages are used to assure the programs can detect user-interaction with the gadget.

### Listing 19-2. BOOLGADGET1.ASM

Boolean gadget demonstration using support code routines.

```
;BOOLGADGET1.ASM BY DANIEL WOLF
;COPYRIGHT 1987 BY COMPUTE! PUBLICATIONS
;09/10/87

 BRA _START

DOS EQU 1
INT EQU 1

WIN EQU 1
GAD EQU 1
TXT EQU 1

 INCLUDE "HEADER"

MAIN
 TST.L ENDFROMWB               ;IF INITIATED FROM WB,  THEN NO ANNOUNCEMENTS YET!
 BNE.S _BUILDAWINDOW
FROMUSER
 DOSPRINT STDOUT,#MYMESSAGE    ;IF INITIATED FROM CLI, THEN OUTPUT TITLE MESSAGE
 ZERO D0
 MOVEA.L COMMAND,A0            ;PUT ADDRESS OF COMMAND LINE IN A0
 CMPI.B #'?',(A0)              ;IF FIRST CHARACTER IS ? THEN
 BNE.S _BUILDAWINDOW
 BRA USAGE

_BUILDAWINDOW
 MAKEWIN #MYWINDOWTITLE,40,15,500,160,ERROR
 MOVE.L D0,WINDOW                     ;WINDOW OPENED HAS ITS POINTER IN D0

_BUILDAGADGET
 LEA MYGADGETEXT,A1
 MOVE.W #20,D4                ;LEFTEDGE FOR GADGET
 MOVE.W #20,D5                ;TOPEDGE FOR GADGET
 BSR MAKEAGADGET              ;MAKE THE GADGET, INTUITEXT, AND BORDER
 MOVE.L WINDOW,A0
 MOVE.L _THISGADGET,A1        ;ROUTINE LEAVES POINTER TO GADGET STRUCTURE HERE
 MOVE.L A1,_FIRSTGADGET       ;ITS THE FIRST ONE, A SPECIAL POINTER FOR WINDOW
 ZERO D0
 MOVE.W #-1,D0                ;THIS ASSURES ITS AT THE TOP OF THE LIST
 INTLIB ADDGADGET             ;ATTACH GADGET TO WINDOW STRUCTURE

 MOVE.L _FIRSTGADGET,A0       ;PASS TWO ADDRESS PARAMETERS TO THE REFRESH ROUTINE
 MOVE.L WINDOW,A1
 INTLIB REFRESHGADGETS        ;NOW MAKE THE GADGET APPEAR!

LOOP
 MOVE.L WINDOW,A0
 MOVE.L WW.USERPORT(A0),A0    ;LISTEN TO PORT ATTACHED TO THIS WINDOW
 SYSLIB WAITPORT              ;WAIT FOR A SPECIFIED MESSAGE TO ARRIVE
 MOVE.L WINDOW,A0
 MOVE.L WW.USERPORT(A0),A0
 SYSLIB GETMSG                ;MESSAGE HAS ARRIVE WITHIN SPECIFICATIONS
 TST.L D0                     ;POINTER TO INTUIMESSAGE COMES BACK IN D0
 BEQ.S RELOOP                 ;NO MESSAGE THERE, SO LOOP
 MOVE.L D0,A1                 ;POINTER TO INTUIMESSAGE CAME BACK, USE IN A1
```

```
 MOVE.L IM.CLASS(A1),D2      ;CLOSEWINDOW AND GADGET MESSAGES APPEAR HERE
 MOVE.W IM.CODE(A1),D3       ;MENU AND MENUITEM APPEAR HERE
 MOVE.W IM.QUALIFIER(A1),D4  ;KEYS APPEAR HERE
 SYSLIB REPLYMSG             ;QUICK, SEND MESSAGE BACK NOW!

 CMP.L #CLOSEWINDOW,D2
 BEQ DONE                    ;IF ITS A CLOSEWINDOW MESSAGE, THEN DO SO...
 CMP.L #GADGETUP,D2
 BNE RELOOP                  ;THIS ISN'T A CLOSE OR A MENUPICK, SO LOOP
 BSR DOGADGET

RELOOP
 BRA LOOP

DONE
 ZERO D0
QUIT
 PUSHREG D0
 MOVE.L WINDOW,D0
 BEQ.S 1$
 MOVE.L D0,A0
 INTLIB CLOSEWINDOW
1$
 PULLREG D0
QUITNOW
 RTS

ERROR
 DOSPRINT STDOUT,#ERRORTEXT
 MOVEQ #21,D0
 RTS
USAGE
 DOSPRINT STDOUT,#USAGETEXT
 BRA DONE

DOGADGET                        ;THIS CODE GETS EXECUTED IF GADGET USED
 RTS

MYWINDOWTITLE
 DC.B ' BoolGadget1  by D. Wolf ',0
 EVENPC
USAGETEXT
 DC.B 'Usage: BoolGadget1',10,0
 EVENPC
ERRORTEXT
 DC.B 10,'Sorry, cannot open window ',10,0
 EVENPC
MYMESSAGE
 DC.B 10,'BoolGadget1 by D. Wolf Copyright 1987 by Compute! Publications',10,0
 EVENPC

WINDOW DC.L 0
RP DC.L 0
_FIRSTGADGET DC.L 0
_THISFONTHITE DC.W 9            ;DEFAULT FONT HEIGHT

MYGADGETEXT                     ;GADGET NULL-TERMINATED TEXT
 DC.B ' PRESS HERE! ',0
 EVENPC
 END
```

The MAKEBGADG macro is illustrated in BOOLGADGET2. Once again, this macro's purpose is to make the use of the MAKEAGADGET subroutine simpler.

## Listing 19-3. BOOLGADGET2.ASM

Boolean gadget demonstration using support code macros.

```
;BOOLGADGET2.ASM BY DANIEL WOLF
;COPYRIGHT 1987 BY COMPUTE! PUBLICATIONS
;09/10/87

 BRA _START

DOS EQU 1
INT EQU 1
GFX EQU 1

WIN EQU 1
TXT EQU 1
GAD EQU 1
DTIME EQU 100

 INCLUDE "HEADER"

MAIN
 TST.L ENDFROMWB              ;IF INITIATED FROM WB,  THEN NO ANNOUNCEMENTS YET!
 BNE.S _BUILDAWINDOW          ;THERE'S NO CONSOLE TO PRINT TO !!!
FROMUSER
 DOSPRINT STDOUT,#MYMESSAGE   ;IF INITIATED FROM CLI, THEN OUTPUT TITLE MESSAGE
 ZERO D0
 MOVEA.L COMMAND,A0           ;PUT ADDRESS OF COMMAND LINE IN A0
 CMPI.B #'?',(A0)             ;IF FIRST CHARACTER IS ? THEN
 BNE.S _BUILDAWINDOW
 BRA USAGE                    ;PRINT USAGE INFORMATION TO USER CLI WINDOW

_BUILDAWINDOW
 MAKEWIN #MYWINDOWTITLE,40,15,500,160,ERROR

 MOVE.L D0,WINDOW                     ;WINDOW OPENED HAS ITS POINTER IN D0
 MOVE.L D0,A0
 MOVE.L WW.RPORT(A0),RP               ;FIND POINTER TO RASTPORT IN WINDOW STRUCTURE

 MAKEITEX GADGMESSAGE,ERROR,GMSG    ;MAKE INTUITEXTS FOR THOSE WHICH WILL BE

 MAKEITEX GADGMESSAGE2,ERROR,GMSG2 ;REPEATED - THEN USE PRINTOLDAT!!!

_BUILDAGADGET
 LEA MYGADGETEXT,A1
 MOVE.W #20,D4               ;LEFTEDGE FOR GADGET
 MOVE.W #20,D5               ;TOPEDGE FOR GADGET
 BSR MAKEAGADGET             ;MAKE THE GADGET, INTUITEXT, AND BORDER
 MOVE.L WINDOW,A0
 MOVE.L _THISGADGET,A1       ;ROUTINE LEAVES POINTER TO GADGET STRUCTURE HERE
 MOVE.L A1,_FIRSTGADGET      ;ITS THE FIRST ONE, A SPECIAL POINTER FOR WINDOW
 ZERO D0
 MOVE.W #-1,D0               ;THIS ASSURES ITS AT THE TOP OF THE LIST
 INTLIB ADDGADGET            ;ATTACH GADGET TO WINDOW STRUCTURE

 MOVE.L _FIRSTGADGET,A0      ;PASS TWO ADDRESS PARAMETERS TO THE REFRESH ROUTINE
 MOVE.L WINDOW,A1
 INTLIB REFRESHGADGETS       ;NOW MAKE THE GADGET APPEAR!

 MOVE.L WINDOW,A1     ;TURN GADGET OFF
 MOVE.L _FIRSTGADGET,A0
 ZERA A2     ;ITS NOT IN A REQUESTER, JUST A WINDOW
 INTLIB OFFGADGET
 PRINTNEWAT WINDOW,OFFMSG,20,40,DONE ;PRINT A MESSAGE THAT ONLY APPEARS ONCE

 MOVE.L #DTIME,D1     ;WAIT 4 SECONDS
 DOSLIB DELAY

 SETAPEN RP,#0
 RECTFILL RP,#2,#10,#200,#35 ;BLANK OUT THE GADGET BEFORE 'ON'

 MOVE.L WINDOW,A1      ;TURN GADGET ON
 MOVE.L _FIRSTGADGET,A0
 ZERA A2      ;ITS NOT IN A REQUESTER
 INTLIB ONGADGET              ;SINCE ONLY ONE GADGET, THIS WORKS TO MAKE IT
     ;APPEAR - THIS ROUTINE CALLS 'REFRESHGADGETS'
```

```
 PRINTNEWAT WINDOW,ONMSG,20,60,DONE    ;PRINT A MESSAGE

LOOP
 MOVE.L WINDOW,A0
 MOVE.L WW.USERPORT(A0),A0  ;LISTEN TO PORT ATTACHED TO THIS WINDOW
 SYSLIB WAITPORT            ;WAIT FOR A SPECIFIED MESSAGE TO ARRIVE
 MOVE.L WINDOW,A0
 MOVE.L WW.USERPORT(A0),A0
 SYSLIB GETMSG              ;MESSAGE HAS ARRIVE WITHIN SPECIFICATIONS
 TST.L D0                   ;POINTER TO INTUIMESSAGE COMES BACK IN D0
 BEQ.S RELOOP               ;NO MESSAGE THERE, SO LOOP
 MOVE.L D0,A1               ;POINTER TO INTUIMESSAGE CAME BACK, USE IN A1
 MOVE.L IM.CLASS(A1),D2     ;CLOSEWINDOW AND GADGET MESSAGES APPEAR HERE
 MOVE.W IM.CODE(A1),D3      ;MENU AND MENUITEM APPEAR HERE
 MOVE.W IM.QUALIFIER(A1),D4 ;KEYS APPEAR HERE
 SYSLIB REPLYMSG            ;QUICK, SEND MESSAGE BACK NOW!

 CMP.L #CLOSEWINDOW,D2
 BEQ DONE                   ;IF ITS A CLOSEWINDOW MESSAGE, THEN DO SO...
 CMP.L #GADGETUP,D2
 BNE RELOOP                 ;THIS ISN'T A CLOSE OR A MENUPICK, SO LOOP

 BSR DOGADGET

RELOOP
 BRA LOOP

DONE
 ZERO D0
QUIT
 PUSHREG D0
 MOVE.L WINDOW,D0
 BEQ.S 1$                   ;LOCAL LABEL 1$ VALID BETWEEN TWO NORMAL LABELS
 MOVE.L D0,A0               ;I.E. BETWEEN QUIT AND QUITNOW
 INTLIB CLOSEWINDOW
1$
 PULLREG D0
QUITNOW
 RTS

ERROR
 DOSPRINT STDOUT,#ERRORTEXT
 MOVEQ #21,D0
 RTS
USAGE
 DOSPRINT STDOUT,#USAGETEXT
 BRA DONE

DOGADGET                        ;THIS CODE EXECUTED IF GADGET GETS CLICKED
 PUSHALL
 SETAPEN RP,#0                  ;SET DRAWING PEN (FOREGROUND) = COL. REG. #0
 RECTFILL RP,#2,#100,#450,#120  ;BLANK OUT THE AREA WHERE MESSAGE WILL APPEAR
 MOVEA.L _FIRSTGADGET,A0        ;NOW CHECK IF GADGET TOGGLED ON OR OFF
 MOVE.W GADG.FLAGS(A0),D0       ;LOOK UP THE FLAGS SLOT OF GADGET STRUCTURE
 BTST.L #7,D0                   ;IS THE GADGET 'SELECTED' ? (FLAG BIT = 1)
 BEQ.S CLRTXT                   ;NO , USE 'SELECT'  MSG
       ;YES, PRINT APPROPRIATE MESSAGE
 PRINTOLDAT WINDOW,GMSG,20,100,ERR_GAD
 ;MOVE.L _FIRSTGADGET,A0
 ;BCLR.W #7,GADG.FLAGS(A0)        ;DE-SELECT IT
 BRA ERR_GAD
 ;LEA GADGMESSAGE,A1              ;YES, USE 'DESELECT' MSG
 ;BRA TEXTOUT
CLRTXT
 PRINTOLDAT WINDOW,GMSG2,20,100,ERR_GAD
 ZERO D0
 ;LEA GADGMESSAGE2,A1
;TEXTOUT
 ;MOVEA.L WINDOW,A0
 ;MOVE.L #20,D0
 ;MOVE.L #100,D1
 ;BSR _PRINTTEXT                  ;JUST FOR DEMONSTRATION, THIS ALLOCATES
ERR_GAD
 PULLALL                        ;MEM EACH TIME, NOT GOOD
 RTS
```

```
;***** TEXT DATA DECLARATIONS *****

MYWINDOWTITLE
 DC.B ' BoolGadget2  by D. Wolf ',0
 EVENPC
USAGETEXT
 DC.B 'Usage: BoolGadget2',10,0
 EVENPC
ERRORTEXT
 DC.B 10,'Sorry, cannot open window ',10,0
 EVENPC
MYMESSAGE
 DC.B 10,'BoolGadget2 by D. Wolf Copyright 1987 by Compute! Publications',10,0
 EVENPC
GADGMESSAGE2
 DC.B ' Now press it again to SELECT ... ',0
 EVENPC
GADGMESSAGE
 DC.B ' and again to DE-SELECT. ',0
 EVENPC
OFFMSG
 DC.B 'OFFGADGET disables and ghosts the Gadget',0
 EVENPC
ONMSG
 DC.B 'ONGADGET enables the Gadget',0
 EVENPC
MYGADGETEXT                      ;GADGET NULL-TERMINATED TEXT
 DC.B ' PRESS HERE! ',0
 EVENPC

WINDOW DC.L 0                    ;POINTER TO WINDOW STRUCTURE
RP DC.L 0                        ;POINTER TO WINDOW'S RASTPORT STRUCTURE
_FIRSTGADGET DC.L 0              ;POINTER TO GADGET'S STRUCTURE IN MEMORY
_THISFONTHITE DC.W 9             ;DEFAULT FONT HEIGHT
GMSG DC.L 0 ;POINTER TO INTUITEXT STRUCTURE
GMSG2 DC.L 0                     ;POINTER TO INTUITEXT STRUCTURE
 END
```

## String Gadgets

String gadgets allow manipulation of a string of text characters. In addition to the other structures needed for a Boolean gadget, a STRINGINFO structure is allocated and linked to the GADG.SPECIALINFO field of the GADGET structure. The MAKEASTRINGADGET subroutine uses a call to the MAKEAGADGET subroutine and some additional code to prepare a complete string gadget with minimum programming overhead. Default values used by the subroutine are easily customized to your unique needs.

Prior to calling MAKEASTRINGADGET, the program source code should provide a text string buffer and an *undo buffer,* which maintains a backup of the text string for the user. An interesting feature of the undo buffer is that only one is needed for all the string gadgets used. There is no need to declare multiple undo buffers. The MAKEASTRINGADGET reuses a single undo buffer.

## The STRINGINFO Structure

Table 19-4 shows the layout of a STRINGINFO structure, with field names and their numerical equivalents.

This special gadget substructure has fields for pointers to the actual text string buffer and the undo buffer, and also specifies the starting character for displaying the string, maximum number of characters for the string, and so on. The MAKEASTRINGADGET subroutine uses standard default values, which display the string starting from its first character, and place the cursor at the first character in both the string and undo buffers.

**Table 19-4. Intuition STRINGINFO Structure for String Gadget**

**Symbol: SI**
**Size: 36 bytes ($24 bytes)**

| *Field Size* | *Name* | *Offset* | *Description* |
|---|---|---|---|
| Long | SI.BUFFER | 0 | Pointer to buffer for string gadget |
| Long | SI.UNDOBUFFER | 4 | Pointer to undo buffer for string gadget |
| Word | SI.BUFFERPOS | 8 | Position of cursor within buffer |
| Word | SI.MAXCHARS | 10 | Maximum number of characters in buffer |
| Word | SI.DISPPOS | 12 | First displayed character buffer position |
| Word | SI.UNDOPOS | 14 | Position of cursor within undo buffer |
| Word | SI.NUMCHARS | 16 | Number of characters currently in buffer |
| Word | SI.DISPCOUNT | 18 | Number of characters visible in string gadget box |
| Word | SI.CLEFT | 20 | Number of pixels from left edge |
| Word | SI.CTOP | 22 | Number of pixels from top edge |
| Long | SI.LAYERPTR | 24 | Pointer to rastport holding gadget |
| Long | SI.LONGINT | 28 | User's typed-in integer value |
| Long | SI.KEYMAP | 32 | Pointer to alternate string gadget keymap |

As was done for the Boolean gadget, a border is drawn for the string gadget. The sizing information for this border is derived from SIZESTRING, a string variable declared in the GADGETS.ASM file (look for it toward the end of Listing 19-1). The border forms a box of a fixed size. You can alter the size of the box, but the default provides for equal-sized boxes for all text strings in a window.

One way to make the box smaller is to insert a 0 somewhere inside the SIZESTRING (between the opening and closing quote). That has the effect of terminating the string with a shorter length because the 0 is detected as the end of the SIZESTRING.

The SIZESTRING can be shorter than the actual text string buffer supplied as the starting value of the string. The string in the gadget scrolls when the cursor reaches an end of the string gadget's display box. It is wise to provide an 80-character string buffer, even if it requires padding the string with spaces at the end. Eighty characters is a typical line of text in many computer applications.

Use the SIZESTRING to dictate the string gadget's size, since exact pixel size declarations sometimes cause part of the image to *ghost*. *Ghosting* is the term used when a region of text is covered with a mask of dots. This has the effect of making the text lighter and harder to read. It's used to dim nonenabled menu items, as well as the titles of all nonactive windows.

Once the string gadget is created, it's added to the list of gadgets by calling ADDGADGET, and is made to appear by calling REFRESHGADGETS. A new feature of Workbench 1.2 is an Intuition routine called ACTIVATEGADGET. A call to this routine activates a string gadget without a mouse click. The cursor appears at the programmed position in a string gadget.

STRGADGET.ASM, Listing 19-4, shows how to declare the null-terminated string and buffers, and then create and display a string gadget. Once again, note the IDCMPFLAGS and IDCMP messages sent if the user deselects the string gadget. The program code can look up the current contents of the string gadget's buffer and take action according to the user's input. This program simply uses PRINTITEXT to print the buffer each time the user alters it.

## Listing 19-4. STRGADGET.ASM

String gadget demonstration using support code.

```
;STRGADGET.ASM BY DANIEL WOLF
;COPYRIGHT 1987 BY COMPUTE! PUBLICATIONS
;09/10/87

 BRA _START

GFX EQU 1

WIN EQU 1
GAD EQU 1
TXT EQU 1
WBC EQU 1     ;ASSURE SOMEWHERE TO PRINT MESSAGES

 INCLUDE "HEADER"

MAIN
 DOSPRINT STDOUT,#MYMESSAGE  ;OUTPUT TITLE MESSAGE REGARDLESS
 ZERO D0
 MOVEA.L COMMAND,A0          ;PUT ADDRESS OF COMMAND LINE IN A0
 CMPI.B #'?',(A0)            ;IF FIRST CHARACTER IS ? THEN
 BNE.S _BUILDAWINDOW
 BRA USAGE

_BUILDAWINDOW
 MAKEWIN #MYWINDOWTITLE,40,15,500,160,ERROR
 MOVE.L D0,WINDOW                ;WINDOW OPENED HAS ITS POINTER IN D0
 MOVE.L D0,A0
 MOVE.L WW.RPORT(A0),RP          ;FIND POINTER TO RASTPORT IN WINDOW STRUCTURE

_BUILDAGADGET
 LEA SGBUFFER,A0
 LEA SGUNDOBUFFER,A1
 MOVE.W #20,D4               ;LEFTEDGE FOR GADGET
 MOVE.W #20,D5               ;TOPEDGE FOR GADGET
 BSR MAKEASTRINGADGET        ;MAKE THE GADGET, INTUITEXT, AND BORDER
 MOVE.L WINDOW,A0
 MOVE.L _THISGADGET,A1       ;ROUTINE LEAVES POINTER TO GADGET STRUCTURE HERE
 MOVE.L A1,_FIRSTGADGET      ;ITS THE FIRST ONE, A SPECIAL POINTER FOR WINDOW
 ZERO D0
 MOVE.W #-1,D0               ;THIS ASSURES ITS AT THE TOP OF THE LIST
 INTLIB ADDGADGET            ;ATTACH GADGET TO WINDOW STRUCTURE

 MOVE.L _FIRSTGADGET,A0      ;PASS TWO ADDRESS PARAMETERS TO THE REFRESH ROUTINE
 MOVE.L WINDOW,A1
 INTLIB REFRESHGADGETS       ;NOW MAKE THE GADGET APPEAR!

LOOP
 MOVE.L WINDOW,A0
 MOVE.L WW.USERPORT(A0),A0   ;LISTEN TO PORT ATTACHED TO THIS WINDOW
 SYSLIB WAITPORT             ;WAIT FOR A SPECIFIED MESSAGE TO ARRIVE
 MOVE.L WINDOW,A0
 MOVE.L WW.USERPORT(A0),A0
 SYSLIB GETMSG               ;MESSAGE HAS ARRIVE WITHIN SPECIFICATIONS
 TST.L D0                    ;POINTER TO INTUIMESSAGE COMES BACK IN D0
 BEQ.S RELOOP                ;NO MESSAGE THERE, SO LOOP
 MOVE.L D0,A1                ;POINTER TO INTUIMESSAGE CAME BACK, USE IN A1
 MOVE.L IM.CLASS(A1),D2      ;CLOSEWINDOW AND GADGET MESSAGES APPEAR HERE
 MOVE.W IM.CODE(A1),D3       ;MENU AND MENUITEM APPEAR HERE
 MOVE.W IM.QUALIFIER(A1),D4 ;KEYS APPEAR HERE
 SYSLIB REPLYMSG             ;QUICK, SEND MESSAGE BACK NOW!

 CMP.L #CLOSEWINDOW,D2
 BEQ DONE                    ;IF ITS A CLOSEWINDOW MESSAGE, THEN DO SO...
 ;CMP.L #GADGETUP,D2
 ;BNE RELOOP                  ;THIS ISN'T A CLOSE OR A MENUPICK, SO LOOP
 BSR DOGADGET

RELOOP
 BRA LOOP
```

```
DONE
 ZERO D0
QUIT
 PUSHREG D0
 MOVE.L WINDOW,D0
 BEQ.S 1$
 MOVE.L D0,A0
 INTLIB CLOSEWINDOW
1$
 PULLREG D0
QUITNOW
 RTS

ERROR
 DOSPRINT STDOUT,#ERRORTEXT
 MOVEQ #CANTOPENWINDOW,D0
 RTS

USAGE
 DOSPRINT STDOUT,#USAGETEXT
 BRA DONE

DOGADGET                           ;THIS CODE EXECUTED IF GADGET TOGGLED
 PUSHALL
 SETAPEN RP,#0                     ;SET DRAWING PEN (FOREGROUND) = COL. REG. #0
 RECTFILL RP,#2,#100,#450,#120     ;BLANK OUT THE AREA WHERE MESSAGE WILL APPEAR
                                   ;PRINT CONTENTS OF STRING GADGET BUFFER
TEXTOUT
 PRINTNEWAT WINDOW,SGBUFFER,20,100,CLRTXT
 ZERO D0
CLRTXT
 PULLALL
 RTS

;***** TEXT DATA DECLARATIONS *****

MYMESSAGE
 DC.B 10,' StrGadget by D. Wolf Copyright 1987 by Compute! Publications ',10,0
 EVENPC
MYWINDOWTITLE
 DC.B ' StrGadget  by D. Wolf ',0
 EVENPC
USAGETEXT
 DC.B 'Usage: StrGadget',10,0
 EVENPC
ERRORTEXT
 DC.B 10,'Sorry, cannot open window ',10,0
 EVENPC
SGBUFFER
 DC.B 'CLICK HERE, PLAY, THEN PRESS RETURN',0  ;INITIAL STRING IN GADGET
 EVENPC
SGUNDOBUFFER
 DCB.B 80,0                        ;UNIVERSAL STRING GADGET 'UNDO' BUFFER

WINDOW DC.L 0                      ;POINTER TO WINDOW STRUCTURE
RP DC.L 0                          ;POINTER TO WINDOW'S RASTPORT STRUCTURE
_FIRSTGADGET DC.L 0                ;POINTER TO GADGET'S STRUCTURE IN MEMORY
_THISFONTHITE DC.W 9               ;DEFAULT FONT HEIGHT
 END
```

## Proportional Gadgets

Proportional gadgets are the most complex gadgets to create and use. You can arrange them vertically, horizontally, or in combinations. You can also attach them to window borders as scroll bars. They provide a variable value to look up in the GADGET structure and use in the program. They are visually elegant and powerful for user interaction, which can obviate the need to type in a number.

## The PROPINFO Structure

Table 19-5 shows the PROPINFO STRUCTURE, which plays the role of SPECIALINFO in proportional gadget programming.

The Proportional gadget needs a SPECIALINFO structure to provide all the additional parameters and data for a Proportional gadget. The PROPINFO STRUCTURE contains fields for special flag bits, 16-bit relative values of the gadget (PI.HORIZPOT or PI.VERTPOT), and a size and increment value (PI.HORIZBODY or PI.VERTBODY) for the slider knob. These values are read during the program to determine the current value of the proportional variable.

**Table 19-5. Intuition PROPINFO Structure for Proportional Gadget**

**Symbol: PI**
**Size: 22 bytes ($16 bytes)**

| *Field Size* | *Name* | *Offset* | *Description* |
|---|---|---|---|
| Word | PI.FLAGS | 0 | Flag bits |
| Word | PI.HORIZPOT | 2 | Sixteen-bit fractional pot value |
| Word | PI.VERTPOT | 4 | Sixteen-bit fractional pot value |
| Word | PI.HORIZBODY | 6 | Sixteen-bit fractional knob size |
| Word | PI.VERTBODY | 8 | Sixteen-bit fractional knob size |
| Word | PI.CWIDTH | 10 | Knob container width |
| Word | PI.CHEIGHT | 12 | Knob container height |
| Word | PI.HPOTRES | 14 | Knob movement/value increment |
| Word | PI.VPOTRES | 16 | Knob movement/value increment |
| Word | PI.LEFTBORDER | 18 | Knob container left border |
| Word | PI.TOPBORDER | 20 | Knob container top border |

The MAKEAPROPGADGET subroutine in GADGETS .ASM (Listing 19-1) provides a simple way to arrange all the bits and pieces of proportional gadgets. It uses the MAKEAGADGET subroutine, but also contains code for allocating and filling in the PROPINFO standard default values. The AUTOKNOB mode lets Intuition create the slider image. MAKEAPROPGADGET uses sizing data passed in registers to specify the length, height, and position of the proportional gadget region.

**Self-adjusting proportional gadgets.** The GRELBOTTOM, GRELRIGHT, GRELWIDTH, and GRELHEIGHT flags insure that the proportional gadget is positioned and sized correctly when the user resizes the window. This relative positioning is often used with scroll bars that remain attached to a window's border and adjust to window size changes. When the GRELBOTTOM flag is set, the relative position passed to MAKEAPROPGADGET is a negative number. For instance, −10 causes the gadget to appear 10 pixels from the window's bottom border. If you want to have a scroll bar at the right edge of a window, 10 pixels wide and extending from the drag bar down to the sizing gadget, set the GRELRIGHT and GRELHEIGHT flags. In this example, set TOPEDGE = 10, LEFTEDGE = −10, WIDTH = 10 and HEIGHT = −20.

The listings provided with this section are PROPGADGET1.ASM and PROPGADGET2.ASM (Listings 19-5 and 19-6). The first features a horizontal proportional gadget. The second features a proportional gadget positioned as a scroll bar inside the window using the GREL*xxxx* (for instance, GETRELWIDTH) flag bits from the GADGET structure. Notice that this gadget is moved and resized correctly over a wide range of window sizes. When the slider is moved, its value (in hexadecimal, between $0000 and $FFFF) is printed out in the CLI window. Again, note the use of IDCMP and the way the PROPINFO data are read by the program code.

## Listing 19-5. PROPGADGET1.ASM

Proportional gadget using support routines.

```
;PROPGADGET1.ASM BY DANIEL WOLF
;COPYRIGHT 1987 BY COMPUTE! PUBLICATIONSS
;09/10/87

 BRA _START

WIN EQU 1
GAD EQU 1
TXT EQU 1

MAT EQU 1
HEX EQU 1
WBC EQU 1                       ;ASSURE WE HAVE STDOUT EVEN IF FROM WORKBENCH
    ;WE CAN ALWAYS DOSPRINT MESSAGES THEN

 INCLUDE "HEADER"

MAIN
 DOSPRINT STDOUT,#MYMESSAGE ;IF INITIATED FROM CLI, THEN OUTPUT TITLE MESSAGE
 ZERO D0
 MOVEA.L COMMAND,A0         ;PUT ADDRESS OF COMMAND LINE IN A0
 CMPI.B #'?',(A0)           ;IF FIRST CHARACTER IS ? THEN
 BNE.S _BUILDAWINDOW
 BRA USAGE

_BUILDAWINDOW
 MAKEWIN #MYWINDOWTITLE,40,15,500,160,ERROR
 MOVE.L D0,WINDOW           ;WINDOW OPENED HAS ITS POINTER IN D0
 MOVE.L D0,A0
 MOVE.L WW.RPORT(A0),RP     ;FIND POINTER TO RASTPORT IN WINDOW STRUCTURE

_BUILDAGADGET               ;DEFAULT WILL BE A HORIZONTAL PROPORTIONAL GADGET
 MOVE.W #20,D4              ;LEFTEDGE FOR GADGET
 MOVE.W #120,D5             ;TOPEDGE FOR GADGET
 MOVE.W #100,D6             ;WIDTH FOR GADGET
 MOVE.W #15,D7              ;HEIGHT FOR GADGET
 BSR MAKEAPROPGADGET        ;MAKE THE GADGET, INTUITEXT, AND BORDER

 MOVE.L WINDOW,A0
 MOVE.L _THISGADGET,A1      ;ROUTINE LEAVES POINTER TO GADGET STRUCTURE HERE
 MOVE.L A1,_FIRSTGADGET     ;ITS THE FIRST ONE, A SPECIAL POINTER FOR WINDOW
 ZERO D0
 MOVE.W #-1,D0              ;THIS ASSURES ITS AT THE TOP OF THE LIST
 INTLIB ADDGADGET           ;ATTACH GADGET TO WINDOW STRUCTURE

 MOVE.L _FIRSTGADGET,A0     ;PASS TWO ADDRESS PARAMETERS TO THE REFRESH ROUTINE
 MOVE.L WINDOW,A1
 INTLIB REFRESHGADGETS      ;NOW MAKE THE GADGET APPEAR!

LOOP
 MOVE.L WINDOW,A0
 MOVE.L WW.USERPORT(A0),A0  ;LISTEN TO PORT ATTACHED TO THIS WINDOW
 SYSLIB WAITPORT            ;WAIT FOR A SPECIFIED MESSAGE TO ARRIVE
 MOVE.L WINDOW,A0
 MOVE.L WW.USERPORT(A0),A0
 SYSLIB GETMSG              ;MESSAGE HAS ARRIVE WITHIN SPECIFICATIONS
 TST.L D0                   ;POINTER TO INTUIMESSAGE COMES BACK IN D0
 BEQ.S RELOOP               ;NO MESSAGE THERE, SO LOOP
 MOVE.L D0,A1               ;POINTER TO INTUIMESSAGE CAME BACK, USE IN A1
 MOVE.L IM.CLASS(A1),D2     ;CLOSEWINDOW AND GADGET MESSAGES APPEAR HERE
 MOVE.W IM.CODE(A1),D3      ;MENU AND MENUITEM APPEAR HERE
 MOVE.W IM.QUALIFIER(A1),D4 ;KEYS APPEAR HERE
 SYSLIB REPLYMSG            ;QUICK, SEND MESSAGE BACK NOW!

 CMP.L #CLOSEWINDOW,D2
 BEQ DONE                   ;IF ITS A CLOSEWINDOW MESSAGE, THEN DO SO...
 CMP.L #GADGETUP,D2
 BNE RELOOP                 ;THIS ISN'T A CLOSE OR A MENUPICK, SO LOOP
 BSR DOGADGET

RELOOP
 BRA LOOP
```

```
DONE
 ZERO DØ
QUIT
 PUSHREG DØ
 MOVE.L WINDOW,DØ
 BEQ.S 1$
 MOVE.L DØ,AØ
 INTLIB CLOSEWINDOW
1$
 PULLREG DØ
QUITNOW
 RTS

ERROR
 DOSPRINT STDOUT,#ERRORTEXT
 MOVEQ #21,DØ
 RTS
USAGE
 DOSPRINT STDOUT,#USAGETEXT
 BRA DONE

DOGADGET                        ;THIS CODE EXECUTED IF GADGET TOGGLED
 PUSHALL
 MOVEA.L _FIRSTGADGET,AØ        ;USE GADGET STRUCTURE TO
 MOVEA.L GADG.SPECIALINFO(AØ),AØ;FIND THE PROPINFO SUB-STRUCTURE POINTER
 ZERO DØ
 MOVE.W PI.HORIZPOT(AØ),DØ      ;AND THE VALUE OF THE 'POT' VARIABLE
 BSR HEXCONVERT                 ;NOW DECODE AND PRINT VALUE TO CLI WINDOW
 PULLALL
 RTS

;***** TEXT DATA DECLARATIONS *****

MYMESSAGE
 DC.B ' PropGadget1 by D. Wolf Copyright 1987 by Compute! Publications ',1Ø,Ø
 EVENPC
MYWINDOWTITLE
 DC.B ' PropGadget1  by D. Wolf ',Ø
 EVENPC
USAGETEXT
 DC.B 'Usage: PropGadget1',1Ø,Ø
 EVENPC
ERRORTEXT
 DC.B 1Ø,'Sorry, cannot open window ',1Ø,Ø
 EVENPC


WINDOW DC.L Ø                   ;POINTER TO WINDOW STRUCTURE
RP DC.L Ø                       ;POINTER TO WINDOW'S RASTPORT STRUCTURE
_FIRSTGADGET DC.L Ø             ;POINTER TO GADGET'S STRUCTURE IN MEMORY
_THISFONTHITE DC.W 9            ;DEFAULT FONT HEIGHT
 END
```

## Listing 19-6. PROPGADGET2.ASM

Proportional gadget scroll bar uses relative positioning within window.

```
;PROPGADGET2.ASM BY DANIEL WOLF
;COPYRIGHT 1987 BY COMPUTE! PUBLICATIONS
;Ø9/1Ø/87

 BRA _START

MAT EQU 1

GAD EQU 1
TXT EQU 1
HEX EQU 1

WBC EQU 1

 INCLUDE "HEADER"
```

```
MAIN
 DOSPRINT STDOUT,#MYMESSAGE ;IF INITIATED FROM CLI, THEN OUTPUT TITLE MESSAGE
 ZERO DØ
 MOVEA.L COMMAND,AØ          ;PUT ADDRESS OF COMMAND LINE IN AØ
 CMPI.B #'?',(AØ)            ;IF FIRST CHARACTER IS ? THEN
 BNE.S _BUILDAWINDOW
 BRA USAGE

_BUILDAWINDOW
 LEA NEWWINDOW,AØ
 INTLIB OPENWINDOW
 TST.L DØ
 BEQ ERROR
 MOVE.L DØ,WINDOW           ;WINDOW OPENED HAS ITS POINTER IN DØ

_BUILDAGADGET                ;DEFAULT WILL BE A HORIZONTAL PROPORTIONAL GADGET
 MOVE.W #Ø,D4                ;LEFTEDGE FOR GADGET
 MOVE.W #-8,D5              ;TOPEDGE FOR GADGET (RELATIVE TO BOTTOM)
 MOVE.W #-15,D6              ;RELATIVE WIDTH, 15 PIXELS LESS THAN WINDOW
 MOVE.W #8,D7
 BSR MAKEAPROPGADGET         ;MAKE THE GADGET, INTUITEXT, AND BORDER
 MOVEA.L WINDOW,AØ
 MOVEA.L _THISGADGET,A1      ;ROUTINE LEAVES POINTER TO GADGET STRUCTURE HERE
 MOVE.L A1,_FIRSTGADGET      ;ITS THE FIRST ONE, A SPECIAL POINTER FOR WINDOW

_CHANGEGADGFLAGS                 ;HERE'S HOW TO USE CUSTOM FLAGS COMBINATIONS
 MOVE.W GADG.FLAGS(A1),DØ        ;IN SPITE OF THE DEFAULT 'MAKEAGADGET' FLAGS
 ORI.W #GRELWIDTH!GRELBOTTOM,DØ ;SET THE RELATIVE WIDTH AND HEIGHT FLAGS
 MOVE.W DØ,GADG.FLAGS(A1)        ;BRING FLAGS OUT, 'OR' AS DESIRED, PUT 'EM BACK
                                 ;THIS COMBO WILL MAKE A SCROLL BAR
_NOWADDTHEGADGET
 ZERO DØ
 MOVE.W #-1,DØ               ;THIS ASSURES ITS AT THE TOP OF THE LIST
 INTLIB ADDGADGET            ;ATTACH GADGET TO WINDOW STRUCTURE'S GADGET LIST

 MOVE.L _FIRSTGADGET,AØ      ;PASS TWO ADDRESS PARAMETERS TO THE REFRESH ROUTINE
 MOVE.L WINDOW,A1
 INTLIB REFRESHGADGETS       ;NOW MAKE THE GADGET APPEAR!

LOOP
 MOVE.L WINDOW,AØ
 MOVE.L WW.USERPORT(AØ),AØ   ;LISTEN TO PORT ATTACHED TO THIS WINDOW
 SYSLIB WAITPORT             ;WAIT FOR A SPECIFIED MESSAGE TO ARRIVE
 MOVE.L WINDOW,AØ
 MOVE.L WW.USERPORT(AØ),AØ
 SYSLIB GETMSG               ;MESSAGE HAS ARRIVE WITHIN SPECIFICATIONS
 TST.L DØ                    ;POINTER TO INTUIMESSAGE COMES BACK IN DØ
 BEQ.S RELOOP                ;NO MESSAGE THERE, SO LOOP
 MOVE.L DØ,A1                ;POINTER TO INTUIMESSAGE CAME BACK, USE IN A1
 MOVE.L IM.CLASS(A1),D2      ;CLOSEWINDOW AND GADGET MESSAGES APPEAR HERE
 MOVE.W IM.CODE(A1),D3       ;MENU AND MENUITEM APPEAR HERE
 MOVE.W IM.QUALIFIER(A1),D4 ;KEYS APPEAR HERE
 SYSLIB REPLYMSG             ;QUICK, SEND MESSAGE BACK NOW!

 CMP.L #CLOSEWINDOW,D2
 BEQ DONE                    ;IF ITS A CLOSEWINDOW MESSAGE, THEN DO SO...
 CMP.L #GADGETUP,D2
 BNE TRYDOWN                 ;THIS ISN'T A CLOSE OR A GADGETUP
 BSR DOGADGET
TRYDOWN
 CMPI.L #GADGETDOWN,D2       ;MAYBE ITS A GADGET DOWN MESSAGE
 BNE RELOOP
 BSR DOGADGET

RELOOP
 BRA LOOP

DONE
 ZERO DØ
QUIT
 PUSHREG DØ
 MOVE.L WINDOW,DØ
 BEQ.S 1$
 MOVE.L DØ,AØ
 INTLIB CLOSEWINDOW
1$
 PULLREG DØ
```

```
QUITNOW
 RTS

ERROR
 DOSPRINT STDOUT,#ERRORTEXT
 MOVEQ #CANTOPENWINDOW,DØ
 RTS
USAGE
 DOSPRINT STDOUT,#USAGETEXT
 BRA DONE

DOGADGET                          ;THIS CODE EXECUTED IF GADGET TOGGLED
 PUSHALL
 MOVEA.L _FIRSTGADGET,AØ          ;USE GADGET STRUCTURE TO
 MOVEA.L GADG.SPECIALINFO(AØ),AØ;FIND THE PROPINFO SUB-STRUCTURE POINTER
 ZERO DØ
 MOVE.W PI.HORIZPOT(AØ),DØ        ;AND THE VALUE OF THE 'POT' VARIABLE
 BSR HEXCONVERT                   ;NOW DECODE AND PRINT VALUE TO CLI WINDOW
 PULLALL
 RTS

;***** TEXT DATA DECLARATIONS *****

MYMESSAGE
 DC.B ' PropGadget2 by D. Wolf Copyright 1987 by Compute! Publications ',1Ø,Ø
 EVENPC
MYWINDOWTITLE
 DC.B ' PropGadget2  by D. Wolf ',Ø
 EVENPC
USAGETEXT
 DC.B 'Usage: PropGadget2',1Ø,Ø
 EVENPC
ERRORTEXT
 DC.B 1Ø,'Sorry, cannot open window ',1Ø,Ø
 EVENPC

WINDOW DC.L Ø                      ;POINTER TO WINDOW STRUCTURE
RP DC.L Ø                          ;POINTER TO WINDOW'S RASTPORT STRUCTURE
_FIRSTGADGET DC.L Ø                ;POINTER TO GADGET'S STRUCTURE IN MEMORY
_THISFONTHITE DC.W 9               ;DEFAULT FONT HEIGHT

NEWWINDOW
 DC.W 1ØØ
 DC.W 2Ø
 DC.W 5ØØ
 DC.W 16Ø
 DC.B -1
 DC.B -1
 DC.L CLOSEWINDOW!GADGETUP
 DC.L WINDOWSIZING!WINDOWDRAG!WINDOWDEPTH!WINDOWCLOSE!SMART_REFRESH
 DC.L Ø
 DC.L Ø
 DC.L MYWINDOWTITLE
 DC.L Ø
 DC.L Ø
 DC.W 14Ø             ;BE CAREFUL MIN HEIGHT AND WIDTH AREN'T
 DC.W 14Ø             ;SO SMALL THAT THE RELATIVE HEIGHT AND WIDTH
 DC.W 64Ø             ;OF THE GADGET CAN BECOME LESS THAN ZERO
 DC.W 4ØØ             ;OR YOU'LL BE SORRY! (COULD ELIMINATE SIZING INSTEAD)
 DC.W WBENCHSCREEN
 END
```

## Programming with Gadgets

Here are some important points to keep in mind when using gadgets: First, Gain as much experience as possible by experimentation. It's not possible to cover the enormous variety of combinations of flags, positioning options, and so on within this text.

Second, changing a gadget in use can be tricky. There are several routines in the Intuition library for this purpose. You may wish to make a gadget disappear, or change the character string used in a string gadget. Here are the functions:

| | |
|---|---|
| ADDGADGET | Adds a gadget to the window's gadget list |
| REMGADGET | Removes a gadget from the window's gadget list |
| MODIFYPROP | Alters a proportional gadget in use |
| REFRESHGADGETS | Displays gadgets on the window's gadget list |

Each of these functions is called with a pointer to the relevant structure in register A0. To alter the features of a string or Boolean gadget, first remove it from the window's gadget list (REMGADGET). The program can then modify fields in the structures associated with that gadget. Next, a call to ADDGADGET and REFRESHGADGETS will redisplay it. ADDGADGET also requires a gadget list position, discussed earlier (see the initial paragraphs of the section on Boolean gadgets).

The MODIFYPROP function changes flags, pot values, and body values without first removing and adding the gadget. More information on the register data and calling sequence for these routines is in the *Amiga Intuition Reference Manual* and the Intuition function call table.

# CHAPTER 20
# Intuition Requesters

After introducing windows, texts, menus, and gadgets, there's only one more major Intuition interactive resource: requesters. Most of what has been applied previously in the construction of INTUITEXT and GADGET structures also applies to requesters. Requesters behave like windows, except the user must respond to them before continuing other work.

Requesters are equipped with some type of close gadget to permit a message to reach the program to remove the requester and allow other work to continue. Just about anything you can do with a menu or gadget in a window is possible using a requester. The requester can't have a real menu, but it can have a variety of gadgets for user interactions. Requesters open in a window and are attached by the system to that window. Therefore, communication with a requester is handled by the Window's I/O port using IDCMPFLAGS and INTUIMESSAGES.

### The Autorequester

With such capabilities, most requesters need a great deal of preparation. The programmer may have to supply BORDER, GADGET, and INTUITEXT structures (perhaps several of each), appropriately linked. Naturally, there is a REQUESTER structure with many fields for pointers to these auxiliary structures. The simplest type of requester, called the autorequester, uses a method that is simpler than filling in an entire REQUESTER structure.

An autorequester presents a *yes/no* or *continue* choice to the user. A special Intuition call (AUTOREQUEST) is used to do most of the work of preparing this one- or two-choice requester.

Programmers may want to use the autorequester most frequently as a warning to users when deleting data or opening a new file. It's common practice to alert a user to the possibility that data will be lost or damaged by user action, and permit the user to back up and safely move to another option. The autorequester is well suited to this warning function.

## The REQUESTER Structure

Table 20-1 has the definition of the REQUESTER structure. The structure fields include the usual positioning data (TOPEDGE, LEFTEDGE, and so on) and pointer fields that point to an existing list of gadgets, a list of borders, and a list of Intuitexts. The lists are actually lists of the structures, each with its own positioning and drawing specifications, and are linked by the NEXT field pointers in each. There is also a field for a pointer to a custom bitmap that can contain imagery for the requester. As with the other complex Intuition structures, the REQUESTER structure also contains a FLAGS field that controls some of its features.

**Table 20-1. Intuition Requester Structure**

**Symbol: REQ Size: 112 bytes ($70 bytes)**

| *Field Size* | *Name* | *Offset* | *Description* |
|---|---|---|---|
| Long | REQ.OLDERREQUEST | 0 | Pointer to older requester |
| Word | REQ.LEFTEDGE | 4 | Number of pixels from left edge |
| Word | REQ.TOPEDGE | 6 | Number of pixels from top edge |
| Word | REQ.WIDTH | 8 | Number of pixels wide |
| Word | REQ.HEIGHT | 10 | Number of pixels high |
| Word | REQ.RELLEFT | 12 | Number of pixels from left relative to pointer |
| Word | REQ.RELTOP | 14 | Number of pixels from top relative to pointer |
| Long | REQ.GADGET | 16 | Pointer to gadget list for requester |
| Long | REQ.BORDER | 20 | Pointer to BORDER structure |
| Long | REQ.TEXT | 24 | Pointer to INTUITEXT structure |
| Word | REQ.FLAGS | 28 | Flag bits |
| Byte | REQ.BACKFILL | 30 | Pen Number for back-plane fill |
| Long | REQ.LAYER | 32 | Pointer to LAYER structure; 32 empty bytes of padding (not used by programs) |
| Long | REQ.IMAGEBMAP | 68 | Pointer to bitmap of predrawn image |

| *Field Size* | *Name* | *Offset* | *Description* |
|---|---|---|---|
| Long | REQ.RWINDOW | 72 | Pointer to window of this requester; 36 empty bytes of padding (not used by programs) |

## Requirements of the Autorequester

The autorequester is the simplest type of requester used by Intuition. It's the easiest requester to program because an Intuition function (AUTOREQUEST) does almost all the work.

When a simple warning or yes/no choice is required of a user, the autorequester is the recommended way to present it. The complete REQUESTER structure does not need to be filled in when creating an autorequester. The Intuition AUTOREQUEST call does most of the work. The program simply provides three null-terminated text declarations:

- A text string for the user's positive choice (*yes*)
- A text string for the user's negative choice (*no*)
- A text string describing the choice (*danger, continue?*)

These are converted to Intuitext strings. The addresses of the three strings are passed to AUTOREQUEST. The AUTOREQUEST function is also supplied with positioning information for the requester.

One more feature of the autorequester is that it creates a new set of IDCMPFLAGS. The programmer can select a combination of IDCMPFLAGS to indicate a positive reply by the user, and other flags for a negative reply. The AUTOREQUEST function puts them into effect automatically. They remain in effect as long as the autorequester is displayed. The previous IDCMPFLAGS are automatically restored when the autorequester is finished with its work.

The AUTOREQUEST function takes the positive and negative INTUITEXT structures and makes them into gadgets. The positive gadget is placed in the lower left of the AUTOREQUESTER and the negative gadget in the lower right. The Intuition system knows where the positive and negative gadgets are, and can send messages to the program in data register D0, indicating which was selected by the user. (See Figure 20-1.)

### Figure 20-1. Autorequester

Note that the autorequester is attached to the Intuition window.

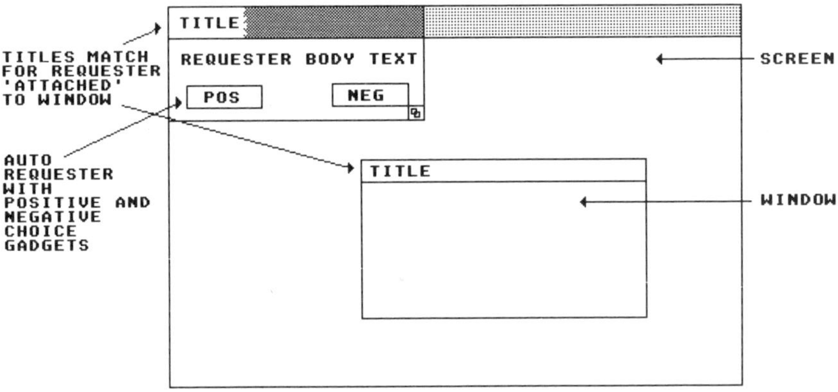


Listing 20-1, REQS.ASM, is an include file with support subroutines and macros for the programs appearing later in this chapter. Enter the file and save it on the DEV disk with the name:

DEV:RAMIT/INCLUDES/REQS.ASM

### Listing 20-1. REQS.ASM

Autorequester support routines and macros.

```
;********************************* REQS.ASM BY DANIEL WOLF
;COPYRIGHT 1987 BY COMPUTE! BOOKS
;03/21/87

;A MACRO TO CREATE REQUESTER INTUITEXTS FROM BODY, POS, AND NEG NTEXTS

MAKEREQ MACRO  ;WINDOW PTR, PTR TO BODY NTEXT, PTR TO POS, PTR TO NEG, ERROR
         ;RESULT IS 3 INTUITEXT ADDRESSES IN A1,A2,A3
 LEA \1,A1
 ZERA A2
 IFNC '\2','0'
 LEA \2,A2
 ENDC
 LEA \3,A3
 BSR SETUPAUTOREQUEST
 TST.L D4
 BNE \4
 ENDM

;A MACRO TO SAVE THE RESULTS OF MAKEREQ (3 INTUITEXTS COME BACK!)

SAVEREQ MACRO              ;LABEL OF HIDING PLACE WITH THREE LONG WORDS RESERVED
 PUSHREG A4
 LEA \1,A4             ;PUT LABEL INTO A4
 BSR _SAVEREQ
 PULLREG A4
 ENDM
```

```
_SAVEREQ
 MOVE.L A1,(A4)+
 MOVE.L A2,(A4)+
 MOVE.L A3,(A4)
 RTS

;A MACRO TO CREATE AND SHOW THE REQUESTER IN A GIVEN WINDOW W/ EXISTING 3 ITEXTS

REQUEST MACRO ;WINDOW,PTR TO REQUESTER ITEXTS, REQXMAX, REQYMAX
 PUSHREG AØ-A4/D2-D3
 MOVE.L \1,AØ
 LEA \2,A4              ;BRING IN THREE ITEXT PTRS FROM HIDING
 IFC '\3',''
 MOVE.L #REQXMAX,D2 ;WIDTH
 MOVE.L #REQYMAX,D3 ;HEIGHT
 ENDC
 BSR _REQUEST
 PULLREG AØ-A4/D2-D3
 ENDM

_REQUEST
 MOVE.L (A4)+,A1
 MOVE.L (A4)+,A2
 MOVE.L (A4),A3
 ZERO DØ               ;TOP
 ZERO D1               ;LEFT
 INTLIB AUTOREQUEST
 RTS

;AUTOREQUEST SUPPORT   ENTER W/ AØ->WINDOW A1,A2,A3->BODY, POS, NEG TEXTS

SETUPAUTOREQUEST                        ;SETS UP FOR USING AUTOREQUESTER
 MOVE.L AØ,_THISREQWINDOW               ;STASH POINTERS WHILE ALLOCATING
 MOVE.L A1,_THISREQBTEXT
 MOVE.L A2,_THISREQPTEXT
 MOVE.L A3,_THISREQNTEXT

_BODREQALLOC
 REMEMBERPUBMEM REMEMBERKEY,#SIZE.IT   ;ALLOCATE FOR AN INTUITEXT
 TST.L DØ
 BEQ ERR_MAKEAREQMEM
 MOVE.L DØ,_THISREQBITEXT               ;THIS IS THE BODY INTUITEXT
 MOVE.L DØ,AØ
 MOVE.L _THISREQBTEXT,A1
 BSR CREATETEXT
 ADD.W #1Ø,IT.TOPEDGE(AØ)
 ADD.W #1Ø,IT.LEFTEDGE(AØ)

_POSREQALLOC
 MOVE.L #Ø,_THISREQPITEXT               ;PROVIDE FOR POSSIBILITY OF NO POSITIVE
 TST.L _THISREQPTEXT
 BEQ.S _NEGREQALLOC
 REMEMBERPUBMEM REMEMBERKEY,#SIZE.IT   ;ALLOCATE FOR AN INTUITEXT
 TST.L DØ
 BEQ ERR_MAKEAREQMEM
 MOVE.L DØ,_THISREQPITEXT               ;THIS IS POSITIVE INTUITEXT
 MOVE.L DØ,AØ
 MOVE.L _THISREQPTEXT,A1
 BSR CREATETEXT
 ADDQ.W #1,IT.TOPEDGE(AØ)
 ADDQ.W #4,IT.LEFTEDGE(AØ)

_NEGREQALLOC
 REMEMBERPUBMEM REMEMBERKEY,#SIZE.IT   ;ALLOCATE FOR AN INTUITEXT
 TST.L DØ
 BEQ ERR_MAKEAREQMEM
 MOVE.L DØ,_THISREQNITEXT               ;THIS IS NEGATIVE INTUITEXT
 MOVE.L DØ,AØ
 MOVE.L _THISREQNTEXT,A1
 BSR CREATETEXT
 ADDQ.W #1,IT.TOPEDGE(AØ)
 ADDQ.W #4,IT.LEFTEDGE(AØ)

 MOVE.L _THISREQWINDOW,AØ
 MOVE.L _THISREQBITEXT,A1
 MOVE.L _THISREQPITEXT,A2
 MOVE.L _THISREQNITEXT,A3
 ZERO DØ
```

```
 ZERO D1
 MOVE.L #25Ø,D2                      ;WIDTH
 MOVE.L #8Ø,D3                       ;HEIGHT
 ZERO D4                             ;CLEAR D4, NO ERROR
 RTS

ERR_MAKEAREQMEM
 MOVE.L #CANTALLOCMEM,D4             ;MOVE ERROR CODE TO D4
 RTS

_THISREQWINDOW  DC.L Ø      ;POINTER TO WINDOW FOR THIS REQUESTER
_THISREQBITEXT  DC.L Ø      ;POINTER TO BODY INTUITEXT
_THISREQPITEXT  DC.L Ø      ;POINTER TO POSITIVE INTUITEXT
_THISREQNITEXT  DC.L Ø      ;POINTER TO NEGATIVE INTUITEXT
_THISREQBTEXT   DC.L Ø      ;POINTER TO BODY NULL-TERMINATED TEXT
_THISREQPTEXT   DC.L Ø      ;POINTER TO POSITIVE NULL-TERMINATED TEXT
_THISREQNTEXT   DC.L Ø      ;POINTER TO NEGATIVE NULL-TERMINATED TEXT
```

**The MAKEAUTOREQUEST subroutine.** The MAKEAUTOREQUEST subroutine in REQS.ASM prepares the structures and performs auxiliary work required to setup for the AUTOREQUEST function call. The programmer supplies three text declarations and positioning information for the requester.

In the MAKEAUTOREQUEST subroutine, no special positive or negative IDCMPFLAGS are specified. A value is returned in register D0, which will inform your program of the user's response.

AUTOREQ (Listing 20-2) shows how to use the REQS.ASM macros to prepare a simple yes/no choice requester. Pay special attention to the way messages are obtained from the requester in the program loop that monitors the IDCMP. The MAKEREQ, SAVEREQ, and REQUEST macros take over almost all the effort of programming the autorequester. These macros also relieve the programmer of monitoring the Intuimessages coming back from the autorequester. TRUE is returned in D0 when the PositiveText was selected; FALSE, when the NegativeText was selected.

The AUTOREQ program shows one way to make the Requester appear. Simply use the REQUEST macro. You may also use the right mouse button (normally used only for Menu selection) to produce a Requester. Review the SETDMREQUEST function in the Intuition Reference Manual. When a program calls that function, an existing Requester is attached to a double-click of the right mouse button. Then if the user double-clicks the right mouse button, the Requester (using its existing REQUESTER STRUCTURE) appears. The usual messages can then be sent to the program, which later calls ENDREQUEST to clear the Requester from the Window. The CLEARDM-REQUEST function unattaches the Requester from a double-click of the mouse. Experimentation with the Double-Mouse Requester (DMRequest) functions is left as an exercise to ambitious readers.

A third alternative for making a Requester appear is the Intuition REQUEST function, which uses an existing REQUESTER STRUCTURE and displays the corresponding Requester image. It also uses the IDCMP for message passing to the program. When you ambitiously design beautiful imagery and Gadget-laden Requesters, the REQUEST function is the most straightforward way to use them. Use of the REQUEST function is left as an exercise for the reader. A routine for allocating the required memory and performing the fill-in function should look something like the MAKEAMENU, MAKEAGADGET, MAKEAWINDOW, and other routines presented in earlier type-in include files.

Listing 20-2 demonstrates using the REQS.ASM routines and macros to make a two-choice autorequester for an Intuition window.

### Listing 20-2. AUTOREQ.ASM

Autorequester demonstration using support from REQS.ASM.

```
;NAME: AUTOREQ.ASM  BY DANIEL WOLF
;COPYRIGHT 1987 BY COMPUTE! PUBLICATIONS
;09/10/87

 BRA _START

TXT EQU 1
REQ EQU 1
WIN EQU 1

REQXMAX EQU 360
REQYMAX EQU 60

 INCLUDE "HEADER"

MAIN

_BUILDAWINDOW

 MAKEWIN #TITLE,40,15,500,40,ERROR,WINDOW

 PRINTNEWAT WINDOW,MESSAGE,5,20,DONE

 MAKEREQ REQMESSAGE,NO,YES,ERROR;USE MACRO TO SET UP AUTOREQUESTER

 SAVEREQ REQ1;SAVE ADDRESSES OF THE INTUITEXTS
```

```
LOOP
 MOVE.L WINDOW,AØ
 MOVE.L WW.USERPORT(AØ),AØ  ;LISTEN TO PORT ATTACHED TO THIS WINDOW
 SYSLIB WAITPORT            ;WAIT FOR A SPECIFIED MESSAGE TO ARRIVE
 MOVE.L WINDOW,AØ
 MOVE.L WW.USERPORT(AØ),AØ
 SYSLIB GETMSG              ;MESSAGE HAS ARRIVE WITHIN SPECIFICATIONS
 TST.L DØ                   ;POINTER TO INTUIMESSAGE COMES BACK IN DØ
 BEQ LOOP                   ;NO MESSAGE THERE, SO LOOP

 MOVE.L DØ,AØ;IF USER PRESSED MOUSE LEFT MOUSE BUTTON THEN
 MOVE.L IM.CLASS(AØ),D7
 MOVE.L IM.CODE(AØ),D6
 MOVE.L AØ,A1
 SYSLIB REPLYMSG
 CMP.L #CLOSEWINDOW,D7;SEE IF USER HAS HIT CLOSEWINDOW BUTTON
 BEQ DONE

HEREITIS;IT WASN'T THE CLOSE GADGET SO ...
 REQUEST WINDOW,REQ1;SHOW THE REQUESTER
 TST.L DØ;WAIT FOR USER REPLY WITH MOUSE
 BNE LOOP;IF USER HIT 'NEGATIVE' BUTTON, THEN DO THIS AGAIN!

ERROR
DONE
 MOVE.L WINDOW,DØ
 BEQ.S QUITNOW
 MOVE.L DØ,AØ
 INTLIB CLOSEWINDOW
 ZERO DØ
QUITNOW
 RTS

 EVENPC

WINDOW DC.L Ø

REQ1 DC.L Ø,Ø,Ø          ;PTR TO BODY ITEXT, POSITEXT, NEGITEXT

_THISFONTHITE DC.W 9

TITLE
 DC.B ' AutoReq  by D. Wolf ',Ø
 EVENPC

MESSAGE
 DC.B ' Please press the left mouse button somewhere in this Window ',Ø
 EVENPC

;**** REQUESTERS **** POSITIVE/NEGATIVE responses

REQMESSAGE
 DC.B ' THIS IS AN AUTOREQUESTER - QUIT ? ',Ø
 EVENPC
YES
 DC.B ' YES ',Ø
 EVENPC
NO
 DC.B ' NO ',Ø
 EVENPC
```

# SECTION 6

# Graphics

# CHAPTER 21

# An Introduction to Amiga Graphics

The Graphics library makes it simple to draw lines, single *pixels* (picture elements, the smallest units of graphics information) of selected colors, fill a window or screen with color, and so on. Some graphics macros are provided in the MACROS.ASM listing and are documented with information about their use. They include:

- READPOINT
- DRAWPOINT
- RECTFILL
- DRAWLINE
- LOADRGB

The macros call Graphics library functions for single pixels, rectangular regions, lines, and color-register maps. They're easy to use. You should be able to learn them quickly by reading through the program examples provided. A complete guide to the Graphics library would require another large book. This section is intended to be an introduction to graphics.

In order for the programs later in this chapter to use the Graphics library routines, the GFXEQUATES.ASM file must be entered. GFXEQUATES.ASM appears in Listing 21-1. Use EMACS or your favorite text editor to type in this equate file. Save it as:

DEV:RAMIT/INCLUDES/GFXEQUATES.ASM

**Listing 21-1. GFXEQUATES.ASM**

```
;******** GFXEQUATES.ASM
;03/24/87

;*** GRAPHICS CONSTANTS

COMPLEMENT   EQU $2
EXTRA_HALFBRITE EQU $80
HAM                 EQU $800
HIRES               EQU $8000
INVERSVID    EQU $4
JAM1                EQU $0
JAM2                EQU $1
LACE                EQU $4
```

```
;*** GRAPHICS LIBRARY ROUTINE OFFSETS (PARTIAL LIST FROM AMIGA.LIB)

LVO.BLTTEMPLATE EQU $FFFFFFDC
LVO.CLEAREOL        EQU $FFFFFFD6
LVO.CLEARREGION EQU $FFFFFDFØ
LVO.CLEARSCREEN EQU $FFFFFFDØ
LVO.DRAW     EQU $FFFFFFØA
LVO.FLOOD    EQU $FFFFFEB6
LVO.GETRGB4         EQU $FFFFFDBA
LVO.LOADRGB4        EQU $FFFFFF4Ø
LVO.MOVE     EQU $FFFFFF1Ø
LVO.POLYDRAW        EQU $FFFFFEBØ
LVO.READPIXEL       EQU $FFFFFEC2
LVO.RECTFILL        EQU $FFFFFECE
LVO.SETAPEN         EQU $FFFFFEAA
LVO.SETBPEN         EQU $FFFFFEA4
LVO.SETDRMD         EQU $FFFFFE9E
LVO.SETRGB4         EQU $FFFFFEEØ
LVO.WRITEPIXEL      EQU $FFFFFEBC

;*** A COUPLE OF RASTPORT STRUCTURE OFFSETS

RP.FGPEN     EQU $19
RP.BGPEN     EQU $1A
RP.OPEN             EQU $1B
RP.DRAWMODE EQU $1C

;*** A COUPLE OF VIEWPORT STRUCTURE OFFSETS

VP.COLORMAP         EQU $4
VP.MODES     EQU $2Ø
```

## The RASTPORT Structure

Most Graphics library routines work with a pointer to a RASTPORT structure. Each window and screen has a RASTPORT structure (WW.RPORT and SCRN.RASTPORT) so the pointer can easily be located by a program.

The RASTPORT structure contains information about the memory layout of the bitmaps in which drawing occurs, and about drawing modes and patterns. The program examples in Listing 21-2 show how to obtain the pointers to a Window's RASTPORT and VIEWPORT.

**Listing 21-2. Examples to identify a Window's RASTPORT and VIEWPORT**

```
;                                                ; EXAMPLE 1. RASTPORT
;                                                ; STRUCTURE POINTER
;                                                ; FROM A WINDOW
            MOVE.L   WINDOW,A0                   ; START WITH WINDOW'S
                                                 ; ADDRESS
            MOVE.L   WW.RPORT(A0),THISRASTPORT   ; GET RASTPORT ADDRESS
                                                 ; FROM WINDOW
;                                                ; EXAMPLE 2. VIEWPORT
;                                                ; STRUCTURE POINTER
;                                                ; FROM A WINDOW
            MOVE.L   WINDOW,A0                   ; START WITH WINDOW'S
                                                 ; ADDRESS
```

```
              INTLIB    VIEWPORTADDRESS              ; GET VIEWPORT ADDRESS
                                                     ; FROM WINDOW
              MOVE.L    D0,THISVIEWPORT
;                                                    ; EXAMPLE 3. BOTH
              MOVE.L    WINDOW,A0                    ; START WITH WINDOW
                                                     ; POINTER
              MOVE.L    WW.RPORT(A0),THISRASTPORT    ; SAVE RASTPORT POINTER
                                                     ; AT LABEL
              MOVE.L    WINDOW,A0                    ; GET WINDOW POINTER
              INTLIB    VIEWPORTADDRESS              ; SAVE VIEWPORT POINTER
                                                     ; AT LABEL
              MOVE.L    D0,THISVIEWPORT
;                                                    ; DATA DECLARATION
;                                                    ; LATER IN PROGRAM
THISRASTPORT  DC.L      0
THISVIEWPORT  DC.L      0
```

## Drawing into a RASTPORT

The Graphics library routines for single-point drawing and line drawing are similar to the operation of a computer plotter. The graphics routines use this plotter metaphor to simplify programming simple drawing.

Imagine the process of drawing a line using a plotter. The plotter's pen is in the up position, not touching the paper. You give the plotter an instruction to move the pen to the starting point of your line. A second command lowers the pen to the paper. A third command moves the pen to the end of the line. Figure 21-1 illustrates this plotter concept.

**Figure 21-1. Plotter Analogy for Graphics Drawing Functions**

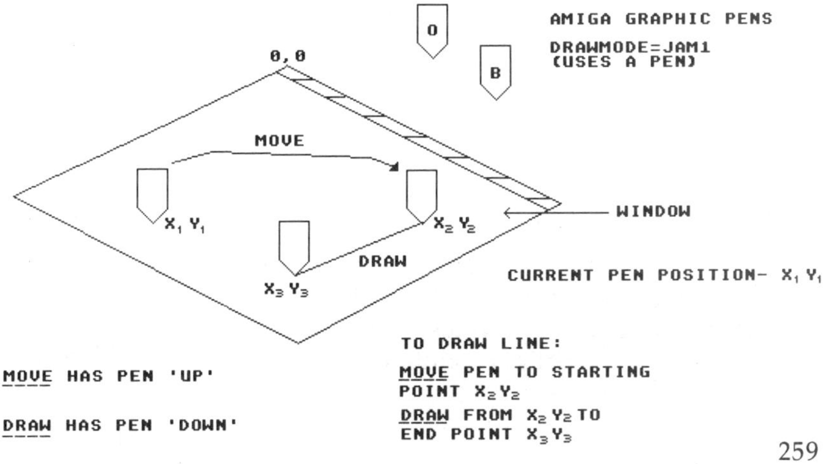

Table 21-2 contains a list of some Graphics library functions with parameter-passing register specifications you can use for more complex graphics. (This table lists only routines used in programs in this book.)

**Table 21-2. Graphics Library Functions with Parameter Register Specifications**

**Drawing Color Control Functions**

| *Function Name* | *Description* | *Parameters* | *Registers* |
|---|---|---|---|
| SETAPEN | Set foreground pen | (RP,Color Reg) | A0,D0 |
| SETBPEN | Set background pen | (RP,Color Reg) | A0,D0 |
| SETOPEN | Set outline pen | (RP,Color Reg) | A0,D0 |
| SETDRMD | Set drawing mode | (RP,Mode) | A0,D0 |

Mode = JAM1, JAM2, COMPLEMENT, INVERSVID

**Line Drawing Functions**

| *Function Name* | *Description* | *Parameters* | *Registers* |
|---|---|---|---|
| MOVE | Move Pen to *x, y* | (RP,*x*,*y*) | A0,D0,D1 |
| DRAW | Draw to *x, y* | (RP,*x*,*y*) | A0,D0,D1 |
| POLYDRAW | Draw List of Lines | (RP,NumPairs,List) | A0,D0,A1 |

**Point Drawing Functions**

| *Function Name* | *Description* | *Parameters* | *Registers* |
|---|---|---|---|
| WRITEPIXEL | Set Pixel Color | (RP,*x*,*y*) | A0,D0,D1 |
| READPIXEL | Read Pixel Color | (RP,*x*,*y*) | A0,D0,D1 |

**Region Filling Functions**

| *Function Name* | *Description* | *Parameters* | *Registers* |
|---|---|---|---|
| FLOOD | Flood within boundary | (RP,Mode,*x*,*y*) | A0,D2,D0,D1 |
| Mode = 0 Fill nonmatching pixels up to boundary of different color | | | |
| Mode = 1 Fill only matching color pixels with new color | | | |
| RECTFILL | Rectangle fill | (RP,*xMN*,*yMN*,*xMX*,*yMX*) | A0,D0–D3 |
| SETRAST | Fill entire raster | (RP,Color Reg) | A0,D0 |

**Color Register Control**

| *Function Name* | *Description* | *Parameters* | *Registers* |
|---|---|---|---|
| SETRGB4 | Set 1 Color Register | (VP,CReg,Red,Grn,Blu) | A0,D0–D3 |
| LOADRGB4 | Set >1 Color Register | (VP, CTable, How Many) | A0,A1,D0 |

Listing 21-3, GFX1.ASM, is a short program that opens an Intuition window and uses the window's RASTPORT structure to draw single pixels and lines. Since all programs are in the Workbench screen, they're limited to four colors.

## Listing 21-3. GFX1.ASM

```
;GFX1.ASM BY DANIEL WOLF
;COPYRIGHT 1987 BY COMPUTE! PUBLICATIONS
;09/10/87

 BRA _START

MAT EQU 1     ;INCLUDE MATH TO GET HEXCONVERT ROUTINE

TXT EQU 1     ;A FEW INTUITEXT MESSAGE WILL APPEAR
HEX EQU 1     ;WE'LL HAVE HEX OUTPUT ON THE PROPORTIONAL GADGET
GFX EQU 1     ;WE NEED THE GRAPHICS LIBRARY AND GFXEQUATES

WBC EQU 1     ;LETS MAKE SURE THERE'S A CONSOLE FOR DOS I/O FROM WORKBENCH

 INCLUDE "HEADER"

MAIN
 DOSPRINT STDOUT,#MYMESSAGE ;IF INITIATED FROM CLI, THEN OUTPUT TITLE MESSAGE
 ZERO D0
 MOVEA.L COMMAND,A0         ;PUT ADDRESS OF COMMAND LINE IN A0
 CMPI.B #'?',(A0)           ;IF FIRST CHARACTER IS ? THEN
 BNE.S _BUILDAWINDOW
 BRA USAGE

_BUILDAWINDOW
 LEA NEWWINDOW,A0
 INTLIB OPENWINDOW
 TST.L D0
 BEQ ERROR
 MOVE.L D0,WINDOW          ;WINDOW OPENED HAS ITS POINTER IN D0
 MOVE.L D0,A0
 MOVE.L WW.RPORT(A0),RP

 PRINTNEWAT WINDOW,MSG1,90,50,DONE     ;A MESSAGE!

 SETAPEN RP,#1                         ;SET COLOR REGISTER #1
 RECTFILL RP,#10,#10,#20,#20;DRAW A RECTANGLE
 SETAPEN RP,#2;COLOR #2
 RECTFILL RP,#15,#15,#30,#30
 SETAPEN RP,#3;COLOR #3
 RECTFILL RP,#25,#25,#70,#70

 PRINTNEWAT WINDOW,MSG2,90,140,DONE;MESSAGE

 SETAPEN RP,#1;COLOR 1
 DRAWPOINT RP,#100,#100;DRAW ONE PIXEL AT 100,100
 SETAPEN RP,#2;COLOR 2
 DRAWPOINT RP,#100,#110
 SETAPEN RP,#3;COLOR 3
 DRAWPOINT RP,#100,#120

 SETAPEN RP,#2
 DRAWLINE RP,#101,#101,#130,#130

LOOP
 MOVE.L WINDOW,A0
 MOVE.L WW.USERPORT(A0),A0  ;LISTEN TO PORT ATTACHED TO THIS WINDOW
 SYSLIB WAITPORT            ;WAIT FOR A SPECIFIED MESSAGE TO ARRIVE
 MOVE.L WINDOW,A0
 MOVE.L WW.USERPORT(A0),A0
 SYSLIB GETMSG              ;MESSAGE HAS ARRIVE WITHIN SPECIFICATIONS
 TST.L D0                   ;POINTER TO INTUIMESSAGE COMES BACK IN D0
 BEQ.S LOOP                 ;NO MESSAGE THERE, SO LOOP
 MOVE.L D0,A1               ;POINTER TO INTUIMESSAGE CAME BACK, USE IN A1
 MOVE.L IM.CLASS(A1),D2     ;CLOSEWINDOW AND GADGET MESSAGES APPEAR HERE
 MOVE.W IM.CODE(A1),D3      ;MENU AND MENUITEM APPEAR HERE
 MOVE.W IM.QUALIFIER(A1),D4 ;KEYS APPEAR HERE
 SYSLIB REPLYMSG            ;QUICK, SEND MESSAGE BACK NOW!

 CMP.L #CLOSEWINDOW,D2
 BEQ DONE                   ;IF ITS A CLOSEWINDOW MESSAGE, THEN DO SO...

 BRA LOOP
```

```
DONE
 ZERO DØ
QUIT
 PUSHREG DØ
 MOVE.L WINDOW,DØ
 BEQ.S 1$
 MOVE.L DØ,AØ
 INTLIB CLOSEWINDOW
1$
 PULLREG DØ
QUITNOW
 RTS

ERROR
 DOSPRINT STDOUT,#ERRORTEXT
 MOVEQ #CANTOPENWINDOW,DØ
 RTS
USAGE
 DOSPRINT STDOUT,#USAGETEXT
 BRA DONE

;***** TEXT DATA DECLARATIONS *****

MYMESSAGE
 DC.B 1Ø,' GFX1 by D. Wolf Copyright 1987 by Compute! Publications ',1Ø,Ø
 EVENPC
MYWINDOWTITLE
 DC.B ' GFX1  by D.Wolf ',Ø
 EVENPC
USAGETEXT
 DC.B 'Usage: GFX1',1Ø,Ø
 EVENPC
ERRORTEXT
 DC.B 1Ø,'Sorry, cannot open window ',1Ø,Ø
 EVENPC
MSG1
 DC.B 'A FEW RECTANGULAR FILLS',Ø
 EVENPC
MSG2
 DC.B 'A FEW PIXELS AND A LINE',Ø
 EVENPC

WINDOW DC.L Ø                   ;POINTER TO WINDOW STRUCTURE
RP DC.L Ø                       ;POINTER TO WINDOW'S RASTPORT STRUCTURE

_THISFONTHITE DC.W 9            ;DEFAULT FONT HEIGHT


NEWWINDOW
 DC.W Ø
 DC.W Ø
 DC.W 64Ø
 DC.W 19Ø
 DC.B -1
 DC.B -1
 DC.L CLOSEWINDOW
 DC.L WINDOWDRAG!WINDOWDEPTH!WINDOWCLOSE!SMART_REFRESH
 DC.L Ø
 DC.L Ø
 DC.L MYWINDOWTITLE
 DC.L Ø
 DC.L Ø
 DC.W 14Ø            ;BE CAREFUL MIN HEIGHT AND WIDTH AREN'T
 DC.W 14Ø            ;SO SMALL THAT THE RELATIVE HEIGHT AND WIDTH
 DC.W 64Ø            ;OF THE GADGET CAN BECOME LESS THAN ZERO
 DC.W 4ØØ            ;OR YOU'LL BE SORRY! (COULD ELIMINATE SIZING INSTEAD)
 DC.W WBENCHSCREEN
 END
```

Listing 21-4, GFX2.ASM, is a program that performs some line and area drawing, then alters the colors used by the window's RASTPORT.

## Listing 21-4. GFX2.ASM

```
;GFX2.ASM BY DANIEL WOLF
;COPYRIGHT 1987 BY COMPUTE! PUBLICATIONS
;09/10/87

 BRA _START

MAT EQU 1     ;INCLUDE MATH TO GET HEXCONVERT ROUTINE

GAD EQU 1     ;WE'LL LET A PROPORTIONAL GADGET CONTROL SOME GRAPHICS
TXT EQU 1     ;A FEW INTUITEXT MESSAGE WILL APPEAR
HEX EQU 1     ;WE'LL HAVE HEX OUTPUT ON THE PROPORTIONAL GADGET
GFX EQU 1     ;WE NEED THE GRAPHICS LIBRARY AND GFXEQUATES

WBC EQU 1     ;LETS MAKE SURE THERE'S A CONSOLE FOR DOS I/O FROM WORKBENCH

 INCLUDE "HEADER"

MAIN
 DOSPRINT STDOUT,#MYMESSAGE ;IF INITIATED FROM CLI, THEN OUTPUT TITLE MESSAGE
 ZERO D0
 MOVEA.L COMMAND,A0         ;PUT ADDRESS OF COMMAND LINE IN A0
 CMPI.B #'?',(A0)           ;IF FIRST CHARACTER IS ? THEN
 BNE.S _BUILDAWINDOW
 BRA USAGE

_BUILDAWINDOW
 LEA NEWWINDOW,A0
 INTLIB OPENWINDOW
 TST.L D0
 BEQ ERROR
 MOVE.L D0,WINDOW          ;WINDOW OPENED HAS ITS POINTER IN D0
 MOVE.L D0,A0
 MOVE.L WW.RPORT(A0),RP
 MOVE.L WINDOW,A0
 INTLIB VIEWPORTADDRESS
 MOVE.L D0,VP

 PRINTNEWAT WINDOW,MSG1,90,50,DONE    ;A MESSAGE!

 SETAPEN RP,#1                         ;SET COLOR REGISTER #1
 RECTFILL RP,#10,#10,#20,#20;DRAW A RECTANGLE
 SETAPEN RP,#2;COLOR #2
 RECTFILL RP,#15,#15,#30,#30
 SETAPEN RP,#3;COLOR #3
 RECTFILL RP,#25,#25,#70,#70

 PRINTNEWAT WINDOW,MSG2,90,120,DONE;MESSAGE

 SETAPEN RP,#1;COLOR 1
 DRAWPOINT RP,#100,#100;DRAW ONE PIXEL AT 100,100
 SETAPEN RP,#2;COLOR 2
 DRAWPOINT RP,#100,#110
 SETAPEN RP,#3;COLOR 3
 DRAWPOINT RP,#100,#120

 MOVE.L #TICKSPERSECOND,D1
 ASL.L #2,D1
 DOSLIB DELAY

 SETAPEN RP,#0;NOW CLEAR THE WHOLE WINDOW
 RECTFILL RP,#10,#10,#630,#180;AND LETS HAVE FUN WITH THE PGADGET

_BUILDAGADGET               ;DEFAULT WILL BE A HORIZONTAL PROPORTIONAL GADGET
 MOVE.W #20,D4              ;LEFTEDGE FOR GADGET
 MOVE.W #20,D5              ;TOPEDGE FOR GADGET
 MOVE.W #-100,D6            ;RELATIVE WIDTH, 100 PIXELS LESS THAN WINDOW
 MOVE.W #-120,D7            ;RELATIVE HEIGHT,120 PIXELS LESS THAN WINDOW
```

```
 BSR MAKEAPROPGADGET           ;MAKE THE GADGET, INTUITEXT, AND BORDER
 MOVEA.L WINDOW,AØ
 MOVEA.L _THISGADGET,A1        ;ROUTINE LEAVES POINTER TO GADGET STRUCTURE HERE
 MOVE.L A1,_FIRSTGADGET        ;ITS THE FIRST ONE, A SPECIAL POINTER FOR WINDOW

_CHANGEGADGFLAGS                       ;HERE'S HOW TO USE CUSTOM FLAGS COMBINATIONS
 MOVE.W GADG.FLAGS(A1),DØ              ;IN SPITE OF THE DEFAULT 'MAKEAGADGET' FLAGS
 ORI.W #GRELWIDTH!GRELHEIGHT,DØ ;(SET THE RELATIVE WIDTH AND HEIGHT FLAGS)
 MOVE.W DØ,GADG.FLAGS(A1)              ;BRING FLAGS OUT, 'OR' AS DESIRED, PUT 'EM BACK

_NOWADDTHEGADGET
 ZERO DØ
 MOVE.W #-1,DØ                 ;THIS ASSURES ITS AT THE TOP OF THE LIST
 INTLIB ADDGADGET              ;ATTACH GADGET TO WINDOW STRUCTURE'S GADGET LIST

 MOVE.L _FIRSTGADGET,AØ        ;PASS TWO ADDRESS PARAMETERS TO THE REFRESH ROUTINE
 MOVE.L WINDOW,A1
 INTLIB REFRESHGADGETS         ;NOW MAKE THE GADGET APPEAR!

LOOP
 MOVE.L WINDOW,AØ
 MOVE.L WW.USERPORT(AØ),AØ     ;LISTEN TO PORT ATTACHED TO THIS WINDOW
 SYSLIB WAITPORT               ;WAIT FOR A SPECIFIED MESSAGE TO ARRIVE
 MOVE.L WINDOW,AØ
 MOVE.L WW.USERPORT(AØ),AØ
 SYSLIB GETMSG                 ;MESSAGE HAS ARRIVE WITHIN SPECIFICATIONS
 TST.L DØ                      ;POINTER TO INTUIMESSAGE COMES BACK IN DØ
 BEQ.S LOOP                    ;NO MESSAGE THERE, SO LOOP
 MOVE.L DØ,A1                  ;POINTER TO INTUIMESSAGE CAME BACK, USE IN A1
 MOVE.L IM.CLASS(A1),D2        ;CLOSEWINDOW AND GADGET MESSAGES APPEAR HERE
 MOVE.W IM.CODE(A1),D3         ;MENU AND MENUITEM APPEAR HERE
 MOVE.W IM.QUALIFIER(A1),D4 ;KEYS APPEAR HERE
 SYSLIB REPLYMSG               ;QUICK, SEND MESSAGE BACK NOW!

 CMP.L #CLOSEWINDOW,D2
 BEQ DONE                      ;IF ITS A CLOSEWINDOW MESSAGE, THEN DO SO...
 CMP.L #GADGETUP,D2
 BNE LOOP                      ;THIS ISN'T A CLOSE OR A GADGETUP
 BSR DOGADGET
 BRA LOOP

DONE
 ZERO DØ
QUIT
 PUSHREG DØ
 MOVE.L WINDOW,DØ
 BEQ.S 1$
 MOVE.L DØ,AØ
 INTLIB CLOSEWINDOW
1$
 PULLREG DØ
QUITNOW
 RTS

ERROR
 DOSPRINT STDOUT,#ERRORTEXT
 MOVEQ #CANTOPENWINDOW,DØ
 RTS
USAGE
 DOSPRINT STDOUT,#USAGETEXT
 BRA DONE

DOGADGET                               ;THIS CODE EXECUTED IF GADGET TOGGLED
 PUSHALL
 MOVEA.L _FIRSTGADGET,AØ               ;USE GADGET STRUCTURE TO
 MOVEA.L GADG.SPECIALINFO(AØ),AØ;FIND THE PROPINFO SUB-STRUCTURE POINTER
 ZERO DØ
 MOVE.W PI.HORIZPOT(AØ),DØ             ;AND THE VALUE OF THE 'POT' VARIABLE
 MOVE.W DØ,POTVALUE
 BSR HEXCONVERT                        ;NOW DECODE AND PRINT VALUE TO CLI WINDOW
 ZERO DØ
 MOVE.W POTVALUE,DØ
 LSR.W #4,DØ
 LSR.W #3,DØ
 MOVE.W DØ,SIZE                        ;NOW DO SOME GRAPHICS BASED ON THE POT VALUE
 SETAPEN RP,#Ø
 RECTFILL RP,#2,#135,#6ØØ,#18Ø  ;CLEAR THE DRAWING AREA
```

```
 SETAPEN RP,#3
 RECTFILL RP,#5,#150,SIZE,#180  ;DRAW RECTANGLE PROPORTIONAL TO POT VALUE
 SETAPEN RP,#2
 DRAWLINE RP,#5,#140,SIZE,#140  ;DRAW LINE PROPORTIONAL TO POT VALUE
 SETAPEN RP,#1
 DRAWPOINT RP,SIZE,#132         ;DRAW PIXEL AT X POSITION PROPORTIONAL TO POT
 ZERO D0
 MOVE.W SIZE,D0
 MOVE.W D0,LASTCOL
 LOADRGB VP,COLRS,4
 ZERO D0
 MOVE.W SIZE,D0
 BSR HEXCONVERT
 PULLALL
 RTS

;***** TEXT DATA DECLARATIONS *****

MYMESSAGE
 DC.B 10,' GFX2 by D. Wolf Copyright 1987 by Compute! Publications ',10,0
 EVENPC
MYWINDOWTITLE
 DC.B ' GFX2  by D. Wolf ',0
 EVENPC
USAGETEXT
 DC.B 'Usage: GFX2',10,0
 EVENPC
ERRORTEXT
 DC.B 10,'Sorry, cannot open window ',10,0
 EVENPC
MSG1
 DC.B 'A FEW RECTANGULAR FILLS',0
 EVENPC
MSG2
 DC.B 'A FEW PIXELS',0
 EVENPC

WINDOW DC.L 0                   ;POINTER TO WINDOW STRUCTURE
RP DC.L 0                       ;POINTER TO WINDOW'S RASTPORT STRUCTURE
VP DC.L 0                       ;POINTER TO WINDOW'S VIEWPORT STRUCTURE
_FIRSTGADGET DC.L 0             ;POINTER TO GADGET'S STRUCTURE IN MEMORY
_THISFONTHITE DC.W 9            ;DEFAULT FONT HEIGHT

POTVALUE DC.W 0
SIZE DC.W 0

COLRS
 DC.W $FFF
 DC.W $000
 DC.W $00F
LASTCOL
 DC.W $0F0

NEWWINDOW
 DC.W 0
 DC.W 0
 DC.W 640
 DC.W 190
 DC.B -1
 DC.B -1
 DC.L CLOSEWINDOW!GADGETDOWN!GADGETUP
 DC.L WINDOWDRAG!WINDOWDEPTH!WINDOWCLOSE!SMART_REFRESH
 DC.L 0
 DC.L 0
 DC.L MYWINDOWTITLE
 DC.L 0
 DC.L 0
 DC.W 140               ;BE CAREFUL MIN HEIGHT AND WIDTH AREN'T
 DC.W 140               ;SO SMALL THAT THE RELATIVE HEIGHT AND WIDTH
 DC.W 640               ;OF THE GADGET CAN BECOME LESS THAN ZERO
 DC.W 400               ;OR YOU'LL BE SORRY! (COULD ELIMINATE SIZING INSTEAD)
 DC.W WBENCHSCREEN
 END
```

# Intuition Screens

One of the limitations of the programs introduced up to this point is that all their windows use the Workbench screen. This screen is configured by the Amiga operating system to have a 640 × 200 resolution and four colors (two bitplanes, each with 640 × 200 pixels) or 640 × 400 pixels, if interlaced.

## Custom Screens for more Colorful Graphics

All windows that open in a screen inherit its resolution and number of available colors. The windows that open in the Workbench screen, therefore, can have, at most, four colors. The Amiga can produce many different combinations of display resolution and many colors. In order to maximize the flexibility of the graphics display in your programs, you can open custom screens with the resolution and colors you desire. Opening a screen is similar to opening a window. A NEWSCREEN structure is filled with appropriate screen data and a call is made to the OPENSCREEN Intuition library function.

## The NEWSCREEN Structure

The NEWSCREEN structure is fairly simple. Like other Intuition display structures, it's composed of fields. Some of these fields are for positioning and sizing parameters. There are also fields to contain a pointer to a title text string and an optional custom bitmap. Another field is an optional pointer to a font for use when text is drawn on the screen. The other field of interest provides for combinations of VIEWMODES flags, which specify the screen resolution and number of bitplanes.

The relationship between colors and bitplanes is as follows: Each additional bitplane multiplies the number of colors available to the screen by two. The minimum number of bitplanes is one for a screen with just two colors (foreground and background). Two bitplanes provide four colors.

To see how Amiga graphics work, pretend that a screen is only two pixels wide by two pixels high and one bitplane deep, like a 2 × 2 array. Any element of the array can hold either a zero or a one. A zero causes that element of the array (pixel) to be drawn in the background color, while a one causes a pixel to be drawn in the foreground color. What really happens is that each element of the array is a *pointer* to a special color register (the Amiga has 32 color registers). A zero points to color register 0 (the background color), and that pixel will be drawn with the color in color register 0. Since this is the background color, it will be invisible. A one will point to color register 1, and that pixel will be drawn in whatever color is in color register 1 (the foreground color). Since each element of the one-bitplane array can hold only a zero or a one, it's limited to pointing to only two color registers. This explains why a one-bitplane screen has only two colors.

Now lets consider what happens if you add another bitplane. You now have two arrays, each two elements wide by two elements high. Think of them as being one right on top of another, with each element in the top array being paired with its corresponding element in the bottom array. Since each individual element can hold a zero or a one, you now have four choices (00, 01, 10, 11—the first number of each pair comes from the top array; the second; from the bottom array). As you can see, with two bitplanes, you can point to four color registers, so you can display four different colors. Each additional bitplane doubles the number of color registers you can point to, thereby doubling the number of possible colors.

Of course, a screen on an Amiga is much larger than two pixels wide by two pixels high, but the idea is exactly the same—just think of much bigger arrays. Each bitplane of a low-resolution, noninterlaced screen is a $320 \times 200$ array, while a bitplane of a high-resolution, interlaced screen is a $640 \times 400$ array. A large number of bitplanes uses a very large amount of memory. Since all of this memory must be chip memory (in the first 512K of the Amiga's memory), you can see why conserving chip memory is so important.

Table 21-3. shows valid combinations of screen parameters to use in the NEWSCREEN structure.

**Table 21-3. Custom Screen Sizes, Parameters, and Memory Usage**

| VIEWMODES | Size (W × H) | Depth | Colors | Memory Usage |
|---|---|---|---|---|
| LORES | 320 × 200 | 1 | 2 | 8K |
| | | 2 | 4 | 16K |
| | | 3 | 8 | 24K |
| | | 4 | 16 | 32K |
| | | 5 | 32 | 40K |
| LORES!INTERLACE | 320 × 400 | 1 | 2 | 16K |
| | | 2 | 4 | 32K |
| | | 3 | 8 | 48K |
| | | 4 | 16 | 64K |
| | | 5 | 32 | 80K |
| HIRES | 640 × 200 | 1 | 2 | 16K |
| | | 2 | 4 | 32K |
| | | 3 | 8 | 48K |
| | | 4 | 16 | 64K |
| HIRES!INTERLACE | 640 × 400 | 1 | 2 | 32K |
| | | 2 | 4 | 64K |
| | | 3 | 8 | 96K |
| | | 4 | 16 | 128K |
| HAM | 320 × 200 | Special mode for 4096 colors | | |

The title is a string of null-terminated text. You should follow certain guidelines for designing screen coordinates:

Standard Intuition screens are the full height and width of the video display area. The standard sizes are: 320 × 200, 320 × 400, 640 × 200, and 640 × 400. The 320-pixel width screens can use up to 32 different color registers, each assigned one of 4096 colors. The 640-pixel width screens are limited to 16 colors. You're free to open a custom screen of nonstandard dimensions (such as a 120 × 120 screen), but there are a few restrictions. See the *Intuition Reference Manual* for details.

The 320-pixel width screen is called *lo-res* (low resolution). The 640-pixel width screen is called *hi-res* (high resolution). A 400-pixel height screen is achieved using *interlace mode*.

Interlace mode is a feature of standard broadcast television. The picture on the monitor is provided by *scan lines* that sweep over the screen many times per second, refreshing the display. In interlace mode, the scanlines are moved very slightly downward on every other *frame*, or sweep of the screen, and another picture is drawn before the phosphors have completely faded from the last scan, providing the illusion of twice the number of lines on the screen. Interlace mode causes the Amiga screen to flicker, but judicious choice of colors can minimize this effect and result in very sharp graphics displays.

The desired combination of LORES, HIRES, and INTERLACE are placed into the VIEWMODES field of the NEWSCREEN structure. If the field is left empty (equal to zero) then a lo-res screen 200 pixels high and 320 pixels wide will appear.

The HAM mode, which allows up to 4096 colors to appear on the screen is a very specialized graphics mode and it will not be covered here.

As with windows, it's a matter of choice for the programmer whether to use a special subroutine to open screens or just declare the NEWSCREEN structure in the source code. Since screens take up large amounts of memory, most programs don't open more than one or two of them.

The NEWSCREEN structure is disposable (it can be deallocated when OPENSCREEN is finished), like the NEWWINDOW structure. It's only used by Intuition when opening the screen. Tables 21-4 and 21-5 list the definitions of the NEWSCREEN and SCREEN structures.

**Table 21-4. Intuition NEWSCREEN Structure**

**Symbol: NS**
**Size: 32 bytes ($20 bytes)**

| *Field Size* | *Name* | *Offset* | *Description* |
|---|---|---|---|
| Word | NS.LEFTEDGE | 0 | Should be 0 |
| Word | NS.TOPEDGE | 2 | Number of pixels from top |
| Word | NS.WIDTH | 4 | Number of pixels wide (320 or 640) |
| Word | NS.HEIGHT | 8 | Number of pixels high (up to 200; or 400, if interlaced) |

| Field Size | Name | Offset | Description |
|---|---|---|---|
| Word | NS.DEPTH | 8 | Number of bitplanes in this screen |
| Byte | NS.DETAILPEN | 10 | Color register number for gadgets and title text |
| Byte | NS.BLOCKPEN | 11 | Color register number for block fills |
| Word | NS.VIEWMODES | 12 | Flags for the screens display modes |
| Word | NS.TYPE | 14 | Workbench, custom screen |
| Long | NS.FONT | 16 | Pointer to font STRUCTURE (0 is the default) |
| Long | NS.DEFAULTTITLE | 20 | Pointer to null-terminated title |
| Long | NS.GADGETS | 24 | Should be 0 |
| Long | NS.CUSTOMBITMAP | 28 | Pointer to your bitmap, if any |

**Table 21-5. Intuition SCREEN Structure**

**Symbol: SCRN**
**Size: 346 bytes ($15A bytes)**

| Field Size | Name | Offset | Description |
|---|---|---|---|
| Long | SCRN.NEXT | 0 | Pointer to next screen structure |
| Long | SCRN.WINDOW | 4 | Pointer to first window in screen |
| Word | SCRN.LEFTEDGE | 8 | Number of pixels from left edge |
| Word | SCRN.TOPEDGE | 10 | Number of pixels from top edge |
| Word | SCRN.WIDTH | 12 | Number of pixels wide |
| Word | SCRN.HEIGHT | 14 | Number of pixels high |
| Word | SCRN.MOUSEX | 16 | Screen mouse position from left edge |
| Word | SCRN.MOUSEY | 18 | Screen mouse position from top edge |
| Word | SCRN.FLAGS | 20 | Screen flag bits |
| Long | SCRN.TITLE | 22 | Pointer to screen title text |
| Long | SCRN.DEFAULTTITLE | 26 | Pointer for window with no screen title |
| Byte | SCRN.BARHEIGHT | 30 | Screen bar height in pixels |
| Byte | SCRN.BARVBORDER | 31 | Vertical border thickness in pixels |
| Byte | SCRN.BARHBORDER | 32 | Horizontal border thickness in pixels |

| *Field Size* | *Name* | *Offset* | *Description* |
|---|---|---|---|
| Byte | SCRN.MENUVBORDER | 33 | Vertical menu border thickness in pixels |
| Byte | SCRN.MENUHBORDER | 34 | Horizontal menu border thickness in pixels |
| Byte | SCRN.WBORTOP | 35 | Top window border thickness in pixels |
| Byte | SCRN.WBORLEFT | 36 | Left window border thickness in pixels |
| Byte | SCRN.WBORRIGHT | 37 | Right window border thickness in pixels |
| Byte | SCRN.WBORBOTTOM | 38 | Bottom window border thickness in pixels |
| Long | SCRN.FONT | 40 | Pointer to FONT structure for screen |
| At this point in the structure is a complete VIEWPORT structure. | | | |
| At this point in the structure is a complete RASTPORT structure. | | | |
| At this point in the structure is a complete BITMAP structure. | | | |
| At this point in the structure is a complete LAYERINFO structure. | | | |
| Long | SCRN.FIRSTGADGET | 326 | Pointer to first gadget structure |
| Byte | SCRN.DETAILPEN | 330 | Drawing pen number for border |
| Byte | SCRN.BLOCKPEN | 331 | Drawing pen number for menu, dragbar |
| Word | SCRN.SAVECOLOR0 | 332 | Used by system to save the background color before a DisplayBeep( ) call |
| Long | SCRN.BARLAYER | 334 | Pointer to screen/menu bar layer |
| Long | SCRN.EXTDATA | 338 | Pointer to external data |
| Long | SCRN.USERDATA | 342 | Pointer to user data |

## Memory Considerations

Memory allocation is automatic when OPENSCREEN is called, but you'll want to know how much is being used. As mentioned previously, it will all be chip memory. To calculate the memory that will be allocated for a screen, use the following formula:

Bytes = (WIDTH × HEIGHT × DEPTH) / 8

A 640 × 200-pixel screen with a depth of three bitplanes (DEPTH = 3) uses 48,000 bytes (3 bitplanes of 16,000 bytes).

The screen that uses the largest amount of memory is a screen of 640 × 400 × 4. It uses 128,000 bytes. Since screen display must be in chip memory (limited to 512K), programmers must provide for circumstances in which a large quantity of memory isn't available. If one program is using a large screen like the one described above, another program may not be able to get the chip memory it needs, causing it to fail.

It's possible to gain some display memory by closing the Workbench screen, but that only works if no windows are open in the Workbench.

> Remember: If your program calls CLOSEWORKBENCH, it must reopen the Workbench later with a call to OPENWORKBENCH.

If a screen can't be opened, the OPENSCREEN function will return a 0 in register D0, which can be detected by your program code. A successful call to OPENSCREEN yields the address of the SCREEN structure in D0. In case of failure, the program can either quit, try to open a screen with smaller memory requirements, or alert the user to close down other applications to provide more memory and try again.

## Closing the Custom Screen

A custom screen is not provided with a close gadget. The drag bar and the front/back gadgets are present (though perhaps not visible) at the top. The drag bar can be used to slide the screen down to reveal the Workbench screen behind it. The front/back gadgets swap screens when clicked with the mouse. You can also type the Left Amiga-N combination (on the Amiga 500, the left Amiga key has been changed to a Commodore logo key) to swap screens.

To close a screen requires a separate call to CLOSESCREEN. Interestingly enough, there is no IDCMP attached to the screen alone, so there's no explicit way to get messages through to the program saying the user wishes to close the screen. To make matters worse, you may not attach any of your own gadgets to the screen.

The SCREEN structure obtained by a call to OPEN-SCREEN contains information that can be used by your program to close the screen: the SCRN.MOUSEX and SCRN.MOUSEY fields in the SCREEN structure. When your program detects certain values in those fields (such as 0 or 639 for SCRN.MOUSEX), the program can react by calling CLOSESCREEN. An alternative is to have a window open up that has an IDCMP for user I/O.

A good combination for convenient display is a screen with a BACKDROP window as large as the screen. A BACK-DROP window is a window that stays behind all other windows on a screen. It does not have a depth arrangement gadget. Needless to say, a screen can have only one BACK-DROP window. Using SMART_REFRESH on the BACKDROP window will protect it from being trashed by menus, requesters, and other objects that are drawn on it by the system. This combination is used in the example program in Listing 21-5. A screen of 640 × 400 × 4 is opened, so its BACKDROP window can display 16 colors. The demo also calls some Intuition routines that manipulate screens, windows, and their title bars. The SETWINDOWTITLES, SHOWTITLE, SCREENTOFRONT, and other routines can add professional polish to programs that have multiple windows and screens.

**Listing 21-5. SCREEN.ASM**

```
;SCREEN.ASM BY DANIEL WOLF
;COPYRIGHT 1987 By COMPUTE! PUBLICATIONS
;09/10/87

 BRA _START

GFX EQU 1

MEN EQU 1
WIN EQU 1
TXT EQU 1
WBC EQU 1

 INCLUDE "HEADER"

;*** EQUATES ***

SCREENWIDTH EQU 640
SCREENHEIGHT EQU 400
SCREENSIZE EQU SCREENWIDTH/8*SCREENHEIGHT
DEPTH EQU 4
MASK EQU (1<<DEPTH)-1
COLRS
 DC.W $FFF,$00F,$00E,$F00
 DC.W $00C,$00B,$00A,$009
 DC.W $008,$007,$006,$005
 DC.W $004,$003,$002,$001

MAIN
```

```
SETUP
 MOVE.L #NEWSCREEN,AØ
 INTLIB OPENSCREEN
 MOVE.L DØ,SCREEN
 BNE.S 1$                ;NO ERROR, GOT AN ADDRESS BACK
 DOSPRINT STDOUT,#NOSCREEN
 MOVEQ #CANTOPENSCREEN,DØ
 BRA ERROR               ;OOPS, NOT ABLE TO OPEN SCREEN

1$
 LEA _THISFLAGS,AØ
 MOVE.L #BACKDROP!BORDERLESS!ACTIVATE!SMART_REFRESH,(AØ)
 LEA _THISCREEN,AØ;SET WINDOW INTO SCREEN
 MOVE.L SCREEN,(AØ)
 LEA _THISTYPE,AØ;CHANGE WINDOW TYPE
 MOVE.W #CUSTOMSCREEN,(AØ)
 MAKEWIN #WINTITLE,Ø,Ø,SCREENWIDTH,SCREENHEIGHT,ERROR   ;NOW MAKE WINDOW
 MOVE.L DØ,WINDOW
 MOVE.L DØ,AØ
 MOVEA.L WW.RPORT(AØ),A1
 MOVE.L A1,RP
 MOVE.L SCREEN,AØ
 LEA SCRN.VIEWPORT(AØ),A1
 MOVE.L A1,VP            ;STASH IMPORTANT POINTERS FOR SCREEN

_MENUS
 MITEMLIST ITEMØØ,ITEMØ1,ITEMØ2,Ø,Ø,Ø,Ø,Ø,2
 MAKEMEN MENØCMDS,MENØMUEX,MENØTITLE,DONE
 MOVE.L D1,_MENUØ
 MOVE.W #5,DØ           ;LEFT POS MENU
 MOVE.W #9Ø,D1          ;WIDTH MENU TITLE
 BSR CREATEMENU

MENUATTACH
 MOVE.L WINDOW,AØ
 MOVE.L _MENUØ,A1
 INTLIB SETMENUSTRIP

LOOP
 MOVE.L WINDOW,AØ
 MOVE.L #$FFFF,DØ
 INTLIB ONMENU
 MOVE.L WINDOW,AØ
 MOVE.L WW.USERPORT(AØ),AØ
 SYSLIB WAITPORT
 MOVE.L WINDOW,AØ
 MOVE.L WW.USERPORT(AØ),AØ
 SYSLIB GETMSG
 TST.L DØ
 BEQ RELOOP
 MOVE.L DØ,A1
 MOVE.L IM.CLASS(A1),D2
 MOVE.W IM.CODE(A1),D3
 MOVE.W IM.QUALIFIER(A1),D4
 SYSLIB REPLYMSG
 CMP.L #CLOSEWINDOW,D2
 BEQ DONE
 CMP.L #MENUPICK,D2
 BNE RELOOP
 ZERO DØ
 MOVE.W D3,DØ
 BSR MENUEVENT

HANDLEMENUØ
 CMPI.W #Ø,DØ
 BNE RELOOP
 CMPI.W #2,D1
 BEQ DONE
 CMPI.W #Ø,D1
 BNE.S 1$
 BSR SDRAW
 BRA RELOOP
1$
 CMPI.W #1,D1
 BNE RELOOP
 BSR ROLLCOLORS
RELOOP
 BRA LOOP
```

```
SDRAW
 MOVE.L WINDOW,AØ
 ZERA A1
 ZERA A2
 INTLIB SETWINDOWTITLES ;CLEAR WINDOW AND SCREEN TITLES

 MOVE.L SCREEN,AØ
 ZERO DØ                ;ZERO HER MEANS SCREEN BAR IN BACK OF BD WINDOW
 INTLIB SHOWTITLE       ;PUT SCREEN BAR IN BACK OF BACKDROP WINDOW

 MOVE.L RP,D7

 LOADRGB VP,COLRS,MASK+1
 SETDRMD D7,#JAM1
 SETAPEN D7,#5
 RECTFILL D7,#Ø,#Ø,#SCREENWIDTH-1,#SCREENHEIGHT-1

 GFXPOINT #3ØØ,#2Ø
 GFXLIB MOVE,D7

 SETOPEN D7,#2
 SETAPEN D7,#2                  ;DRAW WITH PEN #2 (SAME AS OUTLINE PEN)

 MOVE.L #9,DØ;THERE WILL BE 9 POINTS
 LEA POINTLIST,AØ
 GFXLIB POLYDRAW,D7             ;NOW DRAW LINES CONNECTING 9 POINT POLYGON
 ;IN OUTLINE PEN COLOR TO CONTROL THE FILL

 SETAPEN D7,#Ø                  ;FILL WITH COLOR #Ø (WHITE)

 GFXPOINT #3ØØ,#22              ;FLOOD FROM THIS POINT OUTWARD
 MOVEQ.L #Ø,D2                  ;IN MODE Ø
 GFXLIB FLOOD,D7                ;FLOOD OUT TO PIXEL COLOR=OUTLINE PEN COLOR

 SETAPEN D7,#2                  ;DRAW WITH SAME COLOR AS OUTLINE PEN
 DRAWLINE D7,#8Ø,#Ø,#52Ø,#Ø     ;TO CONTAIN THE FILL WHICH COMES BELOW
 DRAWLINE D7,#52Ø,#Ø,#52Ø,#2ØØ
 DRAWLINE D7,#52Ø,#2ØØ,#8Ø,#2ØØ
 DRAWLINE D7,#8Ø,#2ØØ,#8Ø,#Ø

 GFXPOINT #9Ø,#1                ;PICK A POINT FROM WHICH TO FLOOD
 MOVEQ.L #Ø,D2                  ;PICK FLOOD MODE
 SETAPEN D7,#3                  ;PICK PEN FOR FLOOD (COLOR #3)
 GFXLIB FLOOD,D7                ;FLOOD OUT TO COLOR=OUTLINE PEN COLOR

 RTS

ROLLCOLORS
 LEA.L COLRS,A3
 ZERO D5
ROLLCOLOR
 MOVEQ.L #2,D3
ADDACOLOR
 ADD.W #$1,Ø(A3,D3.W)
 ADDQ.W #2,D3
 CMPI.W #32,D3
 BLT.S ADDACOLOR
 MOVE.L #TICKSPERSECOND/32,D1
 DOSLIB DELAY
 LOADRGB VP,COLRS,MASK+1
 ADDQ.W #1,D5
 CMPI.W #$1ØØ,D5
 BLT.S ROLLCOLOR
 MOVEA.L SCREEN,AØ
 TST.W SCRN.MOUSEX(AØ)
 BEQ.S ROLLCOLORS
ENDROLLCOLORS
 RTS

DONE
QUIT
 MOVE.L _MENUØ,DØ
 BEQ.S 1$
 MOVE.L WINDOW,AØ
 INTLIB CLEARMENUSTRIP
1$
 MOVE.L WINDOW,DØ
 BEQ.S 3$
```

```
 MOVE.L DØ,AØ
 INTLIB CLOSEWINDOW
3$
 MOVE.L SCREEN,DØ
 BEQ.S 4$
 MOVE.L DØ,AØ
 INTLIB CLOSESCREEN
4$
DONEALL
 ZERO DØ
ERROR
 RTS

;*** DATA STUFF ***

 EVENPC

USAGE
 DC.B 1Ø,'usage : SCREEN',1Ø,Ø
 EVENPC
NOSCREEN
 DC.B 1Ø,'Sorry, could not open the 7ØØx44Øx4 screen.',1Ø,Ø
 EVENPC
MYMESSAGE
 DC.B 1Ø,'SCREEN by D. Wolf Copyright 1986 by Compute! Publications',1Ø,1Ø,(
 EVENPC

STACK DC.L Ø

NEWSCREEN DC.W Ø,Ø,SCREENWIDTH,SCREENHEIGHT,DEPTH
 DC.B MASK,Ø
 DC.W HIRES!LACE
 DC.W CUSTOMSCREEN
 DC.L Ø,Ø,Ø,Ø

 EVENPC

SCREEN DC.L Ø
VP DC.L Ø
RP DC.L Ø
OUTPUT DC.L Ø
XWIDTH DC.L $CØØØØØ42
YWIDTH DC.L $CØØØØØ42

SCREENX DC.W Ø
SCREENY DC.W Ø
COUNT DC.W Ø

MAXIMUM DC.W 16
LASTCOL DC.W Ø
 EVENPC

MENØTITLE
 DC.B 'PROJECT',Ø
 EVENPC
ITEMØØ
 DC.B '   DEMO         ',Ø
 EVENPC
ITEMØ1
 DC.B '   ROLLCOLORS   ',Ø
 EVENPC
ITEMØ2
 DC.B '   QUIT         ',Ø
 EVENPC
MENØCMDS
 DC.B 'DRQ'
 EVENPC
MENØMUEX
 DC.L $6,$5,$3
 EVENPC
WINDOW DC.L Ø
_MENUØ DC.L Ø
_MYLACE DC.L Ø
WINTITLE DC.B ' SCREEN  by D. Wolf ',Ø
 EVENPC

_THISFONTHITE DC.W 9
```

```
POINTLIST
 DC.W 300,20
 DC.W 350,80
 DC.W 500,90
 DC.W 350,100
 DC.W 300,160
 DC.W 250,100
 DC.W 100,90
 DC.W 250,80
 DC.W 300,20
```

# SECTION 7

# Amiga Floating-Point Math

# CHAPTER 22

# Using Floating-Point Numbers

The Amiga has three libraries of routines for floating-point math operations on floating-point numbers. While integers represent whole numbers within a circumscribed range, floating-point numbers (at some expense of accuracy), can represent real numbers within a much larger range. The range of a 16-bit integer is −32768 to 32677, whereas an FFP format floating-point number can represent a real number in the range −9.22337177E18 to 9.22337177E8.

The Amiga system programmers took better care of the requirements of C language programmers than those of machine language programmers. They provided C language support routines to convert ASCII character representations into the correct 32-bit floating-point number format, for instance, but the machine language routines were not provided. The MATH.ASM listing provided in this book includes ASCIITOFFP, a subroutine to convert ASCII to the Amiga 32-bit FFP (Fast Floating-Point) format, and HEXCONVERT, which prints out the HEXADECIMAL contents of the register D0 to the CLI window.

The illustration in Figure 32-1 shows the 32-bit fast floating-point format that can be used with both the MathFFP (simple arithmetic) library and the MathTrans library (the library of transcendent functions, such as trigonometry, logarithms, and so on). The IEEEDOUBLE (double-precision, 64-bit) format is not covered here. Its use is restricted to the MathIEEEDoubBas library, which has only simple arithmetic capabilities.

**Figure 22-1. 32-bit Fast Floating-Point (FFP) Number Representation**

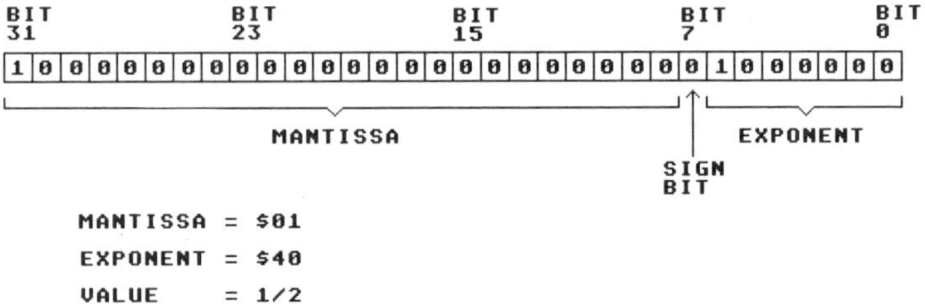


There are two additional requirements for this format: every number (except 0) has a 1 in the most significant (leftmost) bit when normalized, and the 7-bit exponent value is increased by $40 (again, except for the number 0). This format can reliably handle a real number of no more than seven digits, so there's some limitation of accuracy with 32-bit math. Use IEEE double-precision when more accuracy is needed.

Table 22-1. shows some common floating-point numbers and their hexadecimal and binary representations in FFP format.

**Table 22-1. Conversion Equivalents Between ASCII Decimal and Fast Floating-Point Format**

| Decimal | Hexadecimal | Binary | | | |
|---|---|---|---|---|---|
| 0.000000 | 00000000 | 00000000 | 00000000 | 00000000 | 00000000 |
| 1.000000 | 80000041 | 10000000 | 00000000 | 00000000 | 01000001 |
| 2.000000 | 80000042 | 10000000 | 00000000 | 00000000 | 01000010 |
| 4.000000 | 80000043 | 10000000 | 00000000 | 00000000 | 01000011 |
| 10.000000 | A0000044 | 10100000 | 00000000 | 00000000 | 01000100 |
| 100.000000 | C8000047 | 11001000 | 00000000 | 00000000 | 01000111 |
| 3.14159 | C90FD042 | 11001001 | 00001111 | 11010000 | 01000010 |
| −1.000000 | 800000C1 | 10000000 | 00000000 | 00000000 | 11000001 |

Note that 0 is treated in a special manner. It's a long word consisting of 32 zero bits. Also note that negation changes only the high bit of the bit in front of the exponent. Doubling an FFP format number simply means increasing its exponent by one.

The CLIFLOAT program in Listing 22-2 passes floating-point numbers to a program by way of the command line. The principles of the CLIECHO program are used to pick up the command tail, and the ASCIITOFFP subroutine is used to make a floating-point conversion, unless there's an error. Then HEXCONVERT is used to print the floating-point version of the number back to the CLI window. The MANDELBROT program also utilizes these routines to pass five different numeric parameters to the program. The same principles of number handling can be used with a string gadget. Since a string gadget has a known buffer location, its address can be provided to the ASCIITOFFP subroutine, and the buffer's numerical contents (converted to FFP format) will appear in D0.

Listing 22-1, MATH.ASM, is the last of the type-in include files for this book. It has support routines for using the 32-bit floating-point math routines in the MATHFFP library of the Amiga. Type in this file and save it as

DEV:RAMIT/INCLUDES/MATH.ASM

This file adds math support routines to the includes directory on your DEV disk.

**Listing 22-1. MATH.ASM**

Support routines and macros for Amiga floating-point math.

```
;******************************** MATH.ASM BY DANIEL WOLF
;COPYRIGHT 1987 BY COMPUTE! BOOKS
;03/10/87

LVO.SPFix     EQU $FFFFFFE2
LVO.SPFlt     EQU $FFFFFFDC
LVO.SPCmp     EQU $FFFFFFD6
LVO.SPTst     EQU $FFFFFFD0
LVO.SPAbs     EQU $FFFFFFCA
LVO.SPNeg     EQU $FFFFFFC4
LVO.SPAdd     EQU $FFFFFFBE
LVO.SPSub     EQU $FFFFFFB8
LVO.SPMul     EQU $FFFFFFB2
LVO.SPDiv     EQU $FFFFFFAC

LVO.SPSincos  EQU $FFFFFFCA
LVO.SPSin     EQU $FFFFFFDC
LVO.SPCos     EQU $FFFFFFD6
LVO.SPTan     EQU $FFFFFFD0
LVO.SPAtan    EQU $FFFFFFE2
LVO.SPSqrt    EQU $FFFFFFA0
LVO.SPAcos    EQU $FFFFFF88
LVO.SPAsin    EQU $FFFFFF8E

 IFND VLENW
VLENW EQU 2
 ENDC

;FFP MATH SUPPORT CODE

 IFD HEX
```

```
ASCIITOHEX          ;ROUTINE TAKES IN MAXHEX DIGITS OF HEX INTO ARRAY  IN MEMORY
                    ;AØ POINTS TO ASCII
               ;A1 POINTS TO LEAST SIGNIFICANT WORD OF HEX RESULT IN MEMORY
 PUSHREG D1-D4/A2
 ZERO DØ
 ZERO D1
 ZERO D2
 ZERO D3
 MOVE.L A1,D4
 ADD.L #2,D4
 SUBA.L #4,A1

FRONTHEX
 MOVE.B (AØ)+,DØ
 CMPI.B #' ',DØ
 BEQ.S FRONTHEX
 CMPI.B #'Ø',DØ
 BEQ.S FRONTHEX
 BRA FIRSTHDIG

HEXINDIG
 MOVE.B (AØ)+,DØ
FIRSTHDIG
 CMPI.B #'F',DØ
 BHI.S NOTHEX
 CMPI.B #'A',DØ
 BLT.S MAYBELOW
 SUBQ #7,DØ
 BRA HEXIT
MAYBELOW
 CMPI.B #'Ø',DØ
 BLT.S NOTHEX
 CMPI.B #'9',DØ
 BHI.S NOTHEX

HEXIT
 ADDQ #1,D3
 CMP.L MAXHEX,D3           ;CHECK FOR TOO MANY INPUT DIGITS
 BEQ TOOMANYHEX
 ANDI.L #$F,DØ             ;ISOLATE THE HEX DIGIT
ROTHEXIT
 MOVEQ #3,D2               ;COUNT FOR FOUR SINGLE BIT ROTATES OF ALL WORDS IN V
ROTINLOOP
 MOVE.L #VLENW-1,D1
 MOVE.L D4,A2              ;A1 POINTS TO L.S. WORD OF MEMORY ARRAY FOR VARIABLE
ROTHEX
 ROXL.W -(A2)              ;ROTATE BY 1 BIT FROM LSWORD TO MSWORD
 DBRA D1,ROTHEX            ;IN THE ARRAY TOWARD THE L.S. WORD (UP IN ADDRESSES!)
 DBRA D2,ROTINLOOP         ;ROTATE BACK FOR D3 WORDS - D4 BITS
 OR.L DØ,(A1)              ;-OR- IN THE NIBBLE DIGIT OBTAINED FROM ASCII
 BRA HEXINDIG              ;GET ANOTHER DIGIT
NOTHEX
 CMPI.B #',',DØ
 BEQ.S ENDHEXOK
 CMPI.B #' ',DØ
 BEQ.S ENDHEXOK
 TST.B DØ
 BEQ.S ENDHEXOK
TOOMANYHEX
 MOVE.L #$FF,DØ
 BRA ENDHEXIN
ENDHEXOK
 PUSHREG DØ                       ;SAVE LAST CHARACTER FOUND
 ADDA.L #4,A1
 MOVE.L -(A1),DØ
 BSR HEXCONVERT
 PULLREG DØ                       ;LAST CHARACTER
ENDHEXIN
 PULLREG D1-D4/A2
 RTS
 ENDC

 IFD FFP
ASCIITOFFP                        ;ENTER W/ AØ POINTING TO ASCII DECIMAL TEXT
 MOVEA.L _MATHBASE,A6
LEADINGSPACE
 CMPI.B #' ',(AØ)
 BNE.S CHEKNEG
```

```
 ADDA.L #1,AØ
 BRA.S LEADINGSPACE
CHEKNEG
 MOVE.L #Ø,NEGATIVE
 CMPI.B #'-',(AØ)              ;IS IT A NEGATIVE NUMBER?
 BNE.S POSITIVPART
 MOVE.L #128,NEGATIVE
 ADDA.L #1,AØ
POSITIVPART
 MOVE.L #Ø,RITODP
 MOVE.L #Ø,LEFTODP
 MOVE.L #Ø,RDPDIGITS
 MOVE.L #Ø,LDPDIGITS
 MOVE.L #Ø,FLOATNUM
 MOVEQ.L #Ø,D4                 ;FIRST LEFT OF DP
 BSR DOPART                    ;EXIT W/ FLOAT IN DØ AND FLOATNUM
 TST.L D1                      ;D1 INDICATES: Ø  OK
 BNE CONVERTERROR              ;              NOT Ø  ERROR!!
 MOVE.L DØ,LEFTODP
 MOVE.L D2,LDPDIGITS
 CMPI.B #'.',(AØ)
 BNE LEFTONLY
 ADDA.L #1,AØ
 MOVE.L #1,D4          ;THEN RIGHT OF DP
 BSR DOPART
 TST.L D1
 BNE CONVERTERROR
 MOVE.L DØ,RITODP
 MOVE.L D2,RDPDIGITS
FINILEFT
 MOVE.L LDPDIGITS,D7
 SUBQ.L #7,D7
 BLE.S FINIRIGHT
 MOVE.L LEFTODP,DØ
 BEQ.S FINIRIGHT
 MOVE.L TEN,D2
1$
 JUST SPMul
 SUBQ.L #1,D7
 BNE.S 1$
 MOVE.L DØ,LEFTODP
FINIRIGHT
 MOVE.L RDPDIGITS,D7
 BEQ.S FINISHCONV
 MOVE.L RITODP,DØ
 BEQ.S FINISHCONV
 MOVE.L TEN,D1
2$
 JUST SPDiv
 SUBQ.L #1,D7
 BNE.S 2$
 MOVE.L DØ,RITODP
FINISHCONV
 MOVE.L RITODP,DØ
 MOVE.L LEFTODP,D1
 JUST SPAdd
LEFTONLY
 MOVEQ #Ø,D1                 ;NO ERROR
 MOVE.L NEGATIVE,D3
 EOR.L D3,DØ
 MOVE.L DØ,FLOATNUM

CONVERTERROR
 RTS

DOPART
 MOVE.L #Ø,INTEGER
 MOVEQ #Ø,DØ
 MOVEQ #Ø,D1
 MOVEQ #Ø,D2
 MOVEQ #Ø,D3
 MOVEQ #Ø,D5           ;# LEADING ZEROS
LEADINGZERO            ;LEADING ZEROS DO COUNT RIGHT OF THE DP!!
 MOVE.B (AØ)+,D3
 CMPI.B #'Ø',D3
 BNE.S FIRSTDIGA
 TST.L D4              ;ONLY ADD TO NUMDIGITS IF RIGHT OF DP
```

```
 BEQ.S LEADINGZERO
 ADDQ.L #1,D5
 BRA.S LEADINGZERO
FIRSTDIG
 MOVE.B (AØ)+,D3
FIRSTDIGA
 CMPI.B #'9',D3
 BHI.S NOMORDIGITS
 CMPI.B #'Ø',D3
 BLT.S NOMORDIGITS
 ANDI.L #$ØF,D3
 LSL.L #1,DØ
 MOVE.L DØ,D1
 LSL.L #2,DØ
 ADD.L D1,DØ
 ADD.L D3,DØ
 ADDQ.L #1,D2
 CMPI.L #7,D2
 BNE.S FIRSTDIG
MORDIGITS
 MOVE.B (AØ)+,D3
 CMPI.B #'9',D3
 BHI.S NOMORDIGITS
 CMPI.B #'Ø',D3
 BLT.S NOMORDIGITS
 TST.L D4               ;DON'T ADD TO # PLACES IF RIGHT OF DP
 BNE.S MORDIGITS        ;JUST MOVE THE ADDR PTR IN AØ ALONG TO
 ADDQ.L #1,D2           ;A NON-DIGIT
 CMPI.L #18,D2
 BNE.S MORDIGITS
TOOMANY
 MOVEQ #1,D1            ;TOO MANY DIGITS ERROR
 BRA AERROREXIT

NOMORDIGITS
 ADD.L D5,D2
 SUBA.L #1,AØ
 MOVE.L DØ,INTEGER
 TST.L DØ
 BEQ PARTDONE
 MOVE.L #97,D1
3$
 SUBQ.L #1,D1
 ASL.L #1,DØ
 BCC.S 3$
 ROXR.L #1,DØ
 ANDI.L #$FFFFFFØØ,DØ
 EOR.L D1,DØ

PARTDONE
 MOVEQ #Ø,D1
AERROREXIT
 RTS
 ENDC

 IFD HEX
HEXCONVERT
 PUSHALL
 LEA.L HEXBUF,A2
 LEA.L HEXDIGITS,A1
 MOVEQ.L #Ø,D3
 MOVEQ.L #Ø,D2
MORHEX
 ROL.L #4,DØ
 MOVE.L DØ,D1
 ANDI.L #$F,D1
 MOVE.B Ø(A1,D1.W),D2
 MOVE.B D2,Ø(A2,D3.W)
 ADDQ.L #1,D3
 CMPI.L #8,D3
 BNE.S MORHEX
 DOSPRINT STDOUT,#HEXBUF
 PULLALL
 RTS
 ENDC
```

```
;*** DATA STUFF ***
 IFD FFP
LEFTODP DC.L Ø          ;FP CONVERTED FIRST 8 DIGITS LEFT OF DP
LDPDIGITS DC.L Ø        ;TOTAL NUMBER OF DIGITS LEFT OF DP
RITODP DC.L Ø           ;FP CONVERTED FIRST 8 DIGITS RIGHT OF DP
RDPDIGITS DC.L Ø        ;TOTAL NUMBER OF DIGITS RIGHT OF DP
FLOATNUM DC.L Ø         ;FINISHED FLOATING POINT NUMBER
INTEGER DC.L Ø          ;INTEGER PART OF ONE SIDE OF DP
TEN DC.L $AØØØØØ44      ;DECIMAL VALUE OF TEN IN FFP NOTATION
NEGATIVE DC.L Ø         ;NEGATIVE FLAG FOR INPUT NUMBER
 ENDC

 IFD HEX
HEXBUF DC.B 65,65,65,65,65,65,65,65,1Ø,Ø
HEXDIGITS DC.B 'Ø123456789ABCDEF'
MAXHEX DC.L Ø
 ENDC

 EVENPC
```

**The ASCIITOFFP subroutine.** This routine in MATH.ASM accepts a series of byte locations provided by a pointer passed in address register A0. If the bytes are the ASCII characters for a floating-point number, they will be converted to a FFP format and returned in register D0. For example, the ASCII characters 3.14159 (pi) are converted to a long-word FFP number of 32 bits.

It works this way:

1. Set up a zero-value register to be the FFP number.
2. Set LEFT OF DECIMAL POINT flag.
3. Scan for and skip over any leading space characters (ASCII $32).
4. If the first nonspace character is a minus sign, set NEGFLAG.
5. Scan for and skip over any leading 0s.
6. For each ASCII digit, multiply existing FFP format number times ten, add appropriate new digit, and increase the LEFT digit count. If the number of digits exceeds seven, count the remaining digits and store in LEFT digit count.
7. When decimal point is reached, store the LEFT OF DECIMAL POINT integer obtained in step 6, and the LEFT digit count. Shift left the number obtained until the leftmost bit is a 1, counting the shifts necessary. Use the shift count to set the exponent portion of the number.
8. Set RIGHT OF DECIMAL POINT flag.
9. Scan for and count any leading 0s (RIGHT digit count).
10. Duplicate step 6, but for digits right of the decimal point.
11. When a nonnumeric ASCII character (letter, space, comma, and so on) is reached, store the RIGHT OF DECIMAL POINT integer obtained in step 10, and the RIGHT digit count. Do the shift procedure outlined in step 7.

12. The LEFT OF DECIMAL POINT integer is an FFP-format number, as is the RIGHT OF DECIMAL POINT integer. The only remaining task is to modify them (the left number may have had more than seven digits and the right number may have had leading digits as well as more than seven itself).
13. If necessary, the left number is multiplied by ten, once for each digit in excess of seven. The right number always represents a number less than one, so it must be divided by ten, once for each of its digits that were counted.
14. The result of step 13 is again two floating-point numbers, which, when they're added, represent the completely converted ASCII digit sequence. Adjustment of the sign finishes the process.

The ASCIITOFFP subroutine has an arbitrary upper limit of 18 digits on either side of the decimal point. It records an error in D4 if the process of conversion fails. It's intelligent enough to recognize integers (there need not be a decimal point at all). It doesn't recognize scientific notation, though. Here are some examples of legal input to the ASCIITOFFP routine:

| | |
|---|---|
| 1.00 | 303.000000456 |
| −1.05555 | −000000002.22222 |
| .00003333 | 120 |
| 000000033.33 | −10 |

The HEXCON routine in MATH.ASM is assembled conditionally according to the three-letter HEX symbol. This routine accepts any 32-bit number in D0 and prints its hexadecimal form to the STDOUT file, using AmigaDOS.

Listing 22-2 is the CLIFLOAT demonstration program. It allows you to type in floating-point numbers as part of a program's command line. It demonstrates ASCIITOFFP as well as HEXCON, and a few of the calls to library math routines.

**Listing 22-2. FPCMD.ASM**

Floating-point conversion and math demonstration.

```
;FPCMD.ASM BY DANIEL WOLF
;COPYRIGHT 1987 BY COMPUTE! PUBLICATIONS
;09/10/87

 BRA _START

MAT EQU 1
FFP EQU 1
```

```
HEX EQU 1

WBC EQU 1

 INCLUDE "HEADER"

MAIN
 DOSPRINT STDOUT,#MYMESSAGE
 TST.L ENDFROMWB
 BEQ FROMUSER
 LEA DEFAULTSTRING,AØ
 BRA FIRSTPARAM

FROMUSER
 MOVEA.L COMMAND,AØ
 CMPI.B #'?',(AØ)              ;IF USER GAVE NO PARAMS, USE DEFAULTS
 BEQ SHOWUSAGE

FIRSTPARAM
 BSR ASCIITOFFP       ;TAKE FIRST COMMAND LINE PARAMETER
 TST.L D1       ;CONVERT IT TO FP
 BNE BADARGS        ;D1=Ø MEANS NO ERROR IN CONVERSION
 MOVE.L DØ,N1        ;FP NUMBER IS IN DØ IF SUCCESSFUL
 BSR HEXCONVERT       ;SHOW US THE RESULTS

 CMPI.B #',',(AØ)+       ;IS NEXT COMMAND LINE CHARACTER A COMMA?
 BNE BADARGS        ;NO, MEANS NO SECOND NUMBER SO QUIT
 BSR ASCIITOFFP
 TST.L D1
 BNE BADARGS
 MOVE.L DØ,N2
 BSR HEXCONVERT

 CMPI.B #',',(AØ)+       ;IS NEXT COMMAND LINE CHARACTER A COMMA?
 BNE NOMORE       ;NOPE, THERE WERE ONLY THE MINIMUM TWO NUMBERS
 BSR ASCIITOFFP
 TST.L D1
 BNE BADARGS
 MOVE.L DØ,N3
 BSR HEXCONVERT

 CMP.B #',',(AØ)+
 BNE BADARGS        ;IF THERE WAS A THIRD NUMBER, THERE MUST BE A
 BSR ASCIITOFFP       ;FOURTH OR ELSE QUIT
 TST.L D1
 BNE BADARGS
 MOVE.L DØ,N4
 BSR HEXCONVERT

 CMPI.B #',',(AØ)+
 BNE NOMORE       ;THE FIFTH NUMBER IS ENTIRELY OPTIONAL
 BSR ASCIITOFFP
 TST.L D1
 BNE BADARGS
 MOVE.L DØ,N5
 BSR HEXCONVERT

NOMORE
 MOVE.L #TICKSPERSECOND,D1;WAIT ONE SECOND
 DOSLIB DELAY

 DOSPRINT STDOUT,#PRODUCT
MULTIPLY;NOW TRY A COUPLE MATHFFP LIBRARY ROUTINES
 MOVE.L N1,DØ
 MOVE.L N2,D1
 MATHLIB SPMul;MULTIPLY FIRST TWO NUMBERS
 BSR HEXCONVERT;SHOW THE RESULTS

 DOSPRINT STDOUT,#QUOTIENT
DIVIDE
 MOVE.L N1,DØ
 MOVE.L N2,D1
 MATHLIB SPDiv;DIVIDE FIRST TWO NUMBERS
 BSR HEXCONVERT;SHOW RESULTS
```

```
DONE
 MOVE.L #TICKSPERSECOND,D1;WAIT 4 SECONDS
 ADD.L D1,D1
 ADD.L D1,D1
 DOSLIB DELAY

 ZERO D0
ERROR
 RTS

BADARGS
SHOWUSAGE
 DOSPRINT STDOUT,#USAGE
 BRA DONE

EVENPC

;*** DATA DECLARATIONS ***

N1 DC.L 0
N2 DC.L 0
N3 DC.L 0
N4 DC.L 0
N5 DC.L 0

USAGE
 DC.B 10,'usage : FPCMD [N1,N2[,N3,N4[,N5]]]',10
 DC.B 10,'sample: FPCMD -2.25,-1.5,3,3,16',10,0
 EVENPC

DEFAULTSTRING
 DC.B '3.14159,2.7182845,1,10,100',0;PI, E, 1, 10, 100 - ALL 5
 EVENPC

MYMESSAGE
 DC.B 10,'FPCMD by Daniel Wolf  Copyright 1987 by COMPUTE! PUBLICATIONS',10,0
 EVENPC

PRODUCT
 DC.B 10,'PRODUCT OF FIRST TWO NUMBERS = ',0
 EVENPC

QUOTIENT
 DC.B 10,'QUOTIENT OF FIRST TWO NUMBERS = ',0
 EVENPC
 END
```

## Other Math Applications

Once a number is in the FFP format for use with the MathFFP library, all the operations of a scientific calculator are available through the use of the MathTrans library.

The FFP format is used by both the MathFFP and the MathTrans libraries. The STARTUP.ASM code opens the MathTrans library if the TRA symbol is defined. Tables 22-2 through 22-5 are lists of MathFFP and MathTrans library routines with specifications for passing parameters in the registers.

As an exercise, you might like to try writing a routine complementary to ASCIITOFFP: one that converts a 32-bit floating-point number back into ASCII characters. You might name such a routine FFPTOASCII.

### Table 22-2. MathFFP Library Routines

Calling specifications for parameters in registers. The result is always in register D0.

| Name | Description | Registers | N (Condition Codes){1} | Z | V |
|---|---|---|---|---|---|
| SPFIX | Convert floating point to integer | D0 | s | s | s |
| SPFLT | Convert integer to floating point | D0 | s | s | 0 |
| SPABS | Absolute value of floating-point number | D0 | 0 | s | 0 |
| SPNEG | Negative of floating-point number | D0 | s | s | 0 |
| SPADD | Add two floating-point numbers | D0,D1 | s | s | s |
| SPSUB | Subtract two floating-point numbers | D0,D1 | s | s | s |
| SPMUL | Multiply two floating-point numbers | D0,D1 | s | s | s |
| SPDIV | Divide two floating-point numbers (D0 / D1) | D0,D1 | s | s | s |
| SPCMP | Compare two floating-point numbers | D0,D1 | 0 | s | 0 |
| SPTST | Test if floating-point number equals zero | D1 | s | s | 0 |

{1} An *s* appearing under the N, V, or Z column means the flag will be set; a 0 means it will be cleared.

### Table 22-3. Values Returned by SPCMP Library Function

| Value | Meaning |
|---|---|
| 1 | if D0 > D1 (D0,D1 here refer to the input floating-point numbers) |
| −1 | if D0 < D1 |
| 0 | if D0 = D1 |

This function also leaves meaningful results in some additional condition codes of the MC68000:

| Result | Meaning |
|---|---|
| GT | if D0 > D1 (D0,D1 here refer to input floating-point numbers) |
| GE | if D0 > = D1 |
| EQ | if D0 = D1 |
| NE | if D0 < > D1 |
| LT | if D0 < D1 |
| LE | if D0 < = D1 |

**Table 22-4. Values Returned by the SPTST Library Function**

| Value | Meaning |
|---|---|
| 1 | if D0 > 0 |
| −1 | if D0 < 0 |
| 0 | if D0 = 0 |

This function also leaves meaningful results in additional condition codes of the MC68000:

| Result | Meaning |
|---|---|
| EQ | if D0 = 0 |
| NE | if D0 < > 0 |
| PL | if D0 > = 0 |
| MI | if D0 < 0 |

**Table 22-5. MathTrans Library Routines**

Calling specifications for parameters in registers. The result is always in data register D0.

| Name | Description | Registers | N | Z | V |
|---|---|---|---|---|---|
| SPASIN | Arcsine of floating-point number | D0 | 0 | s | 0 |
| SPACOS | Arccosine of floating-point number | D0 | 0 | s | 0 |
| SPATAN | Arctangent of floating-point number | D0 | 0 | s | 0 |
| SPSIN | Sine of floating-point number | D0 | s | s | s |
| SPCOS | Cosine of floating-point number | D0 | s | s | s |
| SPTAN | Tangent of floating-point number | D0 | s | s | s |
| SPSINCOS | Sine and cosine of floating-point number | D0,(D1) | s | s | s{1} |
| SPSINH | Hyperbolic sine of floating-point number | D0 | s | s | s |
| SPCOSH | Hyperbolic cosine of floating-point number | D0 | s | s | s |
| SPTANH | Hyperbolic tangent of floating-point number | D0 | s | s | s |
| SPEXP | Exponential of floating-point number | D0 | 0 | s | s |
| SPLOG | Natural logarithm of floating-point number | D0 | s | s | s |
| SPLOG10 | Base 10 logarithm of floating-point number | D0 | s | s | s |
| SPPOW | Power of floating-point number | (D0, power; D1, number) | 0 | s | s |
| SPSQRT | Square root of floating-point number | D0 | 0 | s | s |
| SPTIEEE | Convert floating-point number to IEEE | D0 | s | s | x |
| SPFIEEE | Convert IEEE to floating-point number | D0 | x | s | s |

{1} In addition to the floating-point number in D0, this function is called with the pointer to a desired cosine result in D1. When the function returns, the sine result is in D0 and the cosine result is in the location pointed to by D1 (even though D1 isn't an address register).

# SECTION 8

# The Applications Programs

# CHAPTER 23
# ASMINT

If you've purchased the companion disk for this book, or if you've typed in Listing 23-1 (ASMINT.ASM), the ASMINT program can be invoked from the CLI by typing its name and pressing Return. ASMINT can also be invoked from the Workbench by double-clicking in its icon.

## ASMINT

ASMINT is a workbench interface for the assembler (called ASM on the disk) that turns your source code, includes, and macros into machine language for your Amiga to execute. The ASMINT screen is made up of several features, each of which is explained below:

**The string gadgets.** Text is entered by way of string gadgets. You will enter such things as source and object file names through string gadgets. To alter the contents of a string gadget, click in it and use the keyboard to modify the string to your satisfaction. Then, press Return.

The string gadgets include:

*Source file.* The default for the Source file string gadget is *source,* but you may click on this gadget and enter any legal filename (for instance, DEV:SOURCES/ASMINT.ASM).

*Object file.* The default for this string gadget is *object,* but you may click here and set the name of your choice.

*Listing file.* The default Listing file value shows NIL: (followed by a space) and then CON:0/0/640/200/ASM_WATCHMEWORK. As it stands, the listing will go to the NIL: device (that is, it won't be listed) and assembly will be uneventful and quiet. If you'd like to watch the assembler work, click on the Listing file gadget and delete *NIL:* and the space that follows it. The listing will be directed to an AmigaDOS window and you'll see the progress of assembly.

If you want an actual file, enter the disk drive, directory path and file name in the Listing file gadget. The assembly will finish and a file will be written containing the listing.

The Listing file is versatile because you can use AmigaDOS conventions like CON:, SER:, and PRT: to direct listings anywhere "on the fly," or just use a conventional ramdisk file to receive the listing and print it later using the List button.

*Include list.* Here you may enter a list of directories of include files for assembly or AUTOLINK. This string is automatically used with the -i flag of ASM68010. If you leave this string blank, the -i flag is ignored. For more information on the -i flag, see Appendix A.

*Edit file.* Here you may enter the name of the file you want EMACS to read when you click the Edit button. If you leave this string gadget blank, EMACS will read whichever file you've named in the source file string gadget.

*Make file.* You can put the name of an AmigaDOS COMMAND file in the Make file string gadget. A COMMAND file is the type normally operated by using EXECUTE at the CLI.

When you try to activate the Assemble or Autolink buttons, the command file will be executed instead. This allows you to enter the name of a long and involved assemble, link, copy, and delete sequence set up in a preexisting command file, and the file will be executed, saving you from a great deal of typing.

**The buttons.** To use a button, click on it once. Be careful to click only once because extra clicks are remembered. They will be executed when the Amiga completes the current task.

*Assemble.* The Assemble button will cause ASM (ASM68010) to assemble the file specified in the source string gadget, to the file specified in the object string gadget. This creates the listing file, using the include list, if one is specified.

> If you've specified a make file, that file will be executed instead of ASM.

ASM produces a nonoperative object module that usually requires linkage to system libraries and support code (using the *ALINK* or *BLINK* linker programs) before it can be executed. ASM should reveal any syntax errors, undefined symbols, and other programming errors.

*Exec obj.* The Exec obj button will activate your finished load module (Autolinked or linked using *ALINK* or *BLINK*). *Load module* is another name for an executable Amiga program.

This button provides an AmigaDOS CLI-type working environment for the program. If you specified Autolink, you can also activate the program by double clicking in the Obj lightning bolt icon.

*List.* The List button will first try to find the listing file. If it's found, it will ask you (using a requester) to choose whether to list to the screen or a printer. Make your choice. Another requester asks you to be sure you really want to list it. Listings can become quite long (easily 100K) if not managed well with NOLIST and LIST assembler directives surrounding uninteresting stretches of code.

To cancel the printout, go offline with the printer using its online switch, or simply turn the printer off. It's recommended to list to the screen first, and list to printer only if you are sure the listing is of an appropriate length.

*Edit.* The Edit button activates EMACS and reads in either the edit file (if there is one) or defaults to read the source file.

*New.* The New button clears all the string gadgets, as well as the command buffer used internally by the program to activate all the other programs (ASM, EMACS, RUN, and so on).

*Autolink.* Autolink is a special flag feature of ASM68010 (use the -a option, if you're working from the CLI). When you activate Autolink, your source file is both assembled and linked (if there are no errors). Normally, this is easy to do. If all symbols are defined within the source code, no further linking is required. To be sure all symbols are defined, provide yourself with comprehensive equate files that define all the symbols used in your programs (look them up in the manuals mentioned frequently in this text).

The result of Autolink is that it produces an executable program, and Autolink makes a copy of the object file to Obj (the program that can be run by clicking in its icon). After

Autolink assembles and links your code, you can use the Exec obj button or the Obj icon to execute your program.

If you want to use the Workbench Obj icon to invoke your finished program, be sure you have provided Workbench startup code in the program. See the STARTUP.ASM listing that provides the minimum requirements for either Workbench- or CLI-based programs.

**The menu.** The menu provides an alternative to the buttons. The menu supports both mouse and keyboard input. To enter a command key, enter the designated key in combination with the right Amiga key.

The only special thing to watch for when using the menu is that ASM and Autolink are combined on a single line. This prevents confusion when they're arranged closely in a menu format. Only one of them can be active, either ASM or Autolink.

The ASM/Autolink menu selection simply activates whichever was last used as a button. That is, if you first activate the assembler function from the menu, it will use ASM (same as the Assemble button). If you've used the Autolink button, the menu will treat an ASM/Autolink selection as if you clicked on the Autolink button. If neither the Assemble nor Autolink buttons have yet been used, the menu selection of ASM/Autolink will default to Assemble.

ASMINT is fun and makes machine language convenient, with minimum typing and (almost) no need for CLI expertise, thanks to Doug Leavitt for the -a (Autolink) option flag in his ASM68010.

### Listing 23-1. ASMINT.ASM

```
 ;NAME: ASMINT.ASM  BY DANIEL WOLF
;COPYRIGHT 1987 BY COMPUTE! PUBLICATIONS
;09/10/87

 bra _START

TXT      equ     1
REQ      equ     1
WIN      equ     1
MEN      equ     1
GAD      equ     1
WBC      equ     1

 include "HEADER"

RBPEN      equu     $0
RFPEN      equ      $1

REQXMAX      equ      300
REQYMAX      equ      65
```

```
STRSIZ      equ      80

;Project Menu Item Codes
PROJ.TEST      equu      $07FF
PROJ.ABOUT      equ      $0000
PROJ.NEW      equ      $0020
PROJ.ASSEM      equ      $0040
PROJ.EXECO      equ      $0060
PROJ.PRINT      equ      $0080
PROJ.EDIT      equ      $00A0
PROJ.QUIT      equ      $00C0

OPENIT MACRO
 move.l #MODE_NEWFILE,d2
 DOSLIB OPEN
 move.l d0,ErrFD
 ENDM

EXECUTIT MACRO
 bsr PRINTOUT
 move.l #ExecBuf,d1
 ZERO d2
 move.l ErrFD,d3
 DOSLIB EXECUTE
 ENDM

MAKOPY MACRO
        lea \1,a0
        lea.l \2,a1
        STRCPY a0,a1
        ENDM

MAKCAT MACRO
        lea \1,a0
        lea.l \2,a1
        STRCAT a0,a1
        ENDM

;         Simple string copy macro
;         Use:      STRCPY      src,dest
STRCPY MACRO
        RSTRCPY \1,\2,\@
        ENDM

RSTRCPY MACRO
\3:
        move.b (\1)+,(\2)+
        bne \3
        endm

;         Simple string append macro
;         Use:      STRCAT      src,dest
STRCAT MACRO
        RSTRCAT \1,\2,\@
        ENDM

RSTRCAT MACRO
\3:
        move.b (\2)+,d0
        bne \3
        subq.l #1,\2
        STRCPY \1,\2
        ENDM

MAIN
 move.l sp,STACK
 tst.l ENDFROMWB              ;IF INITIATED FROM WB,  THEN NO ANNOUNCEMENTS YET!
 bne.s _BUILDAWINDOW
FROMUSER
 DOSPRINT STDOUT,#MYMESSAGE   ;IF INITIATED FROM CLI, THEN OUTPUT TITLE MESSAGE
 ZERO d0
 movea.l COMMAND,a0           ;PUT ADDRESS OF COMMAND LINE IN A0
 cmpi.b #'?',(a0)             ;IF FIRST CHARACTER IS ? THEN
 bne.s _BUILDAWINDOW
 bra USAGE                    ;PRINT OUT THE USAGE TEXT
```

```
_BUILDAWINDOW
 move.l #CLOSEWINDOW!MENUPICK!GADGETUP,_THISIDCMP
 move.l #ACTIVATE!WINDOWDRAG!WINDOWDEPTH!WINDOWCLOSE!SMART_REFRESH,_THISFLAGS
 MAKEWIN #ASMINTITLE,40,15,500,160,ERROR,WINDOW

_BUILDMENU

 MITEMLIST MITEM0,MITEM1,MITEM2,MITEM3,MITEM4,MITEM5,MITEM6,0,6,150
 MAKEMEN MYCMDKEYS,MYMUEXES,ASMWMENUTITLE,DONE
 move.l d1,_THISMENU        ;MAKEAMENU RETURNS WITH POINTER TO MENU IN D1
 move.w #5,d0               ;LEFEDGE  FOR THIS MENU
 move.w #120,d1             ;WIDTH    FOR THIS MENU
 bsr CREATEMENU             ;THIS CREATES THE ACTUAL MENU ATTACHED TO THE MITEMS

_MENUATTACH
 move.l WINDOW,a0           ;SUPPLY POINTER TO WINDOW  IN A0
 move.l _THISMENU,a1        ;SUPPLY POINTER TO MENU #0 IN A1
 INTLIB SETMENUSTRIP        ;AND ATTACH THE MENU TO THE WINDOW

_BUILDASMGADGETS
 lea GTEXT1,a1
 move.w #10,d4
 move.w #140,d5
 bsr MAKEAGADGET
 move.l d0,a1
 move.l a1,_FIRSTGADGET
 move.l WINDOW,a0
 bsr ADDNEWGADG

 NEWBGADG GTEXT2,110,140,WINDOW
 NEWBGADG GTEXT3,210,140,WINDOW
 NEWBGADG GTEXT4,270,140,WINDOW
 NEWBGADG GTEXT5,330,140,WINDOW
 NEWBGADG GTEXT6,390,140,WINDOW

 NEWSGADG SGBUF1,UBUF,10,20,WINDOW
 NEWSGADG SGBUF2,UBUF,10,40,WINDOW
 NEWSGADG SGBUF3,UBUF,10,60,WINDOW
 NEWSGADG SGBUF4,UBUF,10,80,WINDOW
 NEWSGADG SGBUF5,UBUF,10,100,WINDOW
 NEWSGADG SGBUF6,UBUF,10,120,WINDOW

 PRINTNEWAT WINDOW,MSG1,330,20,ERROR
 PRINTNEWAT WINDOW,MSG2,330,40,ERROR
 PRINTNEWAT WINDOW,MSG3,330,60,ERROR
 PRINTNEWAT WINDOW,MSG4,330,80,ERROR
 PRINTNEWAT WINDOW,MSG5,330,100,ERROR
 PRINTNEWAT WINDOW,MSG6,330,120,ERROR

 move.l _FIRSTGADGET,a0
 move.l WINDOW,a1
 INTLIB REFRESHGADGETS

 MAKEREQ NOPrtVerb,R_PosVerb,R_NegVerb,ERROR
 SAVEREQ REQ1
 MAKEREQ NOLstVerb,R_PosVerb,R_NegVerb,ERROR
 SAVEREQ REQ2
 MAKEREQ NoErrWVerb,R_PosVerb,R_NegVerb,ERROR
 SAVEREQ REQ3
 MAKEREQ DoneErrWVerb,0,R_ContVerb,ERROR
 SAVEREQ REQ4
 MAKEREQ NoExecWVerb,R_PosVerb,R_NegVerb,ERROR
 SAVEREQ REQ5
 MAKEREQ DoneExecWVerb,0,R_ContVerb,ERROR
 SAVEREQ REQ6
 MAKEREQ AboutVerb,0,R_ContVerb,ERROR
 SAVEREQ REQ7
 MAKEREQ ListVerb,PrtVerb,ScrnVerb,ERROR
 SAVEREQ REQ8
 MAKEREQ ListRVerb,R_ContVerb,R_NegVerb,ERROR
 SAVEREQ REQ9

LOOP
 move.l WINDOW,a0
 move.l #$FFFF,d0            ;WAKE UP THE WHOLE MENU NOW
 INTLIB ONMENU
 move.l WINDOW,a0
 move.l WW.USERPORT(a0),a0  ;LISTEN TO PORT ATTACHED TO THIS WINDOW
 SYSLIB WAITPORT             ;WAIT FOR A SPECIFIED MESSAGE TO ARRIVE
```

```
 move.l WINDOW,aØ
 move.l WW.USERPORT(aØ),aØ
 SYSLIB GETMSG                   ;MESSAGE HAS ARRIVE WITHIN SPECIFICATIONS
 tst.l dØ                        ;POINTER TO INTUIMESSAGE COMES BACK IN DØ
 beq LOOP                        ;NO MESSAGE THERE, SO LOOP

 move.l dØ,aØ
 move.l IM.CLASS(aØ),d7
 move.w IM.CODE(aØ),d6
 move.w IM.MOUSEX(aØ),d5
 move.w IM.MOUSEY(aØ),d4
 move.l aØ,a1
 SYSLIB REPLYMSG
 cmp.l #CLOSEWINDOW,d7
 beq DONE
                                   ;**** CHECK FOR MENU OPTIONS
 cmp.l #MENUPICK,d7
 bne chkgadget                     ; Not a Menu pick, Check gadgets
 cmp.w #MENUNULL,d6
 beq LOOP                          ; Ignore
 and.w #PROJ.TEST,d6
 cmp.w #PROJ.QUIT,d6
 beq DONE
 cmp.w #PROJ.ABOUT,d6
 bne chknew
 jsr projabout
 bra LOOP
chknew:
 cmp.w #PROJ.NEW,d6
 bne chkprint
 jsr projnew
 bra LOOP
chkprint:
 cmp.w #PROJ.PRINT,d6
 bne chkassem
 jsr projprint
 bra LOOP
chkassem:
 cmp.w #PROJ.ASSEM,d6
 bne chkexecobj
 jsr projassem
 bra LOOP
chkexecobj:
 cmp.w #PROJ.EXECO,d6
 bne chekedit
 jsr projexecobj
 bra LOOP
chekedit:
 cmp.w #PROJ.EDIT,d6
 bne LOOP
 jsr projedit
 bra LOOP

                              ;**** CHECK FOR GADGET information
chkgadget:
 cmp.l #GADGETUP,d7
 bne LOOP                     ; Not a gadget, ignore
 cmp.w #14Ø,d4
 ble LOOP                     ;cant be a Boolean gadget, Y is too low
dogadg1:
 cmp.w #11Ø,d5
 bge dogadg2
 jsr projassem1
 bra LOOP
dogadg2
 cmp.w #21Ø,d5
 bge dogadg3
 jsr projexecobj
 bra LOOP
dogadg3:
 cmp.w #27Ø,d5
 bge dogadg6
 jsr projprint
 bra LOOP
```

```
dogadg6:
 cmp.w #330,d5
 bge dogadg7
 jsr projedit
 bra LOOP
dogadg7:
 cmp.w #390,d5
 bge dogadg8
 jsr projnew
 bra LOOP
dogadg8
 jsr projauto
 bra LOOP

;**** SUBROUTINES
                                ;Tells user what asm/asi are
projabout:
 REQUEST WINDOW,REQ7
 rts

projedit:
 MAKOPY CDSTRING,ExecBuf
 MAKCAT EMACSTRING,ExecBuf
 tst.b SGBUF5                   ;IS THERE A SEPARATE EDIT FILE?
 beq defeditstr
 MAKCAT SGBUF5,ExecBuf
 bra projednow
defeditstr:
 MAKCAT SGBUF1,ExecBuf          ;no, just assume same as assembly source

projednow:                      ;**** OPEN an output file for error messages

 move.l #Edout,d1
 OPENIT
 bne projed2
 REQUEST WINDOW,REQ3
 tst.l d0
 bne projednow                  ; RETRY
 rts                            ; ABORT

          ;**** Try to execute the assembler curse if it fails
projed2:
 EXECUTIT
 move.l ErrFD,d1
 DOSLIB CLOSE
 rts

projauto
 move.w #1,Absflag
 bra projassem

projnew:
 PUSHREG a2-a6
 moveq #(STRSIZ/2)-1,d0
 lea.l SGBUF1,a0
 lea.l SGBUF2,a1
 lea.l SGBUF3,a2
 lea SGBUF4,a3
 lea SGBUF5,a4
 lea SGBUF6,a5
 lea UBUF,a6
 moveq #0,d1
1$:
 move.w d1,(a0)+        ; Clear Ibuf1
 move.w d1,(a1)+        ; Clear Ibuf2
 move.w d1,(a2)+        ; Clear Ibuf3
 move.w d1,(a3)+        ; Clear Ibuf4
 move.w d1,(a4)+        ; Clear Ibuf5
 move.w d1,(a5)+        ; Clear Ibuf6
 move.w d1,(a6)+        ; Clear Ubuf
 dbf d0,1$

 move.l _FIRSTGADGET,a0
 move.l WINDOW,a1
 ZERA a2
 INTLIB REFRESHGADGETS
 PULLREG a2-a6
 rts
```

```
projprint:                              ;Print listing file if it exists
                                        ;**** Try to open the listing file
prtl:
 MAKOPY DSTRING,ExecBuf
 MAKCAT SGBUF3,ExecBuf
 move.l #ExecBuf,dl
 move.l #MODE_OLDFILE,d2
 DOSLIB OPEN
 move.l dØ,LstFD
 bne prt2
 REQUEST WINDOW,REQ2             ;file not found
 tst.l dØ
 bne prtl                        ; RETRY
 bra prt6                        ; ABORT

prt2:
 REQUEST WINDOW,REQ8             ;choose printer or screen
 tst.l dØ
 bne prtoprt
 bra prtocon
prtoprt:                         ;OPEN the printer
 move.l #Prtstr,dl
 bra prt22
prtocon:
 move.l #Constr,dl               ;or console
prt22:
 move.l #MODE_OLDFILE,d2
 DOSLIB OPEN
 move.l dØ,PrtFD
 bne prt3
 REQUEST WINDOW,REQl             ;not successful on OPEN
 tst.l dØ
 bne prt2                        ; RETRY
 bra prt5                        ; ABORT

prt3:
 REQUEST WINDOW,REQ9             ;REALLY PRINT THE WHOLE THING?
 tst.l dØ
 beq prt4                        ;user clicked ABORT
                                 ;user clicked CONTINUE, so
prt33:                           ;Print the listing file
 move.l LstFD,dl
 move.l #ExecBuf,d2
 move.l #512,d3
 DOSLIB READ
 tst.l dØ
 ble prt4
 move.l PrtFD,dl
 move.l #ExecBuf,d2
 move.l dØ,d3
 move.l d3,d6
 DOSLIB WRITE
 cmp d6,dØ
 bne prt4
 bra prt33
                          ;**** CLOSE everything and exit
prt4:
 move.l PrtFD,dl
 DOSLIB CLOSE
prt5:
 move.l LstFD,dl
 DOSLIB CLOSE
prt6:
 rts

projasseml:
 move.w #Ø,Absflag        ;got here via ASSEM gadget, so just ASSEM!
projassem:                ;Start a new assembly with the latest params
 tst.b SGBUF6             ;do ASM or ASM -a depending on how got here
 beq projØ                ;check for MAKE file
projmake:
 MAKOPY CDSTRING,ExecBuf
 MAKCAT EXECSTRING,ExecBuf
 MAKCAT SGBUF6,ExecBuf
 bra proj4
```

```
proj0:                          ;no MAKE file
 MAKOPY CDSTRING,ExecBuf
 MAKCAT Asmstr,ExecBuf          ;put default dir in execbuf
defasmdir:
 tst.w Absflag                  ;check for AUTOLINK origin
 beq proj1
 MAKCAT Absstr,ExecBuf
proj1:
 MAKCAT SGBUF1,ExecBuf          ; Source file string gadget
 tst.b SGBUF2                   ; Object file string gadget exists?
 beq proj2
 MAKCAT Objstr,ExecBuf
 MAKCAT SGBUF2,ExecBuf
proj2:
 tst.b SGBUF3                   ; Use Listing file if it exists
 beq proj3
 MAKCAT Listingstr,ExecBuf
 MAKCAT SGBUF3,ExecBuf
proj3:
 tst.b SGBUF4                   ; Add Include list if it exists
 beq proj4
 MAKCAT Inclstr1,ExecBuf
 MAKCAT SGBUF4,ExecBuf
 MAKCAT Inclstr2,ExecBuf

proj4:                          ;**** OPEN an output file for error messages

 move.l #Errout,d1
 OPENIT
 bne proj5
 REQUEST WINDOW,REQ3
 tst.l d0
 bne proj4                      ; RETRY
 rts                            ; ABORT

             ;**** Try to execute the assembler curse if it fails
proj5:
 EXECUTIT

;put code to COPY OBJECT PROGRAM a pre-existing D:PRG icon here

 tst.w Absflag
 beq AFTERCOPY
 MAKOPY CDSTRING,ExecBuf
 MAKCAT ICONSTRING1,ExecBuf
 MAKCAT SGBUF2,ExecBuf
 MAKCAT ICONSTRING2,ExecBuf
 EXECUTIT
AFTERCOPY:
 REQUEST WINDOW,REQ4
 move.l ErrFD,d1
 DOSLIB CLOSE
 rts

projexecobj:                            ;EXECUTE the object program
 MAKOPY CDSTRING,ExecBuf
 MAKCAT SGBUF2,ExecBuf

proje2:              ;**** OPEN an output file for error messages

 move.l #Execout,d1
 OPENIT
 bne proje1
 REQUEST WINDOW,REQ5
 tst.l d0
 bne proje2                             ; RETRY
 rts                                    ; ABORT

                     ;**** Try to execute obj code  curse if it fails
proje1:
 EXECUTIT
 REQUEST WINDOW,REQ6
 move.l ErrFD,d1
 DOSLIB CLOSE
 rts
```

```
DONE
 move.l WINDOW,d0
 tst.l d0
 beq.s DONEALL
 move.l d0,a0
 INTLIB CLEARMENUSTRIP
DONEALL
 ZERO d0
QUIT
 move.l STACK,sp
 move.l d0,-(sp)
 move.l WINDOW,d0
 beq.s 1$
 move.l d0,a0
 INTLIB CLOSEWINDOW
1$
 move.l (sp)+,d0
 rts
QUITNOW
 move.l STACK,sp
 rts

ERROR
 DOSPRINT STDOUT,#ERRORTEXT
 moveq #CANTOPENWINDOW,d0
 bra QUITNOW

USAGE
 DOSPRINT STDOUT,#USAGETEXT
 ZERO d0
 bra QUITNOW

PRINTOUT
 DOSPRINT ErrFD,#ExecBuf
 DOSPRINT ErrFD,#LINE
 rts

 EVENPC

STACK dc.l 0
WINDOW dc.l 0

REQ1 dc.l 0,0,0          ;PTR TO BODY ITEXT, POSITEXT, NEGITEXT
REQ2 dc.l 0,0,0
REQ3 dc.l 0,0,0
REQ4 dc.l 0,0,0
REQ5 dc.l 0,0,0
REQ6 dc.l 0,0,0
REQ7 dc.l 0,0,0
REQ8 dc.l 0,0,0
REQ9 dc.l 0,0,0

_FIRSTGADGET                      ;POINTER TO TOP OF GADGET LIST
 dc.l 0
_THISMENU
 dc.l 0                           ;POINTER TO TOP OF MENU LIST

ErrFD:
 dc.l 0
PrtFD:
 dc.l 0
LstFD:
 dc.l 0
Absflag:
 dc.w 1                           ; Generate ABS code by default
_THISFONTHITE
 dc.w 9

SGBUF1                            ;STRING GADGET BUFFERS
 dc.b 'Source'
 dcb.b 74,0
 EVENPC
SGBUF2
 dc.b 'Object'
 dcb.b 74,0
SGBUF3
 dcb.b 80,0
```

```
SGBUF4
 dcb.b 80,0
SGBUF5
 dcb.b 80,0
SGBUF6
 dcb.b 80,0
UBUF                                 ;UNIVERSAL STRING GADGET UNDOBUFFER
 dcb.b 80,0

ExecBuf:
 dcb.b 512,0                         ; EXECUTE command buffer
 EVENPC

ASMINTITLE
 dc.b ' AsmInt  by D. Wolf ',0
 EVENPC
USAGETEXT
 dc.b 'Usage: asmint',10,0
 EVENPC
ERRORTEXT
 dc.b 10,'Sorry, cannot open window ',10,0
 EVENPC
MYMESSAGE
 dc.b 10,'AsmInt by Daniel Wolf  Copyright 1988 by Compute! Publications',10,0
 EVENPC

GTEXT1                           ;GADGET TEXTS
 dc.b ' ASSEMBLE ',0
 EVENPC
GTEXT2
 dc.b ' EXEC OBJ ',0
 EVENPC
GTEXT3
 dc.b ' LIST ',0
 EVENPC
GTEXT4
 dc.b ' EDIT ',0
 EVENPC
GTEXT5
 dc.b ' NEW ',0
 EVENPC
GTEXT6
 dc.b ' AUTOLINK ',0
 EVENPC

ASMWMENUTITLE
 dc.b ' AsmInt ',0
 EVENPC
MITEM0
 dc.b '   ABOUT      ',0
 EVENPC
MITEM1
 dc.b '   NEW        ',0
 EVENPC
MITEM2
 dc.b '   ASM/AUTO   ',0
 EVENPC
MITEM3
 dc.b '   EXECUTE    ',0
 EVENPC
MITEM4
 dc.b '   LIST       ',0
 EVENPC
MITEM5
 dc.b '   EDIT       ',0
 EVENPC
MITEM6
 dc.b '   QUIT       ',0
 EVENPC
MYCMDKEYS
 dc.b 'WNAXLEQ'
 EVENPC
MYMUEXES
 dc.l $7E,$7D,$7B,$77,$6F,$5F,$3F

MSG1
 dc.b ' Source File ',0
 EVENPC
```

```
MSG2
 dc.b ' Object File ',0
 EVENPC
MSG3
 dc.b ' Listing File ',0
 EVENPC
MSG4
 dc.b ' Include List ',0
 EVENPC
MSG5
 dc.b ' Edit File ',0
 EVENPC
MSG6
 dc.b ' MAKE File     ',0
 EVENPC

DAsmstr:
 dc.b 'dfl:',0
 EVENPC
Asmstr:
 dc.b 'asm ',0
 EVENPC
Absstr:
 dc.b '-a ',0
 EVENPC
Objstr:
 dc.b ' -o ',0
 EVENPC
Listingstr:
 dc.b ' -l ',0
 EVENPC
Inclstrl:
 dc.b ' -i "',0
 EVENPC
Inclstr2:
 dc.b '"',0
 EVENPC
Edout:
 dc.b 'CON:0/60/400/100/Asm(1.8) EDIT Window ',0
 EVENPC
Errout:
 dc.b 'CON:0/25/640/150/Asm(1.8) ASM Window ',0
 EVENPC
Execout:
 dc.b 'CON:0/60/640/120/Asm(1.8) EXEC Window ',0
 EVENPC
Constr:
 dc.b 'CON:0/0/640/200/Asm(1.8) LIST Window ',0
 EVENPC
Prtstr:
 dc.b 'PRT:',0
 EVENPC
EXECSTRING
 dc.b 'EXECUTE ',0
 EVENPC
EMACSTRING
 dc.b 'EMACS ',0
 EVENPC

;**** REQUESTERS **** POSITIVE/NEGATIVE responses

R_PosVerb:
 dc.b 'RETRY',0
 EVENPC
R_NegVerb:
 dc.b 'ABORT',0
 EVENPC
R_ContVerb:
 dc.b 'CONTINUE',0
 EVENPC
ScrnVerb:
 dc.b 'SCREEN',0
 EVENPC
PrtVerb:
 dc.b 'PRINTER',0
 EVENPC
```

```
;**** REQUESTER BODY MESSAGES

NoAsmVerb:
 dc.b 'Cannot Find Asm',0
 EVENPC
NoExecWVerb:
NoErrWVerb:
 dc.b 'Cannot OPEN Message Window',0
 EVENPC
DoneExecWVerb:
DoneErrWVerb:
 dc.b 'Done With Message Window?',0
 EVENPC
NOPrtVerb:
 dc.b 'Cannot OPEN Output Device',0
 EVENPC
NOLstVerb:
 dc.b 'Cannot OPEN Listing File',0
 EVENPC
AboutVerb:
 dc.b 'Asm Interface by Daniel Wolf',0
 EVENPC
ListVerb:
 dc.b 'List  To  Screen  or  Printer ?',0
 EVENPC
ListRVerb:
 dc.b 'List REALLY ??',0
 EVENPC
CDSTRING:
 dc.b 'C:CD D:',10,'CD',10,0
 EVENPC
DSTRING:
 dc.b 'D:',0
 EVENPC
LINE:
 dc.b 13,10,10,0
 EVENPC
ICONSTRING1:
 dc.b 'COPY '
 EVENPC
ICONSTRING2
 dc.b ' to Obj'
 EVENPC
 END
```

## POLYFRAC.ASM

POLYFRAC.ASM is a demonstration of fractal line drawing using the graphics library. POLYFRAC draws five different line fractals, including the dragon sweep, Hilbert curve, and three kinds of fractal trees. The menu selection has alternate command keys and mutual exclude provisions.

When the program begins, it opens a window and draws the dragon sweep curve first. Each curve is drawn in several levels of detail and remains static in the window. This program demonstrates the speed and efficiency of machine language graphics programming on the Amiga. In the tree fractals, the Amiga produces many lines per second.

An interesting feature of the window used in POLYFRAC.ASM is its automatic adaptation to an interlaced screen. The interlace (400-line) screen can be activated through the Preferences program on the Workbench disk. When the window is opened, a check is made of the mode of the screen. If interlace is the chosen mode, then the SIZEWINDOW Intuition function is used to double the window's height. The window adapts automatically to the screen height.

The code for this program is a good example of combining a window, menu, and graphics features into one application.

**Listing 23-2. POLYFRAC.ASM**

```
 ;POLYFRAC.ASM by Daniel Wolf
;COPYRIGHT 1988 BY COMPUTE! PUBLICATIONS
;09/10/87

 bra _START

GFX equ 1
MAT equ 1
TRA equ 1

MEN equu 1
WIN equ 1
TXT equ 1
FFP equ 1

 include "HEADER"

MAIN
 move.l SP,STACK
 tst.l ENDFROMWB
 bne.s MENUWINDOW
FROMUSER
 DOSPRINT STDOUT,#MYMESSAGE
 ZERO D0
MENUWINDOW
 MAKEWIN #DRAGTITLE,40,4,522,195,ERROR
 move.l D0,WINDOW

 move.l WINDOW,A0
 move.l WW.RPORT(A0),RP
 INTLIB VIEWPORTADDRESS
 move.l D0,A2
 move.w VP.MODES(A2),D0
 and.w #LACE,D0
 tst.w D0
 beq.s FRACLACESET
 move.l #1,MYLACE
 ZERO D0
 move.l #195,D1
 move.l WINDOW,A0
 INTLIB SIZEWINDOW
FRACLACESET
 MITEMLIST ITEM0,ITEM1,ITEM2,ITEM3,ITEM4,ITEM5,0,0,5
 MAKEMEN MYCMDKEYS,MYMUEXES,MYMENUTITLE,ERROR

 move.l D1,_THISMENU
 move.w #5,D0
 move.w #120,D1
 bsr CREATEMENU

_MENUATTACH
 move.l WINDOW,A0
 move.l _THISMENU,A1
 INTLIB SETMENUSTRIP

 move.l #TICKSPERSECOND/2,D1
 DOSLIB DELAY

 bsr DRAGONDRAW
```

```
LOOP
 move.l WINDOW,A0
 move.l #$FFFF,D0
 INTLIB ONMENU
 move.l WINDOW,A0
 move.l WW.USERPORT(A0),A0
 SYSLIB WAITPORT
 move.l WINDOW,A0
 move.l WW.USERPORT(A0),A0
 SYSLIB GETMSG
 tst.l D0
 beq MYTIME
 move.l D0,A1
 move.l IM.CLASS(A1),D2
 move.w IM.CODE(A1),D3
 move.w IM.QUALIFIER(A1),D4
 SYSLIB REPLYMSG

 cmp.l #CLOSEWINDOW,D2
 beq DONE
 cmp.l #MENUPICK,D2
 bne MYTIME
 ZERO D0
 move.w D3,D0
 bsr MENUEVENT
 cmpi.w #5,D1
 beq DONE
CHKDRAGON
 cmpi.w #0,D1
 bne.s CHKHILBERT
 move.l WINDOW,A0
 bsr _CLEARWINDOW
 bsr DRAGONDRAW
 bra MYTIME
CHKHILBERT
 cmpi.w #1,D1
 bne.s CHKTTREE
 move.l WINDOW,A0
 bsr _CLEARWINDOW
 bsr HILBERTDRAW
 bra MYTIME
CHKTTREE
 move.l #255,FIRSTX
 move.l #128,FIRSTY
 cmpi.w #2,D1            ;TRI
 bne.s CHKFTREE
 move.l #3,NANGLES
NOWTREE
 move.l WINDOW,A0
 bsr _CLEARWINDOW
 bsr FRACBRANCH
 bra MYTIME
CHKFTREE
 move.l #100,FIRSTY
 cmpi.w #3,D1            ;QUAD
 bne.s CHKFITREE
 move.l #4,NANGLES
 bra.s NOWTREE
CHKFITREE
 cmpi.w #4,D1            ;QUINT
 bne MYTIME
 move.l #5,NANGLES
 bra.s NOWTREE

MYTIME
 bra LOOP

DONE
 move.l WINDOW,A0
 INTLIB CLEARMENUSTRIP
DONEALL
 ZERO D0
QUIT
 move.l STACK,SP
 move.l D0,-(SP)
 move.l WINDOW,D0
 beq.s 1$
 move.l D0,A0
```

```
 INTLIB CLOSEWINDOW
1$
 move.l (SP)+,D0
 rts
QUITNOW
 move.l STACK,SP
 rts

ERROR
 DOSPRINT STDOUT,#ERRORTEXT
 moveq #21,D0
 bra QUITNOW

FRACBRANCH
 PUSHALL
 move.w #1,LEVELO
 move.l #7,LOGLEN
 tst.l MYLACE
 beq.s BRANCHCONST
 move.l #8,LOGLEN

BRANCHCONST
 move.l FIRSTX,D0
 MATHLIB SPFlt
 move.l D0,XOFP
 move.l FIRSTY,D0
 tst.l MYLACE
 beq.s NOLACETREE
 asl.l #1,D0
 move.l D0,FIRSTY
NOLACETREE
 JUST SPFlt
 move.l D0,YOFP

 move.l NANGLES,D7
 move.l D7,D0
 JUST SPFlt
 move.l D0,D1
 move.l TWOPI,D0
 JUST SPDiv
 move.l D0,PHWHOLE
 move.l TWOFP,D1
 JUST SPDiv
 move.l D0,PHOVER2
 move.l PIOVER2,D1
 JUST SPAdd
 move.l D0,STARTANGLE
 move.l D0,ANGLE
 lea ANGLEARAY,A3
 move.l D0,(A3)+
 move.l PHWHOLE,D1
ADDANOTHERANGLE
 JUST SPAdd
 move.l D0,(A3)+
 SUBQ.L #1,D7
 tst.l D7
 bne.s ADDANOTHERANGLE

BRANCHDRAW
 move.l WINDOW,A0
 move.l #$FFFF,D0
 INTLIB OFFMENU
BRANCHDR
 tst.l MYLACE
 bne.s LEVISSEVEN
 cmpi.w #7,LEVELO
 beq DONEBRANCH
LEVISSEVEN
 cmpi.w #8,LEVELO
 beq DONEBRANCH
 move.l XOFP,CURXFP
 move.l YOFP,CURYFP
 move.l WINDOW,A0
 bsr _CLEARWINDOW
 SETAPEN RP,#0
 RECTFILL RP,#185,#1,#330,#20
 SETAPEN RP,#1
```

```
ONEBRANCH
 move.l STARTANGLE,ANGLE

 lea NARAY,A4
 lea XINCARAY,A2
 lea YINCARAY,A3

 move.w LEVELO,DØ
 asl.w #1,DØ
 move.w DØ,LEVEL               ;LEVEL=2*LEVELØ TO POINT TO WORDS IN ARRAYS
 bsr DRAWB
 move.l #TICKSPERSECOND,D1
 DOSLIB DELAY
 addi.w #1,LEVELO
 bra BRANCHDR

DRAWB
 subi.l #1,LOGLEN
 subi.w #2,LEVEL               ;LEVEL=LEVEL-1
 move.w LEVEL,DØ
 clr.w Ø(A4,DØ.W)              ;N(LEVEL)=Ø
DDRAWB
 addi.w #1,Ø(A4,DØ.W)          ;N(LEVEL)=N(LEVEL)+1
 bsr SUBDRAWB
 move.w LEVEL,DØ
 move.w Ø(A4,DØ.W),D1
 move.l NANGLES,D2
 cmp.w D2,D1
 bne.s DDRAWB
WINDUPB
 addi.w #2,LEVEL
 addi.l #1,LOGLEN
 rts

SUBDRAWB
 move.l LOGLEN,D4
 movea.l _MATHTRANSBASE,A6
 move.l ANGLE,DØ
 move.l #COSANGLE,D1
 JUST SPSincos
 add.l D4,DØ               ;MULTIPLY LENFP*SINANGLE=DØ
 move.l COSANGLE,D6
 add.l D4,D6
 tst.l MYLACE              ;DOUBLE XINC IF NOT INTERLACED
 bne.s NOXDOUBLE
 addq.l #1,D6
NOXDOUBLE
 move.w LEVEL,D2
 asl.w #1,D2
 move.l DØ,Ø(A3,D2.W)
 move.l D6,Ø(A2,D2.W)
 move.l CURYFP,D1
 MATHLIB SPAdd
 move.l DØ,NEWYFP              ;NEWYFP=CURYFP+YINC(LEVEL)
 JUST SPFix
 move.w DØ,D3   ;NEWY
 move.l D6,DØ
 move.l CURXFP,D1
 JUST SPAdd
 move.l DØ,NEWXFP              ;NEWXFP=CURXFP+XINC(LEVEL)
 JUST SPFix
 move.w DØ,D2   ;NEWX
CONVERTPOINTS
 move.l CURYFP,DØ
 JUST SPFix
 move.w DØ,D4   ;CURY
 move.l CURXFP,DØ
 JUST SPFix
 move.w D4,D1
 DRAWLINE RP
 move.l NEWXFP,CURXFP
 move.l NEWYFP,CURYFP
 tst.w LEVEL
 beq.s NEWXNEWY

 bsr DRAWB
```

```
NEWXNEWY
 move.w LEVEL,D2
 asl.w #1,D2
 move.l Ø(A2,D2.W),D1
 move.l CURXFP,DØ
 MATHLIB SPSub
 move.l DØ,CURXFP
 move.l Ø(A3,D2.W),D1
 move.l CURYFP,DØ
 JUST SPSub
 move.l DØ,CURYFP
 add.w #1,ANGLENUM
 move.w ANGLENUM,DØ
 move.l NANGLES,D1
 cmp.w D1,DØ
 bne.s NEXTANGLE
 moveq.l #Ø,DØ
 move.w DØ,ANGLENUM
NEXTANGLE
 asl.w #2,DØ
 lea ANGLEARAY,A5
 move.l Ø(A5,DØ.W),D1
 move.l D1,ANGLE
 rts

DONEBRANCH
 PULLALL
 rts

STARTANGLE dc.l Ø
FIRSTX     dc.l 25Ø
FIRSTY     dc.l 128
FIRSTYLACE dc.l 256
ANGLE      dc.l Ø
PIWHOLE    dc.l $C9ØFDB42
PIOVER2    dc.l $C9ØFDB41
TWOPI      dc.l $C9ØFDB43
PHWHOLE    dc.l Ø
PHOVER2    dc.l Ø
CURXFP     dc.l Ø
CURYFP     dc.l Ø
NEWXFP     dc.l Ø
NEWYFP     dc.l Ø
TWOFP      dc.l $8ØØØØØ42
XOFP       dc.l Ø
YOFP       dc.l Ø
NANGLES    dc.l Ø
COSANGLE   dc.l Ø
LOGLEN     dc.l Ø
LEVEL      dc.w Ø
LEVELO     dc.w Ø
ANGLENUM   dc.w Ø

XINCARAY   ds.l 16
YINCARAY   ds.l 16
NARAY      ds.l 16
ANGLEARAY  ds.l 16
 EVENPC

HILBERTDRAW
 PUSHALL
 move.l WINDOW,AØ
 move.l #$FFFF,DØ
 INTLIB OFFMENU
 move.l WINDOW,AØ
 tst.l MYLACE
 beq.s ONLYSEVEN
 cmpi.w #8,J
 beq DONEHILBERT
 bra.s ONEH
ONLYSEVEN
 cmpi.w #7,J
 beq DONEHILBERT
ONEH
 addi.w #1,J
 tst.l MYLACE
 beq.s ONLYSEVEH
 cmpi.w #8,J
```

```
 beq DONEHILBERT
 bne.s SETITNOWH
ONLYSEVEH
 cmpi.w #7,J
 beq DONEHILBERT
SETITNOWH
 move.l WINDOW,A0
 bsr _CLEARWINDOW
 move.w J,R
 moveq #0,D0
 move.w R,D0
 move.l #128,D1
 lsr.w D0,D1
 move.w D1,Q

 SETDRMD RP,#JAM1
 SETAPEN RP,#1
 move.w #8,X
 move.w #30,Y
 tst.l MYLACE
 beq.s NOTYHEIGHTH
 move.w #30,Y
NOTYHEIGHTH
 DRAWPOINT RP,X,Y
 bsr HILFRAC
 move.l #TICKSPERSECOND,D1
 ;asl.w #1,D1
 DOSLIB DELAY
 bra ONEH

HILFRAC:
 PUSHALL
 subq.w #1,R
 eori.w #1,T
 bsr HILARITH
 tst.w R
 ble.s M0
 bsr HILFRAC
M0
 bsr DOALINE
 eori.w #1,T
 bsr HILARITH
 tst.w R
 ble.s M1
 bsr HILFRAC
M1
 bsr DOALINE
 tst.w R
 ble.s M2
 bsr HILFRAC
M2
 bsr HILARITH
 eori.w #1,T
 bsr DOALINE
 tst.w R
 ble.s M3
 bsr HILFRAC
M3
 bsr HILARITH
 eori.w #1,T
 addq.w #1,R
 PULLALL
 rts

HILARITH
 moveq #0,D0
 move.w Q,Z
 tst.w T
 bne.s PLUSP
MINUSP
 sub.w P,D0
 move.w D0,Q
 move.w Z,P
 rts
PLUSP
 move.w P,Q
 sub.w Z,D0
 move.w D0,P
 rts
```

```
DOALINE
 moveq #Ø,DØ
 move.w P,DØ
 asl.w #2,DØ
 add.w X,DØ
 move.w DØ,L
 move.w Y,DØ
 add.w Q,DØ
 tst.l MYLACE
 beq.s NOTDOUBLEY
 add.w Q,DØ
NOTDOUBLEY
 move.w DØ,M
 DRAWLINE RP,X,Y,L,M
 move.w L,X
 move.w M,Y
 rts

DONEHILBERT
 PULLALL
 move.w #Ø,J
 moveq #Ø,DØ
QUITH
 rts

 EVENPC

X  dc.w Ø
Y  dc.w Ø
L  dc.w Ø
M  dc.w Ø

J  dc.w Ø
Q  dc.w 128
R  dc.w 1
T  dc.w 1
Z  dc.w Ø
P  dc.w Ø

 EVENPC

DRAGONDRAW
 PUSHALL
 move.l WINDOW,AØ
 move.l #$FFFF,DØ
 INTLIB OFFMENU
 move.w #7,MAXLEVEL
 tst.l MYLACE
 beq.s NOTMAXEIGHT
 move.w #8,MAXLEVEL
NOTMAXEIGHT
 move.w MAXLEVEL,DØ
 cmp.w NB,DØ
 beq DONEDRAGON

ONEED
 move.w #1,NB
ONED
 move.l WINDOW,AØ
 bsr _CLEARWINDOW
 moveq #Ø,DØ
 move.w NB,DØ
 move.l DØ,D1
 asl.w #1,D1
 move.w D1,NC
 addq.w #1,D1
 move.w D1,ND
 move.l #128,D4
 lsr.w DØ,D4
 move.w D4,DY
 asl.w #1,D4
 move.w D4,DX
 tst.l MYLACE
 beq.s SHORTY
 move.w DY,D4
 asl.w #1,D4
 move.w D4,DY
```

```
SHORTY
 SETDRMD RP,#JAM1
 SETAPEN RP,#1
 move.w #150,XX
 move.w #120,YY
 tst.l MYLACE
 beq.s HIWHY
 move.w #225,YY
HIWHY
 DRAWPOINT RP,XX,YY

 lea SARAY,A4
 moveq #0,D0
 move.w #32,D0
ZERORAY
 clr.w 0(A4,D0.W)
 subq.w #2,D0
 tst.w D0
 bpl.s ZERORAY

FRACLOOP
 move.l #SARAY,A4
 move.l #SARAY,A3
 adda.l #2,A3
 moveq #1,D1
 moveq #0,D0

MAKED
 cmpm.w (A3)+,(A4)+
 bne.s DPLUSONE
 subq.w #2,D0
DPLUSONE
 addq.w #1,D0
 bpl.s CHEKIFATE
 move.l #7,D0
CHEKIFATE
 cmpi.w #8,D0
 bne.s CPLUSONE
 moveq.l #0,D0
CPLUSONE
 addq.w #1,D1
 cmp.w ND,D1
 bne.s MAKED

 moveq #0,D2
 moveq #0,D3
 move.w XX,D2
 move.w YY,D3
 tst.w D0
 beq.s RIGHT
 cmpi.w #2,D0
 beq.s UP
 cmpi.w #4,D0
 beq.s LEFT
DOWN
 sub.w DY,D3
 bra.s TWO
UP
 add.w DY,D3
 bra.s TWO
LEFT
 sub.w DX,D2
 bra.s TWO
RIGHT
 add.w DX,D2

TWO
 move.w D2,XN
 move.w D3,YN
 DRAWLINE RP,XX,YY,XN,YN
 move.w D2,XX
 move.w D3,YY

 moveq #0,D0
 move.w NC,D0
 asl.w #1,D0
 move.l #SARAY,A4
 addi.w #1,0(A4,D0.W)
```

```
ARAYLOOP
 cmpi.w #2,Ø(A4,DØ.W)
 bne.s THREE
 clr.w Ø(A4,DØ.W)
 subq.w #2,DØ
 addi.w #1,Ø(A4,DØ.W)
 tst.w DØ
 bne.s ARAYLOOP

THREE
 move.w SARAY,DØ
 beq FRACLOOP
 move.l #TICKSPERSECOND,D1
 DOSLIB DELAY
 addi.w #1,NB
 move.w MAXLEVEL,DØ
 cmp.w NB,DØ
 bne ONED

DONEDRAGON
 PULLALL
 move.w #1,NB
 moveq #Ø,DØ
QUITNOWD
 rts

 EVENPC

MAXX dc.w Ø
MAXY dc.w Ø

DX dc.w Ø
DY dc.w Ø
XN dc.w 2ØØ
YN dc.w 1ØØ
XX dc.w 2ØØ
YY dc.w 1ØØ
NB dc.w 1
NC dc.w Ø
ND dc.w Ø
MAXLEVEL dc.w 8
 EVENPC
SARAY DS.W 32
 EVENPC

USAGETEXT
 dc.b 'Usage: POLYFRAC',1Ø,Ø
 EVENPC
ERRORTEXT
 dc.b 1Ø,'Sorry, cannot open new window.',1Ø,Ø
 EVENPC
MYMESSAGE
 dc.b 1Ø,1Ø,' POLYFRAC by Daniel Wolf  Copyright 1988 by',1Ø
 dc.b ' Compute! Publications ',1Ø,Ø
 EVENPC

STACK dc.l Ø
WINDOW dc.l Ø
RP dc.l Ø
MYLACE dc.l Ø
_THISMENU dc.l Ø

DRAGTITLE dc.b ' POLYFRAC BY D.WOLF ',Ø
 EVENPC
MYMUEXES dc.l $1E,$1D,$1B,$17,$F,Ø,Ø,Ø
MYMENUTITLE          ;THIS IS A MENU!!
 dc.b 'POLYFRAC',Ø
 EVENPC
ITEMØ
 dc.b '  DRAGON   ',Ø
 EVENPC
ITEM1
 dc.b '  HILBERT  ',Ø
 EVENPC
ITEM2
 dc.b '  TRITREE  ',Ø
 EVENPC
```

```
ITEM3
 dc.b '   QUADTREE ',Ø
 EVENPC
ITEM4
 dc.b '   QUINTREE ',Ø
 EVENPC
ITEM5
 dc.b '   QUIT      ',Ø
 EVENPC
MYCMDKEYS
 dc.b 'DH345Q',Ø
 EVENPC
_THISFONTHITE
 dc.w 9
 END
```

## LENS.ASM

This is a simple graphic program that combines an adapting window (see POLYFRAC.ASM) with a routine that magnifies a selected region surrounding the pointer. Wherever the pointer is located on the screen becomes the center of the magnified image. A proportional gadget slider control allows you to select eight different magnification factors.

When the program begins, the magnification factor is preset to half its maximum and the window is filled with a magnified view of wherever the pointer is. After the window fills, you can change magnification factors or size the window. No change will result from these operations. To activate the magnification routine, press the right mouse button. If the usual left button select mechanism had been used, you might have had to wait for a magnification operation every time you resized your window. This way, you can use the left mouse button to manipulate the window and slide control, and then move the pointer where you wish and press the right button to start the magnification routine.

You can also call this program from the CLI. Try using LENS ? to make the program print out its own command format. You'll see from the code that it's easy to make a program *see* the question mark. Many programs have a standard *?* mechanism for printing their own command formats. It's easy and it adds a professional touch to any program called from the CLI.

### Listing 23-3. LENS.ASM

```
 ;LENS.ASM by Daniel Wolf
;Copyright 1988 by Compute! Publications
;Ø9/1Ø/87

 bra _START

DOS equ 1
GFX equ 1
INT equ 1
```

```
WIN equ 1
TXT equ 1
GAD equ 1

 include "HEADER"

MINX equ 4
MINY equ 11

MAIN
 move.l SP,STACK
 REMEMBERCHIPMEM REMEMBERKEY,#16          ;THIS ARRAY MUST BE IN CHIP MEM!
 lea TEMPLATE,AØ
 move.l DØ,(AØ)
 bne.s ARRAYOK
 moveq #22,DØ
 bra QUIT
ARRAYOK
 move.l #-1,DØ
 movea.l TEMPLATE,AØ
 move.l DØ,(AØ)+
 move.l DØ,(AØ)+
 move.l DØ,(AØ)+
 move.l DØ,(AØ)

CHKFROMCLI
 tst.l ENDFROMCLI
 beq LENSFROMWB
 DOSPRINT STDOUT,#MYMESSAGE
 move.l COMMAND,AØ
 cmp.b #'?',(AØ)         ;SEE IF THIS CHAR IS A ASCII ?
 bne.s CHKGRID
 beq USAGE               ;SHOW USAGE
CHKGRID
 cmp.b #'G',(AØ)         ;SEE IF COMMAND LINE CHAR IS ASCII G
 bne.s CHKMAG
 move.w #1,GRID          ;SET GRID FLAG
 adda.l #2,AØ
CHKMAG
 clr.l DØ
 move.b (AØ),DØ          ;SEE IF THIS OR NEXT CHAR IS ASCII 1-8
 cmp.b #'8',DØ
 bhi.s LENSFROMWB
 cmp.b #'1',DØ
 blt.s LENSFROMWB
 andi.b #$ØF,DØ
 move.w DØ,MAG           ;YES, SAVE IT AS MAG FACTOR

LENSFROMWB
 lea _THISIDCMP,AØ
 move.l #MENUPICK!CLOSEWINDOW,(AØ)
 MAKEWIN #LENSTITLE,24Ø,65,16Ø,6Ø,MYERROR
 move.l DØ,WINDOW
 move.l DØ,AØ
 move.l WW.RPORT(AØ),A1
 move.l WW.WSCREEN(AØ),A2
 lea SCRN.RASTPORT(A2),A3
 move.l A1,RP
 move.l A2,SCREEN
 move.l A3,SCRP
 SETDRMD A1,#JAM1
 INTLIB VIEWPORTADDRESS
 move.l DØ,AØ
 move.w VP.MODES(AØ),D1
 and.w #LACE,D1
 beq.s NOTLACEHEIGHT
 move.l #1,MYLACE
 move.l WINDOW,AØ
 move.w WW.HEIGHT(AØ),D1
 ZERO DØ
 INTLIB SIZEWINDOW
 move.l #TICKSPERSECOND/4,D1
 DOSLIB DELAY
```

```
NOTLACEHEIGHT
 clr.l D3
 move.w #Ø,D4
 move.w #-8,D5
 move.w #-12,D6
 move.w #8,D7
 bsr MAKEAPROPGADGET                     ;HORIZONTAL GADGET
 move.l WINDOW,AØ
 move.l _THISGADGET,A1
 move.l A1,_BAR
 move.w GADG.FLAGS(A1),DØ
 ori.w #GRELBOTTOM!GRELWIDTH,DØ
 move.w DØ,GADG.FLAGS(A1)                ;SET FLAGS FOR HORIZONTAL BOTTOM BAR
 move.l GADG.SPECIALINFO(A1),A2
 move.w #$2ØØØ,PI.HORIZBODY(A2)          ;SET BODY TO 1 EIGHTH
 move.w #$1FFF,D1
 move.w MAG,DØ
 mulu D1,DØ
 move.w DØ,PI.HORIZPOT(A2)
 ZERO DØ
 move.w #-1,DØ
 INTLIB ADDGADGET                        ;ADD THE GADGET
 move.l _BAR,AØ                          ;SAVE POINTER TO  BAR  GADGET
 move.l WINDOW,A1
 INTLIB REFRESHGADGETS                   ;MAKE IT APPEAR

GETNEWPARAMS
 bsr LENSWPARAMS
 bra BLITLOOP

LOOP
 move.l WINDOW,AØ
 move.l WW.USERPORT(AØ),AØ
 SYSLIB WAITPORT
 move.l WINDOW,AØ
 move.l WW.USERPORT(AØ),AØ
 SYSLIB GETMSG
 tst.l DØ
 beq.s BLITLOOP                     ;NO MESSAGE, SO DO THE COPY LOOP
 move.l DØ,A1
 move.l IM.CLASS(A1),D2
 SYSLIB REPLYMSG
 cmp.l #CLOSEWINDOW,D2
 beq DONE
 bra GETNEWPARAMS                   ;IF MESSAGE NOT CLOSEWINDOW, THEN DO BLIT

BLITLOOP
 PUSHALL
 movea.l SCREEN,A1
 move.w SCRN.MOUSEX(A1),MOUSEX
 move.w SCRN.MOUSEY(A1),MOUSEY
 move.l TEMPLATE,A3
 move.l RP,A4
 move.l SCRP,A5
 move.w MAG,D4
 move.w D4,D5
 ZERO D7               ;SCREENY = Ø
 move.w MOUSEY,D7
 sub.w SCSTARTY,D7           ;SCREENY = SCREENY + MOUSEY
 move.w #MINY,D3             ;WPOSY = MINY
LOOPY
 ZERO D6               ;SCREENX = Ø
 move.w MOUSEX,D6
 sub.w SCSTARTX,D6           ;SCREENX = SCREENX + MOUSEX
 move.w #MINX-1,D2           ;WXPOS = MINX
LOOPX
 cmp.w SWID,D6                  ;IF SCREEN WIDTH  < SCREENX FORGET IT
 bge.s BLITNOW                  ; USE ZERO COLOR
 cmp.w SHIT,D7                  ;IF SCREEN HEIGHT < SCREENY FORGET IT
 bge.s BLITNOW                  ; USE ZERO COLOR
 READPOINT A5,D6,D7             ;GET SCREEN PIXEL COLOR AT POSITION  D6,D7
BLITNOW
 SETAPEN A4                     ;SET WINDOW DRAWING PEN WITH THIS COLOR
 ZERO DØ                      ;DØ = Ø
 moveq #2,D1                    ;D1 = 2
 move.l A3,AØ                   ;TEMPLATE POINTER IN AØ
 move.l A4,A1                   ;LENS WINDOW'S RASTER PORT POINTER IN A1
```

```
 JUST BLTTEMPLATE              ;BLIT IT!!
 addq.w #1,D6              ;SCREENX = SCREENX + 1
 add.w SKIPX,D2            ;WXPOS = WXPOS + SKIPX
 cmp.w WLIMX,D2            ;IF WPOSX < WLIMX THEN
 bls.s LOOPX                 ; ANOTHER X PIXEL
 addq.w #1,D7              ;SCREENY = SCREENY + 1
 add.w SKIPY,D3            ;WYPOS = WYPOS + SKIPY
 cmp.w WLIMY,D3            ;IF WPOSY < WLIMY THEN
 bls LOOPY                 ; ANOTHER Y LINE
 PULLALL
 bra LOOP

DONE
 clr.l D0
QUIT
 move.l STACK,SP
 move.l D0,-(SP)
 move.l WINDOW,D0
 beq.s 1$
 move.l D0,A0
 INTLIB CLOSEWINDOW
1$
 move.l (SP)+,D0
 rts

LENSWPARAMS
 PUSHALL
 move.l WINDOW,A0
 move.w WW.WIDTH(A0),D0
 subq.w #3,D0
 move.w D0,MAXX             ;MAXX = LENS WINDOW WIDTH - 4
 move.w WW.HEIGHT(A0),D1
 subq.w #2,D1
 subq.w #8,D1               ;COMPENSATE FOR SCROLL BAR
 move.w D1,MAXY             ;MAXY = LENS WINDOW HEIGHT - 2

 movea.l _BAR,A0
 movea.l GADG.SPECIALINFO(A0),A1
 clr.l D0
 clr.l D1
 move.w PI.HORIZPOT(A1),D0
 lsr.l #8,D0
 lsr.l #5,D0
 addi.w #1,D0
 move.w D0,MAG

 add.w GRID,D0
 move.w D0,SKIPY            ;SKIPY = MAG + GRID
 add.w GRID,D0
 move.w D0,SKIPX            ;SKIPX = MAG + 2*GRID
 clr.l D7                   ;SCREENY = 0
 move.w MAXY,D7             ;SCREENY = MAXY
 sub.w #MINY-1,D7           ;SCREENY = MAXY - (MINY-1)
 divu SKIPY,D7              ;SCREENY = (MAXY - (MINY-1))/SKIPY
 lsr.w #1,D7                ;SCREENY = SCREENY/2
 move.w D7,SCSTARTY
 clr.l D6                   ;SCREENX = 0
 move.w MAXX,D6             ;SCREENX = MAXX
 sub.w #MINX-1,D6           ;SCREENX = MAXX - (MINX-1)
 divu SKIPX,D6              ;SCREENX = (MAXX - (MINX-1))/SKIPX
 lsr.w #1,D6                ;SCREENX = SCREENX/2
 move.w D6,SCSTARTX
 movea.l SCREEN,A1          ;LENS' SCREEN STRUCTURE POINTER IN A1
 move.w SCRN.WIDTH(A1),SWID
 move.w SCRN.HEIGHT(A1),SHIT
 moveq.l #0,D0
 move.w MAXX,D0                   ;D0 = MAXX
 sub.w MAG,D0                     ;D0 = MAXX - MAGFACTOR
 addq.w #1,D0                     ;D0 = MAXX - MAGFACTOR +1
 move.w D0,WLIMX
 moveq.l #0,D1
 move.w MAXY,D1                   ;D1 = MAXY
 sub.w MAG,D1                     ;D1 = MAXY - MAGFACTOR
 addq.w #1,D1                     ;D1 = MAXY - MAGFACTOR +1
 move.w D1,WLIMY
 PULLALL
 rts
```

```
MYERROR
 DOSPRINT STDERR,#ERRORTEXT
 moveq #20,D0
 bra QUIT

USAGE
 DOSPRINT STDERR,#USAGETEXT
 clr.l D0
 bra QUIT

MYMESSAGE
 dc.b 10,'LENS  by Daniel Wolf   Copyright 1988 by Compute! Publications',10,0
 EVENPC
ERRORTEXT
 dc.b 'Cannot open window',0
 EVENPC
USAGETEXT
 dc.b 'Usage: LENS [G Grid] [# Mag(1-8)]',10,0
 EVENPC
LENSTITLE
 dc.b ' LENS  by D.Wolf ',0
 EVENPC

STACK     dc.l 0
WINDOW    dc.l 0
SCREEN    dc.l 0
RP        dc.l 0
SCRP      dc.l 0
TEMPLATE  dc.l 0
_BAR      dc.l 0
MYLACE    dc.l 0
MAXX      dc.w 0
MAXY      dc.w 0
MOUSEX    dc.w 0
MOUSEY    dc.w 0
SHIT      dc.w 0
SWID      dc.w 0
SKIPX     dc.w 0
SKIPY     dc.w 0
WLIMX     dc.w 0
WLIMY     dc.w 0
SCSTARTX  dc.w 0
SCSTARTY  dc.w 0
MAG       dc.w 4
GRID      dc.w 0
_THISFONTHITE dc.w 9
 EVENPC
 END
```

## QUADRIX.ASM

QUADRIX.ASM is a 3-D graphics generation program that draws quadric surfaces (paraboloid, hyperbolic paraboloic, hyperboloid, ellipsoid, and cone). The program combines a window, menu, and three proportional (slider) gadgets with floating-point and transcendental (trigonometric) math routines. This program uses all the libraries discussed in this book, including AmigaDOS, Intuition, Graphics, MathFFP, and MathTrans.

The slider gadgets partly control the angle of view for the three-dimensional solid shape. Since the angle of view partly determines how large the shape is drawn, there will be occasions when the surfaces may seem too large or too small for the window. You can adjust the SCALE factors. These factors are well-commented in the source code. Scale factors were selected to make the ellipsoid fill the window.

When the window is resized, the image is not redrawn. You'll have to select from the menu again to get a new image. Redrawing the image takes several seconds, in some cases, and might make an aggravating delay when all you want to do is resize. It's the same tradeoff as in LENS.ASM, which also does not redraw the image until commanded by the user.

The reason for the program's length is the math involved in calculating equations for all five quadric surface shapes. The extensive calculations are commented so that you can see how they could be translated into other languages.

### Listing 23-4. QUADRIX.ASM

```
 ;QUADRIX.ASM by Daniel Wolf
;COPYRIGHT 1988 BY COMPUTE! PUBLICATIONS
;09/10/87

 bra _START

;FOR LIBRARIES IN STARTUP.ASM (INCLUDED BY HEADER)
GFX equ 1
MAT equ 1
TRA equ 1

;FOR INCLUDES HEADER
WIN equ 1
TXT equ 1
GAD equ 1
MEN equ 1

;MATHTYPES FOR MATH.ASM
FFP equ 1
HEX equ 1

 include "HEADER"

MAIN
 move.l SP,STACK
 move.l ENDFROMWB,DØ
 beq.s FROMUSER
 bra.s NOWTHEWINDOW
FROMUSER
 DOSPRINT STDOUT,#MYMESSAGE
NOWTHEWINDOW
 move.l #4,SHAPE
 move.l #Ø,HMIN
 move.l #Ø,LMIN

 MAKEWIN #DRAGTITLE,5,3Ø,43Ø,158,ERROR

 move.l #43Ø,HMAX
 move.l #158,LMAX
 move.l DØ,WINDOW

 move.l DØ,AØ
 move.l WW.RPORT(AØ),RP             ;SAVE POINTER TO RASTPORT OF WINDOW
 INTLIB VIEWPORTADDRESS             ;GET POINTER TO VIEWPORT OF WINDOW
 move.l DØ,AØ
 move.w VP.MODES(AØ),D1
 and.w #LACE,D1                     ;ARE WE IN INTERLACE MODE?
 beq.s NOWMAKEQMENU
 move.l #1,MYLACE
 move.l WINDOW,AØ
 moveq.l #Ø,DØ
 moveq.l #Ø,D1
```

```
 move.w WW.HEIGHT(AØ),D1          ;IF SO, DOUBLE WINDOW HEIGHT
 INTLIB SIZEWINDOW

NOWMAKEQMENU
 MITEMLIST ITEMØ,ITEM1,ITEM2,ITEM3,ITEM4,ITEM5,Ø,Ø,5
 MAKEMEN MYCMDKEYS,MYMUEXES,MYMENUTITLE,ERROR
 move.l D1,_THISMENU
 move.l #5,DØ
 move.l #75,D1
 bsr CREATEMENU

 move.l WINDOW,AØ
 move.l _THISMENU,A1
 INTLIB SETMENUSTRIP

YANGLEBAR
 move.b #'V',D3
 move.w #-15,D4
 move.w #1Ø,D5
 move.w #15,D6
 move.w #-18,D7
 bsr MAKEAPROPGADGET
 move.l WINDOW,AØ
 move.l _THISGADGET,A1
 move.l A1,_YBAR
 move.w GADG.FLAGS(A1),DØ
 ori.w #GRELRIGHT!GRELHEIGHT,DØ
 move.w DØ,GADG.FLAGS(A1)
 clr.l DØ
 move.w #-1,DØ
 INTLIB ADDGADGET
ZANGLEBAR
 move.b #'V',D3
 move.w #Ø,D4
 move.w #1Ø,D5
 move.w #15,D6
 move.w #-18,D7
 bsr MAKEAPROPGADGET
 move.l WINDOW,AØ
 move.l _THISGADGET,A1
 move.l A1,_ZBAR
 move.w GADG.FLAGS(A1),DØ
 ori.w #GRELHEIGHT,DØ
 move.w DØ,GADG.FLAGS(A1)
 clr.l DØ
 move.w #-1,DØ
 INTLIB ADDGADGET
XANGLEBAR
 clr.l D3
 move.w #Ø,D4
 move.w #-8,D5
 move.w #-15,D6
 move.w #8,D7
 bsr MAKEAPROPGADGET
 move.l WINDOW,AØ
 move.l _THISGADGET,A1
 move.l A1,_XBAR
 move.w GADG.FLAGS(A1),DØ
 ori.w #GRELBOTTOM!GRELWIDTH,DØ
 move.w DØ,GADG.FLAGS(A1)
 clr.l DØ
 move.w #-1,DØ
 INTLIB ADDGADGET

 move.l _YBAR,AØ
 move.l WINDOW,A1
 INTLIB REFRESHGADGETS

ANNOUNCEMENT
 movea.l WINDOW,A5
 moveq #Ø,DØ
 moveq #Ø,D1

 PRINTNEWAT A5,TEXT1,3Ø,2Ø,ERROR
 PRINTNEWAT A5,TEXT2,4Ø,3Ø,ERROR
 PRINTNEWAT A5,TEXT3,5Ø,4Ø,ERROR
```

```
 move.l #TICKSPERSECOND/2,D1
 DOSLIB DELAY

NEWWPARAMS
 clr.l DØ
 move.l WINDOW,AØ
 move.w WW.HEIGHT(AØ),DØ
 move.l DØ,LMAX
 sub.w #15,DØ
 move.w DØ,LMAXW
 move.w WW.WIDTH(AØ),DØ
 move.l DØ,HMAX
 sub.w #15,DØ
 move.w DØ,HMAXW

LOOP
 move.l WINDOW,AØ
 move.l #$FFFF,DØ
 INTLIB ONMENU
 move.l WINDOW,AØ
 move.l WW.USERPORT(AØ),AØ
 SYSLIB WAITPORT
 move.l WINDOW,AØ
 move.l WW.USERPORT(AØ),AØ
 SYSLIB GETMSG
 tst.l DØ
 beq.s LOOP
 move.l DØ,A1
 move.l IM.CLASS(A1),D2
 move.w IM.CODE(A1),D3
 move.w IM.QUALIFIER(A1),D4
 SYSLIB REPLYMSG
 cmpi.l #CLOSEWINDOW,D2
 beq DONE
 tst.l FIRSTTIME
 beq QMYTIME
 cmpi.l #NEWSIZE,D2
 beq NEWWPARAMS

CHKQMENU
 cmpi.l #MENUPICK,D2
 bne QMYTIME
 moveq.l #Ø,DØ
 move.w D3,DØ
 bsr MENUEVENT
 cmpi.w #5,D1
 beq DONE
CHKPARAB                        ;PARABOLOID 1
 cmpi.w #Ø,D1
 bne.s CHKHYPPAR
 move.l #1,SHAPE
 bsr QSURFACE
 bra QMYTIME
CHKHYPPAR                       ;HYPERBOLIC PARABOLOID 2
 cmpi.w #1,D1
 bne.s CHKHYPHYP
 move.l #2,SHAPE
 bsr QSURFACE
 bra QMYTIME
CHKHYPHYP
 cmpi.w #2,D1                   ;HYPERBOLOID ONE SHEET 3
 bne.s CHKELLIP
 move.l #3,SHAPE
 bsr QSURFACE
 bra QMYTIME
CHKELLIP
 cmpi.w #3,D1                   ;ELLIPSOID 4
 bne.s CHKCONE
 move.l #4,SHAPE
 bsr QSURFACE
 bra.s QMYTIME
CHKCONE
 cmpi.w #4,D1                   ;CONE 5
 bne.s QMYTIME
 move.l #5,SHAPE
 bsr QSURFACE
```

```
QMYTIME
 move.l #1,FIRSTTIME
 bra LOOP

QSURFACE
 move.l #Ø,NEGNECESSARY
 move.l #Ø,DENSE
 move.l WINDOW,AØ
 move.l #$FFFF,DØ
 INTLIB OFFMENU
 PUSHALL
 movea.l _MATHTRANSBASE,A5          ;POINTER TO MATHTRANS LIBRARY IN A5
 movea.l _MATHBASE,A4               ;POINTER TO MATH LIBRARY IN A4
 move.l A4,A6                       ;USE THE MATH LIBRARY NOW
 move.l HMAX,DØ
 sub.l HMIN,DØ
 move.l DØ,HRES                     ;HRES = HMAX - HMIN
 move.l LMAX,DØ
 sub.l LMIN,DØ
 move.l DØ,LRES                     ;LRES = LMAX - LMIN
 move.l HRES,DØ
 lsr.l #1,DØ
 add.l HMIN,DØ
 move.w DØ,HC                       ;HC = 2*HRES + HMIN
 move.l LRES,DØ
 lsr.l #1,DØ
 add.l LMIN,DØ
 move.w DØ,LC                       ;LC = 2*LRES + LMIN
 move.l DØ,D1                       ;DØ = LC
 lsr.l #1,D1                        ;D1 = 2*LC
 move.l SHAPE,D7                    ;D7 = SHAPE
 cmp.l #1,D7
 bne.s YINCOK                       ;IF SHAPE <>1
 add.l D1,DØ                        ;DØ = DØ + D1
YINCOK
 move.w DØ,LC                       ;LC = 3*LC
 move.l #4Ø,DØ
 JUST SPFlt
 move.l DØ,D7
 move.l HMAX,DØ
 JUST SPFlt
 move.l D7,D1
 JUST SPDiv
 move.l DØ,SCALEH                   ;SCALEH = HMAX/4Ø
 move.l #125,DØ
 JUST SPFlt
 move.l DØ,D7
 move.l LMAX,DØ
 JUST SPFlt
 move.l D7,D1
 JUST SPDiv
 move.l DØ,SCALEV                   ;SCALEV = LMAX/125
BARSETTINGS
 movea.l _YBAR,AØ
 move.l GADG.SPECIALINFO(AØ),AØ
 move.w PI.VERTPOT(AØ),GYANGLE
 movea.l _XBAR,AØ
 move.l GADG.SPECIALINFO(AØ),AØ
 move.w PI.HORIZPOT(AØ),GXANGLE
 movea.l _ZBAR,AØ
 move.l GADG.SPECIALINFO(AØ),AØ
 move.w PI.VERTPOT(AØ),GZANGLE

SHAPECHANGES
 move.l SHAPE,D7
 cmp.l #4,D7             ;RESET SCALES FOR ELLIPSOID
 bne.s TWONSHAPE
 move.l #7,DØ
 JUST SPFlt
 move.l SCALEH,D1
 JUST SPMul
 move.l DØ,SCALEH        ;SCALEH = 3*SCALEH
 move.l #25,DØ
 JUST SPFlt
 move.l SCALEV,D1
 JUST SPMul
 move.l DØ,SCALEV        ;SCALEV = 13*SCALEV
```

```
 move.l #1,NEGNECESSARY
 move.l #1,DENSE
TWONSHAPE
 cmp.l #3,D7
 bne.s THIRDNSHAPE
 move.l TWOFP,D0
 move.l SCALEV,D1
 JUST SPMul
 move.l D0,SCALEV         ;SCALEV = 2*SCALEV
 move.l #1,NEGNECESSARY
THIRDNSHAPE
 cmp.l #5,D7
 bne.s CORNERANGLES
 move.l TWOFP,D0
 move.l SCALEV,D1
 JUST SPMul
 move.l D0,SCALEV         ;SCALEV = 2*SCALEV
 move.l #1,NEGNECESSARY

CORNERANGLES
 clr.l D0
 move.w LC,D0
 sub.l LMIN,D0
 JUST SPFlt
 move.l D0,LCMINLMIN
 move.l LMAX,D0
 sub.w LC,D0
 JUST SPFlt
 move.l D0,LMAXMINLC
 move.l HMAX,D0
 sub.w HC,D0
 JUST SPFlt
 move.l D0,HMAXMINHC
 move.w HC,D0
 sub.l HMIN,D0
 JUST SPFlt
 move.l D0,HCMINHMIN

 move.l LCMINLMIN,D0
 move.l HMAXMINHC,D1
 JUST SPDiv
 move.l A5,A6
 JUST SPAtan
 move.l D0,C1
 move.l A4,A6
 move.l LCMINLMIN,D0
 move.l HCMINHMIN,D1
 JUST SPDiv
 move.l A5,A6
 JUST SPAtan
 move.l D0,C2
 move.l A4,A6
 move.l LMAXMINLC,D0
 move.l HCMINHMIN,D1
 JUST SPDiv
 move.l A5,A6
 JUST SPAtan
 move.l D0,C3
 move.l A4,A6
 move.l LMAXMINLC,D0
 move.l HMAXMINHC,D1
 JUST SPDiv
 move.l A5,A6
 JUST SPAtan
 move.l D0,C4
 move.l A4,A6             ;REGMATH
 move.l PIWHOLE,D0
 move.l D0,D7
 move.l C2,D1
 JUST SPSub
 move.l D0,C2
 move.l D7,D0
 move.l C3,D1
 JUST SPAdd
 move.l D0,C3
 move.l D7,D0
 add.l #1,D0
```

```
 move.l C4,D1
 JUST SPSub
 move.l D0,C4

SETXYZANGLES
 move.l #16384,D0
 JUST SPFlt
 move.l D0,D7
 move.l PIWHOLE,D6

 clr.l D0
 move.w GXANGLE,D0
 JUST SPFlt
 move.l D7,D1
 JUST SPDiv
 move.l D6,D1
 JUST SPMul
 move.l D0,XANGLE            ;ANGLE = PROPGADGET/16384 * PI
 clr.l D0
 move.w GYANGLE,D0
 JUST SPFlt
 move.l D7,D1
 JUST SPDiv
 move.l D6,D1
 JUST SPMul
 move.l D0,YANGLE
 clr.l D0
 move.w GZANGLE,D0
 JUST SPFlt
 move.l D7,D1
 JUST SPDiv
 move.l D6,D1
 JUST SPMul
 move.l D0,ZANGLE

 move.l XANGLE,D0
 move.l #COSXA,D1
 move.l A5,A6            ;TRANSMATH
 JUST SPSincos
 move.l D0,SINXA

 move.l YANGLE,D0
 move.l #COSYA,D1
 JUST SPSincos
 move.l D0,SINYA

 move.l ZANGLE,D0
 move.l #COSZA,D1
 JUST SPSincos
 move.l D0,SINZA

 move.l A4,A6
 move.l #26,D0
 JUST SPFlt
 move.l HUNDFP,D1
 JUST SPDiv
 move.l D0,STEP1
 subi.l #1,D0
 move.l D0,STEP2
 subi.l #1,D0
 move.l D0,STEP3

DRAWSURFACE
 SETAPEN RP,#1
 move.w #14,D0
 move.w #10,D1
 move.l WINDOW,A0
 move.w WW.WIDTH(A0),D2
 subi.w #14,D2
 move.w WW.HEIGHT(A0),D3
 subi.w #10,D3
 RECTFILL RP

 move.l A4,A6
 tst.l MYLACE
 bne.s LACESCALE
 subi.l #1,SCALEV
```

```
LACESCALE
 move.l #6,DØ                      ;FOR TY = -6 TO +6  STEP .4
 JUST SPFlt
 move.l DØ,LASTTY
 move.l DØ,PLUSIX
 JUST SPNeg
 move.l DØ,MINSIX
 move.l MINSIX,A3
NEXTYY1
 move.l #Ø,DØ
 move.l DØ,A2
 move.l STEP1,DØ
 tst.l DENSE
 beq.s NOTDENSE
 move.l STEP2,DØ
NOTDENSE
 move.l DØ,STEPTY
 move.l DØ,STEPTX
 move.l PLUSIX,LASTTX                    ;FOR TX = Ø TO 6  STEP STEPTTX
 SETAPEN RP,#2
NEXTXX1
 move.l A2,DØ
 move.l A3,D1
 bsr PROSCALE
 DRAWPOINT RP,MH,MV
 move.l A4,A6
 tst.w MH
 beq.s CONTXX1
 tst.l NEGNECESSARY
 beq.s CONTXX1
 move.l A1,DØ
 JUST SPNeg
 bsr FUNCDONE
 DRAWPOINT RP,MH,MV
 move.l A4,A6
CONTXX1
 move.l A2,DØ
 move.l STEPTX,D1
 JUST SPAdd
 move.l DØ,A2
 move.l DØ,D1
 move.l LASTTX,DØ
 JUST SPCmp
 bgt NEXTXX1
 move.l MINSIX,A2
 move.l #Ø,DØ
 move.l DØ,LASTTX
 move.l STEP2,DØ
 tst.l DENSE
 beq.s NOTDENS2
 move.l STEP3,DØ
NOTDENS2
 move.l DØ,STEPTX               ;FOR TX = -6 TO Ø  STEP STEPTX
 SETAPEN RP,#3
NEXTXX2
 move.l A2,DØ
 move.l A3,D1
 bsr PROSCALE
 DRAWPOINT RP,MH,MV
 move.l A4,A6
 tst.w MH
 beq.s CONTXX2
 tst.l NEGNECESSARY
 beq.s CONTXX2
 move.l A1,DØ
 JUST SPNeg
 bsr FUNCDONE
 DRAWPOINT RP,MH,MV
 move.l A4,A6
CONTXX2
 move.l A2,DØ
 move.l STEPTX,D1
 JUST SPAdd
 move.l DØ,A2
 move.l DØ,D1
 move.l LASTTX,DØ
 JUST SPCmp
 bgt NEXTXX2
```

```
 move.l A3,DØ
 move.l STEPTY,D1
 JUST SPAdd
 move.l DØ,D1
 move.l DØ,A3
 move.l LASTTY,DØ
 JUST SPCmp
 bgt NEXTYY1
 PULLALL
 rts

PROSCALE
FUNCDEF                         ;FUNCVAL = DØ*DØ+D1*D1 FLOATING POINT
 move.l A4,A6
 move.l D1,D7
 move.l DØ,D1
 JUST SPMul
 move.l DØ,D6                   ;D6 = TX SQUARED
 move.l D7,DØ
 move.l DØ,D1
 JUST SPMul                     ;DØ = TY SQUARED
 move.l D6,D1                   ;D1 = TX SQUARED
 move.l SHAPE,D5

 cmp.l #1,D5
 beq PARABOLOID
 cmp.l #2,D5
 beq HYPPARABOLOID
 cmp.l #3,D5
 beq HYPERBOLOID
 cmp.l #4,D5
 beq ELLIPSOID
 cmp.l #5,D5
 beq CONE

PARABOLOID
 JUST SPAdd
 bra FUNCDONE

HYPPARABOLOID
 JUST SPSub
 bra FUNCDONE

HYPERBOLOID
 JUST SPAdd
 move.l TWOFP,D1
 JUST SPSub
 move.l A5,A6
 JUST SPSqrt
 move.l A4,A6
 addq.l #1,DØ
 bra FUNCDONE

ELLIPSOID
 move.l D1,D6
 move.l DØ,D7
 JUST SPAdd
 move.l TENFP,D1
 JUST SPCmp
 blt.s MORELLIPSE
 move.w #Ø,MH
 rts

MORELLIPSE
 move.l TENFP,DØ
 move.l D6,D1
 JUST SPSub
 move.l D7,D1
 JUST SPSub
 move.l A5,A6
 JUST SPSqrt
 move.l A4,A6
 bra FUNCDONE
```

```
CONE
 JUST SPAdd
 move.l A5,A6
 JUST SPSqrt
 move.l A4,A6
 addq.l #1,DØ

FUNCDONE
 move.l DØ,A1
 move.l A2,DØ
 move.l COSXA,D1
 JUST SPMul
 move.l DØ,D7
 move.l A3,DØ
 move.l COSYA,D1
 JUST SPMul
 move.l DØ,D6
 move.l A1,DØ
 move.l COSZA,D1
 JUST SPMul
 move.l D6,D1
 JUST SPAdd
 move.l D7,D1
 JUST SPAdd
 move.l SCALEH,D1
 JUST SPMul
 JUST SPFix
 add.w HC,DØ
 move.w DØ,MH

 move.l A2,DØ
 move.l SINXA,D1
 JUST SPMul
 move.l DØ,D7
 move.l A3,DØ
 move.l SINYA,D1
 JUST SPMul
 move.l DØ,D6
 move.l A1,DØ
 move.l SINZA,D1
 JUST SPMul
 move.l D6,D1
 JUST SPAdd
 move.l D7,D1
 JUST SPAdd
 move.l SCALEV,D1
 JUST SPMul
 JUST SPFix
 move.w LC,D1
 sub.w DØ,D1
 move.w D1,MV
 rts

DONE
 move.l WINDOW,AØ
 INTLIB CLEARMENUSTRIP
DONEALL
 moveq #Ø,DØ
QUIT
 move.l STACK,SP
 move.l DØ,-(SP)
 move.l WINDOW,DØ
 beq.s 1$
 move.l DØ,AØ
 INTLIB CLOSEWINDOW
1$
 move.l (SP)+,DØ
 rts
QUITNOW
 move.l STACK,SP
 rts

ERROR
 DOSPRINT STDOUT,#ERRORTEXT
 moveq #2L,DØ
 bra QUITNOW
```

```
USAGETEXT
 dc.b 'Usage: QUADRIX',10,0
 EVENPC
ERRORTEXT
 dc.b 10,'Sorry, can not open new window.',10,0
 EVENPC
MYMESSAGE
 dc.b 10,'QUADRIX  by Daniel Wolf  Copyright 1988 by Compute! Publications ',10,10,
 EVENPC
TEXT1
 dc.b ' Quadric Surface Generator ',0
 EVENPC
TEXT2
 dc.b ' Contol Angles with Sliders, then ',0
 EVENPC
TEXT3
 dc.b ' Select Shape from Menu and Enjoy! - DW ',0
 EVENPC
DRAGTITLE
 dc.b ' QUADRIX  by D.Wolf ',0
 EVENPC

STACK      dc.l 0
WINDOW     dc.l 0
RP         dc.l 0

MH         dc.w 0
MV         dc.w 0
HC         dc.w 0
LC         dc.w 0
HMAXW      dc.w 0
LMAXW      dc.w 0
ONEFP      dc.l $80000041
TWOFP      dc.l $80000042
FIVEFP     dc.l $A0000043
TENFP      dc.l $A0000042
HUNDFP     dc.l $C8000047
PIWHOLE    dc.l $C90FDB42
PIOVER2    dc.l $C90FDB41
NEGPIOVER2 dc.l $C90FDBC1
MYLACE     dc.l 0
LASTTX     dc.l 0
LASTTY     dc.l 0
STEPTX     dc.l 0
STEPTY     dc.l 0
HMIN       dc.l 0
LMIN       dc.l 0
HMAX       dc.l 0
LMAX       dc.l 0
C1         dc.l 0
C2         dc.l 0
C3         dc.l 0
C4         dc.l 0
XANGLE     dc.l 0
SINXA      dc.l 0
COSXA      dc.l 0
YANGLE     dc.l 0
SINYA      dc.l 0
COSYA      dc.l 0
ZANGLE     dc.l 0
SINZA      dc.l 0
COSZA      dc.l 0
HRES       dc.l 0
LRES       dc.l 0
LCMINLMIN  dc.l 0
LMAXMINLC  dc.l 0
HMAXMINHC  dc.l 0
HCMINHMIN  dc.l 0
DDR        dc.l 0
SCALEH     dc.l 0
SCALEV     dc.l 0
MINSIX     dc.l 0
PLUSIX     dc.l 0
GZANGLE    dc.w 0
GYANGLE    dc.w 0
GXANGLE    dc.w 0
STEP1      dc.l 0
```

```
STEP2       dc.l Ø
STEP3       dc.l Ø
SHAPE       dc.l 4
NEGNECESSARY dc.l Ø
DENSE       dc.l Ø
 EVENPC

_THISMENU
 dc.l Ø
MYMENUTITLE          ;THIS IS A MENU!!
 dc.b 'QUADRIX',Ø
 EVENPC
ITEMØ
 dc.b '  PARABOLOID  ',Ø
 EVENPC
ITEM1
 dc.b '  HPARABOLOID ',Ø
 EVENPC
ITEM2
 dc.b '  HYPERBOLOID ',Ø
 EVENPC
ITEM3
 dc.b '  ELLIPSOID   ',Ø
 EVENPC
ITEM4
 dc.b '  CONE        ',Ø
 EVENPC
ITEM5
 dc.b '  QUIT        ',Ø
 EVENPC
MYCMDKEYS
 dc.b 'PHYECQ'
 EVENPC
MYMUEXES
 dc.l $1E,$1D,$1B,$17,$F,Ø,Ø,Ø
FIRSTTIME
 dc.l Ø
_THISFONTHITE
 dc.w 9
_XBAR dc.l Ø            ;POINTER TO FIRST GADGET
_YBAR dc.l Ø            ;POINTER TO SECOND GADGET
_ZBAR dc.l Ø            ;POINTER TO THIRD GADGET
 END
```

# Appendices

# APPENDIX A

# Motorola MC68000/MC68010 Instruction Set and ASM Directive Definitions

Key to abbreviations used in this appendix.

| | |
|---|---|
| * | Used to indicate that a condition code flag is affected by an operation |
| 0 | Indicates that condition code is always cleared (set to 0) |
| 1 | Indicates that condition code is always set (set to 1) |
| { } | Indicates an optional part of the statement |
| — | Used to indicate that a condition code flag is not affected by an operation |
| ? | Used to indicate that a condition code flag has an undefined result |
| **ADST** | Address register as destination |
| **ASRC** | Address register as source |
| **[B/L]** | Either a byte or long word may be used by appending .B or .L to the opcode |
| **[B/W/L]** | Either a byte, word, or long word may be used by appending .B, .W, or .L to the opcode |
| **C** | Carry flag |
| **CCR** | Condition code register |
| **<DATA>** | Value |
| **DDST** | Data register as destination |
| **DFC** | Destination function register |
| **DSRC** | Data register as source |
| **<EA>** | Effective address |
| **<LABEL>** | Label |
| **N** | Negative flag |
| **PC** | Program counter |
| **RDST** | Either a data or an address register as a destination |
| **[R/L]** | Right or left |
| **RSRC** | Either a data or an address register as source |
| **SFC** | Source function register |

| | |
|---|---|
| **[S/L]** | Either a short or a long word may be used by appending .S or .L to the opcode |
| **SR** | Status register |
| **USP** | User stack pointer |
| **V** | Overflow flag |
| **VBR** | Vector base register |
| **[W/L]** | Either a word or a long word may be used by appending .W or .L to the opcode |
| **X** | Extend flag |
| **Z** | Zero flag |

# Opcodes

## ABCD Instruction

**Action:** Add decimal with extend
**Condition Codes:** X: * N: ? Z: * V: ? C: *
**Opcode Forms:** ABCD
**Assembler Syntax:**

| | |
|---|---|
| ABCD | DSRC,DDST |
| ABCD | −(ASRC),−(ADST) |

**Description:** Add the source operand to the destination operand using Binary Coded Decimal (BCD) arithmetic. Store the result in the destination operand.

## ADD Instruction

**Action:** Add binary
**Condition Codes:** X: * N: * Z: * V: * C: *
**Opcode Forms:** ADD, ADD.B, ADD.W, ADD.L
**Assembler Syntax:**

| | |
|---|---|
| ADD{.[B/W/L] } | <EA>,DDST |
| ADD{.[B/W/L] } | DSRC,<EA> |
| ADD{.[W/L] } | <EA>,ADST |
| ADD{.[B/W/L] } | #<DATA>,<EA> |

**Description:** Add the source operand to the destination operand using binary arithmetic. Store the result in the destination operand. This opcode may be used with any of the legal ADD binary addressing modes. This opcode does not generate the ADDQ{.[B/W/L] } instruction for those special cases.

## ADDA Instruction

**Action:** Add binary address
**Condition Codes:** X: – N: – Z: – V: – C: –
**Opcode Forms:** ADDA, ADDA.W, ADDA.L
**Assembler Syntax:**
ADDA{.[W/L]}        <EA>,ADST
**Description:** Add the source operand to the destination operand using binary arithmetic. Store the result in the destination operand. This opcode is a subset of the ADD opcode, and requires that the destination be an address register.

## ADDI Instruction

**Action:** Add binary immediate
**Condition Codes:** X: * N: * Z: * V: * C: *
**Opcode Forms:** ADDI, ADDI.B, ADDI.W, ADDI.L
**Assembler Syntax:**
ADDI{.[B/W/L]}      #<DATA>,<EA>
**Description:** Add the source operand to the destination operand using binary arithmetic. Store the result in the destination operand. This opcode is a subset of the ADD opcode, and requires that the source be an immediate value.

## ADDQ Instruction

**Action:** Add binary quick
**Condition Codes:** X: * N: * Z: * V: * C: *
**Opcode Forms:** ADDQ, ADDQ.B, ADDQ.W, ADDQ.L
**Assembler Syntax:**
ADDQ{.[B/W/L]}      #<DATA>,<EA>
**Description:** Add the source operand to the destination operand using binary arithmetic. Store the result in the destination operand. This opcode requires that the source be an immediate value with a data range between one and eight.

## ADDX Instruction

**Action:** Add extended
**Condition Codes:** X: * N: * Z: * V: * C: *
**Opcode Forms:** ADDX, ADDX.B, ADDX.W, ADDX.L
**Assembler Syntax:**
ADDX{.[B/W/L]}      DSRC,DDST
ADDX{.[B/W/L]}      –(ASRC),–(ADST)

**Description:** Add the source operand and the extend bit to the destination operand using binary arithmetic. Store the result in the destination operand.

## AND Instruction

**Action:** Logical and
**Condition Codes:** X: — N: * Z: * V: 0 C: 0
**Opcode Forms:** AND, AND.B, AND.W, AND.L
**Assembler Syntax:**

| | |
|---|---|
| AND{.[B/W/L] } | <EA>,DDST |
| AND{.[B/W/L] } | DSRC,<EA> |
| AND{.[B/W/L] } | #<DATA>,<EA> |
| AND{.B} | #<DATA>,CCR |
| AND{.W} | #<DATA>,SR |

**Description:** Logically AND the source operand to the destination operand. Store the result in the destination operand. This opcode may be used with any of the legal AND addressing modes.

## ANDI Instruction

**Action:** And immediate
**Condition Codes:** X: — N: * Z: * V: 0 C: 0
**Opcode Forms:** ANDI, ANDI.B, ANDI.W, ANDI.L
**Assembler Syntax:**

| | |
|---|---|
| ANDI{.[B/W/L] } | #<DATA>,<EA> |
| ANDI{.B} | #<DATA>,CCR |
| ANDI{.W} | #<DATA>,SR |

**Description:** Logically AND the source operand to the destination operand. Store the result in the destination operand. This opcode is a subset of the AND opcode, and requires that the source be an immediate value.

## ASL/ASR Instruction

**Action:** Arithmetic shift left/right
**Condition Codes:** X: * N: * Z: * V: * C: *
**Opcode Forms:** ASL/ASR, ASL.B/ASR.B, ASL.W/ASR.W, ASL.L/ASR.L
**Assembler Syntax:**

| | |
|---|---|
| AS[R/L] {.[B/W/L] } | DSRC,DDST |
| AS[R/L] {.[B/W/L] } | #<DATA>,DDST |
| AS[R/L] {.W} | <EA> |

**Description:** Arithmetically shift the destination operand left or right N bits. The explicit or implied source operand determines N, the number of bits to be shifted. An arithmetic shift with an implied shift count, shifts the specified memory destination location one bit only, in the specified direction.

## B*cc* Instruction

**Action:** Branch conditionally
**Condition Codes:** X: — N: — Z: — V: — C: —
**Opcode Forms:** B*cc*, B*cc*.S, B*cc*.L
**Assembler Syntax:**
B*cc*{.[S/L]}    <LABEL>
**Description:** Continue program execution at the specified label, if the specified condition is met. The .S version of this instruction forces an 8-bit displacement to be generated. This means that the relative offset of the label must be in the range of −128 to 127 bytes in distance from the current program counter. The .L version of this instruction forces an 16-bit displacement to be generated. This means that the relative offset of the label must be in the range of −32768 to 32767 bytes in distance from the current program counter. The current program counter is defined to be the current instruction location plus two. If the B*cc* instruction is used, the assembler automatically decides which of the two displacements is most appropriate, and generates that instruction. This is sometimes known as *automatic branch shortening.*

The following conditions are recognized:

<table>
<tr><th>Condition</th><th>Signed</th><th>Meaning</th><th>Flags Affected</th></tr>
<tr><td>CC</td><td></td><td>Carry Clear</td><td>\C</td></tr>
<tr><td>HS</td><td>*</td><td>High or Same</td><td>\C</td></tr>
<tr><td>CS</td><td></td><td>Carry Set</td><td>C</td></tr>
<tr><td>LO</td><td>*</td><td>LOw</td><td>C</td></tr>
<tr><td>EQ</td><td>+</td><td>EQual</td><td>Z</td></tr>
<tr><td>GE</td><td>+</td><td>Greater or Equal</td><td>(N&V) | (\N&\V)</td></tr>
<tr><td>GT</td><td>+</td><td>Greater Than</td><td>(N&V&Z) | (\N&\V&\Z)</td></tr>
<tr><td>HI</td><td>*</td><td>HIgh</td><td>\C&\Z</td></tr>
<tr><td>LE</td><td>+</td><td>Less or Equal</td><td>Z | (N&\V) | (\N&V)</td></tr>
<tr><td>LS</td><td>*</td><td>Low or Same</td><td>C | Z</td></tr>
<tr><td>LT</td><td>+</td><td>Less Than</td><td>(N&\V) | (\N&V)</td></tr>
<tr><td>MI</td><td>*</td><td>MInus</td><td>N</td></tr>
<tr><td>NE</td><td>+</td><td>Not Equal</td><td>\Z</td></tr>
</table>

| Condition | Signed | Meaning | Flags Affected |
|---|---|---|---|
| PL | * | PLus | \N |
| VC | | oVerflow Clear | \V |
| VS | | oVerflow Set | V |

+ = Signed comparisons
* = Unsigned comparisons
\ = NOT
& = AND
| = OR

## BRA Instruction

**Action:** Branch always
**Condition Codes:** X: − N: − Z: − V: − C: −
**Opcode Forms:** BRA, BRA.S, BRA.L
**Assembler Syntax:**
BRA{.[S/L] } <LABEL>
**Description:** Continue program execution at the specified label. The .S version of this instruction forces an 8-bit displacement to be generated. This means that the relative offset of the label must be in the range of −128 to 127 bytes in distance from the current program counter. The .L version of this instruction forces a 16-bit displacement to be generated. This means that the relative offset of the label must be in the range of −32768 to 32767 bytes in distance from the current program counter. The current program counter is defined to be the current instruction location plus two. If the BRA instruction is used, the assembler automatically decides which of the two displacements are most appropriate, and generates that instruction. This is sometimes known as *automatic branch shortening.*

## BCHG Instruction

**Action:** Test a bit and change
**Condition Codes:** X: − N: − Z: * V: − C: −
**Opcode Forms:** BCHG, BCHG.B, BCHG.L
**Assembler Syntax:**
BCHG{.[B/L] } DSRC,<EA>
BCHG{.[B/L] } #<DATA>,<EA>

**Description:** Place the value of the specified bit, from the destination address, in the Z condition code, and then complement the specified bit in the destination address. If the specified destination address is a data register, then the specified bit offset is modulo 32. If the specified destination address is a memory location, then the specified bit offset is modulo 8, and then the offset is applied to the byte location.

## BCLR Instruction

**Action:** Test a bit and clear
**Condition Codes:** X: – N: – Z: * V: – C: –
**Opcode Forms:** BCLR, BCLR.B, BCLR.L
**Assembler Syntax:**
BCLR{.[B/L]}    DSRC,<EA>
BCLR{.[B/L]}    #<DATA>,<EA>
**Description:** Place the value of the specified bit, from the destination address, in the Z condition code, and then clear the specified bit in the destination address to 0. If the specified destination address is a data register, the specified bit offset is modulo 32. If the specified destination address is a memory location, the specified bit offset is modulo 8, and then the offset is applied to the byte location.

## BSET Instruction

**Action:** Test a bit and set
**Condition Codes:** X: – N: – Z: * V: – C: –
**Opcode Forms:** BSET, BSET.B, BSET.L
**Assembler Syntax:**
BSET{.[B/L]}    DSRC,<EA>
BSET{.[B/L]}    #<DATA>,<EA>
**Description:** Place the value of the specified bit, from the destination address, in the Z condition code, and then set the specified bit in the destination address to 1. If the specified destination address is a data register, the specified bit offset is modulo 32. If the specified destination address is a memory location, the specified bit offset is modulo 8, and then the offset is applied to the byte location.

## BSR Instruction

**Action:** Branch to subroutine
**Condition Codes:** X: — N: — Z: — V: — C: —
**Opcode Forms:** BSR, BSR.S, BSR.L
**Assembler Syntax:**
BSR{.[S/L]} <LABEL>
**Description:** The long word address of the instruction immediately following this instruction is pushed on the stack, and program execution then continues at the specified label. The .S version of this instruction forces an 8-bit displacement to be generated. This means that the relative offset of the label must be in the range of −128 to 127 bytes in distance from the current program counter. The .L version of this instruction forces a 16-bit displacement to be generated. This means that the relative offset of the label must be in the range of −32768 to 32767 bytes in distance from the current program counter. The current program counter is defined to be the current instruction location plus two. If the BSR instruction is used, the assembler automatically decides which of the two displacements are most appropriate, and generates that instruction. This is sometimes known as *automatic branch shortening*.

## BTST Instruction

**Action:** Test a bit
**Condition Codes:** X: — N: — Z: * V: — C: —
**Opcode Forms:** BTST, BTST.B, BTST.L
**Assembler Syntax:**
BTST{.[B/L]} DSRC,<EA>
BTST{.[B/L]} #<DATA>,<EA>
**Description:** Place the value of the specified bit, from the destination address, in the Z condition code. If the specified destination address is a data register, the specified bit offset is modulo 32. If the specified destination address is a memory location, the specified bit offset is modulo 8, and then the offset is applied to the byte location.

**CHK Instruction**

**Action:** Check register against bounds
**Condition Codes:** X: — N: * Z: ? V: ? C: ?
**Opcode Forms:** CHK, CHK.W
**Assembler Syntax:**
CHK{.W}    <EA>,DDST
**Description:** The contents of the specified data register are compared to the upper bound effective address and 0. If the value of the data register is not between 0 and the upper bounds, the processor initiates exception processing. The CHK instruction vector is used as the address to continue processing.

**CLR Instruction**

**Action:** Clear an operand
**Condition Codes:** X: — N: 0 Z: 1 V: 0 C: 0
**Opcode Forms:** CLR, CLR.B, CLR.W, CLR.L
**Assembler Syntax:**
CLR{.[B/W/L] }    <EA>
**Description:** The specified destination address is cleared to 0.

**CMP Instruction**

**Action:** Compare
**Condition Codes:** X: — N: * Z: * V: * C: *
**Opcode Forms:** CMP, CMP.B, CMP.W, CMP.L
**Assembler Syntax:**
CMP{.[B/W/L] }    <EA>,DDST
CMP{.[W/L] }    <EA>,ADST
CMP{.[B/W/L] }    #<DATA>,<EA>
CMP{.[B/W/L] }    (ASRC)+,(ADST)+
**Description:** Subtract the source operand from the destination operand and set the condition codes accordingly. This instruction does not modify the destination address. This opcode may be used with any of the legal CMP addressing modes.

**CMPA Instruction**

**Action:** Compare address
**Condition Codes:** X: — N: * Z: * V: * C: *
**Opcode Forms:** CMPA, CMPA.W, CMPA.L

**Assembler Syntax:**
CMPA{.[W/L]}        <EA>,ADST
**Description:** Subtract the source operand from the destination operand and set the condition codes accordingly. This instruction does not modify the destination address. This opcode requires that the destination be an address register.

## CMPI Instruction

**Action:** Compare immediate
**Condition Codes:** X: — N: * Z: * V: * C: *
**Opcode Forms:** CMPI, CMPI.B, CMPI.W, CMPI.L
**Assembler Syntax:**
CMPI{.[B/W/L]}     #<DATA>,<EA>
**Description:** Subtract the source operand from the destination operand and set the condition codes accordingly. This instruction does not modify the destination address. This opcode is a subset of the CMP opcode, and requires the source to be an immediate value.

## CMPM Instruction

**Action:** Compare memory
**Condition Codes:** X: — N: * Z: * V: * C: *
**Opcode Forms:** CMPM, CMPM.B, CMPM.W, CMPM.L
**Assembler Syntax:**
CMPM{.[B/W/L]}   (ASRC)+,(ADST)+
**Description:** Subtract the source operand from the destination operand and set the condition codes accordingly. This instruction does not modify the destination address. This opcode is a subset of the CMP opcode, and requires that the source and destination operands are both indirect with postdecrement mode.

## DB*cc* Instruction

**Action:** Test, decrement, and branch
**Condition Codes:** X: — N: — Z: — V: — C: —
**Assembler Syntax:**
DB*cc*                    DSRC,<LABEL>
**Description:** If the specified condition is false, decrement the destination data register, and then compare the destination data register with −1. If the destination data register doesn't equal −1, continue instruction processing at the

specified label. If either of the conditions fail, then continue instruction execution with the next instruction. This instruction uses a 16-bit displacement as a label offset. This means that the relative offset of the label must be in the range of −32768 to 32767 bytes in distance from the current program counter.

This instruction provides a primitive looping construct similar to the REPEAT UNTIL looping construct of Pascal. The DB*cc* instruction may be thought of as a REPEAT loop UNTIL either the condition becomes true, or the loop counter goes below 0. This, of course, is assuming that the destination data register was initially set to a positive value. (This instruction uses the bottom 16 bits of the destination data register for a loop counter.)

On the MC68010 microprocessor, the DB*cc* instruction will go into loop mode when the relative offset of the instruction is −4. This means that any word-length MC68010 instruction used as the inside part of the loop will run substantially faster because the MC68010 will not keep refetching the loop instruction and the DB*cc* instruction. This allows for very fast block move routines like the one below:

```
        LEA.L    SOURCEADDRESS,A0
        LEA.L    DESTINATIONADDRESS,A1
        MOVE.W   #LENGTHOFMOVE,D0
LOOP:
        MOVE.B   (A0)+,(A1)+
        DBEQ     D0,LOOP
```

For complete condition codes, see the B*cc* instruction.

## DIVS Instruction

**Action:** Signed divide
**Condition Codes:** X: − N: * Z: * V: * C: 0
**Opcode Forms:** DIVS, DIVS.W
**Assembler Syntax:**
DIVS{.W} <EA>,DDST
**Description:** Divide the source operand by the destination operand using a signed divide. Store the result in the destination operand. The destination operand is expected to be a 32-bit value, and the source operand is expected to be a

16-bit value. The 16-bit quotient is placed in the lower 16 bits of the destination operand. The 16-bit remainder is placed in the upper 16 bits of the destination operand. Division by zero will cause a processor trap. If overflow is set, the operands remain unaffected.

## DIVU Instruction

**Action:** Unsigned divide
**Condition Codes:** X: — N: * Z: * V: * C: 0
**Opcode Forms:** DIVU, DIVU.W
**Assembler Syntax:**

```
DIVU{.W}              <EA>,DDST
```

**Description:** Divide the source operand by the destination operand using an unsigned divide. Store the result in the destination operand. The destination operand is expected to be a 32-bit value, and the source operand is expected to be a 16-bit value. The 16-bit quotient is placed in the lower 16 bits of the destination operand. The 16-bit remainder is placed in the upper 16 bits of the destination operand. Division by zero will cause a processor trap. If overflow is set, the operands remain unaffected.

## EOR Instruction

**Action:** Exclusive OR Logical
**Condition Codes:** X: — N: * Z: * V: 0 C: 0
**Opcode Forms:** EOR, EOR.B, EOR.W, EOR.L
**Assembler Syntax:**

```
EOR{.[B/W/L]}         DSRC,<EA>
EOR{.[B/W/L]}         #<DATA>,<EA>
EOR{.B}               #<DATA>,CCR
EOR{.W}               #<DATA>,SR
```

**Description:** Exclusive OR the source operand to the destination operand. Store the result in the destination operand. This opcode may be used with any of the legal EOR addressing modes.

## EORI Instruction

**Action:** Exclusive OR Logical Immediate
**Condition Codes:** X: — N: * Z: * V: 0 C: 0
**Opcode Forms:** EORI, EORI.B, EORI.W, EORI.L

**Assembler Syntax:**
EORI{.[B/W/L]} #<DATA>,<EA>
EORI{.B} #<DATA>,CCR
EORI{.W} #<DATA>,SR
**Description:** Exclusive OR the source operand to the destination operand. Store the result in the destination operand. This opcode is a subset of the EOR opcode, and requires that the source be an immediate value.

## EXG Instruction

**Action:** Exchange registers
**Condition Codes:** X: – N: – Z: – V: – C: –
**Opcode Forms:** EXG
**Assembler Syntax:**
EXG{.L} RSRC,RDST
**Description:** Exchange the contents of source and destination registers. All 32-bits are always exchanged. Any two registers may be specified.

## EXT Instruction

**Action:** Sign Extend
**Condition Codes:** X: – N: * Z: * V: 0 C: 0
**Opcode Forms:** EXT, EXT.W, EXT.L
**Assembler Syntax:**
EXT{.[W/L]} DSRC
**Description:** Extend the sign bit of a register from an 8-bit value to a 16-bit value, EXT.W, or from a 16-bit value to a 32-bit value, EXT.L. If the instruction EXT.W is used, then bit 7 is copied into bits 8–15. If the instruction EXT.L is used, then bit 15 is copied into bits 16–31.

## ILLEGAL Instruction

**Action:** Take Illegal Instruction Trap
**Condition Codes:** X: – N: – Z: – V: – C: –
**Opcode Forms:** ILLEGAL
**Assembler Syntax:**
ILLEGAL
**Description:** This instruction will always generate an illegal instruction exception.

### JMP Instruction

**Action:** Jump
**Condition Codes:** X: – N: – Z: – V: – C: –
**Opcode Forms:** JMP
**Assembler Syntax:**
JMP <EA>
**Description:** Continue program execution at the new address specified by the instruction.

### JSR Instruction

**Action:** Jump to subroutine
**Condition Codes:** X: – N: – Z: – V: – C: –
**Opcode Forms:** JSR
**Assembler Syntax:**
JSR <EA>
**Description:** Push the long-word address of the instruction immediately following the JSR instruction onto the stack, and then continue program execution at the new address specified by the instruction.

### LEA Instruction

**Action:** Load effective address
**Condition Codes:** X: – N: – Z: – V: – C: –
**Opcode Forms:** LEA, LEA.L
**Assembler Syntax:**
LEA{.L} <EA>,ADST
**Description:** Load the calculated (*effective*) address into the destination address register.

### LINK Instruction

**Action:** Link and allocate
**Condition Codes:** X: – N: – Z: – V: – C: –
**Opcode Forms:** LINK, LINK.W
**Assembler Syntax:**
LINK{.W} ADST,#<DISPLACEMENT>
**Description:** Push the current contents of the destination address register onto the stack. Load the contents of the stack pointer into the destination address register. Add the immediate value to the stack pointer.

This instruction is commonly used at subroutine entry to allocate a new frame pointer and local temporary storage. This is normally done with a negative displacement.

## LSL/LSR Instruction

**Action:** Logical shift left/right
**Condition Codes:** X: * N: * Z: * V: 0 C: *
**Opcode Forms:** LSL/LSR, LSL.B/LSR.B, LSL.W/LSR.W, LSL.L/LSR.L
**Assembler Syntax:**

| | |
|---|---|
| LS[LR] {.[B/W/L] } | DSRC,DDST |
| LS[LR] {.[B/W/L] } | #<DATA>,DDST |
| LS[LR] {.W} | <EA> |

**Description:** Logically shift the destination operand left or right N bits. The explicit or implied source operand determines N, the number of bits to be shifted. A logical shift with an implied shift count, shifts the specified memory destination location one bit only, in the specified direction.

## MOVE Instruction

**Action:** Move data
**Condition Codes:** X: — N: * Z: * V: 0 C: 0
**Opcode Forms:** MOVE, MOVE.B, MOVE.W, MOVE.L
**Assembler Syntax:**

| | |
|---|---|
| MOVE{.[B/W/L] } | <EA>,<EA> |
| MOVE{.[W/L] } | <EA>,ADST |
| MOVE{.W} | <EA>,CCR |
| MOVE{.W} | <EA>,SR |
| MOVE{.W} | SR,<EA> |
| MOVE{.L} | ASRC,USP |
| MOVE{.L} | USP,ADST |

**Description:** Copy the source operand to the destination operand. The upper byte of data is ignored when moving data to the condition code register. The move instructions that load and store the user stack pointer from and to an address register may only be executed while in supervisor mode. On the 68010 microprocessor, the move instructions that load and store the status register may only be executed while in supervisor mode.

## MOVEA Instruction

**Action:** Move address
**Condition Codes:** X: — N: — Z: — V: — C: —
**Opcode Forms:** MOVEA, MOVEA.W, MOVEA.L

**Assembler Syntax:**
MOVEA{.[W/L] }    <EA>,ADST
**Description:** Copy the source operand to the destination operand. This opcode is a subset of the MOVE opcode, and requires that the destination be an address register. If the value is loaded as a 16-bit word value, this value is automatically sign-extended.

## MOVEC Instruction

**Action:** Move control register (MC68010/MC68020)
**Condition Codes:** X: — N: — Z: — V: — C: —
**Opcode Forms:** MOVEC, MOVEC.L
**Assembler Syntax:**
MOVE{.L}    RSRC,SFC
MOVE{.L}    RSRC,DFC
MOVE{.L}    RSRC,USP
MOVE{.L}    RSRC,VBR
MOVE{.L}    SFC,RDST
MOVE{.L}    DFC,RDST
MOVE{.L}    USP,RDST
MOVE{.L}    VBR,RDST
**Description:** Copy the source operand to the destination operand. This instruction is used to load and store the various control registers that exist on the MC68010 and the MC68020. The RSRC and RDST registers may be any 32-bit address or data register. This instruction is privileged, and may only be executed in supervisor mode. The following is the list of the special registers available on the MC68010.

| Special Register | Full Name |
|---|---|
| SFC | Source Function Register |
| DFC | Destination Function Register |
| USP | User Stack Pointer |
| VBR | Vector Base Register |

## MOVEM Instruction

**Action:** Move multiple registers
**Condition Codes:** X: — N: — Z: — V: — C: —
**Opcode Forms:** MOVEM, MOVEM.W, MOVEM.L
**Assembler Syntax:**
MOVEM{.[W/L] }    <REGISTER LIST>,<EA>
MOVEM{.[W/L] }    <EA>,<REGISTER LIST>

**Description:** Transfer the selected registers from the register list to or from the consecutive memory locations starting at the memory location specified by the effective address. The register list is evaluated to a mask that specifies the list of registers to be transferred.

## MOVEP Instruction

**Action:** Move peripheral data
**Condition Codes:** X: – N: – Z: – V: – C: –
**Opcode Forms:** MOVEP, MOVEP.W, MOVEP.L
**Assembler Syntax:**
MOVEP{.[W/L]} DSRC,X(AN)
MOVEP{.[W/L]} X(AN),DDST
**Description:** Copy the source operand to the destination operand. This instruction transfers data in alternate bytes to or from memory. The starting address is specified by the displacement of the specified address register, and the remaining addresses are specified by incrementing the transfer location by two. This instruction is designed to facilitate the transfer of data between 8-bit devices and the 16-bit data bus.

## MOVES Instruction

**Action:** Move address space (MC68010/MC68020)
**Condition Codes:** X: – N: – Z: – V: – C: –
**Opcode Forms:** MOVES, MOVES.B, MOVES.W, MOVES.L
**Assembler Syntax:**
MOVES{.[B/W/L]} RN,<EA>
MOVES{.[B/W/L]} <EA>,RN
**Description:** Copy the source operand to the destination operand. This instruction uses the SFC or DFC registers to generate the necessary function code values to the function code pins of the MC68010 and MC68020 chips when the data is being transferred. The SFC register is used when the data is being transferred to the general purpose register, and the DFC register is used when the data is being transferred to a memory location.

## MOVEQ Instruction

**Action:** Move quick
**Condition Codes:** X: — N: * Z: * V: 0 C: 0
**Opcode Forms:** MOVEQ, MOVEQ.L
**Assembler Syntax:**
MOVEQ{.L} #<DATA>,DDST
**Description:** Copy the source operand to the destination operand. This opcode requires that the source be an 8-bit immediate value. The immediate value is sign-extended before loading it as a 32-bit number into the specified data register.

## MULS Instruction

**Action:** Signed multiply
**Condition Codes:** X: — N: * Z: * V: 0 C: 0
**Opcode Forms:** MULS, MULS.W
**Assembler Syntax:**
MULS{.W} <EA>,DDST
**Description:** Multiply the source operand and the destination operand generating a signed value. Store the result in the destination operand. Both operands are expected to be 16-bit values, and the destination operand receives a 32-bit result.

## MULU Instruction

**Action:** Unsigned multiply
**Condition Codes:** X: — N: * Z: * V: 0 C: 0
**Opcode Forms:** MULU, MULU.W
**Assembler Syntax:**
MULU{.W} <EA>,DDST
**Description:** Multiply the source operand and the destination operand generating an unsigned value. Store the result in the destination operand. Both operands are expected to be 16-bit values, and the destination operand receives a 32-bit result.

## NBCD Instruction

**Action:** Negate decimal with extend
**Condition Codes:** X: * N: ? Z: * V: ? C: *
**Opcode Forms:** NBCD
**Assembler Syntax:**
NBCD <EA>

**Description:** Subtract the destination operand and the extend bit from zero, and store the result back in the destination location. This produces a tens complement if the extend bit is 0, a nines complement if it is set. This is a byte operation only.

## NEG Instruction

**Action:** Negate
**Condition Codes:** X: * N: * Z: * V: * C: *
**Opcode Forms:** NEG, NEG.B, NEG.W, NEG.L
**Assembler Syntax:**
NEG{.[B/W/L]} <EA>
**Description:** The destination operand is subtracted from zero, and the result is placed back in the destination location.

## NEGX Instruction

**Action:** Negate with extend
**Condition Codes:** X: * N: * Z: * V: * C: *
**Opcode Forms:** NEGX, NEGX.B, NEGX.W, NEGX.L
**Assembler Syntax:**
NEGX{.[B/W/L]} <EA>
**Description:** The destination operand and the extend bit are subtracted from zero, and the result is placed back in the destination location.

## NOP Instruction

**Action:** No operation
**Condition Codes:** X: – N: – Z: – V: – C: –
**Opcode Forms:** NOP
**Assembler Syntax:**
NOP
**Description:** This instruction does not affect the processor state other than to update the program counter to continue execution at the next instruction.

## NOT Instruction

**Action:** Logical complement
**Condition Codes:** X: – N: * Z: * V: 0 C: 0
**Opcode Forms:** NOT, NOT.B, NOT.W, NOT.L

**Assembler Syntax:**

| | |
|---|---|
| NOT{.[B/W/L]} | <EA> |

**Description:** The ones complement of the destination operand is calculated and placed back in the destination location.

## OR Instruction

**Action:** Logical inclusive OR
**Condition Codes:** X: – N: * Z: * V: 0 C: 0
**Opcode Forms:** OR, OR.B, OR.W, OR.L
**Assembler Syntax:**

| | |
|---|---|
| OR{.[B/W/L]} | <EA>,DDST |
| OR{.[B/W/L]} | DSRC,<EA> |
| OR{.[B/W/L]} | #<DATA>,<EA> |
| OR{.B} | #<DATA>,CCR |
| OR{.W} | #<DATA>,SR |

**Description:** Inclusive OR the source operand to the destination operand. Store the result in the destination operand. This opcode may be used with any of the legal OR addressing modes.

## ORI Instruction

**Action:** Logical immediate inclusive OR
**Condition Codes:** X: – N: * Z: * V: 0 C: 0
**Opcode Forms:** ORI, ORI.B, ORI.W, ORI.L
**Assembler Syntax:**

| | |
|---|---|
| ORI{.[B/W/L]} | #<DATA>,<EA> |
| ORI{.B} | #<DATA>,CCR |
| ORI{.W} | #<DATA>,SR |

**Description:** Inclusive OR the source operand to the destination operand. Store the result in the destination operand. This opcode is a subset of the OR opcode and requires that the source be an immediate value.

## PEA Instruction

**Action:** Push effective address
**Condition Codes:** X: – N: – Z: – V: – C: –
**Opcode Forms:** PEA, PEA.L
**Assembler Syntax:**

| | |
|---|---|
| PEA{.L} | <EA> |

**Description:** Push the calculated (effective) address onto the stack.

## RESET Instruction

**Action:** Reset external devices
**Condition Codes:** X: – N: – Z: – V: – C: –
**Opcode Forms:** RESET
**Assembler Syntax:**
RESET
**Description:** The reset line on the processor is asserted, causing all external devices to be reset. This instruction does not affect the processor state other than to update the program counter to continue execution at the next instruction.

## ROL/ROR Instruction

**Action:** Rotate left/right
**Condition Codes:** X: – N: * Z: * V: 0 C: *
**Opcode Forms:** ROL/ROR, ROL.B/ROR.B, ROL.W/ROR.W, ROL.L/ROR.L
**Assembler Syntax:**
RO[LR] {.[B/W/L] }   DSRC,DDST
RO[LR] {.[B/W/L] }   #<DATA>,DDST
RO[LR] {.[B/W/L] }   <EA>
**Description:** Rotate the destination operand left or right N bits. The explicit or implied source operand determines N, the number of bits to be rotated. A rotate with an implied shift count rotates the specified memory destination location one bit only, in the specified direction.

## ROXL/ROXR Instruction

**Action:** Rotate left/right with extend
**Condition Codes:** X: * N: * Z: * V: 0 C: *
**Opcode Forms:** ROXL/ROXR, ROXL.B/ROXR.B, ROXL.W/ROXR.W, ROXL.L/ROXR.L
**Assembler Syntax:**
ROX[L/R] {.[B/W/L] }   DSRC,DDST
ROX[L/R] {.[B/W/L] }   #<DATA>,DDST
ROX[L/R] {.[B/W/L] }   <EA>
**Description:** Rotate the destination operand left or right N bits. The extend bit is included as part of the rotation. The explicit or implied source operand determines N, the number of bits to be rotated. A rotate with an implied shift count rotates the specified memory destination location one bit only, in the specified direction.

## RTE Instruction

**Action:** Return from exception
**Condition Codes:** X: * N: * Z: * V: * C: *
**Opcode Forms:** RTE
**Assembler Syntax:**
RTE
**Description:** Load the exception state information from the top of stack and continue with execution. This instruction reloads the status register stack pointer and program counter in the appropriate manner for the chip, and continues execution at the old program counter address. It should be noted that this function, although similar for both the MC68000 and the MC68010, is different because the exception frames are organized differently for the two processors.

## RTD Instruction

**Action:** Return and deallocate
**Condition Codes:** X: – N: – Z: – V: – C: –
**Opcode Forms:** RTD (MC68010/MC68020)
**Assembler Syntax:**
RTD #<DISPLACEMENT>
**Description:** Load the old program counter from the stack and then add the 16-bit displacement, which has been sign extended to 32-bits, to the stack pointer. Proceed to execute the next instruction at the updated program location. The displacement field is a twos complement value.

## RTR Instruction

**Action:** Return and restore condition codes
**Condition Codes:** X: * N: * Z: * V: * C: *
**Opcode Forms:** RTR
**Assembler Syntax:**
RTR
**Description:** Load the condition code and a new program counter from the stack. Proceed with execution at the new program counter address.

## RTS Instruction

**Action:** Return from subroutine
**Condition Codes:** X: – N: – Z: – V: – C: –
**Opcode Forms:** RTS

**Assembler Syntax:**
RTS
**Description:** Load a new program counter from the top of the stack, and proceed with execution at this new address.

## SBCD Instruction

**Action:** Subtract decimal with extend
**Condition Codes:** X: * N: ? Z: * V: ? C: *
**Opcode Forms:** SBCD
**Assembler Syntax:**

| | |
|---|---|
| SBCD | DSRC,DDST |
| SBCD | −(ASRC),−(ADST) |

**Description:** Subtract the source operand from the destination operand using binary coded decimal (BCD) arithmetic. Store the result in the destination operand.

## S*cc* Instruction

**Action:** Set according to condition codes
**Condition Codes:** X: − N: − Z: − V: − C: −
**Opcode Forms:** S*cc*
**Assembler Syntax:**

| | |
|---|---|
| S*cc* | <EA> |

**Description:** Set the specified byte address to 0*x*FF if the condition is met, or to 0*x*00 if the condition is not met. For a complete list of valid condition codes, see the B*cc* instruction.

## STOP Instruction

**Action:** Load status register and stop
**Condition Codes:** X: * N: * Z: * V: * C: *
**Opcode Forms:** STOP
**Assembler Syntax:**

| | |
|---|---|
| STOP | #<DATA> |

**Description:** Load the immediate data into the status register, advance the program counter to the next instruction, and make the microprocessor pause. The processor resumes executing instructions when a trace, interrupt, or reset exception is initiated. If an interrupt request arrives whose priority is higher than the current processor priority, an interrupt exception occurs; otherwise, the interrupt request has no effect.

## SUB Instruction

**Action:** Subtract binary
**Condition Codes:** X: * N: * Z: * V: * C: *
**Opcode Forms:** SUB, SUB.B, SUB.W, SUB.L
**Assembler Syntax:**

| | |
|---|---|
| SUB{.[B/W/L] } | <EA>,DDST |
| SUB{.[B/W/L] } | DSRC,<EA> |
| SUB{.[W/L] } | <EA>,ADST |
| SUB{.[B/W/L] } | #<DATA>,<EA> |

**Description:** Subtract the source operand from the destination operand using binary arithmetic. Store the result in the destination operand. This opcode may be used with any of the legal SUB addressing modes. This opcode does not generate the SUBQ{.[B/W/L] } instruction for those special cases.

## SUBA Instruction

**Action:** Subtract binary addresses
**Condition Codes:** X: – N: – Z: – V: – C: –
**Opcode Forms:** SUBA, SUBA.W, SUBA.L
**Assembler Syntax:**

| | |
|---|---|
| SUBA{.[W/L] } | <EA>,ADST |

**Description:** Subtract the source operand from the destination operand using binary arithmetic. Store the result in the destination operand. This opcode is a subset of the SUB opcode, and requires that the destination be an address register.

## SUBI Instruction

**Action:** Subtract binary immediate
**Condition Codes:** X: * N: * Z: * V: * C: *
**Opcode Forms:** SUBI, SUBI.B, SUBI.W, SUBI.L
**Assembler Syntax:**

| | |
|---|---|
| SUBI{.[B/W/L] } | #<DATA>,<EA> |

**Description:** Subtract the source operand from the destination operand using binary arithmetic. Store the result in the destination operand. This opcode is a subset of the SUB opcode, and it requires that the source be an immediate value.

### SUBQ Instruction

**Action:** Subtract binary quick
**Condition Codes:** X: * N: * Z: * V: * C: *
**Opcode Forms:** SUBQ, SUBQ.B, SUBQ.W, SUBQ.L
**Assembler Syntax:**
SUBQ{.[B/W/L]} #<DATA>,<EA>
**Description:** Subtract the source operand from the destination operand using binary arithmetic. Store the result in the destination operand. This opcode requires that the source be an immediate value with a data range of 1–8.

### SUBX Instruction

**Action:** Subtract binary with extend
**Condition Codes:** X: * N: * Z: * V: * C: *
**Opcode Forms:** SUBX, SUBX.B, SUBX.W, SUBX.L
**Assembler Syntax:**
SUBX{.[B/W/L]} DSRC,DDST
SUBX{.[B/W/L]} −(ASRC),−(ADST)
**Description:** Subtract the source operand and the extend bit from the destination operand using binary arithmetic. Store the result in the destination operand.

### SWAP Instruction

**Action:** Swap register halves
**Condition Codes:** X: − N: * Z: * V: 0 C: 0
**Opcode Forms:** SWAP, SWAP.W
**Assembler Syntax:**
SWAP{.W} DDST
**Description:** Exchange the upper 16 bits of the destination data register with the lower 16 bits of the same register. Store the result in the destination data register.

### TAS Instruction

**Action:** Test and set
**Condition Codes:** X: − N: * Z: * V: 0 C: 0
**Opcode Forms:** TAS, TAS.B
**Assembler Syntax:**
TAS{.B} <EA>

**Description:** Test the byte address specified in the destination, and set the N and Z condition codes appropriately. Set the high order bit of the operand. These operations are performed using read-modify-write memory cycles and are guaranteed indivisible operations. This instruction is useful for synchronization between multiple processors.

### TST Instruction

**Action:** Test
**Condition Codes:** X: — N: * Z: * V: 0 C: 0
**Opcode Forms:** TST, TST.B, TST.W, TST.L
**Assembler Syntax:**
TST{.[B/W/L]}  <EA>
**Description:** Compare the specified operand to zero, and set the condition codes. The destination address is left unmodified.

### UNLK Instruction

**Action:** Unlink
**Condition Codes:** X: — N: — Z: — V: — C: —
**Opcode Forms:** UNLK
**Assembler Syntax:**
UNLK  ADST
**Description:** Load the stack pointer from the destination address register, then pop the long value from the new top of the stack and place it in the destination register. This instruction is commonly used at subroutine exit to restore an old frame pointer and free up any local temporary storage.

## Pseudo-ops

### ALIGN Pseudo-op

**Action:** Align the program counter to any boundary
**Condition Codes:** X: — N: — Z: — V: — C: —
**Opcode Forms:** ALIGN
**Assembler Syntax:**
ALIGN  <VALUE>

**Description:** This directive aligns the current section on a modulo <value> boundary. Zero to <VALUE> − 1 bytes of zero data will be generated to properly change the alignment as requested. This pseudo-op allows the user to align the instruction counter on any boundary. The following example aligns the instruction counter on a four-word boundary:

```
ALIGN 4
```

This is equivalent to the following CNOP pseudo-op:

```
CNOP 0,4
```

## ASCII Pseudo-op

**Action:** Define a constant string
**Condition Codes:** X: − N: − Z: − V: − C: −
**Opcode Forms:** ASCII
**Assembler Syntax:**
ASCII <STRING>
**Description:** This pseudo-op generates a series of bytes of data the same length as the specified string. The generated data is a set of bytes whose ASCII values are represented by the characters in the string. This series of bytes is not null-terminated.

## ASCIZ Pseudo-op

**Action:** Define a constant null-terminated string
**Condition Codes:** X: − N: − Z: − V: − C: −
**Opcode Forms:** ASCIZ
**Assembler Syntax:**
ASCIZ <STRING>
**Description:** This pseudo-op generates a series of bytes of data one byte longer than the specified string. The generated data is a set of bytes whose ASCII values are represented by the characters in the string. A null-termination character is generated with this directive.

## CNOP Pseudo-op

**Action:** Conditional no operation
**Condition Codes:** X: − N: − Z: − V: − C: −
**Opcode Forms:** CNOP
**Assembler Syntax:**
CNOP <VALUE>,<VALUE>

**Description:** This pseudo-op aligns the instruction counter to a boundary. The first expression <VALUE> specifies the amount to increase the instruction counter after the instruction counter has been moved to the proper alignment boundary. The second expression <VALUE> specifies the alignment boundary to be used. The following example aligns the instruction counter one byte after the nearest eight-byte boundary:

```
CNOP    1,8
```

## COMM Pseudo-op

**Action:** Define a common storage/BSS (Block Storage Section) block
**Condition Codes:** X: — N: — Z: — V: — C: —
**Opcode Forms:** COMM
**Assembler Syntax:**
COMM <LABEL>,<VALUE>
**Description:** This directive places the given symbol <LABEL> into the BSS section with a size of <VALUE> bytes long.

## DC Pseudo-op

**Action:** Define constant
**Condition Codes:** X: — N: — Z: — V: — C: —
**Opcode Forms:** DC, DC.B, DC.W, DC.L
**Assembler Syntax:**
DC{.[B/W/L]} <VALUE>{,<VALUE>. . .}
**Description:** This pseudo-op generates constant values specified in the arguments into the object module so that they may be placed in memory at the specified instruction counter locations at the start of program execution. All data values are treated as 32-bit signed values. These values are truncated when necessary, as determined by the size specifier for the pseudo-op. The assembler automatically aligns the current program counter to an even boundary if the specified constant is either a word or a long-word value, and the current program counter is on an odd boundary.

## DCB Pseudo-op

**Action:** Define constant block
**Condition Codes:** X: — N: — Z: — V: — C: —
**Opcode Forms:** DCB.W, DCB.L
**Assembler Syntax:**
DCB{.[B/W/L]}      <EXP1>,<EXP2>
**Description:** This pseudo-op generates <EXP1> number of memory locations in the object module. These memory locations contain the value specified in <EXP2>. The <EXP2> value is treated as a 32-bit signed value that's truncated when necessary, as determined by the size specifier for the pseudo-op.

## DS Pseudo-op

**Action:** Define storage
**Condition Codes:** X: — N: — Z: — V: — C: —
**Opcode Forms:** DS, DS.B, DS.W, DS.L
**Assembler Syntax:**
DS{.[B/W/L]}      <VALUE>
**Description:** This pseudo-op allocates the specified number of memory locations into the object module. When a DS pseudo-op is used and the current section is either a text or data section, the DS pseudo-op forces the allocated bytes to contain a 0 value. This assembler automatically aligns the current program counter to an even boundary if the specified storage is either a word or a long-word value, and the current program counter is on an odd boundary. One method of aligning the program counter to an even boundary is to generate the line:

```
DS.W    0
```

Other alignment methods include using the EVEN, ALIGN, and CNOP pseudo-ops.

## ELSE Pseudo-op

**Action:** Reverse current conditional assembly condition
**Condition Codes:** X: — N: — Z: — V: — C: —
**Opcode Forms:** ELSE
**Assembler Syntax:**
ELSE

**Description:** This pseudo-op changes the true/false condition of the currently active IF pseudo-op. This pseudo-op does not have arguments. ELSE pseudo-ops may be nested just like other IF*xx* pseudo-ops. When ELSE pseudo-ops are nested, the current ELSE pertains to the most recent IF pseudo-op. For example:

```
IFEQ     1
ADDQ.L   #1,D0
ELSE
MOVEQ    #0,D0
ENDC
```

will assemble the MOVEQ instruction.

### END Pseudo-op

**Action:** End of program
**Condition Codes:** X: — N: — Z: — V: — C: —
**Opcode Forms:** END
**Assembler Syntax:**
END
**Description:** This statement is currently optional. Its purpose is to specify the last line of an assembly file. All source code statements following this line will be ignored.

### ENDC Pseudo-op

**Action:** End conditional assembly
**Condition Codes:** X: — N: — Z: — V: — C: —
**Opcode Forms:** ENDC
**Assembler Syntax:**
ENDC
**Description:** This pseudo-op terminates the current nesting level of conditional assembly. This pseudo-op may be used with any of the conditional IF pseudo-ops.

### ENDM Pseudo-op

**Action:** End macro definition
**Condition Codes:** X: — N: — Z: — V: — C: —
**Opcode Forms:** ENDM
**Assembler Syntax:**
ENDM

**Description:** This pseudo-op signals the assembler to terminate the current macro definition. After this pseudo-op is processed, the assembler returns to normal input line processing.

### EVEN Pseudo-op

**Action:** Align the program counter to an even boundary
**Condition Codes:** X: – N: – Z: – V: – C: –
**Opcode Forms:** EVEN
**Assembler Syntax:**
EVEN
**Description:** This directive aligns the current section on an even boundary by generating one byte of data, if necessary, or no data if the current section is already aligned.

### FAIL Pseudo-op

**Action:** Generate a user error
**Condition Codes:** X: – N: – Z: – V: – C: –
**Opcode Forms:** FAIL
**Assembler Syntax:**
FAIL
**Description:** This pseudo-op tells the assembler to flag a user error on this assembly statement.

### FORMAT Pseudo-op

**Action:** No action taken
**Condition Codes:** X: – N: – Z: – V: – C: –
**Opcode Forms:** FORMAT
**Assembler Syntax:**
FORMAT
**Description:** This pseudo-op is currently parsed and accepted by the assembler, but totally ignored.

### GLOBAL Pseudo-op

**Action:** Set a label to be externally defined
**Condition Codes:** X: – N: – Z: – V: – C: –
**Opcode Forms:** GLOBAL, GLOBL, XDEF
**Assembler Syntax:**

```
GLOBAL     <LABEL>{,<LABEL>...}
GLOBL      <LABEL>{,<LABEL>...}
XDEF       <LABEL>{,<LABEL>...}
```

**Description:** This pseudo-op sets the specified list of labels to become globally-defined labels. This assembler lifts the restriction that these labels must be defined in the current file. Instead, this pseudo-op is kept for backward capability and is used as a flag, to the assembler, that the label names, which are listed as arguments, are globally defined symbols that exist in the current assembly. The XDEF, GLOBL, and GLOBAL pseudo-ops are kept for compatibility with other assembly language formats.

## IDNT Pseudo-op

**Action:** Name program unit
**Condition Codes:** X: – N: – Z: – V: – C: –
**Opcode Forms:** IDNT
**Assembler Syntax:**

```
IDNT                <STRING>
```

**Description:** This pseudo-op sets the name of the program unit. By default a program unit has no name, which is equivalent to using this pseudo-op with a null string. An IDNT pseudo-op is not required for proper functioning of the program or the assembler, but is provided for reasons of compatibility.

## IF*xx* Pseudo-op

**Action:** Control conditional assembly
**Condition Codes:** X: – N: – Z: – V: – C: –
**Opcode Forms:** IFEQ, IFNE, IFGT, IFGE, IFLT, IFLE
**Assembler Syntax:**

```
IFEQ                <VALUE>
IFNE                <VALUE>
IFGT                <VALUE>
IFGE                <VALUE>
IFLT                <VALUE>
IFLE                <VALUE>
```

**Description:** These pseudo-ops, depending on the value of the expression and the pseudo-op used, enable or disable assembly. If the condition of the expression is false, assembly of the input stream will be disabled until a balancing ENDC pseudo-op is detected. IF conditionals may be nested. The current nesting level is 16 deep. The appropriate number of nested ENDC pseudo-ops must be reached before the assembler will continue processing statements. See also the ELSE conditional for reversing the current enable/disable assembly level. As an example:

```
IFEQ    3
MOVEQ   #0,D0
ENDC
```

will not assemble the MOVEQ instruction.

## IFC/IFNC Pseudo-op

**Action:** Assemble with respect to string comparison
**Condition Codes:** X: – N: – Z: – V: – C: –
**Opcode Forms:** IFC, IFNC
**Assembler Syntax:**
IFC <STRING>,<STRING>
IFNC <STRING>,<STRING>
**Description:** These pseudo-ops will enable or disable assembly depending on the equality or inequality of the two strings. If the condition of the string comparison evaluates to false, assembly of the input stream will be disabled until a balancing ENDC pseudo-op is detected. IF conditionals may be nested. The current nesting level is 16 deep. The appropriate number of nested ENDC pseudo-ops must be reached before the assembler will continue processing statements. See also the ELSE conditional for reversing the current enable/disable assembly level. As an example:

```
IFC     'FOO','BAR'
MOVEQ   #0,D0
ENDC
```

will not assemble the MOVEQ instruction.

## IFD/IFND Pseudo-op

**Action:** Assemble with respect to defined/undefined label
**Condition Codes:** X: – N: – Z: – V: – C: –
**Opcode Forms:** IFD, IFND
**Assembler Syntax:**
IFD <SYMBOL>
IFND <SYMBOL>
**Description:** Depending on whether the specified symbol is defined or undefined, these pseudo-ops will enable or disable assembly. If these conditionals evaluate to false, then assembly of the input stream will be disabled until a balancing ENDC pseudo-op is detected. These IF conditionals may be nested. The current nesting level is 16 deep. The appropriate number of nested ENDC statements must be reached before the assembler will continue processing statements. See also the ELSE conditional for reversing the current enable/disable assembly level. As an example:

```
IFND    MAIN
MOVEQ   #0,D0
ENDC
```

will not assemble the MOVEQ instruction if the symbol MAIN is defined.

## INCLUDE Pseudo-op

**Action:** Include an external file
**Condition Codes:** X: – N: – Z: – V: – C: –
**Opcode Forms:** INCLUDE
**Assembler Syntax:**
INCLUDE <FILENAME>
**Description:** This pseudo-op notifies the assembler that the current input stream should now be extracted from the named file, until either further notice from another INCLUDE statement, or until the end of the named input file.

This capability allows the programmer to cleanly separate definitions or common code from program specific details. Some uses of this pseudo-op are including header files of common definitions, including header files of common macros, and including program specific code into the middle of machine-independent startup files.

The assembler will search for the include file in both

the current directory as well as the specified include list denoted by the -i flag. INCLUDE pseudo-ops may be nested a maximum of eight deep with this release of the ASM68010 assembler.

## LIST Pseudo-op

**Action:** Turn on listing
**Condition Codes:** X: — N: — Z: — V: — C: —
**Opcode Forms:** LIST
**Assembler Syntax:**
LIST
**Description:** This pseudo-op tells the assembler to continue listing from this point onward. This pseudo-op does not appear in the listing file.

## LLEN Pseudo-op

**Action:** Set line length
**Condition Codes:** X: — N: — Z: — V: — C: —
**Opcode Forms:** LLEN
**Assembler Syntax:**
LLEN <VALUE>
**Description:** This pseudo-op sets the length of the output line sent to the listing file. This pseudo-op expects a value, which represents the number of characters in the line (between 60 and 132). The default value for this pseudo-op is 80 characters. This pseudo-op does not appear in the listing file.

## MACRO Pseudo-op

**Action:** Define a macro
**Condition Codes:** X: — N: — Z: — V: — C: —
**Opcode Forms:** MACRO
**Assembler Syntax:**
LABEL MACRO
**Description:** This pseudo-op starts a macro definition. This pseudo-op tells the assembler to absorb input lines until an ENDM pseudo-op is encountered. The ENDM pseudo-op tells the assembler that the macro definition is completed. The next time the assembler sees the label given to the macro, it will insert the contents of the absorbed lines into the input stream. These lines will at that time be processed

by the assembler. The absorbed lines may contain any regular input line or macro calls; however, they may not contain other macro definitions.

The backslash symbol has special meaning when the assembler is reprocessing lines that have been generated as the result of an instance of a macro label. Whenever the assembler parses a number preceded by a backslash, (such as \1 or \6), the assembler substitutes these characters with the corresponding argument in the macro expansion (the first and sixth in this example). For example, if the assembler sees a \6, then it will replace these two characters with the sixth argument to the macro call. If this argument does not exist, then the assembler simply removes these two characters.

The second special sequence is \@. Whenever an \@ is found in the input line during a macro expansion, it will automatically be replaced with a *.n*, where *n* is a unique number. These numbers are generated by incrementing a counter every time this combination of characters is found in a macro expansion. This is normally used to generate unique labels in a macro. Macro calls may be nested as many as 16 deep. There is also an upper limit to the number of arguments in a macro call. This upper limit is currently set to 24 arguments.

## MASK2 Pseudo-op

**Action:** No action taken
**Condition Codes:** X: — N: — Z: — V: — C: —
**Opcode Forms:** MASK2
**Assembler Syntax:**
MASK2
**Description:** This pseudo-op is currently parsed and accepted by the assembler, but totally ignored.

## MEXIT Pseudo-op

**Action:** Exit from macro expansion
**Condition Codes:** X: — N: — Z: — V: — C: —
**Opcode Forms:** MEXIT
**Assembler Syntax:**
MEXIT

**Description:** When this macro is invoked during a macro expansion it signals the assembler to stop expanding the current macro. This macro is most commonly embedded within condition statements inside macro definitions.

### NARG Pseudo-op

**Action:** Special symbol name
**Condition Codes:** X: — N: — Z: — V: — C: —
**Opcode Forms:** NARG
**Assembler Syntax:**
NARG
narg
**Description:** NARG contains the number of arguments passed to a macro expansion.

### NOFORMAT Pseudo-op

**Action:** No action taken
**Condition Codes:** X: — N: — Z: — V: — C: —
**Opcode Forms:** NOFORMAT
**Assembler Syntax:**
NOFORMAT
**Description:** This pseudo-op is currently parsed and accepted by the assembler, but totally ignored.

### NOLIST Pseudo-op

**Action:** Turn off listing
**Condition Codes:** X: — N: — Z: — V: — C: —
**Opcode Forms:** NOLIST, NOL
**Assembler Syntax:**
NOLIST
NOL
**Description:** These pseudo-ops tell the assembler to halt listing output from this point onward. This directive does not appear in the listing file.

### NOOBJ Pseudo-op

**Action:** Disable object code generation
**Condition Codes:** X: — N: — Z: — V: — C: —
**Opcode Forms:** NOOBJ
**Assembler Syntax:**
NOOBJ

**Description:** This statement flags the assembler not to generate any object code.

### NOPAGE Pseudo-op

**Action:** Disable page header generation
**Condition Codes:** X: − N: − Z: − V: − C: −
**Opcode Forms:** NOPAGE
**Assembler Syntax:**
NOPAGE
**Description:** This pseudo-op turns off paging capability. This forces the assembler to generate a listing file without headers, footers, and other page numbering information, when the listing option is enabled. This pseudo-op does not appear in the listing file.

### OFFSET Pseudo-op

**Action:** Define offsets
**Condition Codes:** X: − N: − Z: − V: − C: −
**Opcode Forms:** OFFSET
**Assembler Syntax:**
OFFSET <VALUE>
**Description:** This pseudo-op is currently parsed and accepted by the ASM68010 assembler, but totally ignored.

### PAGE Pseudo-op

**Action:** Enable page header generation
**Condition Codes:** X: − N: − Z: − V: − C: −
**Opcode Forms:** PAGE
**Assembler Syntax:**
PAGE
**Description:** This pseudo-op reenables the paging feature of listing output. This option is turned on by default every time the listing option of the assembler has been enabled. When this option is enabled, the assembler listing file will contain headers and footers around each page break. This pseudo-op does not appear in the listing file.

### PLEN Pseudo-op

**Action:** Set page length
**Condition Codes:** X: − N: − Z: − V: − C: −
**Opcode Forms:** PLEN

**Assembler Syntax:**
PLEN <VALUE>
**Description:** This pseudo-op sets the length of an output page sent to the listing file. This pseudo-op expects a value, which represents the number of lines in a page (between 24 and 100). The default value for this pseudo-op is 66 lines. This pseudo-op does not appear in the listing file.

## REG Pseudo-op

**Action:** Set register list
**Condition Codes:** X: – N: – Z: – V: – C: –
**Opcode Forms:** REG
**Assembler Syntax:**
REG <VALUE>
**Description:** This pseudo-op is currently parsed and accepted by the assembler, but totally ignored.

## RORG Pseudo-op

**Action:** Set relative origin
**Condition Codes:** X: – N: – Z: – V: – C: –
**Opcode Forms:** RORG
**Assembler Syntax:**
RORG <VALUE>
**Description:** This pseudo-op is currently parsed and accepted by the assembler, but totally ignored.

## SECTION Pseudo-op

**Action:** Program section
**Condition Codes:** X: – N: – Z: – V: – C: –
**Opcode Forms:** SECTION
**Assembler Syntax:**
SECTION <NAME>{,<TYPE>}
**Description:** The SECTION directive is used to establish starting points for programs and subroutines. It is used to create relocatable program sections and operates in conjunction with the linkage editor to create executable programs.

The type field may be any one of the following keywords:

| | |
|---|---|
| CODE (default) | Continue with the code section |
| DATA | Continue with the data section |
| BSS | Continue with the BSS section |

### SPC Pseudo-op

**Action:** Space blank lines
**Condition Codes:** X: — N: — Z: — V: — C: —
**Opcode Forms:** SPC
**Assembler Syntax:**
SPC <VALUE>
**Description:** This pseudo-op generates the specified number of blank lines in the assembly listing file. This pseudo-op does not appear in the listing file.

### TEXT/CODE/DATA/BSS Pseudo-op

**Action:** Text/Code/Data/BSS program section
**Condition Codes:** X: — N: — Z: — V: — C: —
**Opcode Forms:** TEXT/CODE/DATA/BSS
**Assembler Syntax:**
TEXT
CODE
DATA
BSS
**Description:** These directives change the current section to become the code, data or BSS section. The text and the code section are considered equivalent. None of the directives takes an operand, and the section name is assumed to the current section name. These directives can be considered shorthands for the section directive.

### TTL Pseudo-op

**Action:** Set program title
**Condition Codes:** X: — N: — Z: — V: — C: —
**Opcode Forms:** TTL
**Assembler Syntax:**
TTL <STRING>
**Description:** This pseudo-op sets the title to be used as part of the heading in each page of the listing file. This string should not be more than 64 characters in length. This pseudo-op does not appear in the listing file.

## XREF Pseudo-op

**Action:** Define an external label
**Condition Codes:** X: — N: — Z: — V: — C: —
**Opcode Forms:** XREF
**Assembler Syntax:**
XREF <LABEL>{,<LABEL>. . .}
**Description:** This pseudo-op gives the assembler a list of labels that may not be defined in this assembler file. The ASM68010 lifts the restriction that these labels must not be defined in the current file. Instead this pseudo-op is kept for backward capability, and is used as a flag to the assembler that the label names listed as arguments may not exist in the current assembly.

# APPENDIX B

# Common Assembly-Time Errors for the Amiga

In almost every program there are bugs. Legend has it that in one of the first computers, the first programming problem found was caused when a moth flew into the computer and not only killed itself, but caused the giant computer to generate the wrong answer to the program it was running. Since that time, whenever there's been a programming mistake, that mistake is known as a *bug*.

Bugs come in two forms. These are *runtime errors* and *compile-* or *assembly-time* errors. A runtime error occurs when a running program does not produce the expected results. An assembly-time error is produced any time a compiler or assembler sees illegal input. Here's a look at some of the possible assembly-time errors that might be seen during the course of writing an assembly language program.

The following assembler errors are some of the most common detected by the *ASM68010* assembler. Most (if not all) of these assembly-time errors are also detected in other Amiga 68000 assemblers. The actual wording of the error message may be different. It may be necessary to consult your specific assembler reference manual for the exact wording of the error.

- ERROR: Invalid opcode

  This error normally occurs when an opcode has been misspelled and the assembler cannot tell what the real opcode should be. For example:

  ```
  MUVE.L   D0,D1      ;COPY D0 TO D1
  ```

  This type of error can be corrected by fixing a spelling mistake.
- ERROR: Multiply defined symbol

  This error normally occurs when there have been two

label definitions for exactly the same label. For example:

```
COPYSTART:
                MOVE.L  #10,D0    ;LOAD THE COUNT
;
;                                 ;... SOME TIME LATER
;
COPYSTART:
```

This type of error can be corrected by changing one of the label names and all the label references to that name.

- ERROR: Wrong number of operands

This error normally occurs when an assembly statement has too many or too few operands. For example:

```
MOVE.L   D0        ; COPY D0 TO D1 WITH TOO FEW
                   ; OPERANDS
TST.L    D0,D1     ; TEST THE RESULT OF D1 WITH TOO
                   ; MANY OPERANDS
```

This error can be corrected by editing the line so that the proper number of operands appear. An MC68000 microprocessor reference manual should provide a list of the legal operands for an instruction.

- ERROR: Invalid operand

This error normally occurs when a statement has the wrong operand for a given instruction. For example:

```
EOR.L    VAL,D0    ; EOR VAL TO D0
```

This error can be corrected by editing the line so that the correct operands are used.

- ERROR: Odd address

This error is generated by the assembler when it tries to assemble an instruction opcode starting at an odd address. Remember, all instructions MUST start on an even address. For example:

```
DS.W     0         ; FORCE AN EVEN ADDRESS (THIS IS
                   ; DISCUSSED LATER)
DC.B     0         ; FORCE AN ODD ADDRESS (THIS IS
                   ; DISCUSSED LATER)
TST.L    D0        ; THIS INSTRUCTION IS NOW ON AN
                   ; ODD ADDRESS
```

This error may be corrected by adding an EVENPC macro or similar even-alignment facility. This bug also may be corrected by removing the code or data that misaligned the instructions.

- ERROR: Include file not found

This error is usually generated when the assembler cannot find an include file, or the include file is named incorrectly. Example:

```
INCLUDE "HEDDR"  ; NOTE THAT INCLUDE NAME IS
                 ; MISSPELLED
```

- ERROR: Macro undefined

This error is usually generated when a macro call is using the wrong name or the macro was never defined.

- ERROR: Nonrelocatable expression

This error is usually generated when an absolute expression is used where only a relative expression is allowed. Examples include using absolute addresses in B*cc* instructions, or performing an illegal arithmetic operation on a value. For example:

```
BRA     LABEL/2  ; LABEL/2 IS AN ABSOLUTE EXPRES-
                 ; SION.
```

This error can be corrected by editing the line and replacing the absolute expression with a relocatable expression.

- ERROR: Offset too large

This error is generated whenever the offset for a B*cc*, DB*cc*, or BSR instruction is larger than the maximum amount allowed. The range is −128 to 127 for short offsets, and −32768 to 32767 for a long offset. For example:

```
BRA.S   FARAWAY  ; POSSIBLY A BRA OR BRA.L WILL
                 ; WORK HERE.
```

First try making the branch a long branch if it is a short branch. Otherwise, rewrite or shorten the file or subroutine. To get this message because the routine itself is too big, the subroutine must be at least 32,768 bytes long. This is far too big for a single subroutine.

- ERROR: Unmatched ENDC pseudo-op or ERROR: No closing ENDC pseudo-op

This error is generated when the assembler cannot match all the IF*xx* pseudo-ops with the same number of

ENDC pseudo-ops. For example:

```
IFEQ     1
TST.L    D0
END                  ; THE END OF THE FILE.
```

An ENDC needs to be added someplace, or an IF*xx* must be removed. Match up all the IF*xx* with ENDCs, and find out which IF*xx* is missing it's ENDC.

- ERROR: Undefined symbol(s), can't fully link load module

  This error message is printed by *ASM68010* when the -a flag is selected and at least one symbol is not defined in the source. If the symbol should have been defined, define it. If the symbol was defined in a different object module, an ALINK/BLINK of the two object files will have to be performed.

## Other Errors

Many other errors can be produced by *ASM68010* and the other Amiga assemblers. Here's a list of many of the other errors from *ASM68010*.

- ERROR: Invalid character

  The assembler found an unexpected character. Check for a mistyped line.
- ERROR: Invalid constant

  The assembler parsed a constant value where there shouldn't have been one. Check for a missing operator (+, −, /, *, or other operator).
- ERROR: Invalid term

  The assembler found an illegal part of an expression as either the left or right side of an operator. Check for a mistyped line.
- ERROR: Invalid operator

  The assembler thinks it should see an operator (+, −, /, *, and so on) but, instead, found a character it couldn't understand. Check for a mistyped line.
- ERROR: Invalid symbol

  The assembler found a symbol, and at least one character in the symbol is not legal. Check for illegal characters (something other than alphanumeric characters) in the symbol.

- ERROR: Invalid pseudo-op; ignored
  This pseudo-op is not understood by this compiler. It has been parsed and ignored. No operation or code has been generated by this line.
- ERROR: Illegal macro definition
  The macro definition line was probably typed incorrectly. The macro name may also be illegal in some manner.
- ERROR: Invalid assignment
  An EQU statement has been typed incorrectly, or it is missing arguments.
- ERROR: User signaled error
  The FAIL pseudo-op was executed by the assembler.
- ERROR: Unmatched ENDM pseudo-op
  This error is generated when the assembler cannot match the MACRO pseudo-ops with the same number of ENDM pseudo-ops.
- ERROR: Illegal macro redefinition
  The user has defined two macros with the same name.
- ERROR: Unmatched else pseudo-op
  This error is generated when the assembler cannot match or is not preceded by an IF*xx* pseudo-op.
- ERROR: Too many nested include files
  The programmer has nested include files too deeply. On *ASM68010,* this depth is eight include files.
- ERROR: Too many nested conditional levels
  The programmer has nested conditional levels too deeply. On *ASM68010,* this depth is 16 levels.
- ERROR: Nested macro too deep
  The programmer has nested macros too deeply. The *ASM68010* allows a maximum depth of 16 levels.

## APPENDIX C

# Guru Meditation Numbers

A guru meditation number decoding table can help debug Amiga-specific programming errors. A guru meditation number has 16 hexadecimal digits and looks like:

81000009.00281002

You can decode such a message this way:

SSGESPER.00ADDRES

| | |
|---|---|
| SS | two-digit subsystem code |
| GE | two-digit general error code |
| SPER | four-digit specific error code |
| ADDRES | six-digit task memory address |

Subsystems:

| Code | Meaning |
|---|---|
| 00 | CPU Trap (see below) |
| 01 | Exec |
| 02 | Graphics |
| 03 | Layers |
| 04 | Intuition |
| 05 | Math |
| 06 | Clist |
| 07 | DOS |
| 08 | RAM |
| 09 | Icon |
| 0A | Expansion |
| 10 | Audio |
| 11 | Console |
| 12 | Gameport |
| 13 | Keyboard |
| 14 | TrackDisk |
| 15 | Timer |
| 20 | CIA Chip |
| 21 | Disk |
| 22 | Miscellaneous |
| 30 | BootStrap |
| 31 | Workbench |
| 32 | DiskCopy |

Sometimes the first digit of the subsystem is an 8 (as in the example above). In that case, ignore the 8, and read the subsystem number as a 1 in our example. That means there was an Exec error.

General Error Codes:

| Code | Meaning |
|---|---|
| 01 | Not enough memory |
| 02 | MakeLibrary |
| 03 | OpenLibrary |
| 04 | OpenDevice |
| 05 | OpenResource |
| 06 | I/O Error |
| 07 | Signal Absent |

Specific Error Codes:

Exec:

| Code | Meaning |
|---|---|
| 0001 | Checksum: exception vector |
| 0002 | Checksum: ExecBase |
| 0003 | Checksum: Library |
| 0004 | No memory for library |
| 0005 | Memory List damaged |
| 0006 | No memory for interrupt server |
| 0007 | InitAPtr |
| 0008 | Damaged Semaphore |
| 0009 | Can't free already-free memory |
| 000A | Bogus Exception |

Graphics:

| Code | Meaning |
|---|---|
| 0001 | No memory for Copper display list |
| 0002 | No memory for Copper instruction list |
| 0003 | Overloaded Copper list |
| 0004 | Overloaded Copper intermediate list |
| 0005 | No memory for Copper list head |
| 0006 | No memory (long frame) |
| 0007 | No memory (short frame) |
| 0008 | No memory for flood fill |
| 0009 | No memory for TmpRas in text operation |
| 000A | No memory for BlitBitmap call |
| 000B | Region Memory |
| 0030 | MakeVPort error |
| 1234 | GfxNoLCM |

Layers:

| Code | Meaning |
|---|---|
| 0001 | No memory |

Intuition:

| Code | Meaning |
|---|---|
| 0001 | Unknown gadget type |
| 0002 | No memory for port |
| 0003 | No memory to allocate item plane |
| 0004 | No memory for sub allocation |
| 0005 | No memory for plane allocation |
| 0006 | Item's top less than RelZero |
| 0007 | No memory to open screen |
| 0008 | No memory to allocate screen raster |
| 0009 | Unknown screen type to open |
| 000A | No memory to add SW gadgets |
| 000B | No memory to open window |
| 000C | Bad state return entering Intuition |
| 000D | Bad message received by IDCMP |
| 000E | Weird echo causing incomprehension |
| 000F | Can't open console device |

DOS:

| Code | Meaning |
|---|---|
| 0001 | No memory at startup |
| 0002 | EndTask didn't end task |
| 0003 | Qpkt quick I/O failure |
| 0004 | Unexpected packet received |
| 0005 | Freevec failure |
| 0006 | Disk block sequence error |
| 0007 | Bitmap damaged |
| 0008 | Key already free |
| 0009 | Checksum error |
| 000A | Disk error |
| 000B | Key out of range |
| 000C | Bad Overlay (may be linker-related) |

RAM

| Code | Meaning |
|---|---|
| 0001 | Bad segment list |

Expansion:

| Code | Meaning |
|---|---|
| 0001 | Bad expansion free |

TrackDisk:

| **Code** | **Meaning** |
|---|---|
| 0001 | Calibration timing seek error |
| 0002 | Timer wait error |

Timer:

| **Code** | **Meaning** |
|---|---|
| 0001 | Bad request |
| 0002 | Bad supply |

Disk:

| **Code** | **Meaning** |
|---|---|
| 0001 | Unit already has disk |
| 0002 | Interrupt; no active unit |

BootStrap

| **Code** | **Meaning** |
|---|---|
| 0001 | System boot code returned error |

CPU Traps are internal microprocessor errors:

| **Code** | **Meaning** |
|---|---|
| 00000002 | Bus error |
| 00000003 | Address error |
| 00000004 | Illegal instruction |
| 00000005 | Divide by zero |
| 00000006 | CHK instruction |
| 00000007 | TRAPV (TrapVector) instruction |
| 00000008 | Supervisor mode privilege violation |
| 00000009 | Trace |
| 0000000A | Line A trap (OpCode 1010) |
| 0000000B | Line B trap (OpCode 1011) |

The CPU trap errors can often be traced back to programming errors like misused instruction sizes. Arranging the program so that words or long words fall on odd memory addresses frequently results in 00000003 or 00000004 errors.

The actual subsystem general and specific errors above are usually traceable to misuse of memory (for instance, trying to free memory that is already free) or the failure of a library function. If a library function call returns an error code and your program doesn't bother to respond to it, the program will usually crash and present you with a guru message. For example, if OpenWindow fails and a program tries later to attach a menu to the nonexistent window, you'll run into problems.

If you try to allocate memory and fail, and then try to use the nonexistent memory, be prepared to visit the Guru. Memory that is not currently allocated, also cannot be freed.

The process of debugging is an art, and a complete discussion of machine language debugging would be larger than this book. The macros and subroutines in our support code files include error checking for library calls. Be sure your own code does the same. The best debugging is bug prevention. The *Amiga ROM Kernel Reference Manual: Exec* has more information on Amiga debugging tools.

The Guru meditation example 81000009:00*xxxxxx* means Exec error (ignore the initial eight), General Error 00 (no general error) and SPecific ERror 0009 (tried to free memory already free.). The *xxxxxx* will be the address of the instruction that caused the error.

# APPENDIX D

# An Introduction to the *ASM68010* Assembler

**Introduction.** *ASM68010* is an MC68010 assembler that's compatible with the AmigaDOS MC68000 ASSEM program provided by *Metacomco,* as well as the MC68010 assembly language specifications provided by Motorola.

This appendix is a reference manual for the *ASM68010* assembler. Any variations between this assembler and the *Metacomco* assembler are noted. For a more thorough discussion of the M68000 family of microprocessors, please see Section 1 of the text.

**How to read this manual.** This manual uses the following conventions throughout:

- Operand sizes are: A byte equals 8 bits, a word equals 16 bits, and a long word equals 32 bits. In many respects, the MC68000 and MC68010 microprocessors are compatible in Amiga systems. If a specific feature pertains to only one of the microprocessors, the appropriate name (MC68000 or MC68010) is used.
- Braces denote optional arguments. Anything inside the braces ({ }) is considered optional to the instruction.
- Brackets ([ ]) denote a choice among options, one of which must be selected.

The statement

```
CLR{.[BWL]}  D0
```

has four valid meanings. These are:

```
CLR    D0
CLR.B  D0
CLR.W  D0
CLR.L  D0
```

**The MC68000 and MC68010 microprocessors.** The M68000 family of microprocessors have 16 general-purpose registers. These registers are general in the sense that specific instructions are not wired to use specific registers (for shift counts or temporary values, for example), and addressing modes are not wired to use specific registers for base and displacement arithmetic. The M68000 series provides eight D (or data) registers and eight A (or address) registers, as well as the program counter and, depending upon the processor type, one or more special system registers.

The data registers are used in arithmetic calculations, and may be used as index values in the various indexed addressing modes. On the MC68000 and MC68010 microprocessors, these registers cannot be used for indirection. The register names are D0–D7.

The address registers normally contain addresses or address constants and are used as pointers to data elements in memory. The register names are A0–A7. Register A7 normally goes by another name. It is the stack pointer (although stack operations are not restricted to this register, as they are in many other microprocessor architectures).

Other specific registers include the program counter (or PC); the status register (SR); and the condition code register (CCR), the bottom half of the status register. On the MC68010 processor, there are some additional registers accessible only in supervisor mode. These include the vector base register (VBR), the source function code register (SFC), and the destination function code register (DFC).

In supervisor mode on both the MC68000 and MC68010 microprocessors, the programmer can access a second user stack pointer. The name of this register is the user stack pointer (USP).

The M68000 series of processors were designed to directly address four gigabytes of memory. The MC68000 and MC68010 microprocessors directly address 16 Megabytes of this address space. Later processors, such as the MC68020, allow direct access to the entire address range.

In the 65*xx* series of microprocessors, the least significant byte comes first. In the MC68000, a long word is four bytes long. If it is contained in bytes 0–3, byte 0 will be the most significant byte, and byte 3 will be the least significant byte.

One memory access restriction exists on the MC68000 and MC68010 microprocessors: Long words must be aligned on even boundaries. There are various techniques to insure this condition, including certain pseudo-ops and a macro provided in this book.

**Writing machine language source code.**

*Format of a machine language statement.* The following template defines the most common form of an assembly statement line:

{label field} {opcode and associated operands} {comments}

This template shows there are three parts to an assembly statement. These parts, all of which are optional, are:

- A label
- An MC68000 or MC68010 microprocessor opcode and its associated operands
- Trailing comments

Blank lines are considered null (empty) comment lines. Because many of the assembler directives have a slightly different format, their specific formats are each discussed individually in the assembler directive definition section.

*Labels and label definitions.* A label, sometimes called a symbol, consists of a string of alphanumeric characters that refer to an absolute constant (or address) or relative constant (or address). A label may consist of upper- or lowercase ASCII characters, as well as any decimal digit, the underscore character, or a period. The first character of the label may not be a number.

The following are examples of legal and illegal labels:

**Legal Labels**

a
Aa
R2d2
Symbol
FooBar
A_Very_Long_but.legal.NAME

| Illegal Labels | Reason |
|---|---|
| 3.141PI | Leading digit |
| Bad?Label | Illegal character (?) |
| quote_notlegal' | Illegal character (') |

*ASM68010* does not impose a limit on the length of a label; however, for backward compatibility with the *Metacomco* assembler, you should limit labels to a maximum of 30 characters. Some labels are predefined by *ASM68010*. The following table lists these predefined labels:

| Label | Definition |
|---|---|
| . | Current location counter (this symbol is not defined by the *Metacomco* assembler) |
| * | Current location counter (approved *Metacomco* symbol) |
| **narg** | Number of arguments sent to a macro invocation (this symbol is not defined by the *Metacomco* assembler) |
| **NARG** | Number of arguments sent to a macro invocation (approved *Metacomco* symbol) |
| **d0–d7, D0–D7, a0–a7, A0–A7, sp, SP, pc, PC, and so on** | All register names are predefined by the assembler |

Labels are used in two different locations. The first is the label definition, and the second is in a label reference. Label definitions take two forms. When the assembler sees an EQU, SET, or REG assembler directive, it will define an absolute symbol whose value contains the appropriate value as defined by the assembler directive, and the value provided in the expression. When the assembler sees an address label definition, it defines a relative address label whose value contains the address of the current location counter. This label may be used to change the flow of execution or as part of some other assembly-time calculation.

An address label definition has two formats. If the first character of the label starts in position one of the input line, the label name will terminate at the first blank character, at a colon, or at the end of the input line, whichever comes first. If the label doesn't start at position one of the input line, the label must be terminated with a colon. Any other form will cause an assembly-time error.

To maintain compatibility with the *Metacomco* assembler, opcodes should not be used as label definitions. Although this is legal in the *ASM68010* assembler, it is very ill-advised. Unlike opcodes, register names, and assembler directives, all labels are *case sensitive,* which means the labels Assem, ASSEM, and AsSeM are all considered to be different by the assembler. If the programmer does not wish to have case sensitivity, the assembler option -c C cancels it. See the section of assembler options for more information.

Labels, as described in the previous paragraphs, may be externally defined or referenced. The assembler directives XDEF, XREF, as well as the *ASM68010* specific directives GLOBL and GLOBAL, signal the assembler that a label is accessible outside the scope of the file. If these directives are not used, the labels must exist within the current assembly input file.

Another type of label, a *local label*, has a much shorter life span. A local label takes the form of a sequence of numbers. Some examples are 3, 1, and 10. The lifetime of these labels lasts only between the definition of two nonlocal labels. The advantage of local labels is that they may be redefined and reused after each normal label definition. The following example shows this:

```
START:
        BRA     BAR     ; GOES TO LABEL BAR
        FOO:
        BRA     1       ; GOES TO NEXT STATEMENT
1:      NOP
        BRA     2       ; LEGAL INSTRUCTION (GOES TO NEXT
                        ; STATEMENT)
2:
BAR:    BRA     1       ; GOES TO NEXT STATEMENT
1:
        BRA     2       ; ILLEGAL (ASSEMBLY TIME ERROR)
                        ; THIS LABEL '2' IS UNDEFINED NOW
QUIT    BRA     START
```

*ASM68010 Instruction Mnemonics/Opcodes.* The second field is the MC68000 or MC68010 microprocessor instruction mnemonic, usually known as an opcode, and its corresponding operands.

The general format of instruction mnemonics is a set of three or more ASCII characters, possibly followed by a period and a size specifier. The following size specifiers are used in MC68000 and MC68010 assembly language:

**B** Signifies to the assembler a byte-sized opcode.
**W** Signifies to the assembler a word-sized opcode.
**L** Signifies to the assembler a long-word-sized opcode.

The *ASM68010* and *Metacomco* assemblers will parse opcodes of both upper- and lowercase letters. Opcodes may not start in the first column of an assembly line. Placing an alphanumeric character in the first column of a line is the signal to the assembler to process a label. Most likely, a syntax error will result from misplacing an opcode in a label's position.

The opcodes and their various formats are discussed individually in Appendix A.

*Operands and Addressing modes.* Operands are the fields in an assembler that specify the data that the MC68000 or MC68010 instruction is going to process. MC68000 and MC68010 microprocessor instructions accept either 0, 1, or 2 operands.

Appendix A specifies the set of legal operands that may be used with each instruction. An operand is a data reference. Operands come in three classes:

- Addressing modes
- Expressions
- Addressing modes, which contain an expression

The following is a list of the legal addressing modes available on the MC68000 and MC68010 microprocessors:

| **Symbol** | **Addressing Mode** |
|---|---|
| **Rn** | Register direct |
| **(An)** | Address register indirect |
| **(An)+** | Address register indirect with postincrement |
| **−(An)** | Address register indirect with predecrement |
| **d16(An)** | Address register indirect with displacement |
| **d8(An,Rn{.[wl] })** | Address register indirect with index and displacement |
| **Value** | Absolute or direct |
| **d16(PC)** | Program counter with displacement |
| **d8(PC,Rn{.[wl] } )** | Program counter with index and displacement |
| **#immediateval** | Immediate data |
| | Inherent |

In this table, *Dn* means any legal data register. *An* means any legal address register. *Rn* means any legal data or address register. *PC* means program counter. The symbols d8 and d16 specify an 8- or 16-bit offset, respectively. The term *immediateval* specifies any expression that may be evaluated as 8, 16, or 32 bits wide.

**Running *ASM68010*.** The command line interface (CLI) syntax for executing *ASM68010* is: ASM [options] SOURCE [options]. Here is a list of the legal options that are available with *ASM68010*:

| **Option** | **Meaning** |
|---|---|
| **-O OBJECT_FILE** | Redirect the output of the object module to the named file. By default if the assembly file has a .s extension, it is converted to a .o extension. If the assembly file has a .asm extension, it is converted to .obj. If the assembly file has neither of these extensions, a .obj extension is appended to the object file name. |
| **-L LISTING_FILE** | Generate a listing file. Place the listing output in the named file. Listing files are not created by default. |
| **-V ERROR_FILE** | Redirect the error output to the named file. By default this output will appear in the current CLI window. |
| **-H HEADER_FILE** | Process the named header file before processing the source file. This command line argument is equivalent to adding an include assembler directive, with the named file as the argument, in the first line of the source file. |
| **-I INCLUDE_LIST** | This argument specifies the list of directories to search when looking for include files. In *ASM68010,* multiple -I flags may be given. The form for listing multiple directories in either assembler is: -I DIR1,DIR2,DIR3, or -I DIR1 + DIR2 + DIR3, or -I "DIR1 DIR2 DIR3". |
| **-Q Quiet Mode** | This tells the assembler not to print the leading copyright banner lines. It is helpful when *ASM68010* is called from another program such as ASMINT. |
| **-C [S D C X Wnum]** | The -C keyword processes a sublist of command line arguments. These subarguments are: |

| | |
|---|---|
| S | Produce a symbol table dump (*Metacomco*-only). |
| D | Do not dump local symbols to symbol table. |
| C | Ignore upper-/lowercase in labels. |
| X | Generate a cross-reference listing (*Metacomco*-only). |
| Wnum | Set aside workspace amount (*Metacomco*-only). |

The *ASM68010* parses all command line arguments, but simply ignores the requests noted as *Metacomco*-only, above.

| | |
|---|---|
| **-E EQUATE_FILE** | Generate an equate file based on the assembled list of absolute symbols in the symbol table. |

**-A AUTO_LINK**

When possible (it is always possible if there are no external references), generate a completely linked load module. The result, if it is fully linked (no errors), is directly executable from the CLI. This flag lets you skip the ALINK/BLINK phase and proceed directly to the execution step, speeding the assemble/test/edit/assemble phase of program development. Use this option only if your source file has all symbols defined (see text). It works well with the files and programs in this book. (This option is in *ASM68010* only).

**-R Force Relative Mode**

This is the opposite of -A. This occurs by default, and the flag is provided simply for consistency.

# APPENDIX E
# ASCII Codes

| Decimal | Hex | ASCII | Note | |
|---|---|---|---|---|
| 0 | 0 | NUL | NULL | |
| 1 | 1 | SOH | CTRL-A | |
| 2 | 2 | STX | CTRL-B | |
| 3 | 3 | ETX | CTRL-C | |
| 4 | 4 | EOT | CTRL-D | |
| 5 | 5 | ENQ | CTRL-E | |
| 6 | 6 | ACK | CTRL-F | |
| 7 | 7 | BEL | CTRL-G | Ring bell |
| 8 | 8 | BS | CTRL-H | Backspace |
| 9 | 9 | HT | CTRL-I | Horizontal tab |
| 10 | A | LF | CTRL-J | Line feed |
| 11 | B | VT | CTRL-K | Vertical tab |
| 12 | C | FF | CTRL-L | Form feed |
| 13 | D | CR | CTRL-M | Carriage return |
| 14 | E | SO | CTRL-N | |
| 15 | F | SI | CTRL-O | |
| 16 | 10 | DLE | CTRL-P | |
| 17 | 11 | DC1 | CTRL-Q | |
| 18 | 12 | DC2 | CTRL-R | |
| 19 | 13 | DC3 | CTRL-S | |
| 20 | 14 | DC4 | CTRL-T | |
| 21 | 15 | NAK | CTRL-U | |
| 22 | 16 | SYN | CTRL-V | |
| 23 | 17 | ETB | CTRL-W | |
| 24 | 18 | CAN | CTRL-X | |
| 25 | 19 | EM | CTRL-Y | |
| 26 | 1A | SUB | CTRL-Z | |
| 27 | 1B | ESC | Escape | |
| 28 | 1C | FS | Cursor right | |
| 29 | 1D | GS | Cursor left | |
| 30 | 1E | RS | Cursor up | |
| 31 | 1F | US | Cursor down | |
| 32 | 20 | SP | Space | |
| 33 | 21 | ! | Exclamation point | |
| 34 | 22 | " | Quotation mark | |
| 35 | 23 | # | Pound sign | |
| 36 | 24 | $ | Dollar sign | |
| 37 | 25 | % | Percent sign | |

| | | | |
|---|---|---|---|
| 38 | 26 | & | Ampersand |
| 39 | 27 | ’ | Apostrophe (close single quote) |
| 40 | 28 | ( | Open parenthesis |
| 41 | 29 | ) | Close parenthesis |
| 42 | 2A | * | Asterisk (multiply sign) |
| 43 | 2B | + | Plus sign |
| 44 | 2C | , | Comma |
| 45 | 2D | - | Hyphen (minus sign) |
| 46 | 2E | . | Period (decimal point) |
| 47 | 2F | / | Slash (divide sign) |
| 48–57 | 30–39 | Digits 0–9 | |
| 58 | 3A | : | Colon |
| 59 | 3B | ; | Semicolon |
| 60 | 3C | < | Less-than sign (left arrow) |
| 61 | 3D | = | Equal sign |
| 62 | 3E | > | Greater-than sign (right arrow) |
| 63 | 3F | ? | Question mark |
| 64 | 40 | @ | At sign |
| 65–90 | 41–5A | Uppercase alphabet A–Z | |
| 91 | 5B | [ | Left bracket |
| 92 | 5C | \ | Backslash |
| 93 | 5D | ] | Right bracket |
| 94 | 5E | ^ | Caret (up arrow) |
| 95 | 5F | _ | Underscore (underline) |
| 96 | 60 | ‘ | Apostrophe (open single quote) |
| 97–122 | 61–7A | Lowercase alphabet a–z | |
| 123 | 7B | { | Left brace |
| 124 | 7C | \| | Vertical stroke |
| 125 | 7D | } | Right brace |
| 126 | 7E | ~ | Tilde |
| 127 | 7F | DEL | Delete |

# GLOSSARY

# Terms Used in Amiga Machine Language Programming

Given the complexity of machine language programming and the Amiga's capabilities, this book presents a large amount of information in a dense format. For some, it may seem that certain concepts spring forth without much explanation. This glossary should help.

**A**
An abbreviation of the word address, as in address register A0.

**Accumulator**
An accumulator is a temporary location used by a computer for saving intermediate results to a computation. Accumulators are normally limited in number, but are much faster than the larger main memory. On an MC68000, the eight data registers and eight address registers can be considered accumulators.

**Address**
A number or symbol standing for a memory location. When a microprocessor performs an instruction, or loads or stores data, it must be told where in memory to find the instruction or data. The microprocessor uses numbers to distinguish the different memory locations. Each memory location has a numerical address. In programs, the numerical addresses can be given symbolic names whenever it is convenient.

**Addressing Mode**
When the MC68000 reads from or writes to a memory location, it can use any 32-bit number as an address (the highest eight bits are ignored). The microprocessor can calculate the address by combining a variety of numbers. In some modes, it adds together two registers to form an address. In other modes, it adds a constant value to a register to form an address. In still other modes, the address of data is represented

by the number held in one of the address registers. The precise method used to combine numbers and registers to form an address is called an *addressing mode*. Each instruction dictates an addressing mode used for that instruction. If the instruction manipulates data in a register, the addressing mode is called *Register Direct*. If the same instruction manipulates data in memory by pointing to the data with an address register, the addressing mode is called *Address Register Indirect*. The MC68000 microprocessor has 11 different addressing modes.

**ASCII**
The American Standard Code for Information Interchange (ASCII) is a coded list of numbers corresponding to all the letters, numerals, punctuation marks, diacritical marks, and spaces, and certain commands like line feeds, carriage returns, and sounding the bell. There are 128 different ASCII codes, so each can be represented by a byte. The first 32 codes are various commands, while the other 96 are printable characters. For example, in ASCII code, the letter *A* is equal to 65, *B* is 66, and so on. A complete ASCII list is available in Appendix E.

**Assembler**
An assembler is a program that reads a file of source code statements and produces a machine language program. Machine language bypasses interpretation and "speaks" to the microprocessor in its own language, thus operating faster than high-level languages like BASIC.

**Binary**
Binary is the base 2 system. This is a system in which numbers are expressed as sequences of 1s and 0s. Any number can be so expressed. Just as neighboring digits of a decimal number are related by a factor of ten, binary digits are related by a factor of two. The number 3 is represented as 11 in binary.

**Bit**
A bit is a formally defined unit of information that distinguishes between two distinct possibilities (such as whether a switch is on or off). A single bit is usually written as a 0 or 1, depending on whether the bit is off or on, respectively. By combining bits in groups, larger numbers of distinct possibilities can be distinguished by each group. For example, two bits can distinguish four distinct possibilities. The result of two successive coin flips has four outcomes: heads-heads,

heads-tails, tails-heads, tails-tails. These would be represented in binary as 11, 10, 01, and 00, respectively. Each combination of on and off bits can represent a unique binary number. Strings of bits (1s and 0s) can be used to represent any number.

**Bitmap**
A bitmap is a region of memory that's treated by a program as a rectangular block of graphic information. Each bit in the memory region is translated to on or off states of a single dot or pixel in the graphic display. When a bitmap contains 8K, it represents 64,000 distinct individual dots. They might be arranged as a 320 × 200 array of pixels, each one on or off. Within the bitmap region in memory, the first 40 bytes would be treated as a single line at the top of the rectangle. Each succeeding 40-byte (320-bit) portion of the memory region would represent the next line of dots on the screen. With proper hardware and software programming, a single 8K block of memory can be manipulated as if it were really 320 separate 40-byte lines of dots.

**Blitter**
The blitter in an Amiga is a specialized coprocessor chip that manipulates memory as a bitmap. The blitter is also a microprocessor that can read and write memory directly. It's usually used to move bitmaps, so a region inside one bitmap can be placed in another region. The blitter's special advantage is its speed. It is roughly four times faster than the MC68000 microprocessor, at moving bitmaps (twice as fast as the MC68010). The blitter can be told to treat any region of chip memory as a rectangular bitmap. It plays an essential role in all Amiga displays and animation graphics.

**Bus Contention**
Although the Amiga has many specialized microprocessors, such as the blitter, in addition to the MC68000 microprocessor, it has only one bus. All information for all the microprocessors must travel along this bus. Therefore, there are times when operations must slow down while the central processing unit waits for the bus to clear. This condition is called *bus contention.*

**Bus Error**
A bus error occurs whenever the MC68000 cannot access something on its processor/memory bus. This usually occurs if a program tries to access a piece of nonexistent memory.

**Byte**
A byte is a group of eight bits. Taken together as a unit, the group can distinguish 256 different combinations of 1s and 0s. Programmers use bytes to represent numbers ranging from 0 to 255 (256 possible choices). A byte may contain graphic data, part of a word or a long word, an ASCII character, or a single value within the range 0–255.

**C and C Compiler**
C is a compiled high-level programming language that closely resembles machine language in many ways. A C compiler is a program that translates the C language into machine language modules. Using a C compiler has the look and feel of a high-level computer language like Pascal or Modula-2, but the C programmer can do things usually reserved for machine language programming.

**Chip Memory**
The lower 512K of memory is accessible to both the MC68000 microprocessor and a variety of specialized chips like the blitter chip. Since all these microprocessors (also called *chips*) must use the same bus for data transfer, their operations are slowed slightly as a result of bus contention. Therefore, using chip memory will cause the Amiga to run slightly slower than using expansion memory (also known as fast memory). Also see *Fast Memory, Public Memory,* and *Bus Contention.*

**Clear**
When a bit is set equal to 0, it is said to be cleared, or reset.

**CLI**
The Amiga's CLI (Command Line Interface) is a program for interaction with the Amiga, using typed-in commands.

**Condition Codes**
Condition codes are bits stored in the computer which reflect the outcome of the last processed instruction. These bits are used by other instructions, such as branches, when deciding if the program should change it's course and start executing code someplace else in memory.

**Condition Code Register**
The condition code register is the lower eight bits of the status register.

**Copper**
The copper is a general purpose coprocessor that resides in one of the Amiga's custom chips. The copper can control nearly the entire graphics system, freeing the MC68000 to execute programs. Among other things, it can control register updates, reposition sprites, change the color palette, update the audio channels, and control the blitter.

**Coprocessor**
A coprocessor is a separate microprocesor that uses the same memory as the main microprocessor, but which is specialized to certain routine tasks. The Amiga uses at least three coprocessors that perform display, sound, and input/output functions more efficiently than the MC68000 main microprocessor.

**CPU**
The term *CPU* stands for Central Processing Unit. The CPU performs the work laid out for the computer in the form of programs.

**Crash**
The condition in which the Amiga finds itself if your program isn't written properly. When a computer is unable to interpret instructions as a result of faulty programming, it will crash. When it crashes, it will probably present you with a Guru meditation, and it will usually require a warm boot before any further action can be taken.

**D**
An abbreviation of the word *data,* as in data register D0.

**Data**
Numbers or symbols stored in memory.

**Decimal**
Decimal is the base 10 counting system. It is the most commonly used base, perhaps because humans have ten fingers.

**Direct Memory Access Device (DMA)**
A piece of hardware capable of directly modifying the computer's memory without using the microprocessor. Non-DMA devices use the microprocessor to transfer data between the device and memory. A DMA device moves the data on its own, freeing the microprocessor to do other useful work at the same time. A computer with DMA devices is usually a higher-performance computer because, in essence, it can do several things at the same time. This means that more work can be done in less time. The net result is that the computer with DMA devices performs better than one without them.

**Fast Memory**
On the Amiga, this is memory beyond the base of 512K. This memory is inaccessible to the specialized chips of the Amiga. This eliminates bus contention, resulting in faster operation when expansion memory is used. Also see *Chip Memory, Public Memory,* and *Bus Contention.*

**Field**
A field is a portion of a data structure. It may contain a byte, a word, or a long word of information used to specify a feature of the structure.

**File**
An Amiga file is simply a sequence of bytes. The sequence can be in memory or on disk. Any stream of bytes can be manipulated as a file. The AmigaDOS operating system provides all the usual tools for manipulating files, including open, close, read, and write routines. Bytes of data can be stored in a file and later retrieved.

**Function**
See *Subroutine.*

**Guru Meditation Number**
When the Amiga crashes, it provides a number that gives you a clue to the nature of the programming error that led to the crash. This number is known as a *Guru meditation number.* The format and meaning of Guru meditation numbers can be found in Appendix C of this book.

**Hexadecimal (also known as HEX)**
A base-16 numbering system. This system uses decimal digits 0–9 and the letters A–F (which stand for the values 10–15). Two hexadecimal digits make up one byte (each digit is four bits). The number F1 in hex is equal to 241 decimal and 11110001 in binary. Hexadecimal is frequently used in machine language programs.

**High-Level Language**
A high-level language is a language that is not directly in touch with the CPU; you don't have to know much about machine-level operations to program in a high-level language. A single statement in a high-level language may take several assembly language instructions to accomplish the same task. High-level languages are friendlier to use than assembly or machine language, but execute more slowly and require more memory.

**Index Value**
An index value is an offset—a number added to the begining address of an array. If the third element of a byte array is to be accessed, the index value is 2. If the fifth element of a long-word array is to be accessed, then the index value is 16 ( ( 5 − 1) * 4 = 16). This simple equation can be thought of as (ELEMENT# − 1) * size of elements in bytes.

**Interrupt**
An Interrupt is a signal to a computer that some external device (such as a floppy disk) has completed it's current task and is ready to talk to the MC68000. This may mean that the disk has data for the MC68000, or that it is ready to write more data, or that the keyboard has a new character for the MC68000 to process. Many types of external devices may interrupt the MC68000.

**Intuition**
An internal library of programs used to manipulate windows, mouse, menus, and so on in the familiar Amiga user interface.

**Library**
A library is a group of related routines organized as a family. The library may have a jump table, which is a list of addresses of routines in the library. Using the library's jump table is a convenient way of accessing the routines.

**Linked List**
Sequences of data can be arranged in memory so that one block is connected to the next, even though they are widely scattered. Each data block contains a pointer to the next block. The linked list can be manipulated as a list of elements, even though they are not contiguous.

**Linker**
A program that merges or links the object code from one program with another. One program part may contain routines or symbol definitions required by the other. The linker's job is to extract whatever information is required from each part, to make one workable program.

**Loader**
A loader finds enough available memory for a program, and then puts it there and adjusts the relocatable addresses accordingly. It then runs (starts) the program.

**Long Word**
A long word is four bytes, or 32 bits. Long-word integers have a numerical range of over 4 billion.

**Machine Language (also called Assembly Language)**
Machine language is the lowest-level language. An assembler reads machine language statements and translates them into machine instructions. Assemblers are designed to perform one-to-one translations of assembly statements to machine instructions.

**Macro**
A macro is a user-defined instruction. Once defined, an assembler replaces any later occurrence of its name with a predefined block of statements known as the macro body. Everything between the MACRO and ENDM pseudo-ops is the macro body. The macro body can contain opcodes, label definitions, and even calls to other macros.

**Octal**
Octal is a base-8 counting system used on some computer systems. Octal is normally used when a computer's instruction word is broken up into many three-bit fields.

**Operating System**
An operating system is a collection of routines that manage a computer. These routines perform some of the more mundane jobs, such as monitoring and collecting input data from external devices (such as keyboards). These routines also do other jobs, such as starting new programs and keeping track of all resources. The operating system of the Amiga decides which program can write to the disk and which program must wait. If two programs tried to write to the disk simultaneously, both data files would be corrupted. Instead, programs request that the operating system write for them, and the operating system actually does the writing to the disk in such a way that all data files are kept separate and uncorrupted.

**Opcode**
Short for *operation code*. An opcode is an instruction for the microprocessor to execute, but the opcode itself is usually described alone—without reference to its operands (see next entry). The MOVE instruction may have various numerical opcodes, depending on its addressing mode and the operands associated with it. Each numerical instruction is a unique opcode.

**Operand**
An instruction can usually manipulate or operate on one or two pieces of data. These pieces of data are the instruction's operands. Addition requires two operands. Clearing a register requires one operand. Operands may be written as numbers or symbols. They may be registers or memory locations.

**Pointer**
A pointer is simply an address. Registers inside the microprocessor can hold addresses and may be called *pointer registers*. Programmers can arrange that certain memory locations contain pointers to other data. Using MC68000 addressing modes, the pointers can be combined to form additional pointers.

**Program Counter**
The program counter is a special register that contains the address of the next instruction. The program counter increases as successive instructions are executed. When a branch or a jump occurs in a program, the program counter is adjusted to the

address to which the branch or jump occurred. The program counter in a MC68000 microprocessor can be used with addressing modes to calculate addresses of other instructions and data in memory.

**PC**
See Program counter.

**Pseudo-Op**
A pseudo-op is a special assembler directive that is not translated into machine language. Although it looks like an opcode (hence the name), it's really a special form of input to the assembler, telling it to set aside a number of bytes, generate a listing, or some other form of instruction.

**Public Memory**
When your program requests public memory from the operating system, the operating system will provide either fast or chip memory. Fast memory will be provided if available, if not, your program will be given chip memory. All memory that is unallocated is *public memory.* At some point in the future, Commodore may release an Amiga operating system that provides for *private memory,* which will allow blocks of memory to be designated for a single use. This is not currently available, however. Also see *Chip Memory* and *Fast Memory.*

**Register**
A register is an internal memory location within the microprocessor. The MC68000 has 16 general-purpose 32-bit registers—eight data and eight address registers. Each address register can point to a different location in memory. Instructions can directly manipulate data in a register or use the register to form the address of data in memory. The results of performing instructions are also kept in a 16-bit status register, while the program counter has its own 32-bit register. Registers are usually limited in number but much faster than main memory.

**Relocatable Code**
Programs can be written so that they must be executed starting at a particular address. Such programs are called *fixed location* code. They must be stored in memory at a particular

address in order to work. Relocatable code can work regardless of where the program resides. Relocatable code usually requires the program counter to act as a relative reference point. The starting address of the program (initial program counter value when the program starts) is used to adjust any necessary addresses in the rest of the program before it runs.

**Reset**
This term has two meanings. When a bit is returned to a 0 value, it's said to be reset. The second meaning of reset is to reboot the computer after a crash by pressing Control-Amiga-Amiga.

**Set**
When a bit is given a value of 1, it is said to be set. When it's set equal to 0, it is reset, or cleared.

**Sign Bit**
A designated bit of a byte, word, or long word can be interpreted as a + or − sign. Usually a 0 value there means +, and a value of 1 means −. While a byte can represent values from 0 to 255, if its leftmost bit is used as a sign, it represents values from −128 (10000000) to +127 (01111111).

**Stack**
Almost all microprocessors have the ability to manipulate one portion of memory as if it were a list, one end for which data can be added to, or removed from. The stack is used to pass parameters to and from procedures, and to hold return addresses. When data is added to the stack, the address of the stack's next available storage position is automatically adjusted by the microprocessor. Similarly, when data is removed from the stack, the next available address is moved back. Stacks may grow either up (increasing memory addresses) or down (decreasing memory addresses). The microprocessor's pointer to the next available stack position is called the stack pointer. The stack pointer is automatically adjusted up or down, depending on whether data is added or removed.

**Stack Pointer**
This register points to the top of the program's stack.

**String**
A string is a sequence of ASCII characters or bytes of data that represent a sequence of ASCII characters. Most strings are null-terminated, which means a 0 byte is appended at the end of the string.

**Structure**
A structure is a table of data consisting of bytes, words, and long words. Each element of a structure is usually given a field name. Each time a particular structure is used, its data appears in a unique ordering of bytes, words, and long words specific to that structure's definition.

**Subroutine**
A subroutine is a set of computer instructions outside of the main portion of the program. It is good programming practice to organize a program into functional units. Each unit usually does one thing, and is called, when necessary, from other subroutines. Subroutines are sometimes called *functions.*

**Warm Boot**
See *Reset.*

**Word**
A word is two bytes or 16 bits. Using a word, it's possible to distinguish 65536 different combinations of 1s and 0s. Programmers use words to represent numbers between 0 and 65535 or, using the leftmost bit as a sign bit (see *Sign Bit*), between −32768 and +32767.

**Workbench**
Workbench is the standard Intuition screen. It is a high-resolution (640 × 200) two-bitplane (four color) screen. Any application program can use the Workbench screen for opening its windows.

# Index

To order your copy of the *COMPUTE!'s Amiga Machine Language Programming Guide Disk,* call our toll-free US order line: 1-800-346-6767 or send your prepaid order to:

*COMPUTE!'s Amiga Machine Language*
*Programming Disk*
**COMPUTE!** Books Customer Service
P.O. Box 2165
Radnor, PA 19089

All orders must be prepaid (check, charge, or money order). PA residents add 6% sales tax.

Send _____ copies of the *Apple Machine Language for Beginners Disk* at $12.95 per copy.

Subtotal $__________

Shipping and Handling: $2.00/disk $__________

Sales tax (if applicable) $__________

Total payment enclosed $__________

□ Payment enclosed
□ Charge □ Visa □ MasterCard

Acct. No. ____________________________ Exp. Date ______
(Required)

Name ____________________________________________

Address __________________________________________

City ______________________ State _______ Zip _______

Please allow 4-6 weeks for delivery.